PRAISE FOR *RELEASING THE MOTHER LOAD*

"If you've ever felt like you're the only one struggling with motherhood, this book is for you. Erica Djossa approaches the weight that modern moms feel with compassion, understanding, and a proactive method to breaking out from under it. You're not alone. You're not failing. And you don't have to carry the weight by yourself!"

EVE RODSKY

New York Times bestselling author of *Fair Play*

"*Releasing the Mother Load* highlights the way that parenting, and specifically mothering, has changed in recent decades and, even more drastically, since the pandemic. Erica Djossa shines the light on the invisible load and how big of an impact it has on maternal mental health. She also provides practical strategies for how to release that load and protect our self-esteem and well-being."

BECKY KENNEDY, PHD

clinical psychologist, #1 *New York Times* bestselling author of *Good Inside*, and CEO and founder of Good Inside

"Erica Djossa does an incredible job unveiling hard truths about mental labor in *Releasing the Mother Load*. Her ability to share impactful research, meaningful stories, and practical tools will leave the reader feeling validated and equipped to take off the backpack that gets handed to us when we become mothers, as she puts it. This book is for the mother who is trying to conceive, the pregnant mom, the first-time mom, veteran mom, or anyone impacted by the mental tasks fighting for space where there is no more to spare."

ASHURINA REAM, PSYD

CEO and founder of Psyched Mommy

"Motherhood can be exhausting and overwhelming—but it doesn't have to be that way. *Releasing the Mother Load* is a practical tool that helps moms identify why they're struggling and let go of the things that hold them back."

LIBBY WARD

digital creator and maternal wellness
advocate at @diaryofanhonestmom

"Erica Djossa offers a refreshing and much-needed take in *Releasing the Mother Load*, helping women and mothers understand the deep cultural origins of their burnout, how change starts inside, and what actionable steps they can take to nurture, not lose, themselves in motherhood."

JILL KOZIOL

cofounder and CEO of Motherly

"So much of motherhood self-help relies on check lists of self-care items that end up just being one more thing we as mothers feel guilty for not getting to. With *Releasing the Mother Load*, Erica Djossa does a masterful job at making mothers from all walks of life feel seen and paints a practical path forward that is compassionate and reachable. I recommend it for any mother or mother-to-be."

KC DAVIS, LPC

USA Today bestselling author of *How to Keep House While Drowning*

"Erica Djossa's new book is a thoughtful and straightforward guide to helping moms everywhere find their inner GPS—because *Releasing the Mother Load* is as much about letting go of unrealistic external expectations as it is about learning who you are and where your values come from."

CATHERINE BIRNDORF, MD

cofounder and CEO, The Motherhood Center of New York

RELEASING THE MOTHER LOAD

RELEASING THE MOTHER LOAD

HOW TO CARRY LESS AND ENJOY MOTHERHOOD MORE

ERICA DJOSSA

sounds true
BOULDER, COLORADO

Sounds True
Boulder, CO

This book is not intended as a substitute for the medical recommendations of
physicians, mental health professionals, or other health-care providers. Rather, it is
intended to offer information to help the reader cooperate with physicians, mental
health professionals, and health-care providers in a mutual quest for optimal well-being.
We advise readers to carefully review and understand the ideas presented and to seek the
advice of a qualified professional before attempting to use them.

Published 2024

Book design by Meredith Jarrett

Printed in Canada

BK06863

Library of Congress Cataloging-in-Publication Data

Names: Djossa, Erica, author.
Title: Releasing the mother load : how to carry less and enjoy motherhood more
    / Erica Djossa.
Description: Boulder, CO : Sounds True, Inc., 2024.
Identifiers: LCCN 2023039928 (print) | LCCN 2023039929
    (ebook) | ISBN 9781649632258 (hardback) | ISBN
    9781649632265 (ebook)
Subjects: LCSH: Motherhood. | Motherhood--Psychological aspects.
Classification: LCC HQ759 .D595 2024 (print) | LCC HQ759
    (ebook) | DDC 306.874/3--dc23/eng/20230030
LC record available at https://lccn.loc.gov/2023039928
LC ebook record available at https://lccn.loc.gov/2023039929

FSC
www.fsc.org
MIX
Paper from
responsible sources
FSC® C016245

TO MOTHERS EVERYWHERE

May we know our worth, advocate for our needs,
and reach for what our hearts desire.

CONTENTS

EXERCISES

These "in-the-moment" exercises are designed to help you stop, take a step back, and reflect on your individual and underlying beliefs that shape the Mother Load. Revisit these exercises periodically as needed.

SKILLS AND TOOLS

These are the skills and tools that you will need to release the Mother Load. Many of these will take time, practice, and revisiting to build up and implement.

INTRODUCTION

The day my volcano of mom rage erupted was the day that changed my entire approach to motherhood.

I was on my third maternity leave, home with my three sons—eight weeks old, just under two, and three and a half. As you can imagine, life was generally chaotic at best.

But the chaos I was experiencing went beyond the stress of herding three little boys. I wasn't just frazzled—I had lost myself.

I woke up every morning feeling irritated, as if I had already hit my limit for the day before I poured my coffee. I felt like I was drowning. The experience of motherhood wasn't the happy, joyous, greeting-card image I had imagined. It was a constant struggle.

But I was determined not to let that show. I wouldn't admit it to myself, let alone anybody else. Instead, I picked myself up every morning, committed to plow through the discomfort—the *pain* I was feeling—with a stiff upper lip. Whenever I would wonder why I found it so difficult, I told myself that I needed to suck it up. This is what motherhood was. Diapers and spit-up and tantrums and stress. I'd signed up for it. I had no right to question it.

Then one morning, it all came crashing down. It was one of those mornings where everything went wrong. Getting three kids out the door is never easy. Inevitably, somebody spills their milk, can't find their shoes, or melts down. But this was a Stroller Fit Boot Camp day—a fitness class for new moms I attended every week. And I desperately needed to get there—it was the one thing that was giving me a sense of normalcy.

I juggled bags and car seats and blankets and corralled the boys out the door to the van. Just as I hit the button to open the door, I heard a snap. The pulley system on the van broke.

The stress started to bubble up, but I pushed it back down. I refused to let this derail my day. I got everyone buckled in, manually closed the door, and pulled out.

In less than a minute, I saw red and blue lights in my mirror. I groaned as I pulled over, working to push down that stress again. I ignored the screams and cries coming from the back seat and tried to be polite as I rolled down my window.

The officer ticketed me for speeding—I'd hit a speed trap and hadn't adjusted in time. But he also wanted to know why I wasn't wearing glasses. I explained that I'd had LASIK but never updated my information. He decided to ticket me for "misrepresenting my license."

The anger started to bubble back up—only this time it was different. This time, I couldn't hold it down.

I snapped at the officer, took my tickets, and managed to contain my rage until I drove back home and pulled into the driveway.

I opened the car door and collapsed, sobbing in a fit of rage, to the point of vomiting.

And, as I felt the volcano bubble over, as I felt myself collapsing and hyperventilating hysterically, I realized that I was not okay. I couldn't keep pretending that I was.

I ended up being diagnosed with postpartum depression and started a journey to recovery. But I also realized that what I was striving for— this image of the perfect mom—was unattainable.

I was shooting for a dangerous bullseye—the *perfect* mom. I thought that I was just not measuring up. And I believed that if I admitted that I couldn't handle it, I was admitting that I had failed at the most import ant job in my life. But I hadn't failed. The perfect mother myth had failed me. It had told me that I needed to strive for something false, something entirely unrealistic. It wasn't until I broke out of that mindset that I truly started to experience joy in motherhood.

After I had my breakdown-turned-breakthrough, I realized that not only is perfect not real—it's smothering. It's unattainable. And it doesn't reward you. As I broke away from that perfect mother myth, I was able to see motherhood in an entirely new way. I started to get curious about why I felt this need to strive for perfection. Where did these beliefs come from? Whose voice was sounding in my head? How had I been led so far astray? Where was I even trying to go?

The more I looked beneath the surface, the more I saw that the construct of motherhood had kept me from being the mom I truly wanted to be. I'd been conditioned to believe that I had to be all the things— the nurturer, the teacher, the schedule tracker, the memory maker, the keeper of the house, on and on and on. A rulebook of motherhood had been handed to me without me realizing it. And that rulebook came with an invisible load—a world of mental and physical tasks that kept me pushing toward perfection while barely being able to breathe.

But I wasn't the only mom that inherited this rulebook. Motherhood researchers have deemed this the era of intensive mothering—an approach to motherhood that is so all-consuming that mothers' identities don't make it out alive. The more we feel we should be present, "on," and centered around our children, the more we take on physically, cognitively, and emotionally.[1]

THE LOAD MOTHERS CARRY

Research reveals that the myths of intensive mothering and the belief in "the perfect mother" are impacting the mental health of moms. Most moms have internalized the idea that motherhood must involve immense sacrifice, that we shouldn't find fulfillment outside of our roles as mothers, and that we are primarily responsible for our children's well-being. The closer we cling to these ideals, the more likely we are to be dissatisfied in motherhood or to develop depression and anxiety.[2]

Other studies have shown a correlation between invisible labor in the home and maternal frustration and unhappiness.[3] It's no wonder we are struggling. We're being saddled with expectations, pressures, and a never-ending list of cognitive labor as we strive for perfection.

Only after I could see the load was I finally able to break out from under it and become the mother I wanted to be. Not one who checked all the imaginary boxes. Not one who always had it together. Not one who could "do it all." But one who was happy—one who actually enjoyed the role. (Although let's be real—I enjoy some days better than others!)

In discussing the load I carry I want to acknowledge my own privilege. I am a heterosexual middle-class white woman with a partner. The labor that I carry is different than what single moms carry, that moms of color carry, or that LGBTQ+ moms carry. I see and appreciate that others' loads are disproportionately weighted from the start. Because the Mother Load is different for marginalized moms, moms in poverty, or other groups of mothers, the process for releasing might be different. This book aims to give you the basis for breaking away from overarching beliefs and expectations that impact us all.

We're at a unique place in the history of motherhood. Moms have an unprecedented amount of knowledge, right at our fingertips. And yet, we are struggling more than ever—battling depression, caving under pressure, and desperately trying to figure out why we aren't measuring up to the ideals we have in our minds.

As a society, although we still have plenty of gains to make, women have come a long way. But our freedoms haven't been carried into the home.

On the surface, we might believe that mothers do share in that freedom. They can choose to have children or not have children. They can choose to stay at home or continue their careers. They have gained influence on finances and decisions that impact the family.

But hiding beneath that freedom is the Mother Load—the invisible tasks that we, as a society, believe that "good moms" do.

HELPING MOMS FEEL SEEN

Before I experienced my breakthrough, I had over seven years of postgraduate education and years of training and experience as a registered psychotherapist under my belt. And yet, postpartum depression, the "perfect mother" myth, and the invisible load snuck up on me. So if I, with all of my expertise, didn't see it coming, it's no surprise that so many other moms don't either.

When I returned to work after maternity leave, I was dedicated to helping moms feel seen and understood in a way that I wish I would have felt. I began specializing in maternal mental health, seeking additional training, including the Perinatal Mental Health Certification (PMH-C) with Postpartum Support International and many others. Now with more than a decade of experience as a therapist and creating psychoeducational content that has been shared by celebrities such as Snoop Dogg and Ashley Graham, I have built a business with one mission in mind—changing the way moms are supported.

In Momwell, my fast-growing and sought-after maternal mental health platform, my clients often express to me that they feel trapped by motherhood, that they experience identity loss, and that they are constantly scrambling, trying to keep up with everything they have to do. When I started speaking out about the invisible load on Instagram, mothers latched onto it. My posts about the mental labor we carry receive more engagement than any of my other content and have reached millions. Moms resonate with this load—even if they don't understand that they're carrying it.

It isn't just that they feel pressured to wash the dishes, vacuum the floors, and fold the laundry. The hidden Mother Load goes beyond these physical household tasks.

It's the invisible care work that exists underneath that labor. Soothing babies. Navigating tantrums. Keeping track of where everything is in the house. Scheduling and remembering appointments. Knowing when new clothes, diapers, wipes, and shoes are needed. Researching nap schedules and milestones and how to respond to children in a firm but gentle way. Creating activities that stimulate and educate our children. Playing Easter Bunny and Tooth Fairy and Santa. Remembering that one of the kids needs their special teddy bear to sleep, one needs three kisses on the forehead, and the other needs to be tucked in like a burrito.

Moms are the ones carrying most of that unseen labor, starting as early as before conception and continuing even as their children become adults.[4] But because they are under so much pressure to become "perfect moms," they often can't even see the load, much less go about releasing it.

Instead, they continue feeling exhausted, struggling to get it all done, and beating themselves up for falling short.

MOMS IN CRISIS

Moms are in crisis—now more than ever.

The pandemic brought a new level of invisible labor into homes. In addition to the unseen labor we were already carrying, we were suddenly navigating making new decisions about our children's health, worrying about protecting them, managing virtual and home school, choosing whether to send them back, putting our lives on hold during quarantine, and worrying about the impact the pandemic will have on our children. (Not to mention other topical emotional burdens—moms are now explaining to their children why they must do active shooter drills and helping them overcome their anxiety. Black mothers are worrying about their children's very existence, scared they will be targeted or that their life is at risk due to the color of their skin.)

Moms were more than twice as likely to report taking on a great deal of childcare labor in the wake of the pandemic than dads. Working moms were more likely to face barriers at work because of family responsibilities, find difficulty balancing work and parenting, and have work interrupted because of childcare than working dads.[5]

Moms also began exiting the workforce in massive numbers, often citing childcare as the primary reason.[6] The Mother Load isn't just stressing moms out—it has real, tangible impact on their mental health, their well-being, and their career trajectory. Mothers who want to remain in their careers are resigning due to the lack of flexibility in the workplace and the cost of childcare. Mothers who want to be home are being forced to work to help provide necessities for their families due to stagnant wages, the cost of living, and inflation. Economics and finances often dictate these "choices" for us, leaving us pinned into a decision one way or another, regardless of personal preference. Moms are all working, all carrying out the brunt of the load, and often struggling because of it.

The pandemic impacted home dynamics as well. Mothers were 42 percent more likely to have increased their time spent at home with their children during the pandemic than dads, and they were also more likely to experience frustration with their children and dissatisfaction with their relationships due to a lack of support.[7]

Maternal mental health has suffered from the pandemic. The rates of postpartum depression and anxiety have almost tripled since 2020.[8] Moms of color are at particular risk—they are up to twice as likely to develop symptoms of postpartum depression or anxiety than white moms, but significantly less likely to receive care for their mental health.[9]

Furthermore, mom rage (anger or irritability experienced by moms, which is often uncharacteristic, intense, and overwhelming) has also increased since the onset of the pandemic.[10] It's important to understand mom rage, why it happens, and why it's increasing. While all people experience anger in some capacity, maternal anger is unique. It is often fueled by burnout, mental health concerns, societal pressure, and a lack of support for moms. But due to the societal norms placed on mothers, it also comes with a deep sense of shame. Mothers are expected to be joyful, loving, patient, and kind. There isn't room in this romanticized ideal for irritability or rage. This disconnect between expectations and the reality of human emotions can leave us feeling as if we are failing in the motherhood role. We're putting moms between a rock and a hard place—expecting them to carry the invisible load alone, pull extra weight since the onset of the pandemic, and do it without struggling with their emotions or showing any signs of struggle.

Two things are clear—that the invisible load contributes to mental health concerns for moms and that the load is ever-increasing, especially in the wake of the pandemic.

But this isn't the way it has to be.

WHO IS THIS BOOK FOR? AN INCLUSIVE LOOK AT THE MOTHER LOAD

As we move forward in this book, I will be addressing motherhood as a construct, but it is important to remember that I am referring to a Western, often heteronormative ideology. There are many ways to mother, which look different based on geographical locations; cultural beliefs and traditions; family size and dynamics; and many other factors. And while all parents carry an invisible load, the Mother Load centered in this book stems from a specific parenting ideology, known as "intensive mothering," which we will dive deeper into in chapter 2. This ideology has become prevalent for moms in Western cultures. Of course, even the terms "Western moms" or "Western cultures" encompass a wide range of cultural beliefs, religious and racial makeups, and individual family dynamics. But research has shown that intensive mothering culture transcends individual cultural dynamics. Mothers in Western cultures often carry the beliefs of intensive mothering, regardless of socioeconomic status, race, ethnicity, relationship status, years in the relationship, number of children, or job status of the mother.[11]

To moms who are single or who are solo parenting right now for any number of reasons—I see you. These statistics referenced in this book often mention "dads" because these studies were centered around two-parent homes in different-sex relationships. But this book is *not* solely for heterosexual partnered moms. In fact, the lessons in this book are built on universal skills and can help *anyone* learn to break away from expectations and traditional roles often carried out in the home. However, our work here is mom-centered and framed in the context of motherhood.

There will also likely be people reading this book who are not in heteronormative relationships. It's important to note that even in non-heteronormative relationships, these dynamics can still play a role. Partners often fall into traditional "masculine" or "feminine" roles, regardless of their gender identity or sexual orientation. However, the distribution of labor between same-sex partners is statistically shared more evenly.[12]

There are likely several factors that play into this—including an openness to discussing gender and roles, and the very fact that gender isn't available as an automatic default for distribution. The studies referenced here did focus on different-sex couples, and it's important to acknowledge that. I value inclusivity, and I believe that moms can break away from female-coded roles formed by gender norms, whether they are in different-sex partnerships, same-sex partnerships, or single or solo parents.

I also know that many of you who are swarmed with this labor do not have a partner to share in this load. You're still in the right place. Throughout this book, we will use the word "partner" at times. This might be a romantic partner, whether they are the same sex or a different sex. But "partner" doesn't have to refer to a romantic relationship. This could be a support partner, a family member, or even a friend—anybody you can lean on to help share the load. Whether you have a romantic partner or the partner you are with is unwilling to share the load, you can still benefit from this book and learn to release the load. In fact, the bulk of this book is intended to be individual work.

If you do have a partner who is unwilling, and if you are trying harder to change someone than they are trying to change themselves, perhaps your relationship needs some support that goes beyond the invisible load and would benefit from couples therapy while you shift your focus to your own needs, mental health, and well-being.

In any case, much of this work is internal. There are skills and tools throughout this book that can be used with a partner to help communicate and share the load. However, the *real* work comes from reshaping our own internalized ideals, expectations, and beliefs around motherhood.

HOW TO RELEASE THE MOTHER LOAD

Motherhood doesn't have to mean being the only one your children need. It doesn't have to mean managing and scheduling and shopping and answering questions and remembering everything. It doesn't have to mean being the default parent for school phone calls and permission slips and haircuts and nail clipping.

It is possible to release the load, but the process of doing that goes beyond what we might think. It's not enough to try to divvy out tasks between you and your partner or your support system. It's not enough to just ask for help. The real glue that keeps you stuck in the Mother Load isn't outside of yourself—it's rooted deep in your beliefs.

That rulebook that I had been given—that all of us have been given—shapes the way we approach our roles as mothers.

Intensive mothering hasn't always been the norm. But in the mid-twentieth century, a shift happened.[13] Most of us can see this development in our own family lines. Our grandmothers were conditioned not to overindulge their children—to stick to schedules and rules and strict discipline. Even rocking and cuddling children to sleep was considered unusual. Now, we're told the opposite—we should respond to every need our children have, even if it interferes with our own. We must be responsive, nurturing, and gentle. But we must also guide and teach our children, fulfilling all their mental, physical, and emotional needs. We have to do it all, and do it perfectly.

If we believe that the perfect mother must sacrifice her own needs for her family's, find fulfillment only in motherhood, be "on" all the time, and act as the joyous, nurturing caregiver in the home, we cannot break out of the patterns that lead us to carry the invisible labor. While those beliefs remain in place, they act as a barrier for true redistribution and equality in the home. Those beliefs keep the invisible load intertwined with our identities—without breaking out of them, we will resist letting go and slip back into old patterns even if we try to share the load with others.

Step 1: Challenging Our Own Beliefs

In the first section of this book, we're going to dive deep into those beliefs—where they come from, the ways they appear, and how to break out of them. I will show you how to sort through those messages, toss out the harmful ones you have been given, and discover your own personal values (not the values given to you by someone else, but the principles that align with who you are as an individual). Those values will become your north star that guides you through the process of releasing the pieces of the Mother Load that don't align with what truly matters to you.

Step 2: Making the Mother Load Visible

After laying that foundation and establishing the values that will guide you through the process, we'll move into a deeper look into the Mother Load itself. Before we can release the Mother Load, we have to make it visible. We know we're exhausted, but we don't understand why until we experience an Aha Mom-ent that allows us to see the labor beneath the tip of the iceberg. And, in order to make that labor visible to our partners and potentially redistribute it, we must first make it visible to ourselves.

The second part of this book highlights the hidden roles moms are carrying and the actual weight of the load we take on by default. As we begin to see how much labor we are truly carrying, we can understand why we feel like we're drowning in a never-ending list of monitoring, planning, research, and other mental and emotional labor.

The loads throughout this book are not a comprehensive list of labor in the home, but they are the ones that I find the most consuming for my clients. As you read through this book, you can choose to follow through in order, or you may choose to skip around to the loads that are weighing most heavily on you and which ones matter the most to you.

The final load included is different than the rest—managing your own mental health (chapter 9). This load involves more emotional labor and often takes the deepest and most unseen toll on us. If you have been conditioned to believe in intensive mothering, I know that the thought of devoting time to your own mental health and true, deep self-care might feel impossible. But as you will see in chapter 9, it is foundational to releasing the Mother Load.

I chose not to start with that load for a reason, however. I know that if you are reading this book, you are probably at a point where you need solutions fast. You're treading water, and you're not sure where to start. I know that you will probably want to reach for the other loads first—the ones that are more tangible, that feel less scary and self-involved. But I urge you not to forsake that work. If you need to triage, I support you in that. However, if you truly want to release the load, the self-work must be done. It is vital. Take care of yourself as you work through this book. Take breaks as needed. Complete the exercises found throughout the book for digestible ways to jumpstart the process. Visit the skills sections toward the end of each load chapter for practical tips and takeaways. And see the "If You Only Remember One Thing" and "If You Only Do One Thing" sections at the very end of each load chapter to keep yourself from getting lost in the work.

CREATE YOUR OWN PATH IN MOTHERHOOD

Throughout this book, you will learn to see the Mother Load in its entirety—all of the invisible labor that keeps you overwhelmed and exhausted without even realizing what's happening. You will also learn how the societal expectations around motherhood have hoisted this load onto our shoulders, and how to break away from the beliefs that are keeping us stuck carrying it. Finally, you'll learn practical skills, tools, techniques, and scripts to begin releasing the Mother Load based on your values—not what you have been conditioned to think a "good mom" does. At the end of the process, you will have gone through the steps of releasing the Mother Load.

This journey might seem intimidating. You'll be doing deep reevaluation of your own beliefs and values. It will take work. But what you will gain, and what you have to lose, make it worth it.

You might be telling yourself you can handle the load—that if you just buckle down and work through it, you'll be fine. You might even think that this isn't a problem for other moms you know—that they are handling it just fine.

But modern mothers are not fine. And you are not alone.

By releasing the Mother Load, we have a lot to gain. We can chart our own journey in a way that is freeing, that feels right to us, and that doesn't leave us collapsing under the weight of something we never asked for.

After you finish this book, you will walk away with new skills, new understanding, and a new guide that will help you forge your own path in motherhood—not one given to you by society or Pinterest or the movies, but one based on what matters to who you are at the core.

I invite you to walk this journey with me—to learn how to shatter the myths that have given you false expectations, to form a new picture of motherhood that lets you parent more freely and with more fulfillment, and to finally release the Mother Load.

PART 1

THE ORIGIN, BELIEFS, AND VALUES THAT FORM THE MOTHER LOAD

1

THE BIRTH OF THE INVISIBLE LOAD

I can still vividly remember the laundry mountain that created my Aha Mom-ent—the moment I finally saw the invisible load of labor I carried.

As a therapist, I felt that motherhood was going to be a challenge I could tackle with grace and ease. I told myself I wasn't going to be the mom who snapped at her husband or kids. I was going to have a handle on the household. After all, I wasn't going to do it on my own. I had communication skills and the understanding of fairness and task-sharing. My husband and I talked openly about the physical tasks in the home and worked to divide them.

Laundry was one of the tasks that we split in a way we thought was fair. He was better at setting a timer and changing the loads over from the washer to the dryer. I took on the responsibility of folding the laundry and putting it away.

When I was postpartum with my third baby, laundry was a massive task for our family of five. Between diaper blowouts, spit-ups, and rough-and-tumble play, the loads piled up quickly.

As we needed laundry, my husband washed it, changed it over, and made a pile in our primary bedroom. But I started to slip behind, and that pile turned into a laundry mountain.

Every day I walked past the mountain multiple times to go to the bathroom or move around the house. And every day, I tried to pretend it wasn't there. As the mountain grew, it felt like my avoidance grew with it.

I was certainly busy . . . juggling the practical demands of having an infant and two toddlers. But my avoidance wasn't just about the time. I felt paralyzed by the thought of tackling the mountainous pile. I just couldn't face it.

Every time I passed by, it consumed my thoughts.

Ugh . . . that pile is growing even bigger.

You really need to fold that laundry today or it's going to be even worse tomorrow.

How come you can't just keep up with the laundry?

It's a simple task—why can't you just do it?

The thoughts grew more and more self-critical. Instead of motivating me, my internal monologue just fanned the flame of shame and inadequacy.

I grew increasingly harsh toward myself that I was letting everything pile up. I told myself that I should be able to handle it, that there was no good reason why it was such a big deal to me.

Everyone else could do it. Everyone else was managing to fold the laundry and take care of the kids. My husband was washing and drying the clothes with no problem. And I felt like I wasn't measuring up. (Little did I know that on top of my postpartum struggles, I also had undiagnosed ADHD, making task initiation and completion even more difficult. The Mother Load can be overwhelming for any mom, but for those of us who are neurodivergent or struggle with our mental health, the burden can feel even heavier.)

The pile became an analogy for how so much of motherhood felt at the time.

I even tried to seek moral support. While I sat there wrestling with this beast in my mind, I reached out to people in my support system to tell them how I was feeling.

But in return, I was met with toxic positivity. Some of it was the usual, "Oh, you'll get through this. Your kids are only little once." Some of it was more extreme. "You should be grateful that you have kids to fold clothes for." Or "At least your husband is willing to help."

I felt guilty, ashamed, confused, and alone. Of course, I was grateful to have children. Of course, I loved being a mom. But my love for being a mom didn't erase the load I was facing. We should be able to hold space for acknowledging what is hard *and* still be grateful for what we have.

Finally, one day as I moved by the pile, instead of kicking myself, I decided to get curious. *Why* couldn't I do it? *Why* was this so hard for me?

I know that you're probably wondering why we're *still* talking about laundry. How could something so routine and mundane bring forth a life-changing revelation for me? But it *did*. And that's because it wasn't just about the laundry. Something more was going on.

On episode 129 of *The Momwell Podcast*, maternal mental health therapist Erin Spahr likens the invisible load to a backpack that gets handed to us when we became mothers—or for many of us BEFORE we even become mothers.[1]

Sometimes this happens as early as trying to conceive—working through fertility treatments if necessary, tracking ovulation, planning when to take pregnancy tests, and muddling through the anticipation of the two-week wait.

For others, this happens when we become pregnant—handling appointments, researching cribs and bottles and car seats. Labor itself comes with plenty of invisible labor—aside from the physical act itself, moms carry most of the research, creating a birth plan, monitoring their own health, worrying about what to ingest and not ingest.

Other moms might not feel the weight until the postpartum period—navigating feeding challenges, night wakings, the pressure to "bounce back," the emotional weight of caring for a baby, and so much more.

It might hit moms at different times, but most of us feel the weight of the backpack handed to us. It's full of more tasks than we would ever imagine possible—more tasks than we even realize we're being given.

Everyone is just moving around, acting like the massive backpack carrying this impossible load isn't even there.

That's what was happening with me. I was carrying an invisible backpack that I felt the weight of but couldn't yet identify. The more curious I became, the more I realized it was more than the pile of clothes in my room. The season was changing from spring into summer. So, before I could put the laundry away, I needed to go through three different dressers, figure out what fit and what didn't fit, sort through everything so the warmer weather clothes were ready to go, and store the rest away somewhere—for three human beings. I also had to determine whether we needed to buy more things, and then shop for all those things.

It wasn't just a simple task of folding. It was four to five hours of additional physical tasks, plus the cognitive planning that I needed to do to make sure that all three kids had the right sizes of fall clothes ready to go.

My resistance had nothing to do with the physical act of folding clothes. It had everything to do with the ripple effect, of the other invisible tasks that came along with it.

> I couldn't see what I was carrying, but it was there—a looming list of unseen tasks, never-ending and smothering.

That was my Aha Mom-ent. I had been living with a distorted view of motherhood, of labor, and of my own reality. I couldn't see what I was carrying, but it was there—a looming list of unseen tasks, never-ending and smothering.

Once I noticed the load, and gave it a name, the weight came crashing down around me. For the first time, I could see what was going on. Even though we had tried to share the labor in the home fairly, I had ended up carrying a load I didn't even see.

I had to see beyond just the physical task at hand. I needed to become curious, to stop criticizing myself and dig a little bit deeper. Instead of telling myself that I was failing, that I was being irrational, that there was something wrong with me if I couldn't do this simple task, I had to investigate my feelings objectively.

When I saw what was really going on—the depths of mental labor that accompanied the task—I was able to make the Mother Load visible.

From there, I was able to work with my partner. We approached it together, him carving out a chunk of time to do the shopping, sharing in that mental load that I was carrying.

Discovering the invisible mountain of work that was hiding behind the mountain of laundry in my bedroom was one of the most important steps I could take to freeing myself as a mother, parenting with my values, and sharing a life more fairly with my partner.

The more steps I took on that journey, the more I came to realize that moms everywhere were struggling with this same thing—they were often bearing the brunt of the cognitive labor by themselves.

WHAT IS COGNITIVE LABOR?

What I experienced with that load of laundry wasn't unique. In fact, it's something that most modern moms in Western cultures face. Moms are disproportionately responsible for the cognitive labor in the home.

Cognitive labor is the mental work that accompanies a task. Think back to writing a research paper in school. Before you actually *wrote* anything, you had to find sources, read them, decide what information was usable, figure out how to organize the data, and plan out how you would approach the paper. All of that "thinking" work came before you ever sat down to write a word. But it was as difficult and necessary as the writing itself.

That concept also applies to family roles. As I realized when it came to laundry, there was so much more than the physical task of folding and putting away. There was an entire series of unrecognized cognitive labor woven in.

Think about how your child got dressed today. Who picked out the clothes? How did they get into the dresser? Who monitored the need for clothing in that size—continually tracking each item of clothing for each child? Who made sure it was weather-appropriate? Who purchased that clothing item and brought it home? Who noticed the child needed new clothing in the first place?

Each household task is the tip of an iceberg. Below it comes a slew of unseen mental tasks. Noticing. Research. Planning. Monitoring. Managing. Organizing. Scheduling. These mental tasks are vital to the way a household functions. And the majority of the cognitive labor, or "thinking work," falls to moms—even in families that actively try to divide tasks fairly.

Imagine sitting down and dividing up every physical task your family needs to do for the week. Perhaps you say you're going to take the cooking and your spouse offers to do the shopping. But then it's shopping day, and your spouse asks you to make a list of what you need. While at the store, they contact you several times to ask about brands, substitutions, and clarifications. They bring the groceries home and start to put them away, but they come to you to ask where things go. By the time the task is done, you almost feel like you did the work. And, in a way, you did. Sure, your spouse did the physical work of shopping. But the cognitive labor still fell to you.

For years, researchers and sociologists have pointed out that women hold an unfair portion of care work. Many studies and articles have identified this unpaid labor and highlighted the way these tasks fall to moms.

However, most of that research has looked at *physical* tasks. Who is doing the dishes? Who is mopping the floors? Who is changing diapers? Who is feeding the baby? It isn't considering who decides where the dishes go in the cabinets, monitoring when cleaning solution needs to be purchased, knowing when the baby is moving up to the next diaper size, or worrying about whether the baby is eating enough.

Part of the reason why these tasks are overlooked, even in the academic and sociological worlds, is that they are abstract. It's difficult to define them. It's even harder to monitor them. As long as it remains undefined, it will remain unbalanced. We can't try to distribute labor fairly if we don't even clearly understand it.

In recent years, researchers have started to unpack cognitive labor more concretely. While more work needs to be done to fully define it, a picture is beginning to emerge. No household task is done without invisible cognitive pre-tasks. This means that cognitive labor should not be looked at as parallel to manual labor. It's not just another task to divide up in the home—it's the foundation of every task that gets accomplished. Researcher Allison Daminger has emerged as one of the voices leading the quest to define and identify mental labor. She breaks it down into four steps—anticipating needs, identifying options to meet those needs, deciding what option to implement, and monitoring the success of that option.[2]

We can break down any household task into those four steps. For example, when bottle-feeding an infant:

1. *Anticipating needs:* As the baby registry is prepared, understanding that bottles will need to be chosen and purchased.

2. *Identifying options:* Reading forums, asking for recommendations on social media, looking into reviews of those options.

3. *Deciding what option to go with:* Picking, searching for, and purchasing the bottle.

4. *Monitoring:* Determining if the baby likes the bottle. If the bottle doesn't work, this process starts back over again.

The results of Daminger's study showed that female-identifying partners carried most of the cognitive load in almost every area in the home. The study also revealed that women took responsibility for all the steps of cognitive labor except decision-making. (She determined that men were more likely to be the final decision-makers.) This is likely because it is the mental task most closely associated with power. Women overwhelmingly took on the steps of anticipation and research.[3]

Another study in *Psychology of Women Quarterly* breaks cognitive labor into six themes—planning/strategizing, monitoring and anticipating needs, knowing, managerial thinking, and self-regulating. Moms in this study overwhelmingly reported that they were responsible for most of the invisible labor in the household.[4]

For our purposes in this book, I will simplify the mental load into three categories—anticipating, research and planning, and management. This will help us begin to see the labor that might be hidden, even to us.

In both studies, the researchers noticed that at first, the moms being interviewed struggled to see, understand, and verbalize the scope of the mental load. But once the language was there, once their eyes were opened, they realized they were solely responsible for most of the thinking work in the home.

Just like me and my laundry mountain, they couldn't even see what was happening at first. They needed the Aha Mom-ent before they even understood the invisible load they carried.

The Mother Load remains hidden, slowly wearing us down over time, leaving us exhausted, confused, and frustrated. When we become first-time moms, we know we're going to have to tackle new physical tasks. But what we don't anticipate is the amount of unseen labor that we are about to take on—all the while being sleep-deprived and malnourished. Then, if we have more children, the load continues to multiply, becoming even heavier, but staying invisible.

THE EMOTIONAL AND THE COGNITIVE

Some researchers separate cognitive responsibilities (for example, planning, organizing, and maintaining) from the emotional load (anticipating and tending to the emotional needs of the family).

They are distinctly different. Regulating your own stress and anger while navigating a toddler tantrum falls under emotional labor. Researching different methods to address tantrums, on the other hand, is a cognitive task. Emotional labor often involves making decisions in the moment to keep everybody calm and happy. We'll dive deeper into emotional labor and mental health in chapter 9.

The emotional and cognitive labor go hand in hand, and both fall disproportionately to moms. In this book, we're discussing the overall mental load—the cognitive and emotional labor that go into running a household.

If we are going to address the invisible elephant in the room, we must gain the right language. That's why it's important to understand that the cognitive and emotional loads are different.

THE REAL WEIGHT OF THE MOTHER LOAD

Reading these studies reaffirmed what I experienced in my own home and what I have seen with so many of my clients. The invisible load is real. When we feel like we're losing our minds, when we feel like motherhood is enveloping us completely, when we feel like we're working more than our spouses, even if it doesn't seem that way on paper, we aren't imagining it.

Mental labor isn't like physical labor. It isn't a one-and-done task. It isn't a checkbox to be ticked or a list to cross off. The anticipating, the research and planning, the management options—those are things that stick with us. Women are far more likely to report cognitive tasks intruding onto their free time, or even paid work time.[5]

Physical tasks are far less likely to pop into our minds. If you know you need to take out the trash, there's no sense worrying about it while you're at work, at the gym, or having coffee with friends. If it does cross your mind, it passes by just as quickly.

But what if you're carrying the mental weight that accompanies it? What if you know you need trash bags, and the last trash bags you purchased were scented and you didn't like them, so now you must find other options? What if you must remember that the bins are getting picked up a day late this week because it was a holiday, so you shift your schedule and make sure that you get them out on the right day? What if you need to also clean out the refrigerator on the same day so that everything gets picked up? It becomes much harder to put those things out of your mind.

That is a large part of why motherhood is so emotionally and mentally exhausting, why it feels like you have lost your identity. It isn't just that you are responsible for more tasks. You're struggling with a mental load you can't get away from. Even if you do carve out time for yourself, time to de-stress, it's hard to keep the invisible load from encroaching on that time.

To compound an already difficult situation, those abstract cognitive tasks so often feel incomplete or unsatisfying. Mental tasks don't even come with the same sense of accomplishment that physical tasks do.[6] They are often ongoing or cyclical and never reach a state of being "done."

Organizing a playroom might make you feel proud and put together. But researching the options for storage and thinking about them while you're in the shower probably doesn't leave you with that same feeling.

The Mother Load is the perfect storm—work that is so hidden, we don't even know about it ourselves. Work that is so abstract, nobody thinks of it as work. Work that is either forever ongoing or accompanied by a host of other mental tasks. Work that can't be put away, because so much of it takes place in our minds. Work that doesn't let us cross something off a checklist and feel accomplished. Work we can never escape from.

THE IMPORTANCE OF THE AHA MOM-ENT

Before you can release the Mother Load, you must recognize it. We can't redistribute something that we don't even know that we're carrying.

Your mom didn't sit down with you and tell you, "Hey, you're going to carry just about every mental task in your household for the rest of your life if you're not careful." (After all, she probably didn't realize it either.)

To make a change, we need the Aha Mom-ent—when it all crashes down and for the first time we understand . . . this is happening.

Once you see it, you can't unsee it. You realize that everything from feeding the baby to planning birthday parties to doing the dishes comes with a heavy load of cognitive labor that isn't being seen.

If you're still not convinced, grab a pencil and paper. Start at the beginning of your day yesterday and write down everything you did. Every physical task you completed. Every emotional task you faced. Every mental task that fell on your shoulders. Every decision you made. Every worry about the household you had.

My guess is you won't even make it through lunchtime before you realize that you're lugging more than you thought you were.

WHY IS THE LOAD FALLING TO MOMS?

So, why is this happening? Have mothers felt this way forever? To answer that question, we need to reflect on the way family dynamics have changed over time. Back in hunter and gatherer societies, the phrase "it takes a village to raise a child" was taken literally. When a baby was born, the entire village flocked to help.

Even though the mother still took on primary childcare responsibilities for an infant, the rest of her cognitive load was lighter. Someone else was there to help cook. Someone else was fulfilling her gathering quota for the day. Someone else was taking any older children to play and work with the other kids in the village. She was allowed to focus on the primary task of caring for the baby, with all the decisions and thoughts that went into it.

Of course, as society advanced, the cognitive load itself grew. No longer were responsibilities limited to care and feeding. We got larger houses, with societal expectations about cleanliness and organization. We started to give our children toys, little by little, until the house became full of small things that create clutter and extra tasks. Finances completely changed—mortgages, utilities, loans, and insurance made their way into our minds, demanding thought and budgeting and planning.

We started working outside the home—first one spouse, then often both. With that came daycare or nanny decisions, bags needing to be packed, schedules juggled for drop-offs and pickups. Playgroups, play dates, social interactions, extracurricular activities—with each social progression came more and more cognitive labor.

At first, most of it fell to moms out of practicality. After all, if the dad was at work all day, it made sense for the mom to manage the household. But as society shifted, and the cognitive labor grew larger and larger, it continued to pile on the shoulders of moms. At the same time, feminist progression brought more possibilities for women. But even as they gained freedom outside of the home, the cognitive burdens at home remained, fueled by generations of societal expectations and gender norms ("rules" for how men and women act).

HOW GENDER NORMS PAVE THE WAY FOR THE MOTHER LOAD

What does it mean to you to be a "good mother"? Take a minute and think about it, or jot down some ideas in a notebook. Does a good mother attend to the needs of her children? Does she find motherhood enjoyable? Does she sacrifice her own needs for those of her family? Does she give her kids the last piece of pie, even when she wants it?

Gender expert Kate Mangino dives into this idea in her book, *Equal Partners: Improving Gender Equality at Home,* theorizing that gender norms are largely responsible for the imbalance of labor in the home.[7]

For most of us, what it means to be a "good mother" is steeped in gender norms—norms we might not have ever thought about consciously or realized we have been absorbing our entire lives.

From the time we are born, we're receiving subtle (and not-so-subtle) messages about gender norms. When we see our moms managing schedules, packing backpacks, and signing permission slips, we internalize that. When we see dads leaving the home or performing physical labor, we internalize that.

In *Equal Partners,* Kate points out that over time, we begin to gender-code behaviors, in and out of the home. We see behaviors as feminine-coded and masculine-coded.[8]

As a society, many emotions and behaviors are gender-coded:

- Women are naturally better multitaskers
- Men carry out the physical labor because they are stronger
- Women are more nurturing

These beliefs take hold, even in those of us who think we "know better," who value equality.

Let's take this a step further from Kate's gender coding and look at how this plays out in parenthood. Many tasks become male-coded or female-coded, which shapes the labor we take on. For example, if you believe that feeding is female-coded, you might not even think to include fathers in the feeding process. A mom might believe she is the one who should handle all the night feeds because that is her role as a woman. This can even create a cycle of gendered behavior—for example, if a dad is never given a chance to give a bottle, the baby might struggle to take one, leading to more labor for a mom.

Taking a Look at Your Own Gender Coding

In order to move forward with releasing the invisible load, you need to get clear on your own associations with gendered roles in the home. Look through the following tasks. Write "MC" (mother-coded) next to any you associate with moms, "FC" (father-coded) next to any you associate with dads, and "N" next to any that you view as neutral or primarily shared:

____ Fixing a toilet

____ Feeding a baby

____ Comforting a child after an injury

____ Cooking

____ Mowing the lawn

____ Decorating for holidays

____ Organizing toy storage

____ Taking out the trash

____ Packing backpacks

____ Grocery shopping

____ Scheduling appointments

____ Trimming trees

____ Washing the car

____ Playing Tooth Fairy

____ Waking up at night with the baby

____ Packing the diaper bag

____ Disciplining the children

____ Cleaning out the refrigerator

____ Organizing the closets

____ Keeping track of what groceries need to be purchased

Now, add up your MCs and FCs and check your association level:

15 or more gender-coded tasks: Rigid—you hold very tightly to gender norms. It will likely take a great deal of unlearning and intention to overcome these norms in your household and work toward a fair distribution of labor.

10-14 gender-coded tasks: Moderate—there are many areas that you hold to gender norms, which is likely impacting the distribution of labor in your home. You have some areas that are considered neutral, but you'll need to work on overcoming beliefs around the rest.

5-10 gender-coded tasks: Intermediate—you don't hold rigidly to traditional gender norms, but they are still present in your home and will need to be addressed internally and with your partner.

0-5 gender-coded tasks: Progressive—gendered behavior is not as prevalent in your home. You still might have an imbalance in labor, but you are starting from a solid foundation.

Now . . . I am going to tell you something that might feel uncomfortable, but it is central both to this book and to how we move forward in the process of releasing the Mother Load.

The majority of tasks in parenthood are gender neutral.

Can we get real for a second? As moms, we often pride ourselves in our work at home. We build our identity around motherhood. And it feels good to be good at it. There's nothing wrong with taking pride in your ability as a mom or valuing the work you do. (In fact, it's important to value your work!)

But if we want equality in the home, we need to understand that we aren't "better" than our partners at raising children. It might seem like these tasks come easier to us. But if we dig down to the root of it, we can see that it isn't that we are biologically better—it's that we have taken on more of the work and are more experienced at it. (We'll break that idea down in the next section).

Most of the tasks in parenthood are not actually intrinsically linked to a specific gender or sex. There are a handful of tasks that require a specific biological sex—birth, carrying a baby inside a uterus, and the physical act of breastfeeding. (Although even those can be shared to some degree—for example, a partner giving a bottle or being an active support person during labor.)

But aside from those few tasks, care work is not biological. Moms aren't *naturally* better at nurturing, soothing, or multitasking.

You might do it better (and in fact, you likely do) but it isn't because you are inherently better at it—it is because you are the one that is ALREADY doing it.

We have been shaped since birth to associate care work with women, these tasks are all too often entangled with the identity of a mother. But you can take pride in your identity as a mom and share the load fairly in the home. In fact, sharing that load will give you more brain space, time, and energy to be the mom and the individual PERSON you want to be (not the one society decided you should be).

It's going to be tempting to hold onto the belief that you are biologically programmed to be better at care work. That belief has likely played into the foundation of your identity as a mom. It might be easier to create a list of chores and ask your partner to take on their fair share without confronting these beliefs—in the short run.

But what I often see with clients who try to divide up the labor without examining the role that gender and socialization have played in their household dynamic is that they eventually slip back into the same patterns—no matter how many chore charts, spreadsheets, or rotations they create.

Why? Because if you believe deep down that care tasks are coded to moms, and that your value as a mother is measured in those tasks, you will likely take them back on your shoulders. Likewise, if your partner holds those beliefs, they will likely fall back into the same behaviors they are fulfilling now.

Whew, how's that for some real talk? The reality is we can't move forward without addressing that gender-coded elephant in the room.

It's also vital to consider how strong of a hold gender norms have, not just on us, but on our partner as well. If you are in a different-sex relationship, care work has likely not been expected of your partner. In fact, they may have been raised to reject or avoid anything associated with femininity or nurturing. From the time men are very young, they are taught to adhere to "masculinity" and abandon anything feminine. While these messages may look different based on individual family dynamics, race, culture, and religion, the end result is often that children are being socialized to adopt certain behaviors and ideals based on their apparent gender.

I could write an entire book about the way young boys are socialized to behave, and the way that ideals of masculinity get passed down, but that's a project for another day. For now, however, here is a quick overview of healthy vs. unhealthy masculinity:

Unhealthy Masculinity

- Promotes detachment from emotions
- Minimizes others' feelings
- Sees care work as "a woman's work"
- Struggles to connect with the nurturing side in parenthood
- Maintains a tough exterior or displays physical aggression
- Expects hyper-independence
- Displays anti-feminist or sexist behavior

Healthy Masculinity

- Allows for the full human spectrum of emotion
- Teaches men to validate others' feelings
- Empowers men to take on care work (benefiting both themselves and their partners)
- Allows men to be emotionally available to all children
- Teaches men to separate the feeling of anger from violence or verbal abuse
- Creates and maintains friendships
- Teaches men to use their male privilege to advocate for others

This is why it's important to think of the Mother Load not just as chores or the tasks at hand or what our partner is not doing versus what we are doing. The problem is so much more complex than that, and it centers largely around the gender norms that have been handed to both you and your partner. Breaking out of those gender norms is going to be a process for you both.

SEPARATING YOUR PARTNER FROM THE PROBLEM

When you're drowning in the invisible load, it's easy to view your partner as the problem. You might think that they should see everything that you do, and jump in willingly with the same initiative that you do. And you're right—in an ideal, fair world, that's how it should be. But the truth is that your partner is living with the same gender norms that you have lived with. Just like you, they've been conditioned to see this work as a mother's work for their entire lives.

Your partner is not the enemy—the system is. If you're going to have a healthy, productive conversation (or many healthy, productive conversations) about sharing this load, it's important to separate your partner from the problem.

Just as you have been handed a backpack full of beliefs that are not your own, messages about what a "good mom" does, and norms and roles you didn't realize you would play out, so has your partner. And just as you have found yourself in these patterns without realizing it, so have they.

The sooner we realize that the lack of shared labor in the home is not something our partner is deliberately doing *to us*, the sooner we can depersonalize the behavior and approach the true issue as a team rather than seeing each other as the problem. We'll get more information on depersonalizing our partner's behavior in chapter 6.

PERFECTION AS A MEASURING STICK

Gender norms aren't the only dynamic shaping the Mother Load. While gender norms have been passed down in our backpacks, we're also carrying something that our moms and grandmothers didn't carry—the ideal of perfection. We're now expected to do and be it all, carrying the burden of the invisible load while also dedicating every ounce of our time and energy to our kids.

Working moms are still juggling the majority of the household mental load, as well as tackling work responsibilities. But mothers who stay home gained more responsibilities too. It is no longer "good enough" to just care for your children and make sure they are happy and healthy. Now, even though they are encouraged to practice "self-care" and take "me time," stay-at-home moms are expected to facilitate outings, educate their children in preparation for school, provide stimulating environments, limit screen time, and never take their eyes off the kids. Single moms might feel even more pressure to be "on" constantly, juggling all this labor alone and still trying to be and do more. Sometimes moms feel so guilty and worried about potentially damaging their children that they stay in abusive or unhealthy relationships for too long, carrying the emotional burden and adding to the load.

In the book *Modern Motherhood and Women's Dual Identities*, Dr. Petra Bueskens writes about this paradox that modern mothers face. On the one hand, we have been freed as women, as individuals. At the same time, we have been constrained as mothers.[9]

We've been conditioned to believe that we must be perfect. We must dote on our children at all times—sacrificing our own needs and identities. We must exhaust ourselves to provide stimulating experiences for our children. We must find fulfillment in our children, and only in our children. We must be invested constantly, never taking time for ourselves. And we must juggle all of the physical, emotional, and mental responsibilities in the home, never questioning the role we've been assigned. (We'll get more into reshaping the measuring stick of motherhood in the skills section of chapter 4.) This concept of the perfect mom (and the series of beliefs that come with it, which we will dive further into in chapter 2) has saddled us with an overwhelming amount of labor—an impossible load to keep up with. Now, we're drowning in it.

MATERNAL KNOWLEDGE AND THE
NOVICE/EXPERT DILEMMA

Another massive factor in the Mother Load is the distribution of knowledge. There is an idea in books and movies, and in most of our minds before we enter motherhood, that these skills are natural, innate, inborn. We think that we will be able to rely on our "maternal instincts" to guide us and make the right decisions.

But there is a difference between instinct and intuition. Instinct is innate—a natural tendency. Intuition, on the other hand, is the ability to know or do something without thinking consciously about it—and this ability comes from experience.

We *think* of parenting as instinctual. But in reality, parenting isn't innate—it's learned. We were all novice parents to begin with. Remember the first time you held your baby? Or changed a diaper? Were you confident? Or shaky on your feet, unsure of exactly what you were doing?

Breastfeeding is a prime example. While it is "natural," countless moms and babies struggle to find their footing if they choose to pursue it. It is often a difficult process with a steep learning curve and many variables that must align and come together.

But over time, tasks get easier. We become more skilled. Eventually, we can change a diaper for a squirming baby with one hand while wiping a toddler's nose with the other hand. We become more confident, capable, and experienced. While we might not call ourselves parenting "experts," at some point we do reach that "expert level." That's where intuition comes into play. We no longer struggle to put on a diaper. We know exactly how to rock the baby. We intuitively know what to do in a crisis—not because we were born to know, but because we have already handled thousands of decisions before.

The idea of expertise has been studied for a long time. Researcher Anders Ericsson conducted several studies to discover how long it takes to become an expert in a field. He found that the answer could lie anywhere from ten thousand to twenty-five thousand hours. However, the more important factor than time is "deliberate practice" (being effortful in nature, with the main goal of personal improvement of performance rather than enjoyment, often performed without immediate reward).[10]

Moms will likely feel a connection to that definition—we work to better ourselves, put forth effort, improve performance over enjoyment and often receive no immediate reward.

If we took Ericsson's expertise level of ten thousand hours to heart (a popular figure used by other authors and researchers) and said that new moms spent only twelve hours a day with "deliberate practice" (and, let's be honest, they spend closer to twenty-four when we factor in mental and emotional labor and night wakings), then by the time their child is two and a half, they have reached expert-level status.

But what if their partner is only available for three hours during weekdays and twelve on weekends? This equates to about forty hours a week, the same as a full-time job. That's less than half of the weekly labor the mom is putting in—meaning it would take more than twice as long for them to reach "expert parenting level."

What often happens is that moms carve out their roles as "expert" parents early on. They become more "intuitive" because they are more experienced. And, once that is established and they have the maternal knowledge, expertise, and deliberate practice under their belts . . . their expertise keeps them trapped in a default parenting role.

It's an easy pattern to fall into. It even seems *logical* on the surface. If one partner is a Michelin-star chef, who would you expect to cook the meals?

But when it comes to parenting, this becomes problematic—it starts a gap that widens with each day, month, and year. Mom knows how to fix the oatmeal to each child's preference. Mom knows where the band-aids are. Mom knows which bins have clean underwear for potty training and which ones need to be washed. And, most importantly, they are doing the bulk of the research.

The gap in knowledge and research often starts before conception. Moms are Googling, researching, and learning. *Which pregnancy tests are the most accurate?*

And it continues during pregnancy. *What do we need on the registry?* Moms are tracking babies' growth and development, counting kicks, watching what they eat, monitoring their weight, and often worrying incessantly in the process.

By the time a baby is born, the gap can already be extremely substantial. The patterns in the mental labor imbalance are already laid down. And they escalate after a baby comes home.

For many moms, communicating and sharing the knowledge, answers, and research feels like just another overbearing task. The famous last words of a mom? "It's easier if I just do it myself."

There is a prevailing belief for moms that they are better at care tasks. But the reason they are better is because they have had the hours, the deliberate practice, to become experts.

It isn't easy to let go of the idea that it's easier to do it yourself. It isn't easy to accept that your partner is going to do things at a different level than you are. But if we never let our partners take on labor, if we take it all on for ourselves because we want it done at expert level, we're shooting ourselves (and our partners) in the foot.

PARENTAL LEAVE AND THE KNOWLEDGE GAP

Parental leave plays a big role in that knowledge gap. When a mom is home on maternity leave and a partner goes back to work, she inherently gets more touchpoints, more experience, and more deliberate practice, leading her to take on that expert role. She knows where everything is. She knows how to entertain the baby during diaper changes. She knows what labor needs to be done—and she does it.

When I was on maternity leave, it truly felt like it had to be me—that I had to be the one to do the care work in the home. Frenel had been "restructured" out of his job when I was six months pregnant with our first son, so when he took a corporate job, one with promising career potential, we were relying on that as a lifeline. He had to keep working, and he couldn't do anything to jeopardize his position.

When our first son was born, he planned to stay home for a week. But when that week was up, I still hadn't found my footing, so he took another week—both from his annual vacation time. He was commuting to downtown Toronto, working twelve-hour days. And I was at home, trying to figure out where my maternal instinct was.

Day by day, I got better at managing everything. And the more I managed, the more it made sense to take on. I started taking on even more of the labor in the home. And while I felt my bond with the baby growing, Frenel's time was limited to bedtime tuck-ins and weekends.

We were creating the novice/expert dynamic, without intention.

Of course, we were grateful and privileged that I was able to stay home. In many countries, moms are still unable to take paid maternity leave, despite its benefits for maternal and infant mental health:

- The United States offers only twelve weeks of unpaid maternity leave—and that only applies to companies with fifty employees or more[11]

- 25 percent of moms in the United States return to work within two weeks of giving birth[12]

- In the United States, more than half of moms return to work within three months[13]

- Short maternity leave places women at increased risk for postpartum depression[14]

- Taking maternity leave improves maternal health and well-being[15]

When moms have the chance to be at home, find their footing as mothers, learn and develop parenting skills, and bond with their babies, they fare better in the postpartum period. However, what's interesting is that, beyond twenty-five weeks, extra maternity leave doesn't seem to add mental health benefits for a mom.[16]

There could be many reasons for this, but we can speculate that isolation, the invisible load, and the pressures of intensive mothering could play a role. Moms in countries with leave might even want to return to work after a certain period of time but feel pressured to take as much leave as is available to them. It's as if moms can't win—they are expected to be home with their babies, and yet in some countries, that time is not protected.

The lack of paid time off is even worse for fathers. Even in the countries where parental leave is prioritized, it is often only offered to the mother, and almost always provides more time for the mother than the father. While maternity leave is undoubtedly important, dads are getting left behind—and it's impacting both partners:

- When fathers take no paternity leave, moms carry more of the household labor[17]

- If fathers take less than two months of paternity leave, no long-term change in the distribution of labor occurs[18]

- Fathers who take more than two months' leave do more household labor than those who take less or no leave, even years after they return to work[19]

- 88 percent of moms in Canada take parental leave, while only 46 percent of fathers do[20]

- In the United States, 70 percent of fathers take ten days of leave or less[21]

- In the United States, only 13 percent of dads who take leave receive pay for it[22]

In countries where paid paternal leave is not offered, dads often take vacation or other leave, paid or unpaid—at a time when families are facing increased expenses and, in the United States, massive medical bills. The financial pressures on dads to forsake leave to work is staggering.

In the United States, if you don't have a corporate job with a big company, *paid* paternity leave is almost unheard of. When a dad is paid by the hour, every moment he spends with his family for leave is a sacrifice, not just of potential career growth but of actual money in the family's pocket—their lifeline. If a mom is missing out on part or all her income due to leave, dads often feel as if they have no choice but to return to work as soon as possible.

Financial concerns aren't the only factor at play. Even if they do have access to leave, they might fear that taking leave will show they aren't dedicated, or put their jobs or advancement opportunities at risk.[23]

Gender norms are often also at play. Dads feel that they must provide for their family. The idea of a man being the breadwinner is coded strongly in many families.

But what if we could change the script? What if, instead of Mom at home while Dad feels pressured to be back at work, we both had time together at home to share in the learned parenting skills? What if we were becoming experts together? Of course, we can't overhaul the entire system with this book. But we can change the system within our homes.

If you're reading this now, chances are you find yourself experiencing an unequal distribution of labor in the home, possibly impacting your mental health, your relationship, your career, and even your satisfaction in motherhood.

This pattern is not your fault, and if you are in a partnership, I will go out on a limb and say it's also not your partner's fault. It might be easy to blame your partner, to resent them for leaving you with the bulk of the labor. But there is more at play than the two of you. You have both been handed a set of expectations, gender norms, ideals, and stereotypes. You have both fallen into the same patterns that so many couples have. You are both subjects of a system and policies that default care work to mothers. But it is possible to push back and release the load.

UNLEARNING THE BELIEFS OF THE MOTHER LOAD

The knowledge that the invisible load is real, and that you are carrying an unfair portion of it, is empowering. It can also be overwhelming. Once you experience your Aha Mom-ent, your eyes are open, but your hands feel tied.

If you feel heavy now, it's because the doom and gloom of the invisible load is still there—you're just able to see it now.

How do you possibly battle socially ingrained behaviors you've carried your entire life? Where do you even begin to tackle the problem? Do you even *want* to change it?

After all, the Mother Load is paradoxically empowering and burdensome. While part of you knows that it's unfair, that you can't go on like this, that something needs to be done to redistribute the burden, part of you might want to continue being the keeper of that maternal knowledge you hold.

Motherhood takes so much control away from us. We are tethered, physically and emotionally, to small beings who rely on us. We no longer get to decide to sleep in, or to go out on a whim, or sometimes even when we get to take a shower. So, we often try to regain control by holding onto things that only weigh us down.

When Dr. Dan Singley appeared on episode 177 of *The Momwell Podcast*, he pointed out that traditional masculine roles, such as working outside the home, are associated with power, while traditional feminine roles, such as caregiving, are not.[24] In a world that often tells us that men wield the power, holding onto the limited control we do have is a natural response. The household is one area where we could traditionally feel a sense of power or control. But is that control worth the cost?

The truth is that once you are aware, you are at a crossroads. You can continue to live with the Mother Load, knowing and seeing that you hold an unfair burden of work. Or you can set off on a path to do things differently, to release the load, the pressure, and the beliefs that are keeping it on your shoulders.

Some of the labor in your home can't be unloaded. Some tasks are being carried not by choice, but by necessity, by life circumstances, and by the season of life you are in. But some of the load can change. Some can go away altogether. And some can be carried by others. When you can evaluate what is essential and what is not, you can unlearn what you've been taught and choose to do things differently.

Both options are hard. It's difficult to thrive when you feel like you're drowning. But it's also extremely hard to make a change. Neither path is easy. But one feels more worth it. At least with the hard work to unlearn the beliefs we've been handed about mental work, we make movement in the right direction.

Because for so many of us, the status quo isn't working. Avoiding the truth about the invisible load feels like the path of least resistance, but could contribute to stress, burnout, anxiety, and depression in the long term. Mothers are struggling, alone, being smothered by the invisible labor that nobody talks about. But with small steps, we as individuals can step out from under the load, take control (where we can), and shine the light on the invisible load. We can make a difference, not only for ourselves, but for those around us.

Releasing labor for yourself isn't going to change society with the sweep of a brush. But we give permission to others when we do things differently ourselves. It creates a ripple effect on our circle of influence.

The decision you make—the path you choose to take—can make a difference: for you and your family, for your marriage, for your relationship with motherhood. It can set a different example for your children, altering the generational cycles of families.

HOW DO WE RELEASE THE LOAD?

When we make the decision to release the load, we free ourselves from undue mental burden. We can gain peace, happiness, and satisfaction in our lives.

Stepping out of survival mode can make us better moms, better partners, and better people. The journey may not be easy, but it will be worth it.

My goal is to show you *how* to release what you're struggling with and what you're pressured to carry so you can free your own mental and emotional space, and breathe. So you can be empowered to consciously decide to parent in a way that aligns more closely with your values.

I know you're ready to let go of the load. You're ready to find some freedom, to ease the burden, to share that mental load and breathe a little bit easier. But before you can do that, you're going to have to look within yourself; you're going to have to tackle the beliefs that are keeping the Mother Load on your shoulders.

2

THE BELIEFS THAT SHAPE THE LOAD WE CARRY

For a long time, the thought of becoming a mother terrified me. I grew up weathering the storms of a high-conflict divorce, and for the longest time I told myself that I didn't want to get married and have children—or that I would at least wait until I was thirty to decide. How did that work out for me? I sit here at age thirty-five writing this book, with three boys ages eight, six, and four, and celebrating my ten-year wedding anniversary this year.

As I look back, my education and career path were just as much for my own healing as they were to help me have a positive impact on others. Doing my own internal work, building safety and security in my relationship, and working through my past wounds helped me feel like I was gaining the roadmap I needed to parent differently. With the skills and tools I learned, I believed I could break cycles, hoping that if I did have children, I wouldn't put them through the same pain I had endured.

Eventually, I came around to the idea. I got married, and I finished my master's degree. I was checking off boxes and looking forward to what was coming next. While part of me was still terrified, another part of me was determined. I had the knowledge to do it *right*. I wanted to be an amazing mother, and I had high expectations of what that role looked like.

Imagine my surprise when reality hit. Motherhood was nothing like I'd imagined. The things that I believed would come easily were a struggle. Feeding my baby was harder than I had ever thought it could be. Sleep was a constant battle. Like most new moms, I was exhausted and overwhelmed. And, if I'm being honest, I missed my old life. On one hand, I had never experienced so much love for a human being, and yet I simultaneously mourned the loss of my life as it was before children—the *person* I was before I had children. I sat at home alone, covered in spit-up while trying to soothe a colicky baby, and hardly recognized myself. This was not the romanticized idea of motherhood that I had pictured. The gap between what I expected and the reality blindsided me.

I didn't know that I would be so all-consumed with this new role—that I would find myself obsessively researching every decision I made. Could I give him a pacifier, or would that cause nipple confusion? How many naps did he need to take? What time did I need to lay him down? Should I wake him to get him on a schedule, or follow his lead? I was in my head all the time, trying so hard to "make the right choice" or be a "good mom," even though I had no idea what I was aiming for at the time. I wanted to mother perfectly. I wanted to prevent the pain that I had experienced. I wanted to prove I was good enough.

But I didn't step back and wonder if there was a different way to mother—I believed this must just be what motherhood *was*. I didn't realize it at first, but I was falling into intensive mothering—the belief that motherhood must take everything we have, that we must focus on our children's needs above our own, that our identities should become consumed by motherhood, that motherhood should fulfill us completely, and that only when we do those things can we become "good mothers."

Looking back, it's not surprising that I fell right into this ideology. I was still wrestling with my childhood trauma and wounds, which were breeding grounds for using perfectionism to try to protect myself. Throw in some anxiety and we've got the makings of an anxious perfectionist overachiever who wants to make everyone happy. Even without childhood trauma or copious amounts of anxiety, most mothers in North

America feel the weight of intensive mothering. And, although it can seem so pervasive because it is everywhere we turn, this construct of motherhood is *not* the way all cultures, races, and societies experience it.

I was able to see this firsthand when we traveled with our first-born to Benin—my husband's native country, in West Africa—to visit our extended family. While I was there, I saw a completely different, eye-opening world of motherhood.

To my surprise, I saw mothers who mothered in a way that didn't entirely orbit around their children. They wrapped their babies in cloth and wore them on their backs as they worked and went about their days.

I saw mothers who mothered in tandem with *their* mothers, with aunties, and with the community—a village of support unlike anything I had seen in Canada.

I saw mothers who mothered with simplicity—without all the gear, the fancy monitors, the expensive bassinets, the parenting apps—free from information overload and constant marketing messages about products. In Benin, mothering didn't appear to be about measuring worth by gear or the possessions one provided for their children.

Instead of rigid nap schedules, blackout curtains, and white noise machines, I saw moms lay their babies across their laps in church services, patting them to sleep while they lived their lives. Motherhood looked unrecognizable to the image that is put forth in North America.

This isn't about comparison. It isn't about saying that one method of mothering is right or preferable. But it is about taking a step back and viewing motherhood with a broader lens in the way sociologists and anthropologists do. Motherhood doesn't just look one way across the globe. There are other ways to mother where motherhood is respected, revered—where mothers are not held to those unrealistic, intensive mothering standards.

You might be wondering what this has to do with the Mother Load. The answer is *everything*. Our belief system, our intensive mothering ideology, is what has laid the groundwork for moms to absorb and carry the invisible load without realization and without question. For moms in Western cultures, it has become the backbone of modern mothering.

This ideology is often adopted without intention, and it strongly dictates the way mothers behave and the choices they make. Now, we don't all mother exactly the same way, of course. For various personal or economic reasons, some of us work outside of the home, full or part-time, while others stay home. Some of us have one child, while others have multiple children. Some of us are Montessori parents, attachment parents, hang-on-for-dear-life-and-try-to-survive parents (a valid parenting approach if you ask me). We bring a variety of personal, family, religious, and racial cultures and upbringings into our homes. We all have different philosophies, and we have a wide range of choices we make within our families.

But intensive mothering transcends parenting styles, individual culture, and social classes.[1] It is the very foundation of our expectations and ideals as moms, and it directly informs the choices we make.

If we want to undo the outcome of intensive mothering—the Mother Load—we must start by looking at the belief system itself.

THE MOTHERHOOD FILING CABINET

The brain of a modern mom is like an endless filing cabinet. From the time we're born, we've been filling it with messages we've been handed about what it means to be a good mom—from our moms and grandmothers, from our friends, from society, from social media influencers, from the internet. Every bit of information has been filed away in this motherhood junk drawer.

We've filed practical advice, positive guidance, and helpful tips. (The things we witnessed in our families, the ones our moms did that we loved or that we definitely did *not* love, the moments that left us feeling great, the lessons we learned from watching our friends become moms.) But we've also filed away a lot of junk. Conflicting opinions. Advice that doesn't align with our values. And a massive stack of societal stereotypes, expectations, and beliefs.

Fast forward to parenthood, where you need to pull on the data in this drawer more than ever. Your brain has been passively gathering information to guide you in motherhood, and plenty of it is useful. The challenge is that there is so much in there that you have no idea where to begin in sorting through what is helpful and what's not.

As you go digging for the information you need, you start to discover the problem. There are messages in there that contradict each other. There are messages in there that don't make any sense at all. And there are messages in there that just don't feel right.

The solution? Clean out and edit the filing cabinet. Examine the beliefs there and categorize them. When you look closely at the beliefs you're carrying, you can start to see where they came from. When you see where they come from, you can evaluate them. What shaped those beliefs? What purpose do they serve? Do they align with what is important to you? What can you let go of?

As you sort, categorize, and organize these beliefs, weeding out what doesn't belong, you are laying the groundwork for alleviating the invisible load. It is only after we do the work within ourselves to discover our own values as parents, to work through the myths that are keeping us loaded down, that we can ever hope to lighten this load.

THE FILES THAT DON'T BELONG

More moms are suffering from mental health issues than ever.[2] I hear from moms all the time who just feel like they are at the end of their rope, that they are constantly on the verge of crumbling. They are stressed, unhappy, and disappointed in themselves.

It isn't that motherhood itself is inevitably linked to stress or negative emotions. It's the *way* we're mothering—the way we've been conditioned to parent—that is impacting our mental health.[3]

There is a difference between motherhood and mothering. Mothering is the actual act of being a mom—the work that we do as we parent our children. But *motherhood* is a social construct. The ideals around motherhood are built by society, by culture, by socioeconomic status, or by whether you're partnered. It's the image of what being a mother does and should look like.

I was fortunate enough to complete The Motherhood Studies Practitioner Certification with sociologist Dr. Sophie Brock. She discussed the difference between mothering and motherhood and then asked a powerful question: "What would mothering look like if it were freed from motherhood as the institution?"[4]

These messages, these beliefs that there is one way to be a "perfect mom," are universally unhealthy. Yet this is the way that Western cultures have constructed motherhood. We build expectations and adopt beliefs about what motherhood should look like. Sacrificial. Consumed. Nurturing. Caring. Joyful. We expect that motherhood will look that way all the time.

Think about the expectations that moms are held to. The "perfect stay-at-home mom" is often projected as rising before her kids, having a cup of coffee, prepping breakfast, waking the kids up with a song and a hug, getting everybody dressed, baking cookies, planning enriching activities, and handling everything flawlessly, resulting in bright-eyed, happy children.

The "perfect working mom" also rises early, packing lunches and day-care bags, dropping the kids off with a smile and a hug, and going to work where she kills it, rising in her career, serving as an equal contributor (or possibly even the breadwinner) in her household. She misses her children, but she excels as a mom and a professional. She just does it all, and with ease. When the workday is done, she rushes away from work to pick her kids up. She bathes them, plays with them, feeds them, and tucks them into bed without missing a beat.

She takes it all on and she's *happy* with it. She's doing what she "should do." It's what most of us think that we want when we enter motherhood. It's what we think that everybody else is doing, with ease. So, when we fall short of that image, we feel like we're failing at our most important job.

This "perfect mother myth" is one of the biggest factors behind the ever-growing Mother Load. In our pursuit of perfection, we take on an overload of cognitive and emotional tasks, almost all of which fall to moms.

Research has shown that the more we subscribe to intensive mothering, the more unequal the division of labor and childcare in the home is.[5] It has also shown that trying to fulfill the societal construct of what it means to be a good mom has a negative impact on a mother's mental health.[6]

As we dive deeper into the Mother Load, I want you to remember that you aren't carrying these beliefs because you have done anything wrong. It wasn't a conscious choice. You are an individual, mothering in the context of a broader system of motherhood. This broader system, the constitution of motherhood, is so ingrained that you've become oblivious to its presence—its beliefs have become a part of the very air you breathe.

The fact that you are carrying the Mother Load means that you want to do what's right by your children. You want to be the perfect mom. (Of course you do—we all do!) But in our quest for perfection, we have lost ourselves, our identities, and our personal values.

> You want to be the perfect mom. (Of course you do—we all do!) But in our quest for perfection, we have lost ourselves, our identities, and our personal values.

Shattering this "perfect mom myth" is vital to the work that we are doing here. Only by removing the unhelpful beliefs can we discover who we really are as mothers. We must do that before we can hope to release some of the invisible labor we carry.

What's the first step you take when you reorganize a closet or a drawer? You *clean it out.* You pull everything out, evaluate what needs to be thrown away, then decide what stays in—and only after you do that do you consider where to put everything. We must take the same approach with the invisible load. We can't let go of the labor while our filing cabinets are jammed with perfect mom myths, gender norms, and unrelenting societal expectations. If we do, we'll end up right back in the same patterns again. How can you release some of the load when you are still subconsciously operating from a belief system you *should* be the one to carry it? When part of you believes that you *must* do those things to be a good mom? But when you clear it out and work through all the noise, all that messaging that doesn't belong, you can find a new way forward in motherhood. What you put back won't be based on what I tell you, or what any parenting approach or philosophy or tradition tells you—it will be based on *your* values (which we'll dive into in chapter 3).

We're about to do some big, life-changing work. We're about to shred lots of junk mail we've internalized about the construct of motherhood. We're about to clean the slate and evaluate the files that have shaped our identities as mothers.

Whew, that's a tall order. Erica, you want me to do what?! *I just want my partner to help me with the dishes.*

It is not lost on me that this is hard introspective work. To unlearn and carve out your own empowered approach to mothering isn't easy—but I promise you, this work is worth it. We don't have to carry the load forever.

We are going to outline five foundational beliefs that play into the perfect mom image—five unrealistic beliefs that we are holding onto. As we work our way through this book, you will see how these beliefs entwine, feeding into each other, re-establishing myths about motherhood, and creating the Mother Load. Like a braided rope, these beliefs come together stronger, more secure, and harder to unravel and break.

My goal is to help you see these beliefs and unravel them, peeling away the layers of motherhood expectations that are keeping you from being the mother you really are. When we have stripped them away, we can stop the search for the perfect mother status and start the act of values-based mothering.

WARNING: MOM-LIFE CRISIS AHEAD

We're going to tackle the beliefs tied to the perfect mother myth in a moment. But before we do, I want you to think back to when you brought your baby home for the first time. Did you feel lost? Overwhelmed?

That time in your life was probably full of more emotions than you can even begin to name. You were entering into something called *matrescence*—a developmental time when you step out of the person you were and start to form a new identity as a mother. For many of us, it can be a shocking transition, especially when the new identity we've set our sights on in motherhood is based on beliefs that form unrealistic ideals.

Some people use the terms *beliefs* and *values* interchangeably, but there is a very important distinction between them. While beliefs are thought-based, values are feeling-based. Beliefs are assumptions we make about the world, things we believe to be true. Our beliefs grow from what we see, what we read about, how we're raised, and what we experience. They do differ from thoughts, however. You may have dozens of thoughts going through your mind at any given time—the things you see, the things you notice, the things that pop into your brain unannounced—but only the ones that become lasting beliefs hold power and influence. A belief is something you interpret as true, something you lean on as knowledge to guide your decisions and actions.

We develop opinions based on these beliefs, and over time those opinions become unmovable. These become our values—the core principles we consider most important, that guide our lives, our decisions, and our interactions. So, we derive our values from our beliefs.

For example, if as you grew up you didn't spend quality time with your family and that hurt you, you might form the belief that spending time with loved ones is important. This can turn into a value for you—the value of presence.

Beliefs also shape your identity and your interpretation of the world, like a layer between us and reality, filtering the information we receive through the lens of our own views. They impact how we choose to behave, how we show up as moms, and who we are at the core. So, as we make changes to these beliefs, we're going to encounter some internal resistance. These beliefs are stitched into the fabric of our identity, and we can't work on one without impacting the other.

If that feels scary, stick with me. I'm not asking you to toss out everything that's important to you. In fact, I'm asking you to do the opposite—to evaluate and explore your beliefs about motherhood, so that you can find what is and is not valuable.

Some of the beliefs you hold in your filing cabinet were put there intentionally, ones that you thought out and are deeply important to you. Those, we keep. You'll simply want to label them and store them back in your filing cabinet, holding them with intention.

Other beliefs, however, have been internalized and stored, but they weren't created deliberately. Some of them are unwanted. Some of them are unrealistic, or even harmful. Those, we want to change—and in doing so, we are going to be doing some identity work. It's two for the price of one. Unload these unhelpful beliefs, and discover yourself along the way. But in order to do that, we will be self-inducing a Mom-Life Crisis of sorts.

Traditionally, a mid-life crisis happens when someone has the realization that the expectations they'd hoped to achieve for themselves by around the midpoint in their lives do not line up with reality. (For example, they thought they'd be richer, more successful, or having more fun—and then when they see the reality of working in a corporate job for the rest of their lives, it becomes too much to bear.) In life, they are not who or where they thought they would be.

This too happens in motherhood. The hopes, ideals, and expectations you laid out for yourself don't match reality. And to move past it, you have two choices:

You can either keep grasping at straws, trying to live up to this perfect ideal, and go out and buy the proverbial Porsche to prove it to yourself and those around you.

Or . . . you can evaluate the set of beliefs that told you the Porsche was the goal to begin with. You can realize that it isn't your fault you haven't achieved that perfect status—it's the expectations that are at fault. And you can evaluate those expectations and adjust them so you can allow your true motherhood identity to emerge.

As you do this, you're likely to feel uncomfortable. The beliefs we are going to address are closely interwoven into your identity. But your identity isn't fixed. It can, and should, evolve over time. As we let go and challenge some of these beliefs, we are going to fill that space by uncovering your values so you can feel anchored and rooted in something that you've defined and that is important to you. Your Mom-Life Crisis doesn't have to be scary. It can be freeing, empowering, and the start of something new.

THE BELIEFS THAT CREATE THE MOTHER LOAD

Intensive mothering is built on five core beliefs:

1. Being a good mom means that I should be the primary caregiver to my child.

2. Being a good mom means finding all of my fulfillment in my motherhood role.

3. Being a good mom means placing my child's needs, wants, and well-being above my own.

4. Being a good mom means I have to give all of my emotional energy, time, and resources to my child.

5. Being a good mom means I have to always be "on" for my child.[7]

These beliefs pop up when we want to take a break, when we yearn for something outside of motherhood, when we feel overwhelmed, annoyed, or frustrated in our role. They keep us carrying the load.

If we step away to have a hot cup of coffee, we're letting them down. If we scroll on our phones, we're neglecting them. And we can never make mistakes—if we lose our cool, we've done irreparable harm. These standards are impossible to adhere to—and they aren't evidence-based.

This shift in parenting, the need for "perfection," the expectation to be ever-present and engaged, happened slowly. As we as a society moved toward attachment and gentle parenting, moms took on more pressure and responsibility. What started in the right direction has led moms down an impossible path. We have come to believe that our children need these things, constantly. If we stray, allowing ourselves enjoyment outside of motherhood, or to prioritize our own needs, or to set boundaries, we're doing something wrong—and we end up with a dose of infamous mom guilt to prove it.

You see, I would love to tell you that after my Aha Mom-ent, everything changed right away—that I was able to release the pressure of carrying the invisible load and everything was great after that. (Wouldn't that be nice?)

But it didn't exactly happen that way. I had to battle these beliefs, but there was something that stood in my way—my own internalized mom guilt.

In Dr. Sophie Brock's Motherhood Studies Practitioner Certification course, she refers to this as the "mom-guilt surveillance crew," our way of policing ourselves into adhering to the social norms of motherhood.[8]

My mom-guilt crew unrolled a long scroll of reasons why I shouldn't do this—why I shouldn't try to release this labor.

First, the crew brought up the "shoulds" of motherhood—those messages of what "good moms" do. I should be the nurturer. I should love every moment of motherhood. I should want to take care of my children and my family. I should be grateful for what I have. We all experience these "shoulds." They're like tiny daggers jabbing into your mind, reminding you of the expectations you had for motherhood, as well as the expectations and pressures from everyone around you.

But the crew wasn't done there. Next, it reminded me of the "fact" that everyone else was managing this labor just fine. It had to be my own flaws—I just wasn't organized enough, motivated enough, or good enough to handle it. The crew tried to sell me the idea that I was the only one struggling with this. This "fact" is more like an illusion. Moms everywhere are struggling, crumbling under the Mother Load. We're all just too afraid to admit to others, or to ourselves, that it's too much.

After all, we aren't conditioned to question the system. We're conditioned to believe in it, to believe that motherhood should be natural and pleasant. Our first instinct is that we are the ones failing—it couldn't possibly be that we've been set up by centuries of societal pressure.

The crew also told me I couldn't possibly change the dynamic—the precedent had already been set. My partner and my family were counting on me to continue carrying the load. If I tried to break the cycle, I'd be letting them down.

Determined to keep me in my place, the crew also told me that I had no right to put my own needs before my children's—that I was selfish to even consider it. I should be able to do it all—maintain everything with poise and grace.

Finally, the crew told me something so frightening that I almost crawled right back under the load willingly. It told me that admitting I couldn't do it all and asking for help was a confession of the ultimate failure of motherhood.

By this point, I could see what was happening. The Mother Load was no longer invisible to me. The tasks were tallying up at an overwhelming rate—I could barely believe I'd been carrying everything alone. I could see it wasn't sustainable. I knew I needed to call in more hands. But something inside of me told me that asking for help meant I had failed at the role I was supposedly biologically made for. What kind of a mom couldn't do this? What kind of a mom couldn't sacrifice for her kids and make it work?

I'd always considered myself a strong woman, and I was determined to prove that I could adjust to—no, that I could *thrive*—in motherhood. I wanted it so badly that I refused to ask for help. But the weight of the load and the labor of caring for three young children was crushing me. I tried to keep it up, driving myself deeper into postpartum depression and anxiety until I hit my breaking point.

> If we want to release the Mother Load, we must conquer the idea that our worth as moms is measured in blood, sweat, and tears.

It wasn't until I confronted the guilt and shame that I was able to move forward on my journey, to find a deeper satisfaction in motherhood. The old saying that you can't pour from an empty cup is fitting for modern moms. We're not just trying to pour from an empty cup—we're trying to *constantly* fill our children's cups, long after we've emptied our own.

If we want to release the Mother Load, we must conquer the idea that our worth as moms is measured in blood, sweat, and tears. Labor isn't what makes you a "good mom." The kids will survive if you provide a pre-packaged lunch, or store their toys in a cardboard box, if you buy the box brownies instead of learning your grandmother's recipe, or if you buy the costume instead of making it.

We think that our labor proves to our children that we love them, that we want everything for them. In reality, all it does is deplete us to the point where we can't give them a true, fulfilled version of ourselves.

We're not doing our children any favors by leading ourselves to a breaking point. But if we can find a way to let go of what's weighing us down, we can give our children the best that we have to offer, and enjoy motherhood more along the way.

As we move through this book, one of the biggest steps to releasing the Mother Load will be to narrow in on what truly matters to us, to our values as parents, and be willing to remove some of the rest. Sometimes that will mean outsourcing. Sometimes that will mean automating. And sometimes, it will simply mean letting it go.

Some of the load that we carry is essential. But there will be plenty that you'll find can be let go if you're willing. You must shatter the beliefs that keep you from seeing the truth—that you are a better mom when you aren't taking on too much, pushing yourself to the brink, and overloading yourself with the Mother Load.

HOW TO MOVE FORWARD WITH VALUES-BASED MOTHERING

The five core beliefs I just mentioned are foundational for the way moms are carrying the load and struggling under it. But they are only some of the hidden beliefs surrounding the perfect mother myth that impact us. We will work through more as we move through the rest of this book.

These hidden beliefs keep us trapped, striving for unrealistic expectations, and feeling disappointed, even devastated, when we can't reach them. So why do we continue to hold onto them? Researchers have theorized that we cling to these beliefs because we think that it makes us better moms. We might know that the pressures are affecting our mental health, but we think that it is a necessary sacrifice for our children."

Personally, I think that we cling to these societal norms because we are grasping for some criteria to measure our performance in our most important role. These beliefs at least provide some kind of formula for us to evaluate ourselves. It makes sense that we want a measuring stick—we want some feedback as to whether we are on the right track. However, the measuring stick of intensive mothering is rigged and will cause us to fail every time.

What if there was another way to approach mothering? What if our kids benefit more from having a mom who is happy than a mom who is perfect? What if freeing ourselves from these beliefs allows us to be more fulfilled and more joyful? What if what we're doing isn't helping at all? What if it's just holding us back from being the moms we were meant to be?

Through this Mom-Life Crisis we are entering, this journey we are on together, we can tap into our values and begin to discover who we really are as mothers and, more importantly, who we truly want to be. These are the guideposts that make up who we are, that direct us in our lives, our relationships, and our mothering. It is from these values that we will discover who we want to be as moms, the criteria by which we measure this, and what our load should actually look like.

I didn't have a guide to take me through this journey of unlearning and releasing the load. But if you are ready to take that journey, to open your mind, to become curious, to overcome the hidden beliefs and guilt, and to redistribute the labor, I am here to help guide you. I can't do the work for you—but I can help you build the skills to battle your own mom-guilt surveillance crew and release the labor that doesn't align with what is truly important to you.

Identifying Our Underlying Beliefs about Motherhood

Sometimes it can be difficult to identify the subconscious beliefs that are driving our actions and behavior. But it's important to uncover these thoughts and where they came from.

Take a moment to complete these sentences and notice what comes to mind. Write down the first thought that comes up and try to reflect on your responses with curiosity instead of criticism:

- Good moms . . .

- Moms should . . .

- I am . . .

- My partner is . . .

- My family should . . .

- My needs . . .

- I should be able to . . .

- The house should be . . .

- The food my kids eat should be . . .

- Organizing my kids' schedules should be . . .

- I know I'm a good mom when . . .

Reflect on your responses. What event contributed to the formation of these beliefs? Who in your life might have held these views? When did you first start noticing you were carrying these beliefs? What subsequent experiences shaped them? How do these beliefs make you feel?

As we move through this book, we're going to question a lot of our beliefs. It's important to remember that these beliefs aren't necessarily wrong or bad—but that doesn't mean they align with our values.

3

VALUES AS YOUR MOTHERHOOD ROADMAP

As we navigate this Mom-Life Crisis, questioning our sense of self, and our place in this motherhood role, we're going to feel unstable. In response, we might want to cling onto other ideologies, other ways to identify ourselves—just as we would with any other identity crisis in life.

Like most of us, I can remember my cringe-worthy phases in adolescence—and I went through quite a few of them. Black hair, red hair, purple hair, blonde. I listened to emo music for a while, then punk music, then rap music. My interests changed as frequently as my boyfriends did. And, consequently, so did the ways that I identified myself.

Motherhood, in many ways, is no different. I started off as a self-proclaimed attachment parent. With each additional child and each stage of development my kids went through, my identity shifted—from Montessori, providing only open-ended toys, to wanting to be the perfect gentle and respectful parent. I was searching for a way to identify myself, a way to make sense of the big, new messy world of motherhood I found myself in. You'll be excited to know that I landed somewhere in between all the labels—focusing on survival, with my main goal to raise kind children while not completely traumatizing them (or myself) in the process.

You might have experienced this search for a label yourself, wondering what philosophy or style to align yourself with. When reevaluating our identities as mothers, it makes sense that we want to try on all the hats and explore the various options that are out there. Sometimes, this helps you clarify your values, providing a sense of confidence.

But for many of us, researching parenting philosophies prescribes yet another set of expectations, more "rules," and a new bullseye to try to hit. This can lead to information overload, overwhelm, and a lack of certainty in our own mothering choices. We might feel shaky without the beliefs that have made up so much of our identity, without something or someone telling us the "right" way to mother. We feel like if we could just learn enough, just stumble onto the right method, just uncover that motherhood manual, we could become perfect moms.

> I'm here to help you discover your own unique identity in motherhood—one based on your values, not one based on external expectations.

As we walk together through this self-induced Mom-Life Crisis, you may find yourself wanting to find a new label, searching for that manual. You might even be reading this now, anxiously awaiting the moment where I tell you what *to do* now that we have unpacked several motherhood myths.

But unlike many other parenting books, I'm not here to prescribe your motherhood experience to you. I'm not here to give you more rules or more criteria for how to be the perfect mom. I'm not here to offer you a new ideology. I'm here to help you discover your own unique identity in motherhood—one based on your values, not one based on external expectations.

WHAT ARE OUR PERSONAL VALUES?

In my practice, I often work with clients to uncover their values. But I have come to realize that not everybody uses the word "values" the same way. As I mentioned in the last chapter, values are not the same as beliefs. Our values aren't religious beliefs, morals, or perfect ideals. They aren't what we think we should be or even what we think we want to be. Values are our core principles, the ones closest to our hearts, that guide us when we are in doubt.

It is important to note here that we are specifically talking about our own personal values as parents—the ones that inform our cognitions and daily decisions. These might include presence, connection, authenticity, adventure—whatever is most important to who we are and how we want to show up in the world. We are not necessarily discussing the values and qualities we want to instill in our children, as that is a different conversation; for instance, we might want to give our children a sense of responsibility, hard work, and dedication. But our personal core values are the ones that guide us, not the ones we are trying to impart to our children.

When we know what our values are, making decisions becomes easier. Our values serve as our compass, showing us the way when we get lost in life. As Dr. Cassidy Freitas said on episode 106 of *The Momwell Podcast*, "values are what matters when nobody else is looking."[1]

We all have values in our lives—in our careers, in our personal lives, in our relationships, and in our mothering. The values we bring into these areas are strongly linked to the ideology we've been raised with and exposed to.

But when we look outside of ourselves, when we try to bring the perfect mom myth to life, we often adopt the values of others around us. As a result, we break trust with ourselves and erode our own intuition.

DRIVING THE ROAD OF MOTHERHOOD

When we become mothers, it's as if we are simply following the flow of traffic. We do this subconsciously, without intentionally evaluating whether the direction of the traffic feels right, without determining our target destination. It seems natural. Do what everyone else is doing. If a stampede happens, we don't take the time to question where everyone is going or why they are running—we just know we ought to follow.

But the status quo of motherhood isn't working. Looking outside of ourselves to determine our direction as mothers leads us astray. The traffic is moving toward the perfect mother myth. And if we keep traveling in that direction, we're going to be driving forever, searching for a destination we can never reach.

Driving with the traffic won't allow us to break away from the pressures, expectations, and ideals that are keeping us stuck carrying the load, all while exhausted and full of doubt. It won't allow us to discover who we truly are as mothers. And it won't allow us to mother with empowerment, security, and confidence.

We can't just go with the flow anymore. Instead, we need to pave our own way.

In order to break out of the pursuit of the perfect motherhood myth, in order to discover who we truly are and mother in an empowered way, in order to truly find joy in our motherhood experience, we need to tap into our own values—we need to mother with our internal GPS.

Mothering with our values allows us to become more mindful of our path forward and empowered in our role, looking inward instead of outward to make the decisions that shape our lives and the lives of our children.

When we drive toward the perfect mother myth, when we leave our cars on autopilot and follow along with the direction everyone else is going, we're basically trying to drive to the moon. We'll never get there—we'll never even get close. And we'll just leave ourselves exhausted and frustrated in the pursuit. But *values-based mothering* is taking our journey off autopilot, turning off the highway, and finding our own destination and our own route through parenthood. It's leaving the gridlocked freeway and taking a more satisfying route. We might all end up at a different destination, mothering in completely different ways, but we will be happier and more fulfilled driving the journey that is right for us as individuals.

> In order to break out of the pursuit of the perfect motherhood myth . . . we need to mother with our internal GPS.

As we prepare to clean out our junk drawers and sort through the beliefs, the messages, and the files that we have gathered over the course of our lives, we need to make sure we have our compass, our *values*, in hand. We can't look externally to see what we need to keep or the roles we need to adopt. Our values will determine what stays in the drawer. Our values will determine what parts of the load we must hold onto. And our values will determine what we can let go of in order to free ourselves.

DIFFERENT PATHS IN MOTHERHOOD

My best friend and the maid of honor at my wedding always wanted to be a stay-at-home mom. She had pictured being a mother since she was a little girl and couldn't wait to start a family. I, on the other hand, was always work-oriented. In fact, I never actually felt a natural pull toward motherhood.

Despite our very different personalities and inclinations toward having children, we both ended up with three. However, our approaches to mothering could not be more opposite.

She loves staying at home with her kids, baking pies from scratch, and hand-sewing Halloween costumes. That image of motherhood is rewarding for her. But for me, motherhood looks different than that. I want to maintain my career. After maternity leave, I was ready to return to work. I wanted to build a company, and I knew I could be a good mom while doing so.

There were times when I saw her image of motherhood and felt a little voice of doubt creeping into my mind. When she posted pictures of her kitchen full of freshly baked goods, part of me wondered . . . *Should I be doing these things? Is that what motherhood is supposed to be?*

I had to take a step back and remind myself that we are entirely different people with completely distinct values.

In other areas of life, we don't hold shame for choosing alternative paths. Some of us go to college, some of us go into a trade, some of us start our own businesses. We are allowed to hold those roles without judgment. But when it comes to motherhood, we feel like we must follow a script or tick certain boxes.

We must remember that underneath all the junk from the outside world, each of our filing cabinets is different. We take in plenty of similar messages—from society, family, friends, social media—and we pile those up. How to feed your baby, how to let your baby sleep, how to handle your pregnancy—we're bombarded with advice, and much of it contradictory.

We can't possibly fulfill all those ideals, those expectations. Some of them are unattainable, some are unrealistic, and others are just plain conflicting. When we try to adhere to all these messages, it leads to cognitive dissonance—mental discomfort when we hold conflicting beliefs.

We know that we can't possibly chase all these ideals at the same time. We must follow what is in our own hearts—our own values.

When we sort through all those messages—the contradictions, the stereotypes, the myths, the beliefs—what's left underneath are our personal core values. Imagine that we all started life as a blank slate . . . that we were able to paint our own canvas, each with unique features, abilities, and strengths. Our values are the distinctive colors and techniques we apply to our canvas—the things that make us truly unique. We shouldn't be striving to look alike or to all be replicas of each other's designs. Instead, we should be embracing our values to create our own unique expression of motherhood. In doing so, we look different from those around us—but that is the beauty in a one-of-a-kind piece.

That's what I had to do whenever that little voice of doubt crept in, telling me that perhaps I should mother more like my friend. I had to edit my own filing cabinet and dig down underneath the junk to my values. As I sorted through my cabinet and removed what didn't belong, what didn't align with my values, I started to see more clearly.

My friend and I have different filing cabinets. Our core values are completely different. And we have made our motherhood decisions based on those values. Our approaches to motherhood could not be more opposite, but it doesn't mean either of us is wrong. I don't need to adopt her way to be a good mother, just as she doesn't have to adopt my way. We each must lean into what is most important to us and edit down our filing cabinets to discover what our values truly are.

WHEN WE DON'T LEAD WITH VALUES

My experience with my friend isn't uncommon. We all see mothers around us choosing different paths. Motherhood is packed to the brim with decisions:

- How should I navigate behavior and discipline?

- Should I try to have another baby?

- What type of childcare should I choose?

We are constantly bombarded with choices of all sizes (many of which are not fully within our control due to medical, economical, and other reasons). When we make those decisions without being anchored in our own personal values, trying to keep up with others in the pursuit of perfection, we can never really be sure our choices are right.

When we don't feel sure in our decisions, when faced with others who parent differently we might feel doubt in our choices. Or we might feel determined to prove our way is right, to defend it.

Our brains and our bodies can tell when we're out of alignment with our values. They give us clues that we aren't mothering in a way that feels good. Here are some clues that your body and brain give you when you are not anchored in your values, clues that might come up when you face different parenting decisions.

Attempting to Prove Our Way is Right

When we encounter other moms making different choices, we might feel threatened. We wrap our identity as mothers in our parenting decisions. An alternate choice feels like someone is challenging our identity. We might be determined to show that our way is the right way to parent or to argue against the other person's choice.

I could have done this when I saw my friend's choice to stay home. Instead of accepting our differences and acknowledging that we were both following our best paths, I could have responded by telling her how much "better" it was to be a working mom, trying to prove it to her (and really, to myself).

When we do this, it comes off as an attack on other moms, but at its core, it's not about being competitive. It comes from us trying to protect ourselves. We feel unsure about our decisions, but if we can prove that we made the "right" choice, we are closer to reaching the perfect mother status—the image we envisioned.

Justifying Our Way of Thinking

If another parent makes a different decision, we also might try to overexplain or justify our choice.

For example, I could have gone to my friend and explained all the reasons I chose to return to work—to continue my career, to gain balance in my life, to help people. In reality, I would have been trying to reassure myself that I had made the right decision.

This reaction may stem from a lack of confidence in our own approach. We doubt our own choice, and we want to seek reassurance. To garner that reassurance, we overexplain so that the other person can see our way.

Becoming a Chameleon

When we aren't rooted in our values, we might try to adopt the values of others. Our parenting decisions might change based on what group of people we are around (much like my music preferences and interests in high school changed with each boyfriend I dated). We doubt our own decisions and try to emulate the other mothers we observe.

I could have made the choice to bake pies and breads from scratch because my friend was doing that. To ease my own discomfort, I could have adopted her values. But I would have gotten a couple steps into the recipe before the boys had flour all over the kitchen and I regretted every choice that led to that moment. Baking is not my thing, and guess what, it's okay! There are several other ways I can engage the kids that don't involve a mess and a rage-y mom.

Holding on too Tightly to One World
View or Parenting Approach

As I mentioned before, we tend to seek out other like-minded moms, joining Facebook groups or forums. There is nothing wrong with seeking a community for support in motherhood—in fact, the right peer support can be protective for our mental health. But we can sometimes cling too tightly, seeking advice from groups for every parenting decision and questioning our own abilities. Sometimes we even take on an identity based on a group, calling ourselves *crunchy moms* or *minimalist moms*. The more that we fall into the pattern of seeking approval and guidance from other moms, the less we trust in ourselves and our own intuition to make decisions.

We might ask other moms in similar circles what toys we should buy, if we should vaccinate, when to give our child medicine, or whether we should send our child to school or homeschool them. As I made the decision to return to work, for example, I could have consulted my friend who was a stay-at-home mom and contemplating homeschooling. If I were feeling unsure or guilty about the decision to send my baby to day-care, my friend's list of reasons for wanting to be home with her baby (which might have included things like being present, being the one to teach them and so on) could have caused me to doubt my own choices.

Asking for advice and tips from trusted sources is helpful, but turning toward others for every decision and doubting our own abilities to make good choices is a sign that we are losing our way and straying from our values. It is the difference between seeking support and knowledge from your community, or asking them whether you should do something, leaving the decision-making up to the values of others. When we take on philosophies or labels that come with a set of expectations for how we should parent and behave, we are only creating another box to confine ourselves. There is a distinction between reading about various parenting approaches to inform your own parenting and wearing a parenting philosophy like an identity. One informs your values, the other overtakes them.

Seeking parents with similar philosophies isn't inherently a bad thing. We are human and crave community, a sense of belonging, and assurance in our decisions. Sometimes it's nice to get advice from people we trust. But we can find that sense of support and camaraderie without adopting labels or titles—without boxing ourselves in and losing our identities. Holding strong in our values allows us to be in communities and still maintain our autonomy to choose what is right for our family, looking for answers within ourselves.

Shaming or Blaming Ourselves

Another clue that we may be trying to embody someone else's values rather than living out our own is constantly wondering why we can't seem to get motherhood "right." That mom-guilt surveillance crew shows up, ready to roll out the scroll and show us we're doing everything wrong.

If we feel like we can never do anything "right," we are trying to stuff ourselves into motherhood pants that don't fit. When this happens, we blame ourselves rather than seeing that the pants weren't made for every mother to begin with.

It would have been easy for me to shame myself for not living the same way my friend chose to. There were moments when I felt like she was being the "better mom" because her choices aligned with an image I had been handed of motherhood. I could have questioned myself, wondering what was wrong with me when I didn't want that same image. But the motherhood that fits me is not of the stay-at-home mom size or variety—and that's okay!

Mom guilt can keep us in a vicious cycle of shame and blame. We experience guilt, so we attempt to course correct, to "do better." But when our decisions aren't rooted in our values, when we're chasing the mirage of the perfect mother, we will constantly feel like we are falling short again, becoming even more upset with ourselves.

Shaming or Blaming Others

On the flip side of the coin, instead of blaming ourselves, we might try to put other moms down to feel better about our own choices. We sometimes gossip or degrade other parents or parenting styles, trying to reassure ourselves that our way is right and we are closer to that perfect mom status. When our beliefs about motherhood are so intertwined with our identity, we sometimes feel the need to defend who we are.

I could have lashed out at my friend, or mocked her choices, laughing at her decision to stay at home to silence my own doubts.

This reaction stems from feeling threatened that someone else is parenting differently. If they are "right," then we must be "wrong." The perfect mother myth tells us that there is only one expression of motherhood—one right way to do things.

But there is no one right way. There is no perfect mother. There is no right way to parent, no perfect method. We must move past this idea of perfection and realize that there are many sizes and styles of motherhood to explore.

USING KNEE-JERK REACTIONS TO UNCOVER OUR VALUES

Instead of defaulting to these reactions, we want to be able to stand firm in our decisions with confidence. When we know that our choices come from the right place, they honor our values and fulfill us. This doesn't mean we won't ever have guilt or doubt, but when we do, we can circle back around to our values and the conscious reasons we made decisions in the first place.

Those knee-jerk reactions and clues our body gives us don't feel good. It doesn't comfort us to lash out at other parents, to question our own decisions, or to try to justify our own behavior. When we see forms of motherhood that "conflict" with ours, it causes us to look into a mirror and evaluate (even for a brief unconscious moment) whether we are on the right path. We get drawn into comparison and wonder, *if they are right, how can I be right (or vice versa)? How can both things be true at the same time?* We're pinned in a state of cognitive dissonance. Our brains don't understand, and we feel forced to pick a side. We either defend our way and our "rightness," or we bend over backward to please others. But neither of those responses brings us comfort in the long term. Instead, we're left feeling even more doubt and uncertainty about our choices.

However, that doesn't mean that these reactions don't serve a purpose. They are clues, signs that our values are being encroached upon. And, if we can recognize those signs, we can use the negative emotions, the guilt and the doubt, to our advantage. We can use them to help uncover our values.

Using Emotions as Allies

When Dr. Cassidy Freitas appeared on *The Momwell Podcast* on episode 106 to talk about values, she said something that resonated with me: "we can use our emotions as allies in the discovery of our values."[2] Our emotions, both negative and positive, are clues about our values. When we feel good about a situation, our values are being fulfilled. When we're left with discomfort, guilt, or pain, it's a sign that our values are not being met.

If you're not sure where to start in uncovering your values, this is a good place. Think of a time when you were truly happy—a memory that always lights you up. What circumstances led up to that moment? Who was there? What was happening? What, specifically, made you feel happy, joyful, or uplifted?

Write down what comes to mind about this moment. This can guide you to what your values are.

But our negative emotions can also be powerful signs that point to our values. Think about a time you had one of those knee-jerk reactions from earlier in this chapter. A time you felt mom guilt, or a time you engaged in gossip, tried to justify your parenting decisions, or adopted the values of others. Think about how you felt in that moment—threatened, unsure, unstable, full of doubt.

What chord did that strike in you? What memories came up? What parenting choices were you feeling insecure about? These are all clues that point to your values. Take a moment to jot down your thoughts.

DISCOVERING OUR CORE VALUES

If we want to break away from the pursuit of perfection and start the practice of values-based mothering, we must be in tune with our values. To do that, we must know what they are. Many of us have never intentionally gone through the process of uncovering those values.

It's something that I work on with my clients often, something that you may have worked through if you have been in therapy before. But otherwise, you probably haven't sat down and determined what your core values are. If you have done this work, take this as an opportunity to reappraise your values, as they are dynamic and evolve with each stage of your life.

I encourage you to slow down and take your time here, working your way through these exercises and tapping into your values. This work is foundational to the process of releasing the load.

We tend to be obsessed with organizing. *Get Organized with the Home Edit* on Netflix had me out buying all the clear bins I could find, organizing everything in my home by the colors of the rainbow. However, all of that organizing and editing overlooks our relationship with stuff to begin with. You can spend all day reorganizing the playroom, but if you're still holding onto teething toys and rattles when your children are ten years old, no amount of organizing will fix the real issue. If you just move parts around without determining the criteria for what stays in a junk drawer, what goes in the house, and what gets donated, the clutter and junk will build right back up again.

In the same way, if we just try to share the load without looking underneath at the values, we're just reorganizing the clutter. Even if we have a partner, we just end up with two overwhelmed parents instead of one exhausted mom. Our values allow us to remove what doesn't belong in the drawer in the first place, to declutter and toss out what we don't need.

It isn't enough to have a vague idea of what your values are. You need to dig deep and gain clarity around them. Then, you will be able to use them to guide you. I recommend grabbing a pen and a notebook, settling in, and getting ready to dive into your own values.

Identifying Values from a List

A list of values is often the best place to start. As you read through this list, circle or write down any that particularly resonate with you. If two words seem similar, look up the definition and really ponder what is important to you. Remember that our values look different in the various roles and relationships we have. You might have a value as an individual that is different from a value you hold as a mother. It can be helpful to break out your values into key areas of your life—individual values, motherhood values, romantic relationship values, and so on.

As you look through these, narrow down your top twenty values. Think about the ones that truly guide you, that matter even if nobody sees you doing them, that you would never want to compromise on. Once you have a top twenty, list or label your top ten values in order from one to ten. You've discovered your core values!

Sometimes it's easier to physically hold your values on cards and sort them. You can visit ericadjossa.com to print this list so you can sort and visualize your values even more clearly.

Abundance	Caring
Acceptance	Change
Accountability	Charisma
Achievement	Clarity
Adaptability	Collaboration
Advancement	Commitment
Adventure	Communication
Affection	Community
Altruism	Compassion
Ambition	Competence
Appreciation	Confidence
Authenticity	Connection
Balance	Contentment
Beauty	Contributing
Belonging	Contribution
Bravery	Cooperation
Care for others	Courage
Career	Creativity

Curiosity

Dependability

Dignity

Discipline

Diversity

Effectiveness

Efficiency

Empathy

Encouragement

Endurance

Enjoyment

Entertainment

Entrepreneurship

Equality

Ethics

Excellence

Excitement

Fairness

Faith

Fame

Family

Finances

Financial stability

Finesse

Fitness

Forgiveness

Freedom

Friendship

Fun

Generosity

Giving back

Gratitude

Growth

Happiness

Harmony

Health

Home

Honesty

Hope

Humanity

Humility

Humor

Inclusion

Independence

Initiative

Innovation

Integrity

Intelligence

Intuition

Invention

Involvement

Joy

Justice	Risk-taking
Kindness	Safety
Knowledge	Security
Leadership	Service
Learning	Simplicity
Legacy	Speed
Leisure	Spirituality
Love	Stability
Loyalty	Stewardship
Making a difference	Strength
Nature	Success
Openness	Teamwork
Optimism	Thrift
Order	Time
Patience	Tradition
Peace	Travel
Perseverance	Trust
Personal development	Truth
Power	Understanding
Pride	Uniqueness
Relationship	Usefulness
Reliability	Vision
Renewal	Vulnerability
Resourcefulness	Wealth
Respect	Wellness
Responsibility	Wisdom

Once you have your values list, work through these reflections, writing down the answers as you go. These prompts will help you gain clarity on how your values show up in your life, and especially in your mothering.

- Write down three things you are grateful for today.
- Write down a moment when you stayed true to your values.
- Write about a moment when you felt proud about your parenting.
- Write about a moment when you felt confident in a decision you made.
- Write about a moment when you experienced guilt.

While impactful when practiced alone, this exercise can be even more powerful when done with a partner to determine values for both your family and your relationship.

IMPORTANT REMINDERS ABOUT VALUES

As we move forward into values-based mothering and prepare to work our way through our beliefs and our load through the lens of our values, keep in mind a few important notes:

Your Values Can Change Over Time

What was once a core value of yours may have shifted, especially as you entered matrescence and became a mother. Your values will likely continue to evolve based on your season of life, your support system, and your relationships. I encourage you to revisit these values periodically, taking note of big changes and what those mean on your motherhood journey.

Sometimes You Must Prioritize Your Values

There will likely be moments when you are forced to temporarily prioritize one value over another, particularly in relation to your values as a mother and your other values in your life. For example, when I was on maternity leave, I chose to prioritize being home with my child over my career and professional development. It felt like a small death to my career values at the time. But I wasn't abandoning them, I simply had to honor other values for a season of my life. It was as though certain values, wants, or desires went dormant for a season—not tossed out altogether, just waiting for their turn again when the time was right. It wasn't easy to do. I consciously understood why I needed to, why some of my values needed to get reprioritized for that season of my life. But that didn't stop me from grieving the fact they weren't present, or from sometimes questioning whether I would ever regain those things.

We often feel dissatisfaction when there is a gap between the reality of our current situation and the values we hold. This is very common in early stages of motherhood when mothering is all-consuming. Out of necessity, we park many of our personal values, and the motherhood values get bumped to the top of our priority lists. It can feel disheartening when we must put other values aside. But temporarily reordering what takes precedence doesn't mean doing away with the individual values that are important to us. It just means that our different values get prioritized at different times and not all values can be given 100 percent of our attention 100 percent of the time. With every developmental stage and each phase of motherhood, we are constantly reorganizing and reprioritizing our values.

The Discovery of a Value Isn't Always Straightforward

Value-sorting exercises can certainly help you uncover your values. But sometimes you must do a little bit more digging.

This happened to me in my third maternity leave. By the time I had my third baby, I'd been in a season of prioritizing my motherhood values because the three boys were born within three and a half years of each other and I couldn't find myself in all of the pregnancies, breastfeeding, lack of sleep, and postpartum anxiety and depression.

I always valued learning, knowledge, education, and professional and self-development. But when I was home with my sons, I had to put these on pause or try to meet them with learning new parenting philosophies and understanding my new role. On my third maternity leave, though, I found myself reflecting on who I was, longing to reconnect with myself and my values in a way that I felt like pregnancy and postpartum wouldn't allow.

I found myself having an identity crisis—again. What was I going to do when I went back to work? Did I even want to go back to work? Should I pursue my PhD like I had always planned to? Or should I branch out and try a career in marketing, which I had always been interested in?

As I searched for the answers within myself, I stumbled into photography. I started taking pictures and spending time on social media, and, although I had never dabbled with creative mediums before, I found myself falling in love with it. I realized that this was the perfect way to blend something I was really enjoying, something that challenged me and gave me growth, with my motherhood experience. I could take pictures of experiences with the kids, or even set up photo shoots with props and lighting. As I took pictures, I learned how to style, frame, and even edit the photos. I was seeking a way to nurture my need for growth and learning, but I also ended up discovering a new value, one that had been dormant my whole life but I had never actually tapped into—creativity. I felt fulfilled when I took pictures of the kids, created an aesthetic on my social media feed, and experimented with new techniques. To my surprise, creativity ended up becoming one of my core values, one I want to express and embody every day. I followed a trail of breadcrumbs to discover a value I didn't even know existed for me, and I am so glad that I did.

Tap into the things that you love, the things that bring you joy. They just might lead you on your own discovery of a new, important value.

The Way You Express a Value Matters

I remember back to starting my Instagram page; back then it was called "Make it to Nap." I posted about the crafts and sensory experiences that I would do with the kids. I knew that I valued presence and making memories with my kids. But I had internalized the belief that it had to look like beautifully curated sensory bins and Pinterest-worthy arts and crafts. I felt like I needed to be the type of mom that created those experiences for my kids.

Fueled by perfectionism and a desire to "do things right," when I actually did those things—preparing crafts, gathering supplies, and gathering the boys to the table to do them—it didn't feel like the peaceful, pleasant image I had created in my mind. In fact, it felt chaotic, stressful, and overwhelming. Something that was meant to bring us joy actually created irritability and frustration. That was a clear indicator to me that I was off track.

Of course, it's much easier to identify in retrospect. But when we adopt an ideal based on expectations, it's important to pause and ask ourselves why we're striving for that and how it really makes us feel. Is it in alignment with our values? And if it is, is the expression of the value the best way for us to fulfill it? In my case, I was trying to fulfill the value of presence, of time with my kids. But I didn't need Pinterest or bins of rice or a mess of glue and craft sticks to be present with my children. There were other experiences I could have with my boys that didn't leave me feeling overwhelmed.

As you recall a time when you felt unhappy or uncomfortable, it could be that your values were being encroached upon. Or, it could be that you were trying to adhere to a specific expression of a value that didn't work for you. It's important to remember that there isn't always a rigid way we "should" engage with our values.

When I was debating whether or not to pursue my PhD after having my three boys, I had to reevaluate the way my values were expressed. I wasn't in a place where I could realistically go out and complete a doctorate—not only was it extremely expensive, but I was also still very much in survival mode at the time. I ended up learning a new skill, photography, which fulfilled that desire for learning and uncovered a new value. But I also could have integrated academic knowledge in a smaller, more digestible way that didn't feel like a burden, by reading books or taking a single class.

If a value seems overwhelming to pursue, especially when you are in the depths of mothering young children, consider how to break it down into bite-sized pieces. You can slowly bring parts of your old identity into your new identity as a mother without abandoning your role and without creating more stress in your life. We need to be flexible with our values and the way we express them.

VALUES-BASED MOTHERING

Once you have identified the values that make up who you are at the core, you have your compass, your own personalized map for motherhood. These values will serve as your GPS. Whenever the road starts to feel bumpy, whenever you feel yourself veering away from what is truly important, you can use them to find your way back.

When we face decisions, we can ask ourselves, "What is most closely in alignment with my values? What will fulfill the core principles I live by?" When your values are clear, those decisions become easier.

The stronger you stand in these values, the easier it will be to let go of guilt, let go of comparisons, and let go of the perfect mother myth. When you feel that twinge of doubt—the same twinge I felt when I saw my friend hand-sewing Halloween costumes—instead of wondering if we should change, we can resist adopting someone else's values by measuring them up against our own.

The real battle is not with other mothers, other parenting philosophies, or unsolicited advice. It is a battle of finding our own values and holding onto them for dear life, of unlearning the values that others have handed us or we have internalized for all these years so we can step out into a more empowered form of mothering.

You may be surprised at how deeply some of the beliefs about the Mother Load weave in with your identity as a mother. We are going to learn more in the next section about how to reevaluate the load, how to make it visible. But most importantly, we need to ask ourselves . . . do these roles that I have taken on align with my values? Are these truly important to me and my family? Or is this something that I can offload and leave behind?

Maybe you don't have to go all out for birthday parties. Maybe you don't have to pack lunches with a note to your child every day. Maybe you don't have to cut fruit into elaborate shapes for your child. Maybe even a small portion of that time and energy can be regained to help you discover *you* again. If we are going to release the load and free ourselves as mothers and as people, we must determine what doesn't belong in our drawers.

So . . . what do we do now? How do we take the knowledge that we have learned here—our values, our beliefs that need to be let go, and our identity as mothers—and move forward to tackle the Mother Load?

We need to identify the mental labor we are carrying, reevaluate it based on the assumptions we will comb through in each of the following chapters, and release what doesn't align with our values.

PART 2

MAKING THE MOTHER LOAD VISIBLE

THE INVISIBLE LOAD OF BEING
THE DEFAULT CAREGIVER

Being the main one who can calm/soothe

Being the one who knows where everything is

Being the one everyone goes to

Struggling to get a break or alone time

Researching feeding options

Researching the "best" gadgets and gear

Feeling like you're always on

Feeling trapped or always needed

Being the one to manage and troubleshoot baby sleep

Being the one to plan for safety and babyproofing

Being the one who knows and tracks milestones

Being the one who responds to meltdowns or tantrums

4

THE DEFAULT CAREGIVER

My parents divorced when I was around ten years old. My father had grown up in a very traditional household, with a mother and older sisters who cooked, took care of the home, and did the bulk of the care work.

So, when it was me and my younger brother at home with my dad after my parents separated, the expectations that fell on me versus my brother felt like a double standard. I was expected to be involved with the cooking, the cleaning, and even a great deal of the care for my brother. I would wake him up for school and make sure he got ready on time.

I was parentified in a way that my brother wasn't because I was older and because I was a girl. I didn't realize at the time how this pattern was perpetuating gender roles that had been passed down generation after generation. I didn't realize the complex reasons why these expectations fell to me, though I often vocalized how they felt unfair. And truthfully, I wouldn't fully unpack those roles for many years to come.

As I got older, I was fairly determined to break out of that double standard and show that as a woman I could be and do anything. I became more progressive, and I believed that in many ways I had left those gender norms behind. But I never understood how deeply ingrained they really were until I entered motherhood.

When I met Frenel and got married, equality in the home seemed easy. We were both progressive, open-minded, forward-thinking people.

In fact, when we were dating, I often told him that if he wanted a house-wife, he'd picked the wrong one and he needed to keep looking.

Gender wasn't a factor in how we divided tasks. I worked late nights seeing clients, so Frenel handled cooking dinner. We both grocery shopped and meal prepped for the week. On weekends, we cleaned our apartment together, putting on music and laughing while we did. We didn't keep score, and the labor felt split pretty evenly.

We were a real team. Like all couples, we had our disagreements—but managing the house wasn't one of them. Sure, he got annoyed when I left my clothes on the side of the hamper instead of putting them all the way in, but for the most part, the household labor didn't negatively impact us much. We did what we had to do, but we did it together.

When we found out that I was expecting our first baby, gender norms and the division of household labor were the furthest things from my mind. If you had asked me, I would have been confident in our team-work, equality, and cooperation.

But having a baby turned that on its head. Almost overnight, it was as if the gender roles we had worked so hard to avoid took hold full force.

Now, at no point while becoming parents did either of us consciously say, "We're going to adopt traditional gender roles in our home." Neither of us wanted that. Neither of us planned for it. But we also didn't ever sit and talk about our perceptions of gender, how the load was distributed in our homes growing up, how that impacted us, or how parenthood would change our responsibilities and roles in the home.

And with me being at home on maternity leave and Frenel at work, we fell into patterns we never intended to create. I was overwhelmed by everything at home, but all I could see was survival. All I could do was function. It was as if society was saying, "This is your new role and identity now."

There was a never-ending to-do list, none of which I felt competent in. But truth be told, I was happy to try to rise to the occasion. The invis-ible load of motherhood wasn't on my radar yet. But what WAS on my radar was the image of a "perfect mom." And in my mind, the "perfect mom" had to do EVERYTHING.

I was experiencing what so many modern moms go through. This wasn't just the birth of my babies—it was the birth of the Mother Load, centered around the subconscious belief that females are biologically programmed to be better caregivers.

This belief has strong roots in intensive mothering, as we previously discussed in chapter 2, and begins as early as birth. Children are given messages from very early on that caregiving is female-coded. Baby girls are often given dolls and baby strollers, priming them to be nurturers, while boys are often given blocks, cars, and trucks—toys that don't center around caregiving. The norms have become so ingrained that we don't realize we are unintentionally saddling little girls with a lifelong burden that isn't being shared equally.

It was the birth of the Mother Load, centered around the belief that females are biologically programmed to be better caregivers.

When families begin preparing to have babies, those longstanding gender norms about caregiving start to take hold. The perinatal season of motherhood (the period of time from pregnancy to postpartum) sets the stage of labor that goes far beyond the physical birthing of a baby. Moms become defaulted into prenatal (pre-birth) and postnatal (post-birth) labor that paves the way for the invisible load to fall on their shoulders for decades to come.

The patterns created in the perinatal season don't break on their own. The labor that moms take on usually stays with them. Moms often find themselves functioning as the "default parent," the go-to for doing all the care tasks in the home.

Even in households where moms work for pay outside of the home, caregiving is typically still female-coded. In the book *Entitled: How Male Privilege Hurts Women*, philosopher Kate Manne describes a phenomenon she calls "leaning down." When needed, we outsource our care work—the act of physically caregiving (via a nanny or daycare), the housekeeping, the cleaning, and the cooking.[1] However, this care work gets passed on primarily to other women (often women of color).[2] It's important to remember this when we think about gender and household labor.

Despite this "leaning down," moms who work outside the home aren't free from caregiving labor. They might not be the physical primary caregiver during the day, but they make up for it. Women who work outside the home often come home and dedicate themselves to house-work, sometimes staying up late into the night to complete it. Arlie Hochschild coined the term "second shift" to describe this extra burden of unpaid household labor.[3]

Many of my clients believe that if they are earning less money, they should do more household labor to "make up for it." But not only does this undervalue care work, this second shift applies no matter how much women earn. In fact, when women out-earn their husbands, they take on an even higher percentage of housework than their spouses.[4] This confirms that gender is shaping the household labor on a level that goes deeper than finances.

Additionally, moms take on the role of *care coordinator* when they work outside the home full-time or part-time. They are still the ones managing care. Moms are interviewing nannies, researching daycares, and coordinating plans for drop-offs and pick-ups—not to mention packing bags, maintaining communication with caregivers, and juggling care on sick days and holidays.

Working moms are ten times more likely to take off work to care for their sick children than working dads.[5] This impacts both their time and money. The "mommy track" continues to grow, widening the wage gap year after year. While unmarried, childfree women earn on average 96 percent of what their male counterparts earn, women with children earn only 76 percent.[6] When women are expected to always be the ones to prioritize their families, it comes at a cost of their financial earnings and their career growth.

BREAKING DOWN THIS LOAD

In many ways, I can't even begin to break down the mental load of daily caregiving. It's *everything*. All the noticing, the decision-making you do thousands of times a day, the problems you solve, the boo-boos you ban-dage, the hugs and comfort and responses you provide. Caregivers are like conductors, directing everyone through morning routines, transitions, nap times, nighttime routines—making sure everything works together. They're synthesizing the anticipation and the research, making decisions on the spot, and keeping everything seamlessly moving. Playtime, baths, snack time, screen time—caregivers are stitching it all together.

The caregiver also often becomes the "default parent." They sign permission slips, provide medicine and nurturing when the children are sick, navigate bumps in the road, answer phone calls and emails from teachers, remember any changes to the routine—the "default parent" becomes the go-to solver of problems, handler of issues, and doer of expected and unexpected tasks.

It can be hard to visualize how to start releasing the load of caregiving—from the outside, it all looks essential. It's a massive task—one full of mental, emotional, and physical labor. It's all-encompassing and exhausting.

But to release the Mother Load, we must pick it apart. In the following chapters, we are going to make the invisible load visible by breaking down the biggest caregiving tasks into the three sections I mentioned in chapter 1—anticipating, research and planning, and managing. This will help us start to see the Mother Load in its entirety. We're also going to look at the assumptions that keep us saddled with the mental labor and what we can do to start releasing what doesn't belong. In this chapter, we're going to look at the tasks associated with caregiving and care coordinating, both in the perinatal season of motherhood and beyond—from how we feed our babies to being the default parent to coordinating daycare.

As we work through these, you'll find "load maps" that break down the mental labor into a visible checklist. These highlight the labor that goes into each task from start to finish, including the mental prep. When you are trying to communicate the invisible labor and how to share it, the load maps will help you set the parameters for what is involved in each task. You might need to tweak my maps to suit your individual family needs and lifestyle, but this should set you on the right path toward redistributing the load. You can also find editable load map templates at Ericadjossa.com. At the end of each of the following chapters, you'll also find a section that breaks down the skills you need to start releasing this load.

INFANT FEEDING

Infant feeding is often one of the earliest loads that becomes imbalanced during the postpartum period, partially due to feeding structure, but also largely due to gender-coding. Some moms choose to breastfeed and believe that they must shoulder all aspects of feeding and night wakings as a result. I fell into this pattern myself—for me, I believed in order to be a "good mom" I had to be the one to feed my baby both day and night, and I held onto that belief very tightly.

But there is a massive invisible load of nursing or bottle-feeding that goes far beyond the act of feeding itself. For every feed, the baby also needs to be burped, their diaper needs to be changed, and baby needs to be resettled—none of which depend on gender. A large part of caregiving for an infant centers around feeding. Whether moms are the primary caregiver staying at home or the care coordinator, they are almost always the ones juggling the mental load of infant feeding. Let's break that mental labor down into our three categories:

Anticipating

They keep track of how many ounces of breastmilk or formula a baby needs. They must know when to supplement, when to pump, how much to pump, and how much milk is in the freezer. They know when bottles and pump parts need to be washed, sanitized, or replaced, and when formula or breastmilk bags need to be restocked.

They are often the ones to know where the formula or breastmilk is, the ones to track when the baby should eat, the ones who know what the next feeding milestone is. When will the baby start solids? When will the baby need bigger bottles? Do we need to introduce allergens?

This pattern gets laid down in the postpartum period but persists well beyond infancy, with moms often being the ones to research and introduce solids, to track potential allergens, to fix plates and spoon-feed, to know when to add water or cow's milk to the mix or what foods to avoid.

Research and Planning

The caregiver doesn't just notice these things, of course—they also research, sometimes endlessly (more on that later in this chapter).

They research breastfeeding tips, lactation consultants, feeding schedules, formula brands, bottle brands, feeding troubleshooting, causes of gas and colic. They create plans for feeding based on this research.

Managing

The actual physical task of feeding is only one small part of the management—although as many of us have experienced, it is hardly a simple task. What feels like it should be "intuitive" is often a difficult process, full of troubleshooting, returning to research and planning to try to work through struggles, and an overwhelming burden of emotional labor.

For breastfeeding moms, the mental and emotional labor involved in the feeding process includes feeling as if they are the only ones who can do it, experiencing being touched out (feeling overwhelmed with constant physical contact and lack of bodily autonomy), worrying about staying hydrated and eating the right foods, worrying that the baby is getting enough, tracking feedings, pumping and labeling milk, handling night wakes, and being unable to leave home for more than a few hours at a time.

For bottle-feeding moms, this load includes cleaning and sanitizing and keeping track of bottles, often experiencing mom guilt for not breastfeeding (and dealing with judgment or feeling like you must explain yourself), finding the right formula brand, the cost of formula, planning ahead to make sure baby has enough, and dealing with "breast is best" comments.

And for the 46 percent of moms who combination feed, the load entails the tasks of both breastfeeding and bottle-feeding, along with decision-making about how much formula to offer, when to breastfeed, and how to balance both. This leaves them saddled with more of the mental load, even when their partner shares in the physical labor.

Our partners can and should be involved in the feeding process when possible. Some moms (and babies) prefer exclusively breastfeeding and are hesitant to incorporate bottles. That is valid—however, it is important to be aware of the patterns we are forming when it comes to carrying this load. If you breastfeed only, then perhaps your partner can be the one to introduce solids and feed the baby when the time comes, handle other night wakings, or take a shift in the early morning while you catch up on some sleep. I would also urge you to remember that if you have committed to a particular way of feeding and this load is beginning to take a negative toll on your mental health, it is important to remain flexible and adjust as the situation evolves.

Beyond the physical tasks of feeding, to truly share in the task of feeding, we have to bring our partners to the mental and emotional side.

Partners can oversee cleaning pump parts, washing bottles, tracking feeds, and researching and selecting formula or bottles. They can bring snacks, contact lactation consultants, and offer support and encouragement to moms, whether they are breastfeeding or bottle-feeding.

Once we move past the idea that feeding is inherently mom-coded, there are many ways to share in the load of feeding.

THE LOAD MAP

You can take these maps as is and discuss them with a partner or support system, or you can tweak and personalize them to suit your family's needs. If you are passing off a task to a partner or another support person, the *entire* task needs to be considered.

The Mother Load is wide and encompassing. Different families have different labor and tasks. This is by no means an exhaustive list. Also keep in mind that these load maps are intended to help you recognize and, when possible, share the labor in your home. But I want to reiterate that the *real* work of this book is within—it's about releasing the labor, not just redistributing it. I hope that the maps are helpful tools for you to see the work that you are doing, understand it, evaluate it, communicate it, and share it.

For editable versions of the load maps, along with blank templates, visit Ericadjossa.com.

INFANT FEEDING

Anticipating

- Tracking how much formula or breastmilk baby needs
- Determining when to supplement
- Knowing how much formula is left or how much breastmilk is in the freezer
- Knowing when breast pump and/or bottle parts need to be washed
- Noticing hunger signs
- Knowing when to implement solids
- Noticing sensitivities to breastmilk or formula
- Only being able to leave for a few hours at a time if breastfeeding

Research and Planning

- How many ounces of milk or formula to offer by age
- How to relieve gas pain
- Breast pumps
- Bottles
- Bottle warmers
- Formula brands and ingredients
- How to navigate tongue and lip ties if necessary
- Latching positions
- Latching troubleshooting
- Lactation consultants
- How to boost milk supply
- What foods to avoid if breastfeeding

Managing

- Selecting and purchasing formula
- Tracking inventory of formula
- Selecting and purchasing bottles
- Selecting and purchasing baby food or ingredients
- Making baby food
- Decision-making (formula, breastfeeding, pumping, or combo? Baby-led weaning or purees?)
- Coping with plugged ducts and mastitis

- Dealing with guilt, judgment, and criticism if bottle-feeding
- Staying hydrated
- Preparing bottles
- Washing pump parts and bottles
- Daytime feedings
- Nighttime feedings
- Dealing with feeding distractions
- Tracking how much milk or formula baby drinks
- Counting and tracking dirty diapers

SLEEP

Sleep struggles can persist beyond the perinatal season, but the patterns get laid down early. Moms are often the ones juggling this labor with infants, continuing to shoulder that labor well into the future.

Anticipating

The caregiver anticipates sleep needs. They look ahead at nap transitions, determining when the baby is going to transition from a bassinet to a crib, when to lower the crib to the next level, and when to move into a toddler bed. They're thinking ahead to when to stop swaddling or when to change to the next size sleep sack.

They keep track of the routine, notice sleep issues, and wonder what adjustments can be made to move toward that all-encompassing goal of "sleeping through the night."

Research and Planning

The caregiver researches sleep struggle troubleshooting, sleep plans, sleep classes, sleep methods, safe sleep practices, brands of sleep sacks and pacifiers and white noise machines (and ALL the sleep gear).

They create schedules and plans to approach nap time, bedtime, night wakings, sleep regressions, and more.

Managing

For many moms, getting up with the baby at night is rigidly mom-coded. My clients often express desperation from sleep deprivation. But they tell me things like:

My partner leaves for work in the morning and needs their sleep.

I'm up anyway breastfeeding; one of us might as well get sleep.

I'm better at resettling the baby—they only want me.

What we don't realize is that many of these justifications are rooted in gender norms. We tell ourselves these things to justify the imbalance, but underneath there is usually a core belief that moms should be the ones caring for the baby.

Does your partner need more sleep? Or do you believe that because care work isn't paid, your time at home with the baby is less valuable?

Are you naturally better at resettling the baby? Or are you just more experienced at it because you believe that your role is to comfort your baby?

Do you really need to be the one taking all the night wakings just because you are breastfeeding? Or is this task just so linked to "mom" in your mind that you haven't sat down to brainstorm ways to share the load with your partner or other support people?

Sleep matters—for moms as well as their partners. Of all the imbalanced labor in the home, this load might have the worst effect on the physical and mental health of moms. Sleep deprivation is linked to increased risk for postpartum depression and postpartum anxiety.[8]

Studies have shown that, to nobody's surprise, sleep deprivation is also linked to irritability, anger, and mom rage. How are you reasonably expected to wake up bright-eyed and bushy-tailed after being up all night? You can create a plan to protect your maternal sleep and preserve your mental health. (See the skills section of this chapter for more.)

THE LOAD MAP

SLEEP

Anticipating

- Noticing sleep patterns
- Tracking upcoming nap transitions
- Anticipating changes in wake windows
- Anticipating when to stop swaddling
- Knowing when baby needs a new size of sleep sack
- Considering the sleep environment and potential adjustments

Research and Planning

- What is "normal" for baby sleep
- Whether you should start a schedule
- What adjustments you can make to wake windows and schedules

- Signs of being overtired and undertired
- When to move baby to a crib or a different room
- What can go in the crib with baby

- What swaddles and sleep sacks to use
- Sleep routines and classes
- Troubleshooting sleep issues
- Planning the sleep routine

Managing

- Tracking time between naps
- Monitoring for tired signs
- Nap routine/putting baby down for naps
- Bedtime routine/ putting baby down for the night
- Handling night wakings

- Adjusting nap time and bedtime routines as needed
- Decision-making (for example, making the choice that it's time to move baby into their own room)
- Coping with sleep deprivation
- Navigating the emotional load of worrying about sleep

COORDINATING CARE

Whether you're staying at home or working outside of the home, you will likely need to carry the labor of coordinating care at some point (even if it's just on occasion for a date night or outing). This comes with its own set of mental labor. For moms who work outside the home, coordinating care can be so extensive it can feel like another separate job. Seeing this load in its entirety and validating it is important:

Anticipating

The care coordinator anticipates holidays and staff development days, keeping track of when the children will need alternative childcare. They also must anticipate sick days, which as you likely know happen at an ungodly frequency especially when first starting daycare or school. They think about what the backup plan will be if random injuries or life events throw a kink in the plans and plan alternative care for date nights or time away from the kids.

When a family has more than one child, these needs compound. More needs arise. More sick days get taken. If one child goes to the doctor, will the other child come, or will they need alternate care? If one child stays at home sick, do they have to ride in the car for drop-off or does one parent stay home with them and one drive the other to school or daycare?

Research and Planning

A great deal of research and planning goes into care coordinating. Moms spend hours upon hours reading reviews, asking other moms for suggestions, joining community groups, checking references, and posting on social media for recommendations. They make plans for drop-off, pick-up, rides, and alternative care for special days and sick days.

Managing

As the care coordinator, moms are still managing a great deal of the care, even without being physically present. They're the default points of contact for daycare. This often happens even if they tell the school or daycare to contact the other parent. Frenel and I have had to tell our boys' school multiple times that HE is the one they should contact.

Moms are the ones managing relationships with their children's teachers, keeping track of forms and paperwork and homework and photos for projects, and knowing when special events are coming up. They're also the ones troubleshooting alternatives and taking off work to provide care.

THE LOAD MAP

COORDINATING CARE

Anticipating

- Keeping track of days without care (holidays, staff development days)

- Anticipating what to do on sick days

- Knowing when alternative care is needed

- Knowing who is going to care for child on which days

- Knowing who is responsible for drop-off and pick-up

- Anticipating when to leave the house to get to daycare on time

Research and Planning

- Interviewing nannies and babysitters

- Touring daycares

- Researching daycare licensing

- Reading reviews

- Asking for recommendations

- Reading daycare websites

- Planning for the transitions

Managing

- Communicating with daycare, nanny, or teachers

- Coordinating schedules

- Drop-off

- Pick-up
- Packing bags

- Tracking special events like dress-up days or school parties

OTHER LABOR OF CAREGIVING

The caregiver is also addressing immediate daily needs, including emotional needs, safety needs, and milestones and development. They are constantly thinking about how to keep their child safe, what stages of life are coming next, and how to provide the best environment along the way, mentally tracking and planning and worrying.

Thinking about babyproofing, car seat safety, crib safety, and safe sleep; each stage brings new safety concerns. When do we turn the car seat around? When do we lower the crib? When do we add baby gates and drawer locks? They're working through child behavior, sensitivities, and tantrums. They are two steps ahead to the "terrible twos" or the "threenagers," anticipating what to expect in the future.

As their children reach these stages, they anticipate how to avoid tantrums, how to support emotional regulation, and how to navigate unwanted behavior. This often becomes a much larger, all-encompassing load of its own, with high stakes, pressure, and an enormous mental and emotional weight. It can feel as if caregivers can never take space for themselves, to relax, to breathe, or to just be present.

Releasing the Mother Load doesn't just give us a brief respite—it fundamentally changes the way we approach motherhood, the way we show up for our children, and how we live our lives.

THE LOAD MAP

SAFETY

Anticipating

- Thinking ahead to the next stage and its safety challenges
- Knowing when baby will become mobile
- Knowing when child will need to turn in the car seat
- Knowing when to lower the crib
- Noticing sharp-edged and hard surfaces
- Noticing potential choking hazards
- Anticipating potential conflict with pets
- Anticipating potential conflict with other siblings

Research and Planning

- Baby gates
- Play pens
- Drawer locks
- Door locks
- Safety recommendations
- Recalls
- Best practices

Managing

- Putting up baby gates
- Installing door and drawer locks
- Reorganizing to move small parts and toys out of reach

- Reorganizing to move knives and sharp objects out of reach
- Remembering car seat safety and monitoring changes

- Turning the car seat when the time comes
- Lowering the crib when the time comes
- Tracking recalls
- In-the-moment decision-making

MILESTONES/DEVELOPMENT

Anticipating

- Thinking ahead to the next stage and milestones
- Knowing what toys and adjustments to the environment will be needed

- Knowing what is "typical" and what red flags to watch out for
- Noticing whether baby is on track

Research and Planning

- Developmental stages
- How much tummy time baby needs

- How to support baby through different stages

Managing

- Adjusting and organizing environment
- Choosing and purchasing toys

- Tracking milestones
- Discussing milestones with doctor

THE "RESEARCH" BLACKHOLE

I don't want us to overlook the burden of research. I remember being a first-time mom and flocking to the internet for every question. How much spit-up is normal? What brand of pacifier won't cause nipple confusion? How often should I be pumping to build my supply? How could I help relieve my baby's gas?

It's difficult to determine when enough is enough. Many of my clients find themselves in a research spiral turned information overload, unsure of how to stop, how to set boundaries around research, and how to trust their own intuition, experience, and abilities.

Part of the reason why researching becomes such a heavy burden is that it is a complex task. Researching isn't as simple as Googling a question. Caregivers must also evaluate sources and information. For example, a simple search of "Should I give my baby a pacifier" will bring a wide range of answers. A mom who searches this will come across forums, studies, and articles that say pacifiers are a great choice—that they lower the risk of SIDS and help satisfy a baby's natural sucking reflex and promote sleep. But they will also come across other forums and articles that say pacifiers cause nipple confusion, that they interfere with breastfeeding, that they impact teeth growth, and that they are unnatural and should be avoided at all costs.

The overload of opposing views and ongoing contradictions can be very taxing and anxiety-provoking. We can become extremely preoccupied and get sucked in. Moms desperately want to make the "right" choices. They often spend hours sorting through pages and pages of articles, suggestions, and conflicting answers and advice.

In the educational world, researchers have determined that there are many levels of learning—some of which require higher-level thinking skills. One of the most popular education frameworks, Bloom's Taxonomy, places knowledge and remembering at the bottom of a learning hierarchy. These are low-level learning tasks: look up a statistic or a fact and recall it. But some of the highest levels include analysis and evaluation—making strategic, justifiable decisions.[9] The researching phase of the mental load involves those higher-level thinking and processing skills. Moms aren't just doing MORE of the mental work—they're doing the mental work that is most demanding and draining.

Even when partners are contributing to the decision-making process, moms are usually the ones weeding through these online recommendations and narrowing them down, then presenting the "best" options. This places the burden of responsibility on their shoulders and comes with an enormous amount of high-stakes pressure.

It might be difficult to let go of this mental labor. When working with my clients, I often advise creating boundaries to contain the research and decision-making. (We'll look at this more in the skills section of chapter 5.) Because research is so open-ended, you need to draw firm boundaries to keep it from running rampant.

ANTICIPATION, RESEARCH, AND
THE LACK OF PRESENCE

In many ways, the caregiver is constantly being forced to live out of the moment, thinking ahead and recognizing problems before they happen, researching best practices, and evaluating the messages that are coming in.

When I chatted with Dr. Cassidy Freitas on episode 143 of *The Momwell Podcast*, she mentioned that many moms feel a ticking time bomb on maternity leave—the anticipation of the end of leave (and all of the care coordinating that comes along with it), sometimes robbing them of being able to enjoy time at home with their babies.[10] The mental load encompasses their spare time and pulls them out of the moment.

It is hard to be present when your brain has a million balls in the air that you don't want to let drop. We're trying to embody the perfect mother by doing it all, without realizing that trying to do it all is what is robbing us of just being with our kids.

I also want to point out that the steps we have covered so far don't include the actual physical caregiving tasks—this is all just prep work. This is the cornerstone of the Mother Load—the fact that most of the work is mental. That is the labor that stays hidden and unrecognized. It's also the labor that is overwhelming, all-encompassing, and exhausting. For each task in the home, the physical labor is half the battle (or less). The hours that go into researching and anticipating matter. That's why we're on this journey: we need to make this work visible—to you, to your partner, to society.

When we can let go of the mental load, we can reclaim those moments and live more in the present.

THE MANAGER (WITH ALL THE BURDEN AND NONE OF THE GLORY)

In the corporate world, managers are highly valued. They keep a high-level, bird's eye view of tasks to be delegated, improved, simplified, and perfected. Even when a manager doesn't physically touch a project, they are respected and revered for their role.

But when it comes to care work, we are undervaluing moms for this same level of responsibility. Because this work isn't recognized by society and doesn't come with a salary, we overlook it.

When you do all the management—all the high-level thinking and processing, from observation to research—it becomes very difficult to share tasks. At best, your partner or support person can be the implementer.

You can ask for help to put up a baby gate, but if you figured out where the gate needed to go, researched baby gates online, asked for input from other moms, made a decision, bought the baby gate, and told your partner where to put it . . . did your partner really take anything off your plate? You still managed the task—you simply handed it off for the final step. This is where many moms find themselves when they start to take on this work. They create chore charts or write out lists of physical tasks to share. But this only further solidifies the manager/employee dynamic in the home.

When we are carrying the knowledge, the research, and understanding the needs behind tasks, we become the subject matter experts. This is how we build the cage of the default parent. This is how the labor gap holds on so strongly.

> When we are carrying the knowledge, the research, and understanding the needs behind tasks, we become the subject matter experts.

Is this something anybody really wants? Do you want to be the manager who carries all the burden and none of the glory? Of course not. Does your partner want to be a lower-level employee in the home? Probably not.

We want to move away from the manager/employee dynamic. We want to share the expertise, the knowledge, the mental labor, and the confidence that comes along with it. But to do that, we have to let go of some beliefs that have a very strong hold.

ASSUMPTIONS THAT REINFORCE THE LOAD WE CARRY

In order to share the load as caregiver or care coordinator, we must first challenge and reframe our internal beliefs.

There are assumptions that we are carrying, often fueled by the intensive mothering beliefs we covered in chapter 2, that will likely get in the way of releasing the load. These are the internal battles we must fight as we work through this load:

Assumption 1

Assumption: Every small decision about gear and gadgets has the same level of significance, and therefore is deserving of my time and attention.
Reframe: If something fulfills my family's needs, it's good enough.

We're likely carrying extra mental labor that nobody truly needs to carry. When it comes to research and decision-making for all the gear and gadgets, unless it's a question of safety, it might not be significant. We want our babies to be safe and healthy. But many of the things we purchase for our children aren't high stakes. If gear is regulated, there isn't necessarily a "right" or "wrong" choice.

Is one brand of bottle safer or better than another? Do we really need to spend hours researching the best muslin baby blanket that's going to be used to wipe spit-up? If a car seat passes safety regulations, can we cut down on the research time and make a quicker decision?

I understand and appreciate the drive to make the best decisions for your baby. But "best" is subjective. We must let go of the idea of "right" gear and gadgets. No amount of research will decide what will work for you, your lifestyle, or your baby.

Assumption 2

Assumption: As a mom, I am the best suited to care for my child.

Reframe: Caregiving is not gendered, and my child benefits from multiple secure attachments.

In the introduction and chapter 1, we discussed the way that gender norms and intensive mothering beliefs set us up to believe we *must* be the ones carrying the load. They weave together to form this assumption—one that is very hard to let go of. It is deeply rooted, and often entwined with our identity as moms. We're proud of our abilities to parent—and we should be!

But when we hold fast to the belief that as moms we are inherently "better" at caregiving, we aren't the only ones who suffer. Without being invited in and empowered in caregiving, our partners remain at novice level, leaving them feeling less confident and competent. Our children also carry these gender assumptions forward, continuing the cycle of the Mother Load.

We can take pride in our abilities as moms, in the skills we have built through our experience, without gatekeeping parenting or assuming that we are the "naturally best" caregivers.

Assumption 3

Assumption: There is a best or right way to parent.

Reframe: There are many ways to parent according to your values.

As we discussed in chapter 2, there is a lot of pressure in motherhood to do things the "right" way. But parenting in alignment with your values matters more than searching for a non-existent "right" way.

There's a lot of noise on the internet about what the "best" parenting decisions are. Letting go of outside messages and expectations and becoming more in tune with you and your family's values and priorities matters.

Assumption 4

Assumption: My partner won't notice everything or see all the needs that I see.

Reframe: My partner deserves the opportunity to build the knowledge that I have built.

Anticipating needs is not a gendered task. There is nothing biological that makes moms better at observation or noticing. We have simply stepped up to the plate because we subconsciously believed we were the best ones to do so.

If you put your partner in a workplace environment, I'm sure they could anticipate the needs that arise in their role. They can, and should, be able to do the same in the home. When they are given the chance to do that, everybody benefits.

Remember that it takes ten thousand hours to become an expert. Our partners or other support people deserve the opportunity to build their own expertise and confidence and to become empowered in caregiving. They need to be given the chance to build their own parental knowledge, to step out of the "employee" role and become equal managers in the home.

Assumption 5

Assumption: "Breast is best."

Reframe: There is no one right way to feed my baby.

Feeding is often one of the first "skill tests" we face in motherhood where we internally judge our performance. We often intertwine the way we feed so heavily with our identity as moms. If I could go back, I would tell myself a few things, and maybe some of you need to hear this too:

- How you feed your baby does not determine your worth or value as a mother.

- How you are adjusting to your new role is not defined by how you feed your child.

- The way your baby is fed is morally neutral; there is no right or wrong way. There is the way that works for your family based on a thousand different variables, and it doesn't matter how others approached it because others have their own variables at play.

- Your fundamental need for sleep is equally as important as baby's need to be fed and cared for, and one does not trump the other.

- To get your needs met, you may need to be flexible with who feeds baby and how, and that's okay.

Assumption 6

Assumption: It's easier just to do it myself than it is to explain how to do it.
Reframe: While it might be more convenient in the short term to do it myself, in the long run it keeps me shouldering the load.

We often resist the thought of passing off caregiving tasks because we tell ourselves it is easier to just do it than to teach someone else how. And in a way, that might be true. It might take more time in the moment to show somebody else how to do something. However, if we want to break away from the load, we must reframe this story in our minds. Sometimes it's worth the initial time or inconvenience to free ourselves in the long run.

It's also important to remember that just because someone else does something differently than us doesn't mean it's wrong. (See the skills section of this chapter for more information.)

Assumption 7

Assumption: In order to get sleep, I need to get baby sleeping through the night.

Reframe: I can develop a plan for maternal sleep separate from baby's sleep.

The adage "sleep when the baby sleeps" is a double-edged sword. On the one hand, it is valid and important to let go of some of the other labor in the postpartum period when possible and prioritize your rest.

However, we often come to believe that we can ONLY sleep when the baby sleeps. This (along with comparisons to other moms or social media promising quick fixes for infant sleep that often leave us more frustrated) leads us to feel pressured to get our babies to sleep through the night, even before they are developmentally ready to do so. And it makes sense to want to hit that milestone so we can get the all-important sleep we need.

But I cannot overstate the importance of shifting the way we view our sleep. Our sleep should not have to rely on baby's sleep. It might take planning and out-of-the-box thinking, but we can prioritize our own sleep. In fact, doing so makes us able to show up better during the day for the valuable work that we do as moms. In the skills section at the end of this chapter, you'll find more on creating a sleep plan for yourself.

SKILLS AND TOOLS FOR RELEASING THIS LABOR

As we work through the invisible tasks that make up the Mother Load, it's important to remember that we are unlearning a lifetime of conditioning. This requires skill, intention, and practice. It might feel uncomfortable at times, and it might not come easily. But there are skills and tools we can learn to help make the transition easier.

In this section, we'll cover skills and tools that include:

- The postpartum adjustment period

- Recognizing our gendered lens of postpartum care tasks

- The help list

- Developing a maternal sleep plan

- Becoming flexible with your approach to feeding—especially at night

- Measuring your worth in motherhood

- Red light vs. green light times to bring up conversations

- Soft conversation starters

At the very end of each chapter, I will leave you with one big take-away and one place to start. If at any point you become overwhelmed, anchor yourself there. We won't release the load in one day, but rather little by little.

The Postpartum Adjustment Period

The postpartum adjustment is often a difficult transition. Overnight, you become an entirely different person—one who is responsible for caring for a tiny human. You might not have experience with children or babies—and yet you are now responsible for meeting all their needs. But the difficult adjustment isn't just about the physical labor, or even the mental labor. There is a massive emotional component as well.

Moms often experience identity shifts and grief over the loss of their old selves and their old lives. They're facing significant shifts in their values and priorities. For potentially the first time, they face barriers for meeting their own physical, mental, and emotional needs—all while often dealing with body changes, postpartum healing, and hormonal shifts. We're coping with all of that *while* juggling the invisible load we've inherited that we weren't prepared for

This time period can be very vulnerable. We go from being supported during our pregnancy to seeing others around us focus on the baby and their needs. And, unfortunately, *we* often fall through the cracks.

One of the biggest challenges during this time is often the change in relationship dynamics. For partnered moms, it can be hard to navigate the new conflict that often arises. Increased conflict is common—in fact, 67 percent of couples report a decline in relationship satisfaction in the first three years of a baby's life.[11] This is likely due to many factors, including resentment regarding the invisible load, physical and emotional intimacy struggles, mental health concerns, lack of time and energy to dedicate to the relationship, and sheer exhaustion. Moms might feel like strangers in their own bodies, experience frustration over barriers to intimacy, or feel like they "should" want to have sex, even when they are still in survival mode.

When you're encountering these difficulties, it can feel very hopeless. It can help to have self-compassion and remember that this is a season—one that will pass and carve the path to a new normal. But this season is a high-risk time for mental health challenges—not just for moms, but for their partners as well.

And for so many of us, it's not what we envisioned. I often encourage moms to create postpartum plans *before* they find themselves in this time period. It can be helpful to consider your individual risk factors that increase your chances of developing perinatal mood disorders,[12] including:

- Previous mental health struggles, including history of depression, anxiety, or bipolar disorder
- Relationship satisfaction prior to baby
- Perfectionism or "Type A" personality
- Lack of social support
- Sensitivity to changes in hormones
- Unplanned or negative attitude toward pregnancy
- Life events or stressors, including financial difficulty or job concerns
- History of sexual abuse
- Disappointment over sex of the baby
- Sleep deprivation and insomnia

Many of the struggles during this time can't be eliminated—but that doesn't mean we can't create supports to help us. It's important to remember that we as moms don't have to carry all the labor.

Recognizing Our Gendered Lens of Postpartum Care Tasks

One of the reasons why we carry this weight so heavily during the postpartum period is that it *feels* like it must be our job as moms. But . . . does it really? Let's revisit the gender-coding activity we did in chapter 1, but this time apply it specifically to the postpartum period.

Look through the following tasks. Write MC (mother-coded) next to any you associate with moms, FC (father-coded) next to any you associate with dads, and N next to any that you view as neutral or primarily shared:

___ Feeding baby

___ Pacing, walking, or bouncing baby

___ Researching bottle types (or other gear)

___ Soothing baby

___ Attending appointments

___ Night wakings

___ Coordinating support

___ Documenting wet diapers, feeds, etc.

___ Skin to skin

___ Changing diapers

___ Burping baby

___ Getting baby to sleep

___ Tracking milestones

___ Troubleshooting issues that arise

___ Bathing baby

___ Deciphering baby's needs

___ Interacting with/ entertaining baby

___ Researching best safety practices

___ Holding baby for contact naps

___ Dealing with diaper blowouts

How many of these tasks do you associate with mom? And how many with dad? For most of us, most of these tasks are mother-coded, while a few might be neutral. (I'm willing to bet that most of these tasks are not father-coded in our minds.) When we see ourselves as the ones primarily responsible to carry these tasks, we take them on without question.

Breaking away from the assumptions found in this chapter can help us begin to see this labor in a different way. From there, we can come up with creative solutions that allow this labor to be shared with a partner person. Postpartum tasks don't have to inherently fall to mom.

For many of us, it might happen without question. After all, if not by gender, how should we divide out tasks?

That answer becomes a little bit tricky. I want to say work together to divide out tasks according to your strengths. However, gender norms are so prevalent that this can also become convoluted. If you have been expected to know how to nurture and provide care, but this hasn't been expected of your partner, it might appear that it's a strength for you but not for them. For example, let's say you are better at soothing the baby . . . so every time the baby cries, you handle the soothing. You become pigeonholed as the baby tamer. You've had more practice soothing the baby. You very well might be stronger at it . . . but that doesn't mean that your partner shouldn't try to learn, or that another support person shouldn't be able to try and figure it out.

When we can break away from the idea that these tasks should fall to us—because of gender, because of socialized strengths, or just because we feel like we must—it becomes easier to share the labor.

But even when you're on board, it can feel overwhelming to divide tasks. It might be tempting to create a fixed list of who does what . . . and to a degree that might be helpful. However, the issue there arises with the mental work. If you divide the physical tasks, mental labor often falls through the cracks. As I mentioned in chapter 1, the maternal knowledge sets the stage for the Mother Load. A task list doesn't share the knowledge. It doesn't always share the anticipating or the research or the management. To truly share the Mother Load, systems and rhythms and routines help more than a fixed list. (We'll dive more into rhythms and routines in the skills section of chapter 6 and talk about sharing and syncing maternal knowledge in the skills section of chapter 7.)

The Help List

Many of us struggle to ask for help. Maybe we lack assertiveness, worry about burdening others, or feel like we should be able to carry it all. Whatever the reason, I find that many of my clients have difficulty in this area. I understand that firsthand—it took my full breakdown/breakthrough to make me realize that I needed to ask for help.

Many moms in my community have shared how a "help list" on the fridge can make it easier to accept support.

In the postpartum season, visits from guests can sometimes feel like added labor and pressure for moms. They often feel as if they need to host or care for their guests. While they might have been doted on during pregnancy, once a baby comes, the focus shifts off mom. Guests might come over and be more interested in holding the baby than checking to see what mom needs.

But often, the people visiting *want* to help—they just don't know what we need. They might feel that holding the baby is a help . . . but you might feel differently.

That's where the help list comes into play. A help list is a list of tasks you need support with that you keep on your fridge so visitors or support people can chip in. It provides clear direction to those who do want to offer support but don't know where to start, and it directs people to help you in a way that you actually need.

Some examples may include:

- Take the dog for a walk
- Fold laundry
- Watch baby while mom naps or showers
- Wash dishes
- Empty the dishwasher
- Play a game with other children/siblings

This list might also include other ways that support people can help during this time, such as drop off a meal, bring a coffee, or pick up your curbside groceries.

Having a list helps to give them concrete ways to support you—and most often, our support systems in our lives appreciate the clarity and guidance.

Developing a Maternal Sleep Plan

Sleep is a fundamental cornerstone of a mother's mental health and well-being. I know I am preaching to the choir—of course you want more sleep. Of course you want to rest. But you can't because of baby's sleep schedule.

We have a mindset that the only way we can get sleep is by problem-solving or controlling our babies' sleep. And while that plays a role, I am an advocate for having a sleep plan for mom that is completely separate and doesn't depend on baby sleeping. Baby sleep is often unpredictable, and if we think that we can *only* sleep when the baby sleeps, our sleep can suffer.

On episode 141 of *The Momwell Podcast*, Dr. Nicole Leistikow outlined a study that highlighted the impact that sleep has on mood and depression postpartum.[13] Through the course of her research on maternal sleep, she came across a recent study centered around a new medication specifically to treat postpartum depression—Brexanalone.

In the study, moms in their first six months of postpartum with symptoms of severe depression were given an IV infusion of either the medication or a placebo. They had to stop breastfeeding for a week, remaining in the hospital for three days. The group that received the medication showed significant improvement within sixty hours. But interestingly, the moms who received the placebo also had a strong, fast, and lasting improvement in symptoms.[14] Dr. Nicole believes that one of the reasons why the placebo group also experienced improvement is that they were able to sleep undisturbed.

Sleep impacts our mental and physical health. It's vital for brain function. And when moms are sleep-deprived, they are more likely to experience severe symptoms of postpartum depression or anxiety. In fact, sleep deprivation for even just one night can impact our brain function.[15]

But protecting our sleep can help improve our mental health greatly. Even one consecutive stretch of four to six hours of sleep can reset and restore our brain, making it easier to cope and function during the day and improving our well-being.[16]

That's why creating a sleep plan for mom separate from baby matters. Not every infant will cooperate with our need for at least four hours of sleep. But we can create a plan to ensure that everyone gets the sleep they need by taking overnight shifts.

Dr. Nicole recommended "musical beds." Have a partner or support person take the first wake up, while mom sleeps with ear plugs or goes to a different room to sleep undisturbed. Later in the night, you can swap so the support partner can get consolidated sleep.[17]

Now, we all know that some babies won't take a bottle, or that some families want to exclusively nurse. But that doesn't mean we can't still protect sleep. If you are nursing, have your support person bring baby to you to nurse so you aren't on alert listening for noise. Then have them take baby to burp, change and resettle while you maximize your sleep between feedings.

The idea of sharing night labor can be difficult for many of us. This comes down largely to our assumptions that we should be the ones to handle this labor. We might believe that our partner needs more rest because they work outside of the home or that we are the ones best suited to soothe baby. I encourage you to challenge these assumptions. Mothers work, whether they leave the home and earn a paycheck or not. Their work is high stakes—caring for, attending, and protecting children 24/7. And we need rest in order to do that.

Sometimes sharing sleep requires creativity. Maybe you don't have a partner. Or your partner travels for work, is deployed, or works a job that doesn't allow them to share in the night labor. Once you have shifted your mindset from "I must sacrifice my sleep and tend to my baby because that is what makes me a good mom" to "I need to make a plan for myself so that I can be well and able to care for my baby in a healthy way," it frees you up to look for creative solutions.

Perhaps grandparents stay for a routine night a week when parents can get a solid chunk of consecutive sleep. Maybe you and your partner find a groove that involves alternative solutions. Or perhaps you can team up with a single or solo parent to partner on the weekend so you can each get restorative, consolidated sleep. If feasible for you, maybe you can hire a night nurse or a postpartum doula.

If none of those solutions is possible for you, maybe that means moving baby to a different room or turning the monitor to its lowest volume, so you aren't disturbed by every grunt or coo.

Whatever your situation, the solution will look unique, but when we can see sleep as king (or queen) in our postpartum adjustment and well-being, we can problem solve in ways that go beyond focusing on sleep training or trying to get baby to sleep through the night before they are ready.

Becoming Flexible with Your Approach to Feeding—Especially at Night

As I mentioned earlier, if I were to do it all over again and have a fourth (which I won't—and, no, to the granny who randomly asked me in the grocery store, it's not time for me to try for a girl), the biggest change I would make is how I approach feeding, specifically at nighttime. I was so anxiously preoccupied with "exclusively breastfeeding" that I did it at the cost of my sleep and mental health.

It took us a while to figure out latching, work through engorgement, and knowing the signs of when baby had had enough. I was feeding, pumping, and tube feeding at the breast . . . and looking back, I understand that the entire experience robbed me of time enjoying my baby.

I've heard similar stories from my community about the pressures of exclusively breastfeeding. I've heard from moms whose mental health suffered because of the pressures. I've heard from moms with mastectomies or other health conditions that prevented breastfeeding who experienced shame and guilt. I've heard from moms who pushed and punished themselves for supplementing or feeding with formula. Feeding doesn't go according to plan for many clients I work with, and the grief and mix of feelings this can bring is complex.

I wish that I would have known then that flexibility matters. I wish I would have supplemented and given myself permission to protect my sleep more. And I wish I would have understood that I didn't have to feed my baby according to one specific ideal.

Flexibility about how we approach feeding, especially at nighttime, is vital to sharing this load and protecting our mental health postpartum. Breastfeeding can be a positive experience for some and therefore add to their experience of motherhood, while for others it can be a negative experience (for a variety of reasons) and therefore can have a negative impact on mental health. It's important to question our expectations and be flexible when something doesn't work for us or our family.

Holding tight to an expectation or ideal you set for yourself before you stepped one foot into the reality of the role is misguided. Being able to adapt, be flexible, and evaluate the approach or ideals you had based on the reality of the circumstances in front of you is courageous, resilient, and healthy.

Measuring Your Worth in Motherhood

What does being a "good mom" mean to you? Does it mean your children aren't fussy? That they sleep through the night? Or that your house is tidy? Or that you made a home-cooked meal for dinner? Many of us are using the wrong measuring sticks to determine our value as moms.

Motherhood is our most cherished and important role; it makes sense that we want a measuring stick that helps us to evaluate how we are doing. But when this measuring stick is oriented to the wrong things— to perfectionist standards, to unrealistic expectations that society has set—whenever we look to it, we feel like we are failing or coming up short. It's time to stop blaming ourselves and change the measuring stick.

Old ways of evaluating ourselves in motherhood

- Children are always well-behaved
- House is clean and tidy
- Home-cooked or balanced meals
- Everything is going according to plan

- Getting your to-do list done
- Having children who are always happy
- Whether your child is a good sleeper
- Whether you were able to breastfeed or not
- How your baby was delivered

New ways of evaluating ourselves in motherhood

- Was I compassionate with myself today?
- Was I attuned to my child's needs?
- Did I breathe before reacting or responding? (And if not, was I compassionate with myself? Did I explore *why* I didn't react the way I wanted?)
- Did I care for my needs today?
- Was I able to be present during a playful moment?
- Did I notice when I needed a break today and take one?
- Was I able to be flexible and adjust my expectations of the day based on the reality of what was happening?

Red Light vs. Green Light Times to Bring Up Conversations

When having big conversations about sharing labor (or any potential conflict or change), choosing the right time matters. The middle of the night when you are sleep deprived and at your breaking point is likely not the best time to launch into a conversation about how your partner doesn't help you enough at night.

The right approach to a conversation matters. Relationship researcher Dr. John Gottman says that 96 percent of the time, the way an argument begins predicts how it ends.[18] It's a pretty telling statistic that gives us a good lesson—if we want our partner to hear us, we have to consider how the message is being delivered.

Many of us launch into arguments out of emotion, to relieve pressure or blow off steam, but these conflicts are rarely productive and can do more harm than good.

Knowing red light and green light signs for serious or emotional conversations can help.

Red Light Signs

- *You haven't tended to your basic needs first.* Think about your needs. Are you hungry? Are you sleep-deprived? Do you need a shower, a breather, or some space from the situation first? This might not be the time to approach the conversation.

- *A heated or emotional moment.* We often bring up conflict when we're heated. It's easy to understand why—that's when it's on our minds and we're looking for a solution. But the moment that you see your partner or a family member do something that triggers your frustration is likely not the best time to have a conversation about it. When you're dysregulated, your nervous system is activated. You're in fight-or-flight and your blood is pumping, making it very hard to keep your logical, rational, problem-solving brain online. Allowing yourself some time and space to calm your body is a must.

- *You're distracted or in the middle of something.* The time for a heart-to-heart is not when you're cooking dinner with children running around and a million noises in the background, especially if you are already feeling escalated. This will most likely lead to overstimulation and miscommunication rather than the resolution you are looking for.

Green Light Signs

- *You've had some space to think about the conversation (instead of just reacting).* When you take time to intentionally bring something up, rather than just reacting in the moment, the conversation is likely going to go better. Choose a time when the kids are asleep, you don't have a time crunch or something to accomplish, or you've carved out some intentional time.

- *You've taken care of your needs.* You've eaten, showered, or relaxed—you don't have pressing needs that are going to keep you from approaching the conversation calmly.

- *You know you have each other's undivided attention.* The kids are not around, you're not on your phones, you aren't watching the new episode of your favorite TV show or an important ball game. You need to be able to give each other undistracted attention for big conversations.

- *You're able to breathe and regulate your body.* If you struggle with this, practice grounding and calming techniques for staying in the moment.

- *You can be intentional about how you start the conversation.* Positive, productive conversation starters can help lead to successful discussion.

Soft Conversation Starters

Bringing up potentially tough conversations about the invisible load can be hard. When we don't view a topic in the same way as our partner, these discussions can get heated. But if we change our approach, it can become easier.

You've likely heard of "I" statements before (framing a conversation from its impact on you, rather than putting the emphasis on what the other person is or isn't doing). These are a valid tool for starting conversations. But it's important to understand why.

As mentioned on page 120, the way a conversation begins often predicts how it ends. So, we want to enter conversations with what Dr. John Gottman calls soft start-ups. This isn't about infantilizing our partners or treating them with kid gloves; it's about approaching them from a position of respect and willingness to hear their perspective.

Here are some ways that Gottman recommends entering conversations:[19]

Take responsibility

- "I can see where I responded harshly when I said . . ."

- "I hear you. Next time I will try to discuss how I am feeling sooner."

- "I agree I could have handled that part better. I'll work on that for next time."

Share how you feel about the specific situation and state a positive need

- "I felt really anxious when you didn't answer the phone when you went to visit your parents with the kids. It's a long drive and I would appreciate it if you'd check in when you get there."

- "I feel really frustrated when I have to remind you to change over the laundry. We agreed it would be your responsibility . . . perhaps you can set a timer on your phone so this doesn't fall on me."

- "I have a really hard time with the way you spoke to the kids this morning. I know the mornings are chaotic, but I'd appreciate if you'd try to be more playful getting them in the car rather than raising your voice."

Start the conversation with "I" instead of "You"

Starting conversations with "you" is placing blame and puts your partner on the defensive.

- "I feel unappreciated when everyone leaves their laundry on the floor for me to pick up. Can we work together on a system to make sure everything ends up in a basket at the end of the day?"

Describe your experience or how you feel without casting judgment or blame

- "From my perspective, when you didn't follow through on the task, it felt like you were expecting me to do it for you."

- "You may not have intended it this way, but when you said . . . it made me feel . . ."

- "I had a hard day at home with kids and was counting down the moments until you got home, so when you stopped by a friend's without checking in, I was frustrated."

Be appreciative and respectful

- "When you handled dinner and cleanup tonight, I felt very seen and valued. Thank you."

- "I noticed that you've been stepping in to change diapers without me asking. I really appreciate you taking initiative and not waiting to be asked."

Don't accumulate offenses

Holding onto things without addressing them is bomb-building, and it's guaranteed to explode at some point.

IF YOU ONLY REMEMBER ONE THING

Whew! That's a lot, isn't it? I know that it can seem overwhelming. We're talking about undoing a lifetime of conditioning here. But I also understand busy mom life. So for each load, I want to leave you with one big takeaway and one starting point—so you can begin the work of breaking away from the Mother Load *now*.

The most important thing to remember: Our worth as moms is not measured by the amount of caregiving labor we provide. Being a "good mom" isn't about the hours we sacrifice, the tasks we do, or being the one who does it all.

IF YOU ONLY DO ONE THING

Start here: If you only have the capacity to do one thing, begin with redefining your measuring stick of what makes you a "good mom." Let go of the old measuring stick and start evaluating your performance by your values and things that truly matter.

THE INVISIBLE LOAD OF FEEDING THE HOUSEHOLD

Knowing everyone's food preferences

Considering nutrition, diet, and allergy needs

Managing food inventory

Researching new meals that everyone will eat

Creating a positive food environment

Planning meals

Shopping for groceries

Coping with the pressure to get kids to eat

Juggling schedules for mealtimes

Making in-the-moment decisions about snack and food requests

Feeling pressure to set a healthy food example

Managing meal prep and cooking

5

FEEDING THE HOUSEHOLD

If you travel to different countries and interact with a range of cultures, one of the first things you will notice is that food is a central part of society almost everywhere in the world.

My husband is originally from Benin. His family and his culture believe in food as an expression of love and affection. When my mother-in-law came to visit in the postpartum period, I observed her spending hours preparing meals for our family, caring for us through food.

Whether we're from a culture that does not condone waste, or grew up in poverty, or ate frozen pizza frequently, or sat around the table eating home-cooked meals, for most of us, food represents so much more than just what we're putting into our bodies.

Food is security, when those of us who grew up without enough are able to fill our fridge and pantry after payday.

Food is comfort, when we take a casserole to someone's home after a loss.

Food is punishment, when we restrict our bodies and count calories because we are unhappy with how we look.

Food is perfectionism, when we spend hours worrying about each individual ingredient, chemicals, and GMOs.

Food is connection, when we value coming together for big family dinners.

Food might be shame, if we've grown up in diet culture, experienced body issues, or if we were made fun of for our culture's dishes.

Food can be love. Food can be hope. Food can be communication.

We all carry internal stories and beliefs around food—past and present experiences that shape the relationship we have with food. And, when we become parents, we often bring those stories, that relationship, with us without realizing it.

We all carry internal stories and beliefs around food—past and present experiences that shape the relationship we have with food.

This is why the act of feeding the house often becomes so ingrained in our identity as moms. Our relationship with food operates in the background, an invisible puppet master pulling our strings.

We might view our children as wasteful, unappreciative, or disrespectful when they don't eat what we make. We might panic or stress about picky eating or food waste. And we might create pressure for ourselves around the act of feeding.

For me, after my parents got divorced, my dad often took the path of least resistance when it came to food. He had rarely made home-cooked meals, and money was tight, so we ate a lot of processed foods—frozen chicken nuggets, French fries—anything that could be popped into the oven and served with ease. So when I became a mom, I wanted to be the opposite. I wanted to hand-craft organic baby food. I wanted to cook big family dinners. I wanted to be the nutritional advocate I didn't have in my own life.

Now, three kids in, I've decided to choose my battles—and serve a fair share of chicken nuggets. For me, it wasn't the food itself that was the actual concern—it was the meaning I associated with mealtimes, the ways food shifted in our home as a result of my parents' divorce and the change in income, and the experiences I had regarding food.

I never took the time to reflect on why I put pressure on myself around feeding my family, and whether it truly aligned with my values. Before the boys were born, Frenel and I shared the labor of preparing meals. But when they came along, something shifted in my mind. I felt like I should be the one to feed everyone, to provide nourishment and connection and security.

This happens in so many families. We want our children to be secure and healthy. But what we don't realize is that there are so many underlying beliefs that go beyond simply health and nutrition wrapped up in our relationship with food. This often comes out in perfectionism and pressure—we associate feeding our children home-cooked meals from scratch with being a good mom.

These beliefs make this load particularly emotionally charged. They also make it very difficult to put the load down. As we work through this load, it's important to reflect on your own relationship with food.

What Does Food Represent to You?

Take a moment to ask yourself these questions:

- What memories come up when you think about mealtimes as a child?

- What were the rules around food in your home growing up?

- How was it handled when you refused to eat something or said you were full?

- How was food talked about in your home? Was it morally neutral or described in terms like "good" or "bad"?

- What emotions come up for you when you think about food?

- What emotions come up for you when you think about your children eating—or NOT eating?

- What parts of feeding your children are triggering for you?

- What does it mean to you when someone cooks you a meal?

- What are you trying to express when you cook a meal for others?

Being a good mom doesn't mean home-cooked meals every day. It doesn't mean that your child always eats the perfect balance of nutrients. It doesn't mean that your child is not a picky eater or never wastes food.

Being a good mom is so much more than how or what you feed your child. Choosing the path of least resistance when it comes to food doesn't mean you are a bad mom.

Think about what a home-cooked meal represents to you. Is it family? Love? Support? Connection? Now, think about alternative routes to get to that destination. Some of you might genuinely love preparing every meal from scratch. There is absolutely nothing wrong with that. But if the act of feeding your children in a specific way is crushing you or impacting your mental health, it's time to take a step back and think about why you are carrying that weight.

Being a good mom is so much more than how or what you feed your child.

In most instances, our children won't suffer if they eat chicken nuggets sometimes (heck, a lot of the time), or if you order takeout, or if you choose to let go of perfection around food. In fact, letting go of some of the expectations you are holding onto around food could give way to more presence, more thoughtfulness, more connection, and more happiness.

The pressures we give ourselves about food come from a good place. Our intentions are pure—we want to feed our children, we want them to be healthy, we want them to grow, we want them to be secure, we want to provide for them, and we want to show our love and strengthen our attachment and bond.

But if we think about our relationship with food like an onion, and we peel back the layers of our food associations, we can see that each desire, each emotion, each outcome we want for our child can be achieved without perfection around food. No research on attachment or relationships shows that a home-cooked meal is a prerequisite. Feeding our children in a specific way is not the only vehicle for care, love, connection, and nurturing.

It's also important to consider the socioeconomic impact of feeding the family. Many families struggle to afford fresh meat, fresh produce, or seafood. Now, facing inflation and supply chain issues as a result of the COVID pandemic, it's harder than ever. We're talking about food in this chapter as a choice. Do we choose home-cooked meals or those made from scratch? Do we choose organic ingredients or not? But for many families, these are not even choices that are available. Processed foods might be a means of survival, which can come with its own load of guilt and shame. I hope that we can release some of those negative emotions through this chapter.

Confronting and reframing the moral beliefs we associate with food is vital if we want to put down the Mother Load and chart a path in motherhood that aligns with our own values.

THE PATTERN OF IMBALANCE IN FEEDING THE FAMILY

Many of us fall into the pattern of becoming the sole or primary feeder of the home during maternity leave, but the roots are often established earlier, during pregnancy. The pattern continues with infant feeding, but it often carries into feeding the entire household. It might make the most sense for the parent who is home to cook most of the meals. However, this often becomes a gateway to a load that grows exponentially as our children or our families grow. When we factor in our internal beliefs, food stories, and pressures, it becomes a perfect storm for an unmanageable load of labor.

As our babies start solids, we might begin on the path of most resistance—buying steamers and blenders, preparing every puree from scratch and freezing them for our babies. When our children become older, we might obsess over nutrition and balance and sugar and organic food and the ingredients in their food, or even trying to appease their preferences (which becomes more complicated with each child added to our family).

These patterns endure even if we return to work—we often continue carrying the mental labor, planning, preparation, and pressure around food. That labor frequently remains unshared, even if we divide the physical labor of cooking. If a mom researches ingredients, plans the menu, creates a shopping list, buys the food, puts it away in the pantry, and monitors the inventory, then asking a partner to cook a meal here and there doesn't ease the load.

To share the load of feeding, we need to take a look within at our expectations and find where we can shift to the path of least resistance, looking at the feeding tasks as a whole and combining all of the mental and emotional labor they encompass.

Anticipating

The feeder of the home recognizes the upcoming food needs—tracking inventory, monitoring their children's preferences, thinking about upcoming meal plans, and trying to prepare healthy, balanced diets that everybody will be willing to eat.

They are also often responsible for navigating allergies and sensitivities if relevant, keeping upcoming holidays or special events in mind, and planning the day around food needs. (If we go to story time at the library in the morning and swim class in the afternoon, when and where will we eat? Do we need to bring snacks? Do we need to come home early to set out dinner to thaw?)

It is in this stage that we often create additional and potentially unnecessary labor for ourselves. We over-anticipate, ultimately leading to over-researching and overmanaging.

I remember noting the difference when we reevaluated the labor in our home and decided that Frenel would take over the bulk of feeding the family. He didn't always worry about the perfect balance of nutrients or every little ingredient. He simply planned a variety of meals and went for functionality.

Watching that was a light bulb moment for me. Some of the labor I was carrying was necessary. But some of it simply wasn't. Those internal messages, the food beliefs, the pressure, were creating a bigger load around feeding. If we are going to share this load, we need to be open to the fact that not every food decision is high stakes. Not every meal needs to be perfectly balanced. There are places where we can, and should, let go.

Research and Planning

In the research phase of feeding the household, moms spend time finding food options to meet the needs of the family. They look up recipes, read about batch meal prep programs and methods, research meal kits. They turn to social media and forums to ask other moms what works for them and their families. When their kids get tired of what they are preparing, or when things get busy, they Google easy lunch and dinner ideas.

If food allergies or sensitivities are involved, they research even more, determining what foods are safe for their children or what might be causing rashes, gas, or other stomach issues. They plan the meals and menus, prep the grocery lists, and plan for when to grocery shop.

Feeding the household also often involves financial planning and couponing, trying to manage the weekly grocery run on a set budget. Moms often feel immense pressure around spending and saving money, especially when they are not working paid jobs.

During the research and planning phase of feeding the household, we can become overexposed to information that might increase our anxiety, bring added pressure, or skew our expectations. For example, if we Google simple lunch ideas but come across Pinterest-mom examples of star-shaped fruit, elaborate lunches, and daily notes in the lunchbox, we might end up taking on even more labor or experiencing guilt if the lunches we make don't look like that. Over-researching can bring even more extraneous standards of perfection—more "shoulds" that we feel we must live up to.

To make matters even harder, researching in this phase also comes with a high level of evaluation, just like in the caregiving and care-coordinating tasks. The internet is full of to-dos, curated images, and contradictory information. For example, you might read online about how sugar will harm your child, then scroll through Instagram and see advice that says to add sugar to your child's plate so that sugar isn't viewed as "special." It can feel impossible to know who is right, which people to follow and listen to, and to live up to the massive expectations to feed our children the "right way."

In many ways, the task of feeding makes moms feel like they need to be dieticians, occupational therapists, child psychologists, and intuitive eating therapists, channeling all the expertise and information online to help their children develop the "best" eating and nutrition habits. We often view feeding as extremely high stakes, believing that if we make mistakes, we will ruin our children's nutritional health and outlook for the rest of their lives. But when we hold onto these feeding ideals, we keep ourselves saddled with the load.

It's also important to remember that there is such a thing as too much information. We think that when we research and learn more, we are becoming more informed and therefore "better" moms. But the more information we take in, the harder it is to evaluate and make decisions that align with our values. The truth is that it is practically impossible to keep up with the level of research, attention to detail, and expectations that surround feeding the household.

When Dr. Sophie Brock was a guest on episode 69 of *The Momwell Podcast*, she and I talked about how much pressure the perfect mother myth creates, and how unattainable and unrealistic it is—especially if you add more children to the mix.[1] Maybe (and that is a strong *maybe)* you can keep your head above water if you have one child, and lots of financial cushion and support. But when you add multiple children to the mix, the Mother Load increases exponentially. It becomes impossible to live up to the perfect mother ideals in our minds. We simply must learn to triage as parents.

To some degree, we figure this out on our own over time, or if we have multiple children. We begin to lean back on what we have learned rather than flocking to the internet to research. We might opt for a squishy pouch instead of preparing our own baby food. We probably introduce sweets a little bit earlier for our second child. But if the perfect mother myth has a hold on us—as long as we are aiming for this unattainable and undefinable target—we will likely experience immense amounts of guilt and shame, even when we understand the necessity of triaging.

The goal here is to learn to prioritize what's most essential based on our own values, based on our own priorities, and based on our own needs, without judgment or comparison or guilt or shame. We must evaluate what is truly important. Do we really need to read every ingredient of every snack and research whether it is acceptable to feed our child? Do we really need to be paralyzed by every parenting decision? Do we really need validation from the online world in what we feed our child?

In the grand scheme of parenting, there are things that matter more than others. And, while feeding your child a healthy diet is certainly admirable, we likely need to set some boundaries around this load. We should be able to make quicker decisions, to choose what matters to us—without hours of online research.

These anticipating and researching tasks come well before the physical task and the management. By the time we have anticipated, researched, planned, and shopped for the food, we have put many hours of mental labor in. We can't simply share this task by asking our partner to do the physical labor. If we do all the prep work, all of the mental labor, and ask them to cook a meal we planned and prepped and shopped for, it does not remove the burden from our shoulders. The exhaustion and burnout moms often feel doesn't come from physical tasks—it comes from all the invisible stages that come before and after them.

After all, if only we carry all the knowledge of the moving parts, our partner is never going to complete the task to the same level that we are. That's why sharing the knowledge is key—your partner must be involved in the research and evaluation to take an active role in this task.

Managing

Leading up to the management phase, we have a lot of control around feeding our children. We have control over the food choices we make, the groceries we buy, the ingredients we choose, the meals we plan. We often want to carry that high level of control into the management phase. The problem is, at the end of the day, we have no control over what our children actually put into their bodies. The management of food with our little ones is often full of battles—battles, I would venture to say, that we typically do not need to fight.

The actual management of feeding should involve cooking or preparing meals, creating an environment for eating, deciding on mealtimes, and putting food on the table at the time that we choose—the rest is up to our child. (The skills section of this chapter provides more insight into this concept, known as the division of responsibility.)

For many of us, the idea of dividing the responsibilities this way, and letting go of control where we truly have none, is anxiety-inducing. It is so tempting to hold onto control over what our children eat. But letting go of the power struggles can bring more peace and freedom into our lives and mealtime routines.

THE LOAD MAPS

For editable versions of the load maps, along with blank templates, visit Ericadjossa.com.

MEAL PLANNING AND MEAL PREP

Anticipating

- Monitoring everyone's preferences
- Noticing potential allergies, reactions, or sensitivities
- Keeping upcoming holidays and special events in mind
- Knowing what changes will come to the routine when on the go
- Anticipating nutritional needs

Research and Planning

- Recipes
- Meal prep programs
- Meal kit services
- Crowdsourcing meal ideas

- Ingredients and nutrition
- Feeding philosophies

- Creating food plans
- Allergen information

Managing

- Creating the actual meal plan for the week
- Prepping food for all the meals
- Accommodating last-minute changes in schedule

- Taking taste preferences into account
- In-the-moment decision-making and adjustment

GROCERY SHOPPING

Anticipating

- Monitoring grocery inventory
- Anticipating time needed for shopping

- Considering meal planning and coordinating with inventory

Research and Planning

- Recipes
- Grocery store availability

- Price comparison
- Budgeting
- Couponing

Managing

- Coordinating the schedule to create time to shop

- Tracking any last-minute additions or changes

- Decision-making/ adjustment for substitutions

- Managing children asking for items throughout the store if they come along

COOKING/PREPARING MEALS

Anticipating

- Monitoring everyone's preferences

- Anticipating nutritional needs

- Noticing where necessary ingredients are

- Monitoring hunger cues of children, other family members, and guests

Research and Planning

- Recipes

- Substitutions

- Different meal plans and diets based on needs and restrictions

- Baby-led weaning versus traditional weaning

- Ways to hide vegetables or sneak in nutritional content

Managing

- Creating a healthy and positive food environment

- Monitoring our children's relationship with food

- Setting out age-appropriate snacks

- Deciding on meal and snack times

- Working with children to expose them to new foods and flavors

- In-the-moment decision-making and adjustment

- Determining how much food and what food is served at which time

ASSUMPTIONS THAT REINFORCE THE LOAD WE CARRY

In order to redistribute the feeding labor in the home, we must first confront the assumptions that are adding labor and keeping us carrying it:

Assumption 1

Assumption: Preparing meals is one of the most important ways I can show love.

Reframe: There are endless ways to show love and build attachment and connection with your child.

Food is likely intrinsically linked to love and security in our minds. But it's important to remember that those emotions are not actually inherently linked to food. We must sort through what we believe about food and what food truly is.

We don't have to prepare complex meals from scratch, perfectly balance every meal, or always say yes to every snack to show our children that they are loved, secure, and safe.

In fact, sometimes choosing the path of least resistance can provide even more opportunity for connection. If we spend an hour trying to cook a meal from scratch for our children while our babies and toddlers fuss, leaving us stressed and overstimulated, is that truly better than ordering pizza and sitting with our children for a relaxed, engaging meal?

That's not to say we should never choose the home-cooked meal—do what you value and enjoy. It just means that we need to reframe our thinking around it. When we let go of some tasks, we can create room for presence, space for connection, and opportunity for bonding and for preservation of our own mental health.

Assumption 2

Assumption: Cooking is a woman's job.

Reframe: Food preparation is not a gendered task.

There is nothing biological about women that programs them to cook. Take Michelin-starred chefs for example—an industry largely dominated by men. In the United States, only 7 percent of Michelin-starred restaurants are run by women.[2] It is clear that the task is not actually tethered to gender. However, when it generates monetary income, men are more likely to do it.

We need to shift away from thinking of cooking as feminine-coded. Our partner is fully capable of sharing or even taking over the task of feeding.

We also need to invite our partner to take part in the anticipating and researching. Sharing the knowledge is vital for sharing the load.

Assumption 3

Assumption: If I'm not perfectly preparing food for my child, with balanced nutrition and home-cooked meals, I'm failing.

Reframe: If my child is fed, I'm doing my part.

A normal diet will provide our children with the nutrients they need to grow and develop. We don't have to make every "right" decision. It's okay to be relaxed about food rules sometimes and take the path of least resistance. In fact, many intuitive eating therapists and dieticians encourage us to listen to our bodies and learn to trust ourselves with food again. We can likewise choose to trust our children with their own bodies.

Sometimes, we must choose the path of ease. Sometimes, done is better than perfect. Putting food on the table doesn't have to come with research, making each ingredient from scratch, and questioning ourselves every step of the way. When we look back ten or twenty years from now, will each of these responsibilities matter? Will we care that we gave our children only organic food? That we hand-blended our infant's purees? What really matters to us, to our values?

Assumption 4

Assumption: We have control over how much food our children eat.
Reframe: We each have a level of responsibility when it comes to mealtimes.

It is not our job to control how much food our children eat. It is our responsibility as parents to provide food for our children and choose when meals are served and what is offered. Our children can and should have a say in what and how much to eat.

Assumption 5

Assumption: My beliefs around food are universally true.
Reframe: We all have unique relationships with food and perspectives on what it means.

You are not wrong if you associate food with certain emotions. However, it is important to keep perspective. Your relationship with food is not necessarily the same as your child's or your spouse's.

Sometimes, different food philosophies can cause friction between partners. It is important to try to see everyone's relationship with food, and to unpack where our beliefs about feeding come from. Ultimately, food is neutral, and the act of feeding our children should not come at the cost of anybody's emotional well-being.

SKILLS AND TOOLS FOR RELEASING THIS LABOR

In this section, we'll cover skills and tools that include:

- Recognizing helpful vs. unhelpful research

- The division of responsibility

- Flexibility based on capacity

- Choosing the path of ease

- Embracing functionality as the standard

- Sharing anticipation labor through shared lists

As we work through these expectations, these beliefs, and these assumptions about food, we can begin to let go of some of the tasks associated with feeding.

We can let go of the idea of perfection. We can choose functionality over Pinterest-perfect presentation. And we can find balance. Perhaps a couple of home-cooked meals a week are adequate. Perhaps breakfast can be simple and easy.

Ultimately, how much you choose to let go of and what to keep comes down to your values and your family's values. This requires discussion, reflection, honest conversation, and the following skills and tools:

Recognizing Helpful vs. Unhelpful Research

We live in a wild world with a wealth of information at our fingertips. This means we can read reviews, check forums, and see what other parents are saying about everything we purchase or do for our children.

But that is not always a good thing. There is such a thing as too much research.

I distinctly remember working with a client who had very high expectations around her child's food. She was concerned with what ingredients were in the food, how it was prepared, how it was served—and anything less than "healthy" felt wrong to her. She was a self-proclaimed perfectionist who wanted the best for her child—she wasn't going to "lower her standards" at the request of her partner or anyone else.

As a result of her food concerns, she spent hours upon hours extensively researching topics related to food such as GMOs, toxins, ingredients, and safety. Through her research, she also read that stress could decrease her milk supply—so she shut down any conversations when her family tried to approach her about this or how it had taken over her life. This level of research was no longer about the food—postpartum anxiety was in the driver's seat, pushing her to search for control.

It's also important to break away from the idea that there is one "right" way to mother. Just because we have access to information doesn't mean there isn't room for nuance. Take "healthy food" as an example. What constitutes a "healthy" diet has been a debated topic for decades and is often a wellness space filled with fads and extremes, with each approach contradicting the next. There have been more rules prescribed to our food than I can count that cause people not to trust themselves and leave them seeing food as being good or bad. Food is not black or white. Our approach doesn't have to be all or nothing.

In my client's case, research had gone *beyond* just information-seeking. Sometimes, research is just research. But other times, research is:

- Trying to find the "right" or "best" way to do something
- Seeking reassurance
- Grasping for certainty
- Feeding your anxiety
- An attempt to soothe your anxiety

I have seen this pattern play out many times with many of my clients. I believe that in many ways intensive mothering prevents us from seeing signs of anxiety. When we interpret perfectionism and the need to avoid mistakes at all costs as being a good mother, we have a lot of pressure to carry. It's no wonder that so many of us find ourselves in the research rabbit hole.

Does that mean all research is bad? Of course not. But we need to learn the difference between when it's helping and when it's not. Researching should be used to provide you with enough information to make an informed decision. It should have boundaries—not be all-consuming.

Here are some signs that your researching is actually hindering you:

- You become very anxious or upset when you scroll and read people's comments, advice, or reviews

- You are very preoccupied with doing things "right" and finding the best way or method

- Even though you are devoting plenty of time to researching the topic, you feel the need to continue to learn more before you can feel confident in your decisions

- You get very stressed out or defensive when others share a differing or opposing view to yours online

- You compare yourself to others or feel pressure to meet external expectations that don't align with your internal values

It isn't easy to break out of the endless cycle of over-researching. It can be helpful to remember that more information isn't always *good* information. There is a mountain of blog posts, articles, forums, information, and opinions on every topic, much of which is conflicting. Sometimes, reading is more confusing than it is enlightening.

Setting limits and boundaries on research, and anchoring yourself in your values, is a necessary way forward.

The Division of Responsibility

When I am the one in charge of meal planning and prep, all the information I've read comes flooding back to me with every "food rule" I should follow. Don't do this; don't say that. Present food this way and not that way. If you just present veggies and fruit cut into little hearts to your children enough times while singing and dancing, then just maybe your children will eat their vegetables. And if they don't, it's because you didn't do enough or do it right. I call BS.

Sometimes when it comes to food, we either over-assume or under-assume our responsibilities. We either try to control our children's eating, pushing "one more bite" or obsessing over how much they put in their bodies, or on the other extreme, we ask our children repeatedly what they want to eat, sometimes creating multiple meals for everyone in the household. (Both of these responses come with good intentions. But both create more labor, stress, and worry for moms—and neither one of them increases what our children eat or provide a healthier lifestyle for them.)

That does *not* mean that we should never involve our children in the process. We can absolutely invite our children to participate in the food preparation. They can help us grocery shop, help us plan meals, and help us cook. In fact, children eat more food when they help with the preparation.[3]

But the in-the-moment decision of what food to make belongs to the parent. This keeps boundaries in place for our children, leaves our responsibilities where they should be, and prevents us from creating five separate meals for every mealtime.

Family therapist and feeding and eating specialist Ellyn Satter coined the phrase "the division of responsibility" when it comes to feeding children.[4] The concept is that children are capable of making their own food decisions.

Your responsibility as a parent when it comes to food is to:
- Feed your children as best you can

- Determine what you are going to serve

- Determine when (and how) you are going to serve it

But it is your child's responsibility to:
- Decide what they will eat (from what you provide)

- Decide how much they will eat

Moms shoulder so much blame when kids don't do things—but children are not little robots taking orders. As I am sure you have experienced, they are their own little wild beings with their own sets of preferences and opinions. Accepting the fact that you can plan and control what to serve and that your child can choose what to eat can help relieve some of the pressure when it comes to feeding.

Frenel and I now serve dinners we know the kids will eat. That often looks like tacos, spaghetti, or meatball wraps. In the middle of the table, we place a "family plate" with different fruits, vegetables, or foods they have never tried before. They can choose to eat from the family plate if they wish. And honestly, I don't do this every night. I reserve the family plate for evenings when the day doesn't feel like total chaos . . . which in a house with three small boys isn't very often. Choose times and opportunities to introduce new, healthy foods to your child. But choose moments that work for you, free from pressure or expectation.

I do encourage taste tests—we often talk about how our tastes change as we grow and it's important to give a new food a fair chance. But if my boys spit out new foods in disgust (which they do, frequently), we simply move on with life.

It can take a lot of self-soothing and training ourselves out of perfection and control to accept the division of responsibility. But it goes a long way in removing some of the pressure and burden off our shoulders.

Flexibility Based on Capacity

A meal plan, a to-do list, or a color-coded schedule can be helpful tools, but if held too rigidly they can also be a source of stress and shame. They can keep us organized, prepared, focused, and productive . . . sometimes. Other times, they can leave us feeling like massive failures who can't get it together.

I've worked with many different clients who will set a plan or create a to-do list during a time when they are feeling good, when they have plenty of capacity (like in the morning before the kids wake up, or the evening after they've had some downtime). But then things don't go according to plan. Maybe the baby is teething or the toddler doesn't settle for a nap, or you were up several times in the night and now you're exhausted and irritated and the plan or expectations that had been set just don't seem so doable.

Flexibility is important. When we make a structured system or create a plan, it's important to remember that it's not set in stone. We likely created that list in a moment with higher capacity, but we didn't have the same data that we have in the actual moment. Embracing flexibility can be a real self-care act. We often need to adjust the expectations of the day and ourselves, without guilt or shame.

When your expectations for the day are not aligning with the reality that your child or life is serving you, give yourself the gift of readjusting.

Choosing the Path of Ease

Another valuable tool for relieving pressure and reducing your burden (both in regard to food issues and other aspects of the Mother Load) is choosing the path of ease—a term I adopted into my toolbox after a conversation on episode 79 of *The Momwell Podcast* with Dr. Quincee Gideon.[5] When we feel the weight of trying to be perfect in motherhood or make the "best" or "right" decisions, we can focus on ease to help us cut through the smothering and sometimes paralyzing pressure.

This can begin in the postpartum period, when the reality is often very crushing for moms. They are going through major life transitions, hormonal changes, and adjusting to caring for tiny newborns, often running on little sleep with no breaks. For moms who struggle with their mental health during this time, there is often a mentality that if they just grit their teeth and white knuckle through the first year, postpartum depression will resolve itself.

But research shows that up to 25 percent of mothers with PPD still experienced symptoms three years later.[6] Waiting it out doesn't mean it will go away. We can't simply push our needs to the side and muddle through. Choosing the path of ease can become particularly valuable in the postpartum period, especially if you are struggling with your mental health. That might look like taking medication, sending your toddler to daycare a few days a week while you are home with the baby, or adjusting your expectations about what you can accomplish in a day.

But choosing the path of ease is a valuable tool far beyond just the postpartum period. We can embrace this tool at all stages of motherhood.

Choosing the path of ease might look like:

Adjusting your plan/routine based on the day

For example:

- Sleeping or doing absolutely nothing during the baby's nap time (instead of trying to cram in more from your to-do list)

- Choosing sandwiches or frozen chicken nuggets for dinner after a hard day

- Skipping evening sports or activities if it has been meltdown central and everyone is too tired

Bringing in help or support

In the form of hired support:

- Cleaning

- Daycare

- Babysitter

- Mother's helper

Or in the form of family or community support:

- Trading off childcare with another mom to give each other a break

- Having grandparents involved (if possible or available) to provide a necessary break

Setting boundaries or saying no

Sometimes choosing the path of ease also means creating space and setting boundaries with family members, friends, or others in our lives who are a source of conflict and distress.

Avoiding food battles

It can feel very difficult to choose the path of ease when it comes to food battles. We often feel the urge to control food—to get our children to eat their vegetables or drink their milk or to take "just three bites." And we might think that these battles are necessary for health and nutrition. But when we take a closer look at our beliefs around food, we can begin to see that there is more to it. We're carrying our own associations with food into these battles. Research has shown that when we try to control our children's food intake, they are more likely to have a negative outlook on food and struggle with self-regulation.[7]

Ultimately, choosing the path of ease is being kind to yourself and making decisions that make things easier for you, not harder.

Embracing Functionality as the Standard

Frenel and I have very different ways of approaching meal planning. His approach is far more functional (hungry children = get food in belly), and mine is much more idealistic/perfectionistic (hungry children = get well-balanced, low-sugar, non-processed food in belly while not over- or underdoing it to ensure I am helping them foster a healthy relationship with food).

Um . . . why do I do that to myself? It's too much. And it leads to so much unnecessary guilt.

Now, don't get me wrong—I want my children to eat well-balanced meals. I don't want to order pizza every single night for dinner. But as I have been letting go of mom-coded behaviors, one of the tasks that has shifted to Frenel is cooking dinner. That means that we've needed to have conversations about a happy medium that we can all live with.

For me to really be able to hand over part of this load, my perfectionism had to go with it.

As Frenel began to take this responsibility over, we had a lot of conversations about what worked (and what didn't) so that we could establish a new norm. This did NOT look like me telling him what to serve or correcting what he was doing. Instead, these conversations were focused on our goals for our family and what we value when it comes to food.

We've also created other shortcuts, like getting takeout once or twice per week (usually one weekday evening and one lunch out when on the go on the weekend) and embracing sandwiches, wraps, or tacos weekly. We have found that we don't need to overcomplicate things. In chapter 6, we will talk about the power of rhythms and routines in sharing the load. For us, a valuable routine was finding seven to ten different meals that the kids will all eat and rotating through them regularly. Convenience and time are major factors in our family as we shuttle children and juggle the demands of running a company—and that is okay.

When we have conversations about food or discuss what to make for dinners and meals, we often ask ourselves these questions:

- Will the kids actually eat it, or will it just be a big fight? (We often embrace the path of ease toward the end of a long, hard week for all of us.)

- Have they had this meal in the past couple of days?

- Do we have the time and ingredients to make this meal?

- If it is a carb-heavy or less-balanced meal, can we serve it with a side or two to boost the nutritional value?

Shared Lists = Sharing the Load of Anticipating

Even when you choose to focus on functionality or you have created a rhythm or routine to help ease the load, there is still anticipating and monitoring labor involved.

If we truly want to share the Mother Load, we must share that labor. One simple hack to do that is creating shared grocery lists.

Frenel and I have a shared Google list. Whoever empties something or notices it getting low adds the item to the list. (We've even set the list up so that we can verbally tell Google to add items to the list while our hands are dirty in the kitchen because the responsibility sits with whoever is using the item or sees it is getting low.)

Even the kids have caught on—if one of them takes the last granola bar from a box in the snack drawer, they will (sometimes) ask one of us to add more to the list!

The shared list establishes an expectation that monitoring and anticipation is a family affair. It helps make the invisible labor visible.

There have been many times that I have gone to look for something I use often, such as ingredients for my lattes, only to realize that I am out. Frenel will remind me that he doesn't drink coffee (how!?!), so he wouldn't know to add them to the list. Ultimately, it is my responsibility to track and monitor my items. It's not fair to expect this of him in the same way that it is not fair for it to be my responsibility to keep track of all the inventory in the house. It's an unrealistic expectation for any one person in a household to be responsible for all the noticing, anticipating, and monitoring.

Consider creating a shared list and having some norms about when and how the list gets used. This is a simple way to shine a light on this invisible labor and begin the process of releasing the Mother Load.

IF YOU ONLY REMEMBER ONE THING
Your viewpoints on feeding the household are about SO much more than the food itself. Food is a vehicle for our expression of love, connection, security, and so much more. Only when we can start to understand that can we recognize where the pressure we are putting on ourselves about food comes from.

IF YOU ONLY DO ONE THING
Explore your own relationship with food. Think about what emotions you associate with food and why (revisit page 129 for reflection questions surrounding food). This will be the key to giving ourselves permission to let go of the beliefs we are holding onto.

THE INVISIBLE LOAD OF KEEPING THE HOUSE

Organizing ALL the toys

Researching storage bins and solutions

Managing the never-ending laundry cycle

Facilitating clean-up from the kids

Anticipating when deep cleans are necessary

Managing the never-ending cycle of dishes

Navigating pressure and judgment about keeping a clean house

Scrambling to clean for last-minute visitors

Knowing where everything belongs

Remembering when bedsheets were changed

Remembering when floors need to be cleaned

Handling ALL the clutter

6

THE KEEPER OF THE HOUSE

For many moms, cleaning the house is ongoing—the thing that always leaves them feeling behind. The thing that they can never seem to get a handle on. The thing that brings shame, guilt, and fear of judgment.

I have heard from so many clients that they dread the thought of someone coming over unannounced—they would be too embarrassed by the state of their home. They feel as though they need to have a perfectly clean or tidy space, or play host when family members come to visit.

There's nothing wrong with setting boundaries and not wanting visitors, especially in the postpartum period. But I'm more concerned with *why* moms feel that they need to always have this state of perfection in their homes. Instead of welcoming the support from visitors, we feel shame, guilt, and fear of judgment. And yet, male partners often don't feel these same emotions or pressures around keeping the house clean. This divide between genders starts before we even have kids (even if we aim to divide household labor fairly).

Picture the stereotypical bachelor pad. It's stark, devoid of decoration, and focused instead on functionality—rather than putting forth effort to create an appealing aesthetic, single men often focus on technology, gadgets, entertainment areas—how the home serves them. This of course is a generalization; some of the best designers and stylists are men. However, the societal expectation is that men focus on function, and they don't face the same pressure to have a clean, tidy, and curated aesthetic. The gender norms we encounter in our upbringing have a strong impact on how we engage and interact as adults.

When I first started dating Frenel and went over to his place, there was a large cardboard box sitting upside down by the couch. I saw him sit down and put a cup on it, and realized this was a box he was deliberately using in place of a side table.

I teased him about it, but it didn't bother him. "Why would I buy a piece of furniture to do what this box does for me?" he asked. I would have been embarrassed to have that setup in my apartment—feeling eyeballs of judgment coming from every direction. But Frenel didn't even care what it looked like, if it worked practically for him.

If you believe that the state of the home reflects your worth as a woman or mother, of course you're going to prioritize it.

Frenel cared about *cleanliness*. His home was always neat and tidy. He would never leave dirty dishes or clothes everywhere. (Have I mentioned that he always put clothes *inside* the hamper instead of laying them over the side haphazardly?) But he had no interest in getting a fancy piece of furniture that served the same purpose as an overturned box.

It's easy to look at that situation and say we just had different priorities—that I cared more about what people thought, or what the home looked like. In reality, the difference was much more deep-seated. I cared about what my home looked like—but not because of my own personal values. I cared because I had been taught since I was a child that the home reflects a woman—that having an unkempt home meant a mom was lazy, while having a clean home meant she had everything together.

In *Equal Partners*, Kate Mangino points out that priorities are not a fair way to divide household labor, and this is why. Our priorities are dictated by gender norms.[1] That's why it doesn't work for our partner to say, "You care about the house more than I do, so that's on you." The truth is that women bear the brunt of the judgment and criticism when a home is messy.

If you believe, even subconsciously, that the state of the home is a reflection on your worth as a woman or a mother, of course you're going to prioritize it. And when you inevitably struggle to keep it clean with multiple little ones running around, you're likely to feel shame and embarrassment. You might even feel like a failure.

Before we unpack what mental, emotional, and physical tasks are involved in keeping the house clean, we must confront those beliefs. We must take a look at why we feel anxious about keeping the house clean, why we feel ashamed if we don't, and why we continue to take on this labor ourselves. For most of us, the answer is deeply rooted in our past, in our identity, and in the myth of the perfect mother.

Women are conditioned to care about the state of the home from childhood. Toy mops and brooms are often in the girls' section of the store. Studies have shown that by age nine, girls are doing more household chores than boys.[2] Those patterns are often carried out into adulthood and reinforced through society. Marketers target women with advertisements about clean homes, preying on socialized perfectionism. Women are inundated with messages about how homes need to look and the pressure to create curated, organized spaces.

I recently created a reading nook in our home. We just had too many books, and Pinterest was full of beautiful tips for tidy spaces that would offer the solution to our problem. So, I researched all the options. We built shelves. I shopped for all the cute furniture that would add a cozy appeal. (I'm still trying to pick everything out.)

But much to my disappointment, creating the nook didn't solve the problem. It just brought different labor—now, I spend time organizing the books, putting them back on the shelves, and clearing out all the things that get put on the empty spaces. Pinterest promised me a solution, but it only brought more labor my way.

In our search for perfection, we strive for the ideal solutions that will lighten our load of housework. The perfect bins. The perfect cleaning schedule. The perfect plan. But perfectionism isn't the path to relief—it's the path to carrying unnecessary labor on our own.

When we cling to perfectionism, we can't realistically invite our partner to share in the cleaning load. If we have unrealistic expectations and standards, and our partner does not, we will likely take this

Perfectionism isn't the path to relief—it's the path to carrying unnecessary labor on our own.

labor back on our own shoulders, frustrated that it doesn't get done perfectly.

That isn't to say that we shouldn't come together and create household standards—we absolutely should. But an even more important part of the conversation is to dig into where those standards come from—to pick apart what cleaning the household means and to reframe it in a way that aligns with our values.

Reflecting on Your Beliefs about Cleaning

Take a minute to reflect on these questions:

- In your childhood home, who was responsible for the household cleaning?

- What standards did your parents have for cleanliness?

- Were household chores divided by gender?

- What emotions arise when you think of a messy house? Or a clean one?

- Do you feel that you will receive judgment if your home is not clean?

- Does a messy house make you feel anxious, stressed, or guilty?

- When someone sends a message that they are stopping by, what comes to your mind?

Keep the answers to these questions in mind as we work through the rest of the chapter—they lay the foundation for how you view your role in the home.

BREAKING AWAY FROM BELIEFS
AROUND CLEANLINESS

One of the biggest questions to ask ourselves when it comes to cleanliness is, what does cleaning actually mean? Therapist KC Davis, known as Domestic Blisters on TikTok and author of *How to Keep House While Drowning*, defines three separate tasks within housework—cleaning, organizing, and tidying. Cleaning is disinfecting, vacuuming, and scrubbing. Tidying is removing clutter. And organizing is making sure everything has a place it belongs and putting it there.[3]

The differences in these terms matter. If we ask our children or our partner to clean the toy room, and they pick up all the toys and dump them in one bin, we might get frustrated. To them, "cleaning" might mean making sure the floor is clear, even if we meant organizing.

Each of these terms has a different function. Each has a different process. And each needs to be considered separately when we talk about cleaning and household standards. Does cleaning the kitchen involve clearing the counters? Or just doing the dishes and wiping the sink? If it is my job to clean the bathroom, do I need to organize the drawers, or just disinfect surfaces and toilets? We need to determine what cleanliness means to us, what is realistic to expect, and, most importantly, what is functional.

When KC appeared on *The Momwell Podcast* on episode 136, she pointed out that for moms, and for women, cleaning is often perceived as moral.[4] The phrase "cleanliness is next to Godliness" captures this idea. We think of having a clean home as a sign of something inherently good, responsible, successful. So, when we end up drowning in spit-up and onesies and diapers and gear, suddenly juggling more things for more people with less time than ever, keeping the home up to the same standards as we did before children doesn't work.

KC argues that we should shift our perspective on cleanliness, viewing household work not as moral, but as functional. We don't exist to serve our home—it exists to serve us. When we approach household tasks from a functional perspective, KC says that we can find new, practical ways to reduce the workload.[5]

We must think beyond the "right" way that we have been taught to do tasks. For example, if the function of laundry is to make sure everybody has clean clothes to wear, there are shortcuts that can be created. For KC, that means sorting clothing into bins instead of folding it and ensuring that every room in the house has a basket of clean and dirty clothes for her children. This eliminates a big hassle for her (folding clothes), achieves the same function, and reduces the need to move back and forth between rooms to get clothes.[6]

KC also observes that when we think of household tasks as being complete or incomplete, we often leave ourselves feeling pressured, stressed, and overwhelmed. Our families are living our lives and interacting with things in our home. There will always be laundry to do, dishes to wash, toys to pick up. We think we have everything "done," but then the day ends, and we have another day's worth of clothing to wash (or a potty accident throws a kink into our plans in the middle of the day)!

These tasks don't reach a magical state of "doneness." No matter how many bins we buy or shelves we assemble, no matter how hard we are on ourselves or how much we promise ourselves we'll never fall behind on the laundry again, we can't escape this load by being more efficient or working harder or reaching the perfect level of organization. These tasks don't end. Instead, we can look at them as cyclical.[7]

For example, the cycle of dishes includes clean dishes that are put away, dirty dishes that need to be washed, and dishes in the dishwasher if we have one. If we can shift our mindset and realize that the dishes, laundry, and housework are rarely "done" (and certainly don't remain "done" for long), we can give ourselves grace and view cleaning in a different, more practical way.

It can be difficult to break away from the idea that there is one right way to keep house—that the standards and processes we have been taught are not the be-all end-all of cleanliness. But the truth is that the weight of keeping a clean house combined with all the mental and emotional labor of motherhood is impossible to keep up with. We must find areas where we can let go and find ways to achieve the necessary functions in an attainable way.

Think about the areas that are the biggest time drains or frustrations for you. What is the function of those tasks? Where can you reframe your standards? How can you streamline your processes? What can you do to make it more feasible and less consuming for you? Do you need a color-coded pantry with perfectly organized snacks? Or can you toss the kids' snacks in a basket for them to choose from? Do you need to hand-wash bottle parts? Or can you put them in a steaming bag or the dishwasher to sterilize them?

This is where we start to release the labor of keeping home—by peeling back the layers and determining where our standards really come from, and uncovering what really matters (and why).

Sometimes, this looks like automation or outsourcing, if that is financially feasible for your family (for example, getting a robot vacuum or hiring a housekeeper or a cleaning company). Sometimes, this looks like calling in a partner—or other support member if available—ensuring that the emotional and mental labor are accounted for and that the standards of cleanliness are agreed upon. This doesn't mean making a chore chart for your partner or handing them a list of tasks. When you must ask for "help" from your partner (which indicates that the job is ours alone), it keeps you as the manager of the household cleaning. You are still the one carrying the labor. You are still the one keeping track of what needs to be done. You are still the one anticipating, researching, and monitoring. When a support person takes an area of household labor, they need to take it entirely with all the labor involved in the task.

Sometimes, this looks like creating a family atmosphere where all members buy in and share the weight of cleaning the home. My boys love pitching in to sweep and mop. We have family cleaning days on the weekends where we put on music and work together to clean the house.

> We start to release the labor of keeping home by . . . determining where our standards really come from, and uncovering what really matters.

This cultivates a sense of shared responsibility and eliminates the need for one family member to be solely in charge of tracking and delegating household tasks.

Sometimes, this looks like systemizing—creating new methods to tackle areas of your home that free up your time and energy and don't always require you to be the one to reset and clean up the home. (We'll go over more tips on systems in the skills section of this chapter.)

And sometimes, it looks like rethinking your own beliefs about how tasks need to be done and charting your own realistic path toward what you want your home to look like and how you want it to function.

UNPACKING THE HOUSEHOLD LABOR

Part of the reason why "cleaning" the home feels so overwhelming is because of the sheer amount of labor involved in it. Our house is full of rooms and responsibilities—things that need organizing and areas that we often become in charge of as moms. We need to break these tasks down in order to shift our thinking around them.

Anticipating

Each area of the home requires mental labor to keep clean, organized, and tidy, beginning with noticing and anticipating what needs to be done.

Laundry

Clothing for the household requires a great deal of anticipation. We anticipate what clothing each family member needs for the week and what loads of laundry need to be washed. But we anticipate so much more than that—size changes, weather and seasonal changes, clothing preferences, sensory issues with certain materials, and when we will need laundry detergent.

We also anticipate special clothing for events (like school activities, sports, meetings, weddings, family pictures, or matching pajamas).

This is why laundry was the straw that broke the camel's back for me, and the catalyst for why this book was even written. It was the overwhelming amount of anticipation labor that made laundry feel impossible for me.

Bathrooms

The keeper of the house anticipates not just when the bathrooms will need to be deep cleaned, but also when the soap will need to be refilled, when the toilet paper roll needs to be changed and when more needs to be purchased, when to change out towels and hand towels. They think about when bath toys need to be disinfected, when toothbrushes need to be changed, and when to refill toiletries.

Kitchen

The keeper of the house also monitors when dishes need to be washed and unloaded, what dishes can't go in the dishwasher, when food needs to be thrown out from the refrigerator, when appliances need to be deep cleaned, and when counters and sinks need to be scrubbed. They also often become responsible for noticing all the piles of stuff that end up accumulating on tables and islands and countertops. They remember when sponges should be changed and when paper towels should be refilled.

Toys

The keeper of the house often takes on the responsibility of noticing when toys need to be reorganized, when new bins need to be purchased, and when toys need to be disinfected. They notice where toys gather so they can brainstorm solutions. They monitor which broken boys need to be thrown away or fixed and where the toys should go.

Clutter

Toys aren't the only thing that ends up out of place or piled up where they shouldn't be. The household cleaner notices the piles of papers that need an organization system, the books that don't fit on the shelves, the shoes that end up cluttering up the floor. They see that the backpacks need a solution, that the knick-knacks need a place to go, that the diaper rash creams need a basket.

Once a family includes kids, the sheer amount of stuff begins to multiply, and with every added item comes more anticipation, more needs, and more mental labor. In many ways, clutter can be one of the most frustrating areas for moms. Clutter can quickly make a tidy room appear messy, and it doesn't always have an easy solution. It often requires a great deal of noticing and problem-solving.

Home Projects

Just like my reading nook, houses are often full of problems that need creative solutions or projects. The household cleaner notices the areas that need solutions and thinks of ways to meet those needs.

Pets

When we have pets in the home, we notice more: when hair needs to be cleaned up, when litter boxes need to be scooped, when we need to set out a puppy pad or wash dog beds.

It can often feel like this additional labor pushes us over the edge, leading to resentment toward our pets, especially in the early postpartum period.

Research and Planning

The household cleaner notices all the problems and messes and clutter in the home, and they also research and plan for how to fix those problems, and for the best way to keep the home clean.

They might turn to Pinterest for home organization and storage methods and sleek clear bins. They might compare laundry detergent and dish soap, double checking ingredients and reading reviews. They might even research chore charts or incentives for the kids to pitch in around the home.

When problems arise, like too many books or scuffs on the wall or fingerprints appearing on the refrigerator, the home cleaner also researches, evaluates, and plans for how to fix them. They troubleshoot clutter and toy storage and where to put all the bags and blankets and washcloths. Sometimes there are so many decisions to make and products to compare, from which bookshelf to buy to which sponge to use, that it can become paralyzing.

The person managing the mental labor likely carries these burdens even if the family outsources labor to a housekeeper or cleaning service. Additionally, they research cleaning services, read reviews, make the decision on who to hire, and coordinate schedules—and they often end up needing to keep the home clean in preparation for service or prepare a list of chores.

Once again, all this labor comes before any physical cleaning. This is all the planning, thinking, noticing—mental labor, problem-solving, and decision-making that is woven into the task of keeping the home clean. This is why when somebody asks you, "What did you do all day?" you feel exhausted, even if you didn't leave the house or physically clean anything. It also explains why delegating doesn't actually take anything off your plate. If you asked your partner to clean the toy closet, but you researched organization methods, bought all the bins, created and printed out labels, and told them where to put everything, the small physical task of sorting out the toys is a drop in the bucket. The mental labor is all-consuming and never-ending, and it takes so much more than just picking up an area of the home.

Managing

In addition to the actual act of cleaning the home (which is packed full of physical tasks such as mopping, vacuuming, sweeping, scrubbing toilets, picking up toys, decluttering, organizing, and wiping down cabinets), the managing consists of ongoing mental labor. As I've said multiple times, even when we outsource or pass off chores, we often end up carrying the mental load alone.

The keeper of the house persistently monitors and maintains every facet of the home. They evaluate the efficiency of each organization system and start the process back over when issues arise. For example: for months, I continually brought up that we needed to get a robot vacuum—one of the fancy ones that mopped and swept and vacuumed. We finally caved and bought one—and it is currently sitting, unused, in a closet. Why? Because to use it, we have to take care of all of the toys and clothes and clutter. It ended up being more work on us than just sweeping the floors myself. For some people, a robot vacuum might be a great solution. For us, it wasn't. This evaluation of solutions and systems is a big part of the labor involved in keeping the house.

That's why cleaning the house with small children often feels like patching holes in a sinking boat. We might get one area clean or organized, but another area is filling up with toys at the same time. There is a certain level of tolerance, of realism, and of acceptance that we need to embrace if we want to free ourselves from the burden of all-consuming cleaning.

THE LOAD MAPS

For editable versions of the load maps, along with blank templates, visit Ericadjossa.com.

KITCHEN/DISHES

Anticipating

- Anticipating when dishes will be needed
- Anticipating deep cleans of appliances
- Noticing when the dishwasher needs to be emptied
- Noticing when dish soap is low
- Knowing when food needs to be thrown out
- Noticing when counters and islands need to be wiped down
- Seeing areas that collect clutter
- Noticing when the trash needs to be emptied
- Noticing when the floors need to be swept or mopped

Research and Planning

- The best kitchen cleaning gear (sponges, paper towels, washcloths, hand towels, cleaning solutions)

- Types of dishwasher pods and dish soap

- Planning chore chart/ rotation

- Planning ahead for when to change over dishes

- Making sure there are clean kid-friendly dishes for lunches, snacks, and daily water intake

Managing

- Wiping and scrubbing counters and islands

- Decluttering

- Clearing piles of mail and paper junk

- Organizing cabinets and drawers

- Deep cleaning accessories

- Cleaning out the refrigerator

- Monitoring expiration dates in the refrigerator and pantry

- Clearing off the table

- Wiping the table down

- Loading and emptying the dishwasher

- Handwashing anything that can't go in the dishwasher

- Taking out the trash

LAUNDRY

Anticipating

- Anticipating what clothing each family member needs

- Noticing what loads of laundry need to be washed

- Tracking weather and seasonal changes

- Monitoring size changes and anticipating the next size

- Knowing whether new items need to be purchased

- Paying attention to sensory and clothing preferences

- Anticipating when laundry detergent and fabric softener will be needed

- Anticipating special events that require specific clothing

- Tracking when sheets need to be washed and changed

Research and Planning

- Shopping through different clothing options

- Planning ahead to make sure everybody has the right amount of seasonal clothing in the right size

- Determining where unused clothes will be stored

- Choosing the best laundry detergent (especially with sensitive skin needs)

Managing

- Gathering laundry from hampers
- Sorting laundry into loads
- Washing the clothes
- Changing the laundry over into the dryer
- Folding the clothes
- Organizing closets
- Organizing drawers
- Removing seasonally inappropriate clothing
- Removing clothing that is too small
- Ensuring that the next size of clothing is ready and available
- Laying out clothing for the family
- Handling emergency laundry accidents

BATHROOMS

Anticipating

- Noticing when the toilet paper roll needs to be changed
- Anticipating when toilet paper will need to be purchased
- Anticipating when toiletries will need to be purchased
- Knowing when the showers and bathtubs need to be cleaned
- Knowing when the toilets need to be cleaned
- Anticipating when cleaning supplies will need to be purchased

- Noticing cluttered areas
- Noticing when the trash needs to be emptied
- Noticing when floors need to be cleaned

Research and Planning

- Bath toy organization options
- Baskets/bins/storage options
- Soap and toiletry ingredients
- Cleaning supply ingredients
- Budgeting or shopping for deals on cleaning supplies
- Tracking time between cleans

Managing

- Cleaning the sinks
- Cleaning the counters and other surfaces
- Cleaning the toilets
- Cleaning the showers and bathtubs
- Organizing toys
- Organizing baskets and toiletries
- Organizing cabinets and drawers
- Troubleshooting organization tips
- Taking out the trash
- Discarding outdated products

TOYS

Anticipating

- Noticing what toys need organization solutions
- Noticing when the toys need to be picked up
- Noticing when toys have ended up in the wrong room

- Anticipating when toys need to be changed out or updated
- Knowing when toys need to be disinfected or sanitized

Research and Planning

- Toy storage solutions and bins
- Chore chart options and incentives
- Labels
- Decluttering tips

- Planning bins and mentally categorizing toys
- Knowing which labels to create and purchase
- Planning chore rotations

Managing

- Putting away toys and/or coordinating toy pickup
- Organizing toys and bins

- Putting together storage shelves
- Ongoing monitoring of toy organization

- Adapting when new toys are added
- Moving toys between rooms
- Keeping floors cleared

- Teaching family members where things go
- Keeping a mental inventory of what items go with what toy sets

CLUTTER

Anticipating

- Noticing areas that build up clutter
- Noticing what the clutter consists of

- Anticipating empty areas that might gather clutter

Research and Planning

- Storage and organization solutions

- Bins, trays, mail sorters
- Tips for decluttering

Managing

- Sorting
- Organizing
- Tidying
- Clearing spaces, tables, and floors

- Purging and deciding what to do with unwanted items
- Teaching family members where things go

OVERALL CLEANLINESS

Anticipating

- Noticing when floors need to be cleaned
- Noticing when surfaces need to be wiped or disinfected
- Seeing marks or scuffs that need to be cleaned
- Tracking when handles, doorknobs, and light switches need to be cleaned
- Anticipating when cleaning supplies will need to be purchased
- Knowing when rags and washcloths will need to be cleaned

Research and Planning

- Cleaning supplies
- Cleaning gadgets (brooms, mops, washcloths)
- Coordinating schedules to clear time to clean
- Researching and vetting cleaning services and housekeepers

Managing

- Dusting
- Mopping
- Sweeping
- Vacuuming
- Troubleshooting/in the moment decisions (cleaning spills, scuffs off walls, sharpic off the couch, etc.)

HOME PROJECTS

Anticipating

- Noticing areas where projects are needed
- Anticipating what goes into the project

Research and Planning

- Shelves
- Storage
- Bins
- Organizational methods
- Planning how to execute the project
- Measuring/ determining what supplies and tools are needed
- Researching where to source supplies and tools

- Determining which projects need to be outsourced
- Researching contractors or maintenance professionals when needed
- Contacting and coordinating schedules with contractors or maintenance professionals when needed

Managing

- Creating projects
- Putting plan into action
- Maintaining projects/troubleshooting when random projects come up (for example, the furnace or air conditioner going out, or the wind damaging a fence)

ASSUMPTIONS THAT REINFORCE
THE LOAD WE CARRY

If we cling to perfection, we will continue to live in a state of frustration about the household labor. If we try to entwine the cleanliness of our home with our value as moms and as people, we will continue to feel flustered and "behind."

But we can reframe the beliefs and assumptions that keep us tethered to those unattainable goals and determine what truly matters to us.

Assumption 1

Assumption: We can achieve a state of "doneness" with household chores.
Reframe: Household chores are often cyclical, always at some stage in the cycle.

As previously mentioned, household chores will never reach a magical state of "doneness." Rather than looking at ourselves as "behind" if these chores are not "complete," we can view them as cyclical, understanding that they move through various stages. This removes unrealistic expectations and pressures.

Assumption 2

Assumption: The state of my house determines my ability and worth as a mom.
Reframe: Your value as a mom is not linked to the cleanliness of your home.

Reflect on the values you discovered in chapter 3. I'm guessing "having a clean house" was not one of them. Do you need to have a clean home in order to be present, loving, and nurturing for your children? Do you need to have a clean home in order to form bonds and attachments? Do you need to have a clean home for your children to live happy and fulfilling lives? The answer is no.

I am not advocating for you to swing the pendulum in the opposite direction and do away with cleaning altogether. There are safety, hygienic, and even just plain practical living reasons for why we care for the space we live in. Tidiness and organization also have value—but that value lies in their function, not in your ability and worth as a mom.

An organized home might make it easier to find what you're looking for—and that's great. It might make it easier to get out of the house on time or give your kids space to play. But if you struggle with your mental health, or you are having a hard time managing it all, your worth and value doesn't change if you let some things slide. You become a good mom by showing up for your children. You become a happy mom by living a life that aligns with your values. Neither of those require a perfectly spotless home.

Assumption 3

Assumption: Women are better at keeping the house.

Reframe: Cleaning is not gendered—all family members play a role in the household.

It is not your job as a woman or a mom to keep the entire family home clean. Chores are not gender specific. Just like there is a division of responsibility around food, there can also be one around cleaning. It is not your job to do the tasks of others who can do it for themselves.

Assumption 4

Assumption: Housework should be done on my leisure time.

Reframe: I deserve time to myself, for myself.

Moms often experience guilt when their houses are not kept up to the standard they have in mind. But they also experience guilt when they take time away from their children in order to do the housework. It's as if moms are supposed to snap their fingers and keep the home clean, without diverting any attention away from being physically present with the kids. We simply can't live up to both standards. So, we often end up sacrificing our free time to catch up on chores, scrambling to get everything done. But in the search to become the perfect housekeeper and the perfectly present mom, we leave no time for ourselves, our interests, or our needs.

It's okay to give your children time and space to play alone while you do the dishes or fold the laundry. But it's also okay to leave those dishes and that laundry for another day. We deserve space to breathe, to live in the moment, and to give ourselves permission to enjoy our lives.

Assumption 5

Assumption: I should always keep my home neat, clean, and tidy.

Reframe: The house exists to serve my family.

Our homes dictate a lot of our time. The floors that need to be mopped, the bathrooms that need to be cleaned, the toys that need to be put away. It's easy to think that we *must* do those things before we let ourselves relax.

But we are the ones in charge—not our homes. We get to decide what needs to be done, when. Our house's function is to serve us—to make our lives easier—not to call us out of every leisure moment to serve it, or to dictate how we will spend every free moment.

We don't have to adhere to arbitrary, old-fashioned rules and standards. Instead, we can carve out our own path for chores and cleanliness.

Assumption 6

Assumption: There is a "right" way to do chores.

Reframe: There are no rules about how to clean a home.

If you don't want to fold laundry, take a page out of KC's book and sort clothing into bins. If you don't like sorting your clothes into colors and washing seventeen different loads, toss them all in together. If it works for you to have a miscellaneous toy bin in every room of the house, go for it! You can find shortcuts, let go of perfection, and clean your home in a way that feels right to you.

This is also a hard pill to swallow, but a good reminder when our partner or our children are the ones doing chores. There is no one way—it is okay if it is not perfect. It's helpful to have a standard of cleanliness so everyone is on the same page, but it doesn't have to be rigid or unrealistic (and it doesn't have to require *us* to be the one to do it). (See the skills section of this chapter for more about the standard of cleanliness.)

Assumption 7

Assumption: If I just find the right solution (organizational system, chore chart, plan, pretty bins), I can lighten the load of housework and stay on top of things.

Reframe: I can work with what I have to keep my home clean and tidy.

You don't need the best mop or the expensive clear bins. We often worry about what our home looks like to others—we fear judgment or criticism or embarrassment. But this is the mom-guilt surveillance crew coming back into action. Most of us are perfectly understanding when we go to someone else's home and it isn't spotless. And yet, we don't extend that grace to ourselves.

We must let go of the idea that the home needs to look perfect, that we need the best, most expensive cleaning equipment, or that every solution in our home needs to be Pinterest-worthy. The function matters more than how everything looks.

Assumption 8

Assumption: If I fall behind in the housework, it means I'm lazy.

Reframe: "Laziness" or a lack of motivation is the symptom of something deeper.

What might appear as "laziness" is usually a symptom of something else. We might be burnt out. We might be crumbling under the invisible load. We might be overstimulated. We might be struggling with something else.

Keeping up with the housework as a parent is hard. There are things and gadgets and toys everywhere, and little kids who actively undo your work behind you. If you fall behind, it's okay—it's completely understandable. Creating systems and routines can relieve some of the pressure so that you don't have to carry everything alone.

SKILLS AND TOOLS FOR RELEASING THIS LABOR

As you reframe your beliefs and start to release this labor, there are skills and tools you will need in your toolbox to communicate effectively and keep yourself from falling back into established patterns and gender norms.

In this section, we'll cover skills and tools that include:

- Keeping house as a family affair

- Creating household routines

- Establishing predictable rhythms

- Systemizing the work

- Finding a tolerable common ground

- Ways to depersonalize your partner's behavior

Keeping House as a Family Affair

One of the best ways to reinforce shared labor in keeping the house is to normalize the fact that this is not solely your responsibility. Everyone in the household plays a hand in keeping it clean.

Working together can establish a sense of teamwork and cooperation, sharing the load between the entire house.

You can:

- Create a fifteen-minute "family clean-up time" where everybody tidies up prior to the bedtime routine or on a weekend afternoon

- Get kids involved by feeding the empty toy buckets or seeing how many items they can pick up

- Play fun music to lighten the mood and get others involved

- Hold challenges or position the cleaning as "kids vs. adults" to encourage participation

- Instill boundaries around toys being picked up or rooms being tidied before screen time is earned

The more that you collectively model the family value that everyone is responsible for keeping the house clean, the easier it will be to share this labor.

Creating Household Routines

When it comes to cleaning, so much of the labor lies in the anticipating and monitoring stages (remembering what laundry needs to be done in which order, when dishes need to be unloaded, etc.).

This requires never-ending scanning and tracking, often hour to hour or even minute to minute. That constant buzz of noticing and tracking is a key contributor to the overwhelm of the Mother Load.

I have found that the "need to do" anticipating labor falling on me doesn't work for me and my family. In fact, Frenel and I have a much different threshold for when things "need to be done." He is more likely to fill the soap dispensers when they are a quarter full, while I might not notice until I'm trying to pump out soap to wash my hands . . . and I might or might not then forget after I leave the room, distracted by something else altogether.

So, rather than waiting until things "need to be done," inevitably placing extra mental labor and potential time-crunch stress on one of us, we have established a routine to incorporate those tasks.

For example, on Saturdays Frenel washes laundry, regardless of how much is dirty. On Sunday, I fold and put the boys' five outfits for the week in an organizer on the back of their door. We don't wait until we are out of clothes—it's just part of the routine. Nobody has to monitor the laundry needs or scramble at the last minute. We don't even need to deal with making decisions on clothing in the moment. (We've come a long way since the laundry mountain Aha Mom-ent!)

Another routine we have established is that the dishwasher gets run every other day, whether it's full or not. It's built into the routine to run it in the evening on those days.

Think about the anticipation labor that you are carrying in your home. Where can you create routines to eliminate or reduce that anticipation labor?

178 Making the Mother Load Visible

Some examples might include establishing:

- Laundry day
- Restocking day
- Grocery day
- Family clean day

As you work to create routines, remember that these should incorporate shared labor—not just fall on mom. These routines can be worked to create the best schedule that works for everyone.

Remember that it might take some trial and error. If you try running the dishwasher at night and that doesn't work for your family, switch it to the morning or afternoon. The goal should be to alleviate pressure, not to create added stress.

Establishing Predictable Rhythms

Just like routines, creating steady rhythms for transition times of the day can help reduce anticipation labor and carve out set responsibilities for everyone in the home. (This is the answer to the "just tell me what to do" conundrum. When you work together to create a rhythm of established expectations, you no longer need to dictate or delegate. You're working as a team to reach a common goal.)

Think of rhythms as a formula:

Clear understanding of the tasks + each person owning their role = a good rhythm

For example, bedtime in our home is 7:00 pm. When it hits that time, Frenel and I both know our roles. We don't have to ask each other to do their part. We are on the same page with the tasks that need to be accomplished—we own our roles and it allows us to function well as a team.

See if you can establish rhythms for:

- Morning routine
- Bedtime routine

- Daily tasks after the kids go to bed (wiping down counters, setting out backpacks, prepping lunches—whatever needs to be done on a regular basis)

- Dinner prep

- After dinner

It can also be helpful to create "opening duties" and "closing duties," a list of tasks that each partner does in the mornings before the kids wake up and in the evenings after the kids go to bed.

I have often heard my mom clients express frustration that at the end of the night, their partner goes to sleep while they pick up toys, check the locks, set the alarm system, and run the dishwasher. Creating opening and closing duties and setting clear expectations can help eliminate that disparity and keep everyone involved. You can choose to tackle these duties together or take turns working through them so everybody gets a chance to have mornings or evenings "off"—whatever feels right for you and your partner.

Rhythms can also be done as a solo parent—but this is harder without other adult hands. Getting children to own their role when they think you are ruining their life by making them get some sleep is rough. Predictability and structure help to bring some order to these chaotic times. But I also understand that when you are exhausted by the load, it can become more difficult to establish and hold boundaries. For example, if everybody sleeps in their own bed but you are exhausted, you might be more likely to cave if your child pushes the bedtime boundary and wants to crawl into your bed.

When solo parenting (or to create smoother transitions in general), it can help to automate the routine and the boundaries that need to be set during these transitions when possible. For example, ending tablet time in the evening was a common struggle in my home. So, we decided to automate the process using a feature that routinely locks their tablets each evening, setting the limit without us needing to be the bad guy (a fight nobody looks forward to when we are all exhausted). Visual timers, alarms, and ok-to-wake clocks, which provide visual cues for our children, can help automate the transition or establish regular limits. It may take some getting used to for everyone to settle into these rhythms, but with consistency, the boundaries and limits will be predictable and easier to enforce.

Systemizing the Work

Anyone who watches *Get Organized with the Home Edit* knows the power of a good system. The girls on the show always say, "It's a system!" when they bring order and functionality to chaos.

I didn't know what a system was until I was in my thirties. If something didn't seem to be working, I didn't understand that I could create something that would ease the process. But now, I understand their power. They provide structure and containment, bring order, and create consistency.

And the best part about systems is that *once they are in place, ANYONE can follow them.* That means that systems make it easier to hand over the load.

Think of systems as hacks, workarounds, or solutions we can put in place to help things run more smoothly.

For example, in my house, the boys will often change clothes in the living room. Their laundry baskets used to be in their rooms, where they "should be." But several times a week, we would end up with clothes on the living room floor—creating extra, unnecessary clean-up labor. I noticed that we needed to change the system. So, now we have laundry baskets on the main floor closer to the living room.

The over-the-door clothing organizer in each room was another system we put in place to help things run more smoothly. I noticed how much time we were spending digging through clean clothes baskets, and realized we could create a system that would eliminate that time and labor altogether.

When creating systems, think about common areas of frustration for you. Take a few minutes to jot them down, then brainstorm solutions.

Are you finding shoes kicked around on the floor because their "go-to" place is out of sight and mind? Create a system that dictates a designated place closer to the door for shoes to go. Are you frustrated by dishes piling up on the counter? Get a dish tub to stick dirty dishes in until someone is available to load the dishwasher. Think about ease, convenience, and practicality—not about cute organizers, expensive solutions, or outside expectations of what household labor traditionally looks like.

If you are partnered, include them in the system creation. You can both bring your unique strengths and perspectives to the table to create efficient, functional solutions. I am great at coming up with systems and not-so-great at the follow-through. Frenel, on the other hand, is a much more methodical, detail-oriented thinker than me. He is likely to help smooth out kinks in the plan and bring in additional solutions I wouldn't have thought of when a system needs to be revised. Together, we have alleviated many unnecessary tasks, backtracking, or clutter-cleaning.

The Load of Creating Systems

Creating a system in and of itself requires anticipation labor. But if you're drowning in household labor, isn't it better to focus that anticipation on something that will eliminate the *ongoing* anticipation? I would much rather spend thirty minutes to an hour noticing an issue and creating a solution than pick up seventeen shirts off the living room floor every week for the next twelve years!

However, it's also important to remember that sometimes, expecting yourself to execute a system perfectly every single day is unrealistic. If you are in the throes of postpartum adjustment or struggling with your mental health, you might not have the capacity to see these systems through—and that's understandable! What might seem easy on days when we are coping well can feel impossible on days when we're in survival mode. In these situations, triaging can be helpful. For example, in the postpartum period, if there's one system you focus on implementing, let it be creating a plan for maternal sleep, on page 116. Establishing a system for laundry or other household chores can wait. Systems are supposed to streamline, to bring ease—not to overwhelm us. They aren't about rules or rigid expectations; we can be flexible depending on our capacity and needs.

Finding A Tolerable Common Ground

As you embark on sharing household labor, whether with a partner or with your children, it's important to remember that there is no one right way to keep a home clean. That applies not just to you, but to everyone in your home.

Just because someone else might not do it the exact way you would doesn't mean it's wrong.

It's important to have conversations about a standard of cleanliness. What counts as "getting the job done"? If it's my night to do the dishes, and I also scrub the counters, sweep the floor, and clean out the refrigerator, but my partner just washes the dishes, I'm going to feel frustrated when the rest of the labor doesn't get done. But if a tolerable or common standard had been discussed, that frustration is less likely to occur.

As you hand over labor or create routines or systems, talk about a tolerable minimum standard. Talk about each task and what it encompasses. If there is a disconnect on the definition of a task, think about where you can compromise or meet halfway.

One partner very well might have to adjust their standards from perfectionist heights, while the other partner might have to agree to take their standards up a notch or two. For example, Frenel has . . . very particular ideas about how the dishwasher should be loaded. I do not. He packs in everything perfectly like Tetris. I pop the dishes in quicker and perhaps a little haphazardly.

We've had to discuss the minimum acceptable standard based on the functionality of the task, The goal is for dishes to come out clean. He has had to accept that I am not going to take the time to play Tetris with the dishes. We had to develop a tolerable compromise that met the goal while avoiding pushing that labor onto him alone because he had higher standards.

Communication is key when talking through distribution of labor. Without it, you might find yourself taking tasks back on your own shoulders rather than troubleshooting and working through the process as a team. As you talk through tasks to share or routines to create, ask yourself and your partner these questions:

- What is the goal and function of this task?

- What corners can we cut to reach the goal with less labor?

- Do we have common ground?

- Is this a task I can tolerate sharing?

- Have we arrived at a shared expectation of what this task should include?

Ways to Depersonalize Your Partner's Behavior

Imagine that you've been working all morning to keep the house clean, shuffling behind the kids and ensuring that everything has been put away properly. Then, your partner makes lunch for your children and leaves the bread on the counter.

That bread might *feel* like so much more than bread. It can feel like your partner is slighting you, provoking you, intentionally leaving behind something that you must deal with. You might even think that bread means that your partner doesn't care about you, respect you, or love you anymore. (Resentment has a way of tricking us into only seeing the bad.)

But I would encourage you in that moment to pause and take a step back. Ask yourself to think of three alternative reasons why the bread could be on the counter, other than your partner deliberately leaving it out to spite you.

Maybe they were about to put it away when an argument broke out at the table, causing complete chaos. (I'm not speaking from experience here or anything . . .)

Maybe the little human boss called out asking for ketchup alongside their grilled cheese, and your partner got derailed.

Maybe everyone is sick and just muddling through in survival mode.

There could be dozens of innocent reasons why the bread is on the counter. Now, I'm not suggesting we should let your partner off the hook or not hold them accountable. Depersonalizing the behavior doesn't mean you just assume the best, never say anything, and pretend it doesn't bother you. It is about giving them the benefit of the doubt that their actions were not a direct assault on you or a reflection of their feelings toward you.

The adage "do unto others as you would have them do unto you" applies here. If you forgot to do something, how would you want your partner to react? You would likely want them to give you a chance to talk it through without assuming the worst in you.

When you find yourself jumping to the worst conclusion or taking your partner's behavior as a personal slight, pause and ask yourself if you are giving them the same benefit of the doubt that you would want them to give to you. Then, when you have let off the initial steam and considered that this wasn't done deliberately to hurt you, you can have a much more productive conversation. You can still hold them accountable—but in a way that lets you both move forward as a team.

When we let resentment take control, we begin to interpret everything our partner does through a negative lens. We create narratives in our mind that aren't necessarily based in reality. If we are living with an unfair distribution of labor in the home, it's easy and common for resentment to build. But it shouldn't be ignored.

It's crucial that we learn to depersonalize our partner's behavior and bring some grace into the situation if we want to see positive change in the way labor is shared. Only when we can have productive conversations will we be able to move the needle on household labor and find a way to share the load fairly.

IF YOU ONLY REMEMBER ONE THING

You don't exist to take care of your house—it is meant to serve you. In order to release the Mother Load, we need to let go of the idea that being a good mom means having a clean, tidy home. Tasks in the home should exist to help us function in our daily lives.

IF YOU ONLY DO ONE THING

Begin challenging the "rules" that you believe about keeping house. There is no "right way." Clothes don't have to be folded if that doesn't work for you. Shoes don't have to be organized in a color-coded, fancy way. We can create our own systems that work for us and our family.

THE INVISIBLE LOAD OF BEING THE SCHEDULER

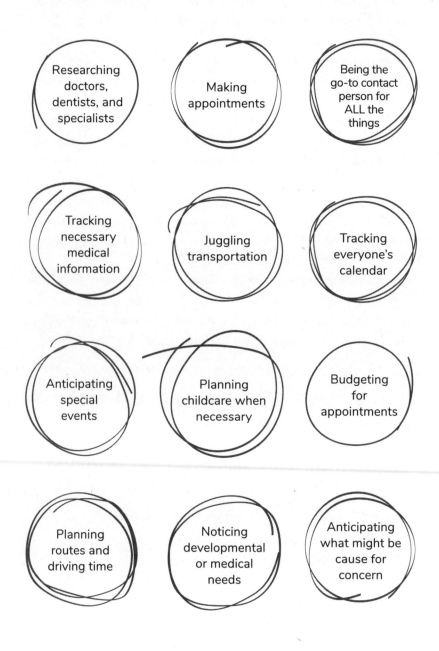

Researching doctors, dentists, and specialists

Making appointments

Being the go-to contact person for ALL the things

Tracking necessary medical information

Juggling transportation

Tracking everyone's calendar

Anticipating special events

Planning childcare when necessary

Budgeting for appointments

Planning routes and driving time

Noticing developmental or medical needs

Anticipating what might be cause for concern

7

THE SCHEDULER

D o you remember the days when you used to just grab your keys and head out the door? Where were you off to? Who knows . . . maybe the mall, maybe to meet up with a friend for lunch, or perhaps just to walk your favorite path—but wherever you were headed, you were in charge and had a sense of autonomy over your choices.

When I think back to before I had children, there are two big differences that stand out in my mind in relation to time.

The first is the freedom and flexibility with my time and calendar. Back then, my time was my own. If I wanted to take a mental health day, I did. If I wanted to be alone, I didn't have to ask anybody for a break. If I didn't feel like doing something, I simply didn't.

I took time for granted if I'm being honest. It wasn't something I thought about in the same way that I do now. Sometimes I was busy. Sometimes plans changed at the last minute. Sometimes I had plenty of free time. It was fluid and flexible in a way that I miss, because once I had kids, that all changed. Overnight, I went from owning my time to my schedule being completely dependent on somebody else's clock (a little somebody with no concept of time whatsoever, I might add).

But the second big difference in my time after I had kids wasn't just about priorities. In many ways, I anticipated that change—I knew that my time would have to be focused in a different way after I had kids.

What I didn't anticipate was how the perception of my time would change. Once I became a mom, it was as if my time was no longer valued at the same level of importance. Without ever intentionally deciding, I became the default time-manager. The one to: make

I went from owning my time to my schedule being completely dependent on somebody else's clock. sure we planned to get out the door on time, make doctor's appointments, track upcoming events, and juggle the logistics of moving through a day.

It happened so subtly that I didn't even notice. And I couldn't figure out why it was so hard to manage.

I'd never been the best with time management, always rushing to make it places on time just to chronically be five minutes late to everything. Getting diagnosed with ADHD in my thirties brought so much into perspective as I began to understand that time blindness is a common experience for neurodivergent folks, leaving them struggling to know how much time has passed. But even with that barrier—that difficulty of organization and executive function—I was able to successfully adult, for the most part. I leaned on tools, like Google Calendar and phone reminders. But I juggled my own schedule and appointments and managed to show up (even if I was regularly a few minutes late). But what I recall most of all was a strong sense of autonomy over my choices and that I was only responsible for getting myself out the door. I never thought about timekeeping, managing, or scheduling as labor. It was simply part of life, and if managed incorrectly, the consequences usually only impacted me.

But now, I wasn't just responsible for my own schedule. I was responsible for the entire family's. My follow-up appointments. My son's doctor's appointments. Any event that included the entire family. It fell to me.

By the time I had three little ones, I felt like I was being torn in a thousand different directions every moment of every day. Managing macro schedules of dentist's appointments, play dates, daycare pickups and drop-offs, birthday parties, outings. Managing micro schedules of when we needed to leave, when we would get back for nap, what time dinner needed to be started—all of which were little tabs left open in my depleted mental computer, draining the RAM of my energy and brainpower.

I berated myself for being so exhausted and resenting my role, for dropping the ball on appointments, for putting off scheduling. This was adulting 101, right? But what I didn't realize at the time was with every event or appointment came a great deal of mental labor—juggling, planning, tracking, decision-making, and remembering. Scheduling is a full-time job—and I was expecting myself to somehow cram it into nap times here and there without batting an eye.

I think that of all the mental labor addressed in this book, it's possible that scheduling and logistics is the one we overlook the most. We don't even realize that it is labor.

It seems like such a little thing—call to schedule an appointment and show up on time. But it is so much more nuanced and complicated than that. For just one routine doctor's appointment, you:

- Research doctors in the area

- Read recommendations

- Make a decision

- Remember to call to schedule the appointment

- Set aside time to make the call without crying children in the background

- Overlook the general daily mess and grind to follow through with making the call

- Have your calendar of events on hand for availability

- Have insurance or benefits information on hand if necessary

- Call and schedule the appointment

- Remember the appointment

- Schedule time off work if relevant

- Discuss talking points for the appointment with your partner

- Decide what to do with your other children if you have multiples

- Coordinate care for the other children or take on the added task of taking everyone with you
- Consider location and traffic to determine when to leave
- Get everybody ready on time
- Leave the home without any unwarranted surprises
- Drive to the appointment
- Fill out paperwork
- Report any important information to the doctor
- Ask questions or share concerns
- Try your hardest not to forget anything
- Take in any important information to share with your partner
- Schedule follow-ups if necessary

Yikes! When we start to unpack this labor, it's no wonder it's exhausting. Maybe scheduling a one-off appointment isn't that big of a deal. But when you, and you alone, are responsible for juggling every appointment for every member of the family, it adds up *fast*. As our family grows, and our children grow, this labor only grows. We add in extra appointments with doctors, dentists, and specialists, along with sports and swim lessons and clubs and activities. It makes me also think of those who have children with special needs or health concerns that require visits with specialists, or ongoing appointments with occupational, speech, or play therapists. With these unique circumstances, this load becomes a full-fledged behemoth to manage. And when you are carrying all those details and remembering every bit of paperwork and the unique needs for every event, it becomes impossible to turn it off. This labor is all-encompassing and never-ending. And yet, we are expected to manage this with the same level of ease that we did before we had children.

In *Fair Play*, Eve Rodsky theorizes that a big reason why this happens is because we value men's time over women's time—we view men's time as "a finite resource (like diamonds), and women's time as abundant (like sand)."[1]

She points out that we often offer up "toxic time messages," things we tell ourselves that delegitimize this labor and keep us trapped in that belief about our time versus our partner's. We say that "time is money," which leads us to believe that if we are not being compensated monetarily, our time is less valuable. We also condition ourselves to protect our partner's time over our own.[2]

When we are trapped in believing that our time is infinite and invaluable, we continue to carry the load of scheduling alone. When we think that managing a schedule is something that "should" be easy, or something that moms must do, we continue to carry this labor alone. When we tell ourselves that other people have it together and we're the only ones struggling, we continue to carry this labor alone. And when we shield our partners from sharing in this labor, protecting their time because we subconsciously believe that it is more valuable than our own, we continue to carry this labor alone.

We must remember that this labor is so much more than a one-off appointment here and there. It's more than a phone call to a doctor's office. It's a massive mental undertaking. It's planning and organizing and orchestrating every day of your family's life, from sunrise to sunset.

Think about the CEO of a major corporation. They don't schedule meetings or track their calendar or plan out their days. In fact, they pay executive assistants hefty salaries to do just that.

Managing and maintaining a schedule is work. And it isn't even mindless, basic work—it's high level labor.

In the corporate world, executive assistants are expected to have their eyes and ears everywhere. These assistants are valued for their major contributions (and given full-time wages and benefits at that). Their job requires a massive set of skills, including:

- Time management
- Organization
- Communication skills

- An ability to multitask and remember many details and nuances at once

- Excellent attention to detail

- Resourcefulness

- Proactive problem-solving

- Critical thinking

- And more

Yet moms are doing the same labor, plus all the other labor we are unpacking in this book. The difference is that we are expected to do this labor for no pay, with no training, and often with no appreciation and no acknowledgment.

We're simply expected to put on the role of "mom" and somehow poof that skill set into existence, keeping the ball rolling for the entire household all day every day.

Most of us didn't have experience juggling three, four, five, or six schedules and calendars in a very limited amount of time. In fact, many of us didn't have the skills to do this efficiently for just ourselves.

Take me for example, with my decades of undiagnosed ADHD. Yes, I managed to get where I needed to go before I had kids, purely out of necessity. But showing up on time put together as a functioning adult? It wasn't easy for me. In fact, most days it was really freaking hard.

Then, when I had kids, I suddenly had to multiply that load for three additional human beings who couldn't even dress themselves, much less tell time, and show up as the executive functioner for everyone else! It was practically impossible.

The definition of executive functioning is "the group of complex mental processes and cognitive abilities (such as working memory, impulse inhibition, and reasoning) that control the skills (such as organizing tasks, remembering details, managing time, and solving problems) required for goal-directed behavior."[3]

Even the dictionary knows these are complex mental processes. But moms should just . . . do this? For multiple people? It is an unrealistic expectation.

Executive functioning for the entire household is a massive undertaking in and of itself. When you add any extenuating factors, like neurodivergence, mental health struggles, sleep deprivation, stress, or overwhelm, you're pushing your brain's RAM power beyond its capability.

Picture those cute little memes that say things like, "that moment when you have so much stuff to do that you decide to take a nap instead." When we have too many tasks to do, our brains get overwhelmed, and we often shut down—especially if we struggle with executive functioning. We are so exhausted we don't even know how to prioritize the load. This results in struggling with initiating tasks even though there is a mountain building up, and watching *The Real Housewives* or scrolling social media instead. Then we end up beating ourselves up because we didn't do anything. But, even just deciding what to tackle or finding the motivation to start can be labor when you're so paralyzed by invisible tasks.

Whether moms are working outside of the home or caring for their children, we're expected to get these tasks done in a very small window of time. If you must call the dentist and the doctor and return a call to the school and set up swim lessons and register for hockey, all on your work break or in your baby's nap time, it's difficult to even break it down into doable chunks. The very act of carrying that to-do list is exhausting—and that's before you even start to knock items off.

I'm not saying all of this to overwhelm you even more. I'm pointing it out because until we see this load for what it is—real labor, full-time labor, labor that must be acknowledged and appreciated and valued—It's like a hidden disease, attacking your body and exhausting you before you even realize it's happening. But if we can shine a light on the disease—if we can acknowledge the labor and understand the accumulation of it—we can start to treat it.

OBJECTIONS TO SHARING THE LOAD

As you read this, you might very well already feel resistance bubbling up about letting go of this load, with "shoulds" and beliefs surfacing that reinforce the idea that this labor should be easy. We do a very good job of minimizing the invisible labor we carry, inadvertently keeping ourselves trapped under it.

We often tell ourselves that this load can't or shouldn't be shared for many reasons. Here are some internal objections we might need to over-come surrounding this load:

Work Flexibility Means I Must Take This Entire Load Myself

Moms often tell themselves that they must be the ones to carry this burden because they have flexibility in their schedule. They are more likely than dads to work part-time or carry flexible hours, likely largely due to societal expectations about being available for their children. The pandemic has exaggerated this work gap—moms cut their hours back four times more than dads did.[4] This trend of moms being the default job-sacrificers impacts their wages and careers in the long-term—31 per-cent of moms *wanted* to continue working after they had children but felt that they couldn't due to a lack of flexible work options.[5]

It also contributes to the default status of moms as caregiver, sched-ule manager, and appointment handler. The pandemic also caused an increase in that trend. More moms reported taking on additional child-care responsibilities than dads did, and working moms were more likely to report feeling as if they couldn't give 100 percent at work due to added responsibilities at home. In fact, more than a third of moms who worked at home reported that they also carried out childcare responsibilities at the same time.[6] And whether the labor itself was unrealistic to keep up with or whether moms were forced to make impossible decisions, the result was the same—a year into the pandemic, 1.4 million more moms than the year before were no longer working.[7]

Either way, the implication is clear—moms are the ones expected to handle it all. They are the ones who ask for flexibility at work, and they are the ones who end up staying at home if that's what must happen—whether they want to or not. This directly reflects the value we carry toward women's time versus men's. Moms are the ones who are function-ing as the default parents.

But work flexibility doesn't mean you should solely carry this labor. Whether you stay home or work, this load doesn't have to be carried by you alone. This is labor that can be shared—but in order to do so, we must realize that our time has value, whether we're being paid or not.

Being the Scheduler Is a Mom's Job

For many of us, we are simply carrying out cycles without realizing it. We saw our moms be the ones to take off work and take us to the doctor. Or we grew up with a stay-at-home mom who did this. Perhaps we have observed soccer moms or sports moms for our entire lives. So, we slip right into the same pattern, unintentionally becoming the default parent because we think it's the right thing to do.

I had a client once who talked about how difficult it was to juggle her child's school ending at 3:00 pm. She worked a regular 9 to 5 job. So, she had to coordinate with her employer on how to take off work and pick up her child in the middle of the workday, then continue her work until 5:00 pm.

But as she expressed her frustration at juggling this pick-up and work schedule, her spouse was never brought up. Just like him, she worked a full-time job. But she was the one sitting there, carrying out all the logistics and mental labor involved. She was the one coordinating her work schedule. And she was the one potentially suffering at work (and beyond) because of it.

This idea of moms being the ones to maintain flexibility, to show up for this labor, is so ingrained we don't even see it.

When Kate Mangino appeared on episode 127 of *The Momwell Podcast*, she discussed gender norms and how deep-rooted they are for so many of us. She shared a little tidbit that I found very helpful: in order to determine if something is gendered behavior, flip the gender in mind and ask yourself if it still makes sense.[8]

Would a man be expected to leave work in the middle of the day and coordinate a pick-up on his own, without help from his wife in the logistics? It's unlikely. That's a good indicator that this behavior stems largely from gender norms.

I'm the One Who Knows Everything, So
It Just Makes Sense for Me to Do It

The scheduling and logistics labor can feel very all-or-nothing. It's easy to think that one person must be the go-to doctor handler. They're the one who knows when the diaper rash started. They're the one who remembers the milestones the doctor said to look for the last time. They're the one who knows the insurance and benefits information. It can feel like sharing the knowledge and labor is harder than just doing it ourselves.

It can feel as if sharing this labor is impossible. We've already trapped ourselves with the maternal knowledge we have gained, and we can't possibly hand over all that knowledge. If we aren't cognizant of this objection, we can easily slip into maternal gatekeeping. Perhaps we don't trust our partner to relay the proper medical information or ask the right questions.

> The more we analyze where our expectations come from, the more we can become intentional about how we distribute tasks in our home.

In this case, we really need to take a step back and look at where our concerns are coming from. Is our partner actually incapable of handling a doctor's appointment? If your partner can handle work meetings and projects, showing up and functioning at a high level at work, they are able to call and schedule a doctor's appointment and show up there.

If you find yourself gatekeeping, I encourage you to become curious. Do you not trust your partner? Or is it, perhaps, stemming from anxiety and a need to know?

Think back to your values. Perhaps you value safety and security. That's not a bad thing. However, you don't have to physically be the one to handle appointments in order to fulfill that value. Can your partner handle the yearly wellness appointment? Or take over the dentist?

Are you holding on to these tasks because they make you feel like you are carrying out social expectations of a "good mom"? What would happen if you shared this labor?

The more we analyze where our expectations come from, the more we can become intentional about how we distribute tasks in our home.

Anticipating

The labor around scheduling and managing logistics in the home often centers around us essentially becoming maternal subject matter experts. We become the all-seeing noticers, anticipating medical needs, abnormalities, typical or atypical behavior. What's "normal" and what should be brought up to the doctor? What are the signs that we need to seek a specialist? Are they meeting all their physical and developmental milestones?

Some of this anticipation information comes from proximity. If moms are more likely to be the stay-at-home parent, they are more likely to have opportunities to notice these things—and because of that, their knowledge will continue to grow.

However, if that were the only factor, then in homes with two working parents, this labor wouldn't be unfairly divided. And yet, it is. Which means that moms are carrying out this anticipation labor whether they are physically there, or there is another caregiver in the mix. And so, they are the ones who are essentially processing and synthesizing information from nannies, babysitters, grandparents, or daycare providers, turning that information into anticipation labor.

When analyzing this labor, it's also important to remember that not all medical appointments require an equal level of anticipation labor. Perhaps if you are a stay-at-home mom or work part-time, you do have a level of proximity that your partner doesn't. In that case, maybe passing off the knowledge about certain medical needs might not be realistic.

However, there are two very different types of medical appointments. Many of them—wellness appointments and regular check-ups—are routine. They go on the schedule and require little more than transporting and filling out paperwork. Daily pick-ups and drop-offs. Yearly wellness appointments. Biannual dentist appointments. Being the appointed daycare/school contact. These pieces don't require a higher level of proximity.

There is plenty of scheduling and logistics labor that doesn't require that build-up of knowledge. We also anticipate upcoming school events, such as holidays, staff development days, or half-days at school, knowing when we will need to coordinate alternative care or make arrangements to stay home. We anticipate parties and homework projects, swim lesson sign-ups and sports practices and games, special events that our children want to attend and places we need to be, weaving it all together into our own internal calendar and knowing what needs to be set up and in place at what time and what day.

In fact, the bulk of this labor is typically mundane and routine. It can be passed off. It can be shared. And it is not gendered. Even stay-at-home parents can share this labor—it just might mean thinking comprehensively and advocating for your time.

Research and Planning

Moms are often the ones researching doctors, dentists, optometrists, and other specialists—Googling, reading reviews, and verifying insurance information. They handle the calls and record times, then plan to be off work to take care of the appointment. They research symptoms and decide if it's serious enough to go to a doctor or if there is an ongoing issue that needs to be addressed at the next well visit. (For example, is this rash normal? Is it common for a baby to spit up after eating? Is there a way to help relieve gas and reflux?)

Researching medical issues can be helpful—it's admirable to want to be equipped with knowledge about our children's health. However, without limits, medical Googling can fuel anxiety. It's easy to get lost in the research black hole of medical questions, local activities, registration deadlines, milestones, events, and more. But having limits around research is important.

Managing

Scheduling and logistics require creating the calendar and maintaining it—we update with changes, track what's coming up the following day and week, and ensure that we have prepared for whatever is coming up. We coordinate childcare for siblings and transport them there, show up where we need to show up with the proper paperwork in hand, and make sure everybody is dressed appropriately for whatever event we attend.

We also often serve as the primary phone number to call—answering calls even when we're working, and juggling, coordinating, and often taking off work.

We also handle the activities and navigate our child's preferences. Do they no longer enjoy piano? We decide between enforcing carrying on with lessons or letting them quit. These in-the-moment decisions require a lot of judgment, weighing and thinking about bigger implications.

In addition to that, we also manage "soccer mom" or "hockey mom" culture, contributing to funds, fundraisers, and parties surrounding clubs and activities. And, in the activities, we juggle the schedule, show up, and navigate changes as they come, troubleshooting traffic or logistics or unexpected situations.

THE LOAD MAPS

For editable versions of the load maps, along with blank templates, visit Ericadjossa.com.

ROUTINE DOCTOR'S AND DENTIST'S APPOINTMENTS

Anticipating

- Remembering when appointments need to be made

- Anticipating what might be asked at the appointment

- Thinking of questions to ask or any concerns to express

- Anticipating developmental milestones

- Choosing dates for the appointment, avoiding other important events

- Anticipating the cost associated with appointments

Research and Planning

- Googling doctors or dentists
- Reading reviews
- Verifying insurance or benefits information
- Planning potential dates and times for an appointment

- Investigating locations and drive time
- Researching appropriate developmental milestones
- Budgeting and coordinating financial needs
- Locating antiracist or inclusive providers

Managing

- Scheduling appointments
- Filling out appointment forms
- Coordinating any other necessary childcare
- Communicating with schools or daycares in advance as necessary

- Arranging transport
- Arriving to the appointment on time
- Filling out any medical paperwork
- Relaying information to the provider
- Asking questions as needed

OUTSIDE-OF-THE-ROUTINE MEDICAL APPOINTMENTS

Anticipating

- Noticing developmental or medical needs

- Discerning what might be cause for concern

- Anticipating what might be asked at the appointment

- Thinking of questions to ask or any concerns to express

- Choosing dates for the appointment, avoiding other important events

Research and Planning

- Googling doctors or dentists

- Reading reviews

- Verifying insurance or benefits information

- Planning potential dates and times for an appointment

- Investigating locations and drive time

- Researching your area of concern

- Researching appropriate developmental milestones

- Budgeting and planning for financial needs

- Tracking your child's behavior or medical information

- Locating antiracist or inclusive providers

Managing

- Scheduling appointment
- Filling out appointment forms
- Coordinating any other necessary childcare
- Communicating with schools or daycares in advance as necessary
- Arranging transport

- Arriving to the appointment on time
- Filling out any medical paperwork
- Relaying information to the provider
- Asking questions as needed
- Advocating for child's needs

SCHOOL AND SOCIAL EVENTS

Anticipating

- Anticipating upcoming events
- Anticipating sign-ups or registration

- Calculating what needs to be purchased, planned, made, or packed

Research and Planning

- Researching events, clubs, and activities

- Decision-making on what activities to sign up for

- Reviewing locations for practices, rehearsals, or games
- Planning loads of laundry to ensure uniforms are clean

- Weighing the cost of school trips or extracurricular activities/adjusting the budget as necessary

Managing

- Registering
- Filling out forms
- Coordinating any other necessary childcare
- Arranging transport

- Arriving to practices, rehearsals, and games on time
- Participating in the parent culture
- Volunteering to join trips/run activities

ASSUMPTIONS THAT REINFORCE THE LOAD WE CARRY

To share this load, we have to understand that this is real, tangible work. Logistics and scheduling are extremely important tasks. But they are not tasks that we have to carry alone. We can, and should, share this labor.

Assumption 1

Assumption: My partner is not as capable of multitasking and juggling schedules.

Reframe: My partner is capable—they have just never been asked or expected to do this work.

Your partner is a capable human being. They have managed their calendar and showed up to places and tended to themselves throughout life. They have simply never had the expectation of doing this labor for the family. But if given the opportunity, they can absolutely share in these tasks (presuming they are willing).

Assumption 2

Assumption: I need to protect my partner's time.

Reframe: My time is as valuable as my partner's, even if I am not exchanging my time for money.

Your time matters—whether you work full time, part time, or stay at home. Either way, you are carrying out an undue burden of labor in addition to this invisible load of logistics and scheduling. What you do is work—paid or unpaid, it is labor, and your time is a finite resource. It isn't unfair or unrealistic for you to call in more hands and to share this labor with your partner.

Assumption 3

Assumption: Because I have been doing this labor, I must be the one to handle it all.

Reframe: My backlog of maternal knowledge does not mean this labor should fall to me.

You have the knowledge because you have been the one carrying this labor. But if you have a partner, they can build the knowledge as well. You are a member of a team, and the two of you together need to share in the knowledge, understanding, and labor involved in this load.

If you don't have a partner, think of other support people. Do you have a family member who you can call in to help research medical concerns? Is there another caregiver who can share in the knowledge? Sometimes, the answer is no—in that case, this might not be an area you can unload.

But it's also important to remember that not all scheduling and logistics requires a backlog of knowledge. Perhaps letting go of bigger medical concerns is not something you are able, or even wish, to do. But routine appointments, clubs, school events—these can all be easily shared with your partner moving forward, with a very minimal amount of knowledge transfer.

Your partner can call the dentist and take your child to a teeth cleaning without your backlog of knowledge. They can attend a school party or field trip without it. They can even handle the wellness appointment without it. And over time, the more that they are invited to be an active participant in the family team, the more they will build their own knowledge.

Assumption 4

Assumption: Handling the family schedule is my role and responsibility as a mom.

Reframe: This labor is not gendered, and it doesn't make me a good mom.

As mentioned earlier in this chapter, scheduling is not a gendered task. And it is not a requirement to be a "good mom." When in doubt, revisit your values. Think about what you identified as the most important. Was it "calls and makes every doctor's appointment and is always the one to drive them"? I doubt it. It might have been safety or security. But you can fulfill those values as a team with your partner—without always being the one physically present, without always being the one picking up the phone and calling, without living with a million dates and details in your head, invading your free time.

Assumption 5

Assumption: This is simple work, and I should be able to keep up with it.

Reframe: Scheduling and logistics are high-level work—it's understandable if I struggle with it.

Executive functioning for an entire household isn't easy, and it isn't realistic to put it all on one person. If you struggle to carry it all alone, that's understandable. You might be carrying too much.

There are also many factors that impact our ability to executive function, like our own brain or mental health, physical health, life stressors, other projects, sleep deprivation, or large-scale events like the pandemic.

SKILLS AND TOOLS FOR RELEASING THIS LABOR

In this section, we'll cover skills and tools that include:

- Syncing household knowledge
- Creating a visual schedule
- Prioritizing the load
- Taking a mental clutter inventory
- Unpacking our mental clutter
- Preventing the load from being handed back to you by society
- Implementing a family calendar

Syncing Household Knowledge

As we discussed in chapter 1, the maternal knowledge we accumulate in our role is something that often lives in our minds, which makes it hard to hand certain tasks over to partners or support people in our lives. Without sharing the knowledge, we cannot share the load. Carving out a routine way that you sync with those who share in parenting with you is essential.

This really boils down to open lines of communication so that everyone in the situation is informed. We need to shift from a top-down delegation, where you hold the knowledge and assign tasks, to a collaborative, team effort, conquering the load together.

Here's how this looks in my home currently:

Weekly Sync

Frenel and I often have a weekly sync where we look at our calendars for the week ahead and decide who is going to do what. Who's taking who to hockey, who is getting groceries, do we have any other social events, birthday parties, or leisure activities to fit in?

This is usually a bird's-eye view of the week, where we divide out the big tasks. It also gives us a chance to discuss overarching needs for the upcoming weeks and months. For example: is one of the kids' birthdays approaching? Where should we book the party? What's the budget? We tap into that knowledge together with a pulse check on big items that are floating around that need some clarity.

Daily Sync

We also do a quick daily sync after dropping off the kids each day about what needs to happen for the day. What are we having for dinner and who is on duty? Does something need to be taken out? Who's doing pickup? This is how we ensure we are both actively in the know, no matter who is doing what.

Situational Syncs

Sometimes other needs arise. Situational syncs are prompted by concerns or observations either of you see, such as fussiness or sleep wakings, behavior concerns, or anything you need to problem-solve together.

Appointment Syncs

Before and after any appointments, we work together to create a list of what needs to be discussed in upcoming appointments. We also connect and debrief with each other after the fact.

There are times when clients have expressed this debriefing or conveying doctors' appointments to partners as an unfair part of the load—and it can be. For example, at the height of the pandemic, one of my clients was going to multiple appointments throughout her pregnancy to determine whether their baby had a genetic disease. She was forced to attend these appointments alone, which was very upsetting already. But one of her biggest fears was that if the doctors gave emotional or devastating news, she would then carry the responsibility of sharing that with her partner.

Whenever possible, we aimed to have her partner present in these appointments via a phone call so that she didn't carry the extra weight of being the one to keep her partner informed when she was emotional and processing herself. This can be a helpful solution for when partners or support people aren't physically present so that they can still be holders and keepers of knowledge.

Syncing knowledge is important, and it requires some flexibility. Some syncs are more set into the ebb and flow of the week and schedule, while others are more fluid and needs-driven. Ultimately what is most important here is figuring out a communication approach that works for your household. Maybe daily check-ins don't work but you can succeed with a big sync on the weekend. Or maybe you need to record information in a shared document. Experiment and discover what works for you.

Creating a Visual Schedule

A recurring struggle that comes up with working with moms is their to-do list is miles long. They often find it difficult to accomplish what they planned for the day. This is more about the micro schedule day to day and what can realistically get accomplished than the macro weekly, monthly, or quarterly schedule.

For example, I worked with a lovely client who had very high expectations of herself. She homeschooled her two boys and explained to me that she could never stick to the schedule and accomplish what she set out for the day. As we worked through the expectations she had for her homeschool day with the kids vs. the reality of what happened, there were not physically enough minutes in the day to accomplish all that she had set out to do. Her list included items such as bake before lunch and get outside to keep with their streak of the 100 days outdoors challenge, but it underestimated the length of these tasks and didn't account for all the other tasks involved in caring for children that we often don't congratulate ourselves for.

Whether you're homeschooling or working full-time or something else entirely, this can become an issue. You think you should be able to do more than you have the capacity or physical minutes in the day for. I find this challenge of overcommitting or underestimating the time tasks take to be particularly challenging for neurodivergent folks like myself, who struggle with seeing all of the steps that are involved in a task and the realistic amount of time each item takes.

Being able to manage time effectively includes skills like:

- Being oriented by time rather than getting lost in thoughts or tasks

- Being able to know how long tasks take

- Being able to see the steps involved in a task and prioritize where to start

- Being able to start and initiate tasks in a timely fashion to keep with the schedule

(All of which I am terrible at!)

For those who also struggle with having an overfilled to-do list, one of the best ways I have found that works for myself and for clients is to intentionally chunk out your tasks in a visual schedule.

With my client, we pulled out a daily calendar broken down by half hours. First, we put in the day-to-day routine care tasks, like meal and nap times. Once those were in, we determined that there were only two chunks of free time, each about an hour and a half to two hours, for homeschool activities or other items.

When reevaluating the baking activity, considering pulling out ingredients, leaving the dough to rise, time in the oven, and cleaning up, we determined that it was an unrealistic task to fit into the two-hour window before lunch and her youngest's nap time. She was able to adjust her expectations when we broke it down.

Prioritizing the Load

For those of us who have brains that work differently, or those who simply look at the sheer volume of tasks we must do and feel completely paralyzed and want to crawl back into bed, it is important to know where and how to start.

I hate to be the one to say it, but the majority of the tabs open in our brain are not urgent. But we struggle to know how to prioritize which one is urgent and which one isn't because all of our energy is spent keeping track of the tabs so we don't drop the ball.

Taking a Mental Clutter Inventory

To really gain an objective view of what needs to be done and when, we have to take a mental clutter inventory—a good old-fashioned brain dump. This brain dump must include all of the mental tabs so we can understand where tasks begin, and therefore prioritize the vital ones from start to finish.

Grab a pen and some paper or open a memo on your phone, set a timer for five minutes, and jot down everything that flows through your mind. It might be tasks, it might be worries, or it might be a memory of a difficult conversation you had. Whatever comes up, jot it down.

After you have your task list, go through the items and ask yourself:

- Does this have to be done today?

- Does this need to be done by me?

- Does this need to be done at all?

If it doesn't have to be done today, chunk it in your visual schedule on a day you have time, or have a discussion with your partner or a support person about owning it. If it does need to be done today, look at your visual schedule and decide where it fits in. If it is urgent, you may have to remove something else you're hoping to accomplish in order to meet the necessary demand.

What I often find when clients do this is that it's not always tasks that are taking up brain power—it's a lot of other mental clutter.

Unpacking Our Mental Clutter

It is easy to attribute our mental clutter to the invisible load, and while that is a large chunk of it, there are different things that clutter our minds. The invisible load is made up of the pervasive tasks and to-do lists that constantly pop into our brain, often during time when we are trying to wind down, have time for ourselves, or relax.

As someone with ADHD, my mental clutter also consists of random thoughts and noise. This is the constant state of my brain. There is a song in the background while a random social interaction from high school pops back into my head while I am trying to listen to a podcast while doing the dishes . . . it's a never-ending stream of noise.

While some of these are invisible load- or work-related, oftentimes the thoughts are just curiosities, daydreams, or even creative ideas. On harder days, they might be intrusive thoughts, or flashbacks of tough moments and negative experiences. Mental clutter might contain anxious worst-case scenarios or scary and intrusive thoughts that pop out of nowhere. It could be stress due to relationship strain or health concerns.

It is an important distinction for us to understand the content of our mental clutter because the treatment isn't the same across the board. The skills I use to help alleviate my intrusive thoughts are not the same skills I use to stay on task, which are not the same skills I use to try to pull myself out of a funk or a bad mood. The brain dump can help us parse everything out and see where our energy is being spent, and what we can let go of. These different types of clutter all weigh on us and impact our capacity, and therefore our ability to cope with the other aspects of the Mother Load.

If you do the mental clutter inventory/ brain dump and realize that it is actually worry, trauma, or something else preoccupying your thoughts, I would encourage you to explore what you need to help support you in those areas.

When Society Tries to Hand the Load Back to You

Sometimes, even if we and our partner are on board with sharing the load, society isn't on the same page.

For example, as Frenel and I worked to divide out this load more, he took over correspondence with the school, scheduling appointments for the boys, etc. But as we began to make this transition, I noticed that most places continued to call me first instead of him. I would come out of a day of back-to-back client sessions to a voicemail from the doctor or school (whom we had repeatedly asked to call Frenel first).

When I was going through university, I worked as an administrative assistant in a psychology clinic, and I remember numerous conversations or comments about preferring to deal with moms for schedules and about calling mom first before dad. The reality is that society reinforces these gender norms and stereotypes. So if we're going to make a shift, we have to be prepared to set boundaries, correct people, and push back when they try to place the load back in our laps.

I recommend preparing some go-to statements, like:

- Please make my partner the primary contact for my child.

- Please call my partner before calling me as I've asked that he be made the primary contact on several occasions.

- Is there somewhere to note that my partner should be called first before reaching out to me?

After several prompts, the school and other professionals got the message and began to call Frenel first. He has gone to the school for things so many times the whole office knows his face and who his kids are. (Meanwhile, I can sneak in and out without being detected because I'm so rarely the one they contact!) This took intention, and it took time. But it was so worth it!

Implementing a Family Calendar

Perhaps this goes without saying, but have a central family calendar. It keeps everyone on the same page, with all the events in one place, and everyone in the family can add to it. That means you are not the keeper of the birthday parties, play dates, and appointments. Everyone is responsible for putting important items on the calendar and keeping the family informed.

In my home, we do this two ways. Frenel and I put family events in a Google calendar that is synced to both of our phones. This is where we put appointments, parties, hockey schedules, important registration dates, etc.—anything that we need to be aware of together.

We also have a whiteboard calendar in our kitchen. This is a visual that the kids can see and read. We add tests, school trips, activities, etc.

We keep this in a high-traffic, visible place so we collectively don't miss or forget about things.

Play around with different methods and visuals that work for you. Finding a practical system to share logistics and scheduling helps distribute this load and create a family buy-in so that this labor doesn't fall solely on your shoulders.

How to Decide If It Should Be Added to the Family Calendar

Many families find themselves busy and overscheduled, committed to events, outings, play dates, parties, and an overwhelming number of activities. We often have more activities or commitments to manage than we have time for.

It is important to have some questions to ask yourself to determine whether something should make it into the family calendar or not:

- Is this activity or event in line with my values?
- Am I doing this out of pressure and what I see others doing or do I sincerely want to do this?
- Am I doing this out of obligation to someone else?
- Which one of my values (or our family values) is driving this choice?
- What is the cost of this commitment? (financial, time investment, etc.)
- Does what we stand to gain outweigh what we stand to lose?

As children get older and activity schedules start to pick up, being mindful about your commitments and what you allow on your calendar is important.

IF YOU ONLY REMEMBER ONE THING

Your time is as valuable as anyone else's—your child's, your partner's, or anybody else you find yourself prioritizing. This is true whether you earn a paycheck outside of the home or not—you are working, you are investing time, and that matters.

IF YOU ONLY DO ONE THING

Challenge the beliefs around time that are keeping you stuck in this self-sacrificial pattern. Scheduling is labor. Your time matters. (Revisit the assumptions section on page 203 of this chapter for more on these beliefs.)

THE INVISIBLE LOAD OF BEING
THE CREATOR OF FUN

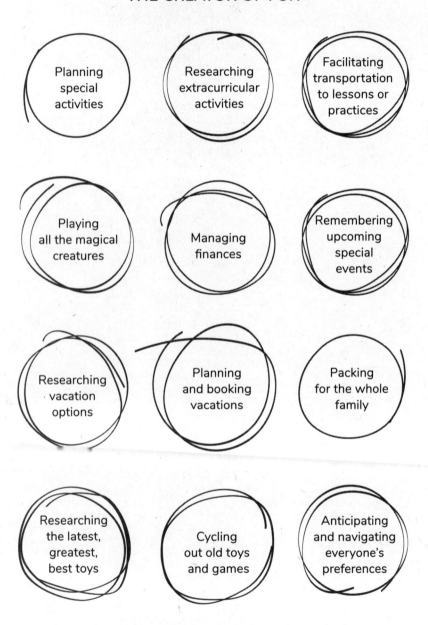

Planning special activities

Researching extracurricular activities

Facilitating transportation to lessons or practices

Playing all the magical creatures

Managing finances

Remembering upcoming special events

Researching vacation options

Planning and booking vacations

Packing for the whole family

Researching the latest, greatest, best toys

Cycling out old toys and games

Anticipating and navigating everyone's preferences

8

THE CREATOR OF FUN

When I was on my first maternity leave, I spent a lot of time on the go. I wanted to create beautiful memories and fill photo albums for my little boy to look back on. And in some ways, it was also a way to preserve my mental health. If I kept myself moving, if I filled my time, if I just kept myself from sitting at home, maybe I could pretend that I wasn't struggling.

So, we did story time and mommy meetups and went to the zoo once a week. And it was fun. Sometimes it was stressful, but it was generally manageable.

With my second and third, I desperately wanted to keep up that same pace. I felt like I had set a precedent and needed to keep up—that my second and third would miss out if I didn't plan fun outings. To add to my feelings, I saw social media posts from other moms on their first maternity leave, doing all the things—and I wanted to do that too.

So, one day when my third was still a tiny baby, I packed all three boys up and headed to the zoo for the day. It was my first time venturing out with all three boys on an adventure this size by myself.

It was a little wild from the start—my two older boys wanted to move and roam free, and I was slowed down by a baby and all the gear. It felt a lot like herding kittens.

After a while, we sat down at a picnic table to eat the lunch I had packed—and that's when the real chaos ensued. I helped my older two get their lunches opened and sat down to nurse the baby. My middle son, being the wiggly little worm he was, leaned too far back out of his seat—and fell and gashed his head on the side of the table.

I became immediately aware that I absolutely did not have enough hands to get the situation under control. He was crying and bleeding, I was juggling the baby, and I couldn't leave to go get help because I had three little ones to wrangle all by myself.

Fortunately, there was another mom nearby who was able to flag down the zoo staff. My head was spinning—what would I do if we needed to go for stitches? How was I even going to get everyone through the five-kilometer walk back to the parking lot? Why had I even put myself in this position? An EMT came and helped clean the wound and gave him ice. And, thankfully, everything was fine. As soon as we were cleaned up and checked out, we beelined all the way out of the zoo to the van to head back home. I didn't take all three of them out by myself again for a very long time.

That ordeal taught me a lot. It taught me that I wasn't Supermom (an unrealistic standard often placed on moms that serves to keep them in the cycle of trying to be and do it all). It taught me that I needed to adjust my expectations. And it taught me that trying to keep up with my perception of what everyone else was doing, or my ideal vision of what life should look like, wasn't worth the potential risk. Everything turned out okay that day . . . but what if it had been more serious? It was clear that it wasn't just stressful to handle outings with all three by myself—it was also potentially unsafe.

I had to let go of comparison. It didn't matter if my friends with one baby, or even if my friends with multiples, posted pictures of fun family events or seemed to have it all together. It likely didn't tell the entire story of those outings—and, ultimately, it didn't change my reality, my capacity, and my family's needs.

I needed to look back on my values for my family and remember that going to the zoo or attending story time or any of those other fun outings didn't make me a good mom. I had to accept that my family had grown, my reality had changed, and even just leaving the house came with a new set of logistical challenges that needed to be conquered.

And it wasn't just local outings that changed. Holidays, travel, and vacations also became more difficult and more encompassing with every child we added. What was once purely about fun now consisted of a mountain of mental labor.

Before we had children, visiting our family in Benin was a relaxing experience. We got away from work and spent a few weeks visiting, resetting, and escaping the stress of our daily lives. After we had one son, we went back for another visit. This time it was different. It involved gear and baby things, more packing, more decisions, and more chaos. It was less rejuvenating—but it was still manageable.

Then, our second son was born. We planned a trip for when he was eight months old. I knew that it would be more difficult . . . what I didn't know was that I would be pregnant (and extremely sick) while we traveled. I was miserable, still nursing the baby while pregnant with another, and dealing with a two-and-a-half-year-old on top of it. Our family support was the only way I got through it.

Now with three, the thought of taking a vacation sometimes fills me with dread. I want to travel, to expose my boys to different cultures, and to show them the wonders of the world. But even just a weekend trip comes with days of prep—laundry, packing bags, figuring out how everything is going to fit in the car and deciding what toys to let each of them bring . . . not to mention the overwhelm of chasing them around during the actual trip!

We just took our first big trip as a family of five. We started with a much closer, shorter trip—I still haven't worked up the nerve to fly back overseas because I remember how hard the last trip was. We enjoyed our trip—but it didn't come without stress, chaos, and pressure.

As moms, we often take on the pressure of being the creators of fun, the makers of memories, the coordinator of travel and social events and experiences. We are the planners and the magical creatures and the toy purchasers and the travel agents, bending over backward to give our children lives full of wonder and joy.

For many of us, these were the things we pictured before we had kids. We romanticized them in our minds. Family trips to the zoo. Vacations. Camping. Santa and the Easter Bunny and the Tooth Fairy. Sporting events. But we likely envisioned the fun part—the joy and the happiness and the connection—not the packing of bags, the juggling of schedules, the chaos of a change in routine, and the constant pressure to do and be more.

We often take on the pressure of being the creators of fun, the makers of memories, the coordinator of travel and social events and experiences.

At some point, we must wonder if it's worth it. That's not to say we shouldn't plan fun things for our kids! It simply means we must weigh the tradeoff. Is the amount of fun or the memories we created or the pictures we captured worth the stress? Sometimes the answer might be yes. Other times, we might opt for more slowness.

But how do we decide what activities or trips or traditions are worth it? The first step is to look at where our expectations came from. Is this something we really want to do? Or is it something we feel like we *must* do? We need to dig into those filing cabinets and unpack our beliefs about the experiences we're trying to create.

The pressure to create memories and capture moments starts before a baby is born. We feel as if we need a cutesy pregnancy announcement, a complicated gender reveal, bump picture updates every week. We're supposed to muddle through extreme fatigue or crippling morning sickness to pose for the camera and come up with creative photos and witty captions.

This continues when we have a newborn. We think we need perfectly curated monthly milestone photos, to the point where we feel guilty if we miss the day or if we don't keep up with the same traditions with every child.

That pressure only grows as our children grow. We feel the need to enroll them in sports or clubs, to document their first day of preschool with a personalized chalkboard sign, and to attend every school party or special event.

When we create fun and memories, we have a highlight reel—photos to show, to share, and to keep. We often do genuinely enjoy looking back at these photos and memories, even if we didn't enjoy the entire experience. But for many of us, there is also often an element of comparison. We feel pressure to check off these boxes to be "good moms" and keep up with the appearances of our social media friends.

We view everyone else's highlight reels and we think that we should do more. But it's important to keep some perspective. Those highlight reels are curated—we have no idea what's going on behind the scenes. That smiling moment might have been snapped right before a full-blown meltdown. The matching pajamas might have gotten stained with juice after the photo was taken. Nobody is sharing the bad. In fact, nobody is even sharing the mundane. They're sharing the highlights— and those highlights don't need to guide your parenting decisions.

It's wonderful to want to create a fun, positive childhood for your kids. Maybe you remember fond moments from your childhood that you want to pass on . . . or maybe your childhood was far from magical and you want to break cycles and be there for your kids in a way that you didn't have. None of that is wrong to want. But when we are carrying so much weight and pressure that we feel exhausted, overwhelmed, or even resentful of the roles we play, it's time to reevaluate the rules we're setting for ourselves.

Bonding, family relationships, fun—these are all great things that are likely very important to you. Those things might be held closely in your family values. There's nothing wrong with that. But when we are holding ourselves to impossible standards, when we are doing these things because we feel that they are what makes us good moms, we need to think more creatively about how to achieve that same function without doing ALL the things.

Can you take a small camping trip instead of a complex, expensive vacation in the summer? Can you create memories at home without spending money? Do we really need to invest every moment of our time, every dollar we have, and every bit of our energy into things we think will make our children happy? Or, perhaps, can we find some value in slowness, in letting go of some of the things to make space for both fun for our children and our own mental health?

We can find the ways we can challenge this perfectionism, this perfect mother myth, and still create meaningful memories without it being so costly to us—both mentally and financially. After all, it's impossible to separate out the conversation of finances from the conversation about the pressure to create fun. Whether we're talking about experiences (like vacations or day trips or outings) or tangible items, we often feel as if we must spend more money in order to give our children more joy.

There is a pressure to buy more (just as there is to be more)—to always have the latest, greatest, flashiest toys and clothes. When we are constantly taking in intensive mothering messages that tell us that "good moms" give all their resources (time, attention, energy, and money) to their children and then pour consumerism messaging on top of that, it's a deadly combination for moms. *We must spend more money to have the latest things in order to give our children what they need and deserve— because that's what good moms do.* But when is it enough? Do our children really need or want these things? Or would they, perhaps, be just as happy to choose less, to choose slow?

Perhaps the things that truly make experiences special are that they are unique, outside of the norm. We can choose to take a special outing once a month or go on a small trip every quarter or pick just one holiday to go all-in on—and our children won't necessarily miss out. Our children don't always need more things, or even more fancy experiences.

There are two big components of this particular invisible load: *fun* and *memories*. *Fun* includes play, physical items/toys, and experiences. *Memories* include traditions, holidays, milestones, achievements, or notable moments. We can find areas in both sections that don't align with our values, things we can choose to let go of.

Everything that we choose to do for our children or buy for our children comes with an investment—of time, energy, and often money. We have been conditioned to believe that the highest investment in these elements will produce the highest impact for our kids—as if time plus money equals memorability. But that formula has been written by intensive mothering ideology and consumerism. And it is not inherently true for every child or every family.

Sometimes the lowest investments come with the highest impact. For example, each Christmas season, I create a holiday advent calendar of experiences—small, manageable experiences. It includes things like having a glow-stick dance party or drinking candy cane hot chocolate by the Christmas tree. This takes me less than twenty minutes to plan and create. Nothing on the list costs a great deal of money. But each of my boys recalls these experiences more than anything they got under the tree. We don't have to invest more to have more impact.

We experienced another moment recently that opened my eyes to the value in simplicity. We were all feeling a little restless at home, so I suggested packing everyone up and going for a weekend at a nearby resort. Frenel suggested we look for something else to do, something with a lower time and money investment. We ended up finding an open fun swim at our local rec center. We took the boys there and they had a blast. One of my sons even managed to earn his own swim pass to show he can go into the deep pool by himself. In fact, he didn't meet the requirements the first day—but the next day he did. He was so proud of himself. He ran up to me, showing me his pass, beaming.

I know that he will remember that moment more than anything we could have bought him at the resort. It wasn't a curated, expensive experience—it only cost us $9.50 for the whole family (compared to a small fortune to stay away for a couple of nights). It was just something he did himself, something to be proud of, a fleeting moment that will likely be etched in his brain forever.

I'm so glad we opted to go to the open swim instead of hauling everyone away for the weekend, especially considering we were coming off Christmas and I was already exhausted. Now, that's not to say we're never going to go on holidays or vacations—I'm sure we'll end up packing up for an adventure before too long! Higher investment activities can be fun and great. But it's freeing to know that the formula isn't so linear—we don't have to always put in more time and money to produce a better experience. We can choose flexibility, balance, and simplicity sometimes. We can choose to do things differently.

It's not always easy to break out of the mindset that more time and money equals more memorability. It can take some work to reframe this and view it in a different way. If you have a partner, this might involve sitting down and discussing boundaries and expectations regarding holidays, travel, or even regular outings. Maybe you each take over one holiday and let some of the others go. Or perhaps you forego a massive family vacation for a mini trip. If you don't have a partner, maybe mapping out small outings once a month seems more doable. Maybe you have a grandparent or a support person to travel with and you can do this work with them. It will look different based on your circumstances, but building some structure can help relieve some of the moment-to-moment pressure to do and be more. Boundary-setting and expectation management can help us remember that not every moment is high stakes, and that it's okay to choose what is right for your family.

There might be times when it's very hard to remember that. When we do something outside of the norm, something that contradicts societal messaging, there will likely be times when we inevitably doubt ourselves. We'll see a social media feed full of expensive Hanukkah or Christmas gifts, and hear a voice that tells us we're not doing enough. If we're going to choose to let some of this pressure go, if we're going to choose to do things differently, we must lean on our values as our compass. When those doubts come up, we'll have to reanchor in our values, battle the mom-guilt surveillance crew, and push comparison away so we can hold onto what truly matters to us.

Anticipating

Being the creator of fun requires plenty of anticipation labor. Moms are often juggling all the magical roles we play—remembering when to switch out the tooth for a quarter, when to order stocking stuffers, when to have Valentines ready to go, and when to move the Elf. We anticipate holidays, traditions, birthdays, and other special events, mentally keeping track of everything we need to do to prepare.

We also anticipate free time and weekends, deciding whether we need to fill breaks from school with camps or outings. While doing this, we notice what our children's interests are, deciding whether we should cultivate those interests by signing up for lessons or clubs, and we anticipate the deadlines to register.

Research and Planning

Moms often are the ones researching different clubs and activities, mapping out locations, thinking about logistics and scheduling, and planning what physical labor will be involved. They fill out the registration forms and research the gear needed, from shin guards to ice skates to art supplies.

They also serve as the travel agents for the family, researching potential vacation spots, thinking about budget and financial needs, planning dates for trips, and creating itineraries. (I feel compelled to point out that there are people who plan for a living—but as moms we are supposed to shove this into our "free time.")

Moms also research toys, gifts, stocking stuffers, and holiday items. They plan where to hide them, when to wrap them, when to sneak them out under the tree. They arrange special activities, like advent calendars, along with research and planning for special holiday events in the community.

It can feel like there is no end to the research and decision-making labor. It's easy to get caught up in information overload, looking up activities or gifts for hours and hours on end. I find that this is particularly true with gift giving. We weigh developmental stages, preferences, longevity, and finances, and spend a great deal of time poring through reviews and product descriptions.

It's important to keep some perspective— there is no one "perfect" gift or activity or vacation for your child. It can be helpful to put a cap on how long you can research or how many pages on Amazon you can check through before making a choice. We sometimes need to set limits to take that pressure of perfectionism off our shoulders.

Managing

Moms often feel as if they must constantly fill our children's time with activities, their spaces with new toys, and their days with never-ending fun.

This requires ongoing management. We find ourselves in a recurring cycle of filling the calendar with things, shuttling our kids back and forth to practices, rehearsals, games, and lessons. This also requires evaluation and decision-making—are we going to sign up for another season or try something new? What do we need to tweak to make this work for us?

We're also frequently purchasing new toys and gadgets as our children hit new developmental stages, which leads to more cleaning and organization labor.

When it comes to vacations, there's packing, managing behavior on the road, navigating airports or transportation, hustling to activities, and trying to document every moment along the way. After a trip, moms are unpacking, washing clothes, and trying to reestablish the routine.

THE LOAD MAPS

For editable versions of the load maps, along with blank templates, visit Ericadjossa.com.

FAMILY VACATIONS

Anticipating

- Considering everyone's schedules and determining when the family will be available

- Thinking ahead on when to start preparing and booking

- Deciding when to start packing

- Discerning and accounting for sleep needs (Do we need to bring a pack and play, a white noise machine, or a toddler cot?)

- Considering child ages and readiness for travel

- Noting and considering everybody's preferences—what will be fun for the entire family?

- Noticing and anticipating clothing and laundry needs

- Noticing and anticipating food/snack needs

Research and Planning

- Destinations
- Hotels/cabins/vacation rentals
- What to pack and bring
- Meals and snacks
- Sleeping arrangements

- Transportation/car seats/strollers
- Budget options/finances
- Entertainment for car rides or flights
- Planning age-appropriate activities/outings

Managing

- Deciding what to bring
- Doing laundry
- Packing bags
- Schedule tracking/time-keeping
- Managing behavior
- Unpacking

- Navigating unexpected moments
- Evaluating everyone's levels of "fun" to make decisions on future trips
- Reestablishing routines and schedules

HOLIDAYS AND TRADITIONS

Anticipating

- Tracking upcoming holidays and anticipating needs
- Anticipating school parties/functions
- Anticipating competing family demands/scheduling conflicts

- Considering children's preferences and interests
- Anticipating upcoming developmental stages and changes to incorporate into gifts

Research and Planning

- Gifts
- Traditions and activities
- Community events
- Budgeting and considering financial implications
- Planning how to hide gifts/keep surprises secret

- Decision-making on gifts and purchasing
- Ensuring that everything is fair and equal
- Creating plans with all of the extended family
- Coordinating gifts with extended family

Managing

- Navigating behavior due to changes in routine

- Creating new traditions and carrying them out

- Carrying out cultural traditions (for example, playing Santa, the Easter Bunny, the Tooth Fairy, Elf on the Shelf, etc., choosing Hanukkah gifts, orchestrating Diwali celebrations, or preparing lucky money for Lunar New Year)

- Wrapping presents

- Tweaking activities and traditions to suit the needs of every child

EXTRACURRICULAR ACTIVITIES

Anticipating

- Noticing preferences and interests

- Considering any special needs or accommodations

- Anticipating sign-ups and registration times

- Considering schedules and logistics

- Anticipating when uniforms or costumes need to be clean and ready

Research and Planning

- Activity options

- Locations of practices, rehearsals, lessons, or games

- Calendar tracking

- Planning schedules to accommodate multiple activities

- Gear, musical instruments, or supplies

Managing

- Decision-making and purchasing all the gear
- Shuttling everyone to events
- Doing laundry
- Packing bags

- Entertaining other children during events
- Fulfilling "sports mom" or "club mom" expectations

OUTINGS

Anticipating

- Noticing preferences and interests
- Considering any special needs or accommodations
- Considering schedules and logistics

- Anticipating upcoming special community events (special nights at the zoo or unique story times)
- Anticipating free time that needs to be filled

Research and Planning

- Community events
- Activities
- Reading reviews

- Determining what is age appropriate and meets the needs and preferences of each child

- Planning day outing schedules

- Assessing costs

Managing

- Transportation
- Packing bags
- Managing behavior

- Troubleshooting when unexpected changes arise

THE GATEKEEPER AND PROVIDER OF TOYS

Anticipating

- Anticipating developmental stages and changes
- Noticing interests and preferences

- Noticing organizational needs or when to cycle out old toys
- Noticing and considering new toy options

Research and Planning

- The newest toys
- Tablet options
- Game options
- Evaluating budget needs

- Reading reviews
- Considering fairness and equality
- Researching quality of toys

Managing

- Purchasing of toys
- Ongoing organization/toy rotation

- Managing behavior/ disputes over toys
- Decision-making when new things are requested

ASSUMPTIONS THAT REINFORCE THE LOAD WE CARRY

In some ways, we might be most hesitant to let go of this labor. These precious, fun moments were what we pictured before we had kids. It's what we looked forward to. But what we looked forward to was a romanticized ideal.

When we find ourselves struggling, we often need to shift away from ideals. Just because something sounds fun, or we see other people doing it, doesn't mean it's right or best for our family. We must make decisions on what labor to take on and what to let go of based on our values and our family's individual needs.

Assumption 1

Assumption: If I spend more time and money on something, it will have a greater impact.

Reframe: Sometimes the lowest investments yield the highest impact for my kids.

You don't necessarily need club-level sports activities or the latest, greatest, flashiest toys. Sometimes the smallest moments create the best interactions with your kids.

There's nothing wrong with big, expensive toys or exciting vacations. But you don't have to choose those things, and you certainly don't have to choose them frequently. More time and money don't necessarily correlate to greater impact.

Assumption 2

Assumption: My child needs more toys, more activities, more outings, and more trips to be happy.

Reframe: There is value in selectivity and in slowness—I don't have to always fill my children's time, or their toy boxes.

A happy childhood doesn't require a playroom full of toys or a calendar packed with extracurricular activities. We can choose less, if that's right for us and our family.

If you are a family that is currently overloaded with extracurricular activities and you want to begin to release some of that labor, start small. Drop one activity or protect one night a week, then continue to build up as it feels right. Find the balance that works for you and your child.

> A happy childhood doesn't require a playroom full of toys or a calendar packed with extracurricular activities.

Assumption 3

Assumption: The fun experiences I create are going to be magical.

Reframe: There will be good moments, good memories, and also stress and chaos.

It's okay to want to create magical moments, great memories, and fun for the family. But we must remember that for every moment we create, there is a mountain of invisible labor leading up to it. Sometimes that labor is worth it, but if we feel pressured to continuously create these moments, we can push ourselves beyond our capacity. We must weigh out what is worth it and what is not, finding areas of compromise, slowness, and simplicity.

It's also important to be realistic with our expectations—not every moment will be fully magical. We can embrace the fun and chaos at times and opt to forego it at other times.

Assumption 4

Assumption: Good moms are constantly creating memories, fun, and experiences for their children.

Reframe: Being a "good mom" doesn't require expensive, curated experiences.

The things that make us "good moms" are the ongoing bonds and connections, the safety and security we create for our children. We all want our children to experience fun and have positive memories of their childhood. But they don't necessarily need fantastical holidays or expensive vacations to do that. In fact, they will likely have a more positive memory of spending time with a happy, fulfilled mom who prioritized her mental health than one who is exhausted, overwhelmed, and resentful.

Assumption 5

Assumption: I must keep up with what everyone else is doing for their children.

Reframe: Just because other moms do it doesn't mean it's right for me or my family.

Remember that what we see on social media or hear about from other moms is part of the highlight reel. We don't know what goes on behind the scenes.

Having a highlight reel is great, but ours doesn't have to look like everyone else's. It doesn't have to include everybody else's ideas or traditions. And it doesn't have to be Pinterest-worthy. Instead, our highlight reel should be created based on our family values.

Assumption 6

Assumption: I have to keep up the same precedent, patterns, experiences, and traditions with each child so nobody misses out.

Reframe: As we add more children to the mix, logistics and practicalities change. It's unrealistic to expect the same of myself.

If you have multiple children, the invisible load multiplies greatly. It takes much more effort, time, energy, and often money to create the exact same experience when you have three children as it did when you had one. It's okay to alter or let go of certain experiences as you have more children. You're in an entirely different situation.

Assumption 7

Assumption: It's my role as a mom to create fun and magic for my child.
Reframe: This labor is not gendered. Other caregivers can play the same role in creating experiences.

We have been conditioned to assign this type of mental labor to moms, to the point where when people see dads wrapping Christmas gifts or taking their child to the park, we shower them with praise. But the bar doesn't need to be that low. There is nothing gendered about this labor.

Often, a mom is behind the scenes doing all the invisible work. Perhaps Mom did all the anticipation of preferences and interests, researched and planned presents for each child, and purchased and hid the gifts before her partner wrapped them. Or maybe Mom planned the outing and packed the bags for her partner before they took the kids to the park.

We often have to overcome the discomfort of passing off the labor and letting our partner play a more active role.

SKILLS AND TOOLS FOR RELEASING THIS LABOR

In this section, we'll cover skills and tools that include:

- Recognizing the true enemy
- Curating your social feeds
- Weighing "shoulds" against our values
- Establishing a rhythm to vacations and adventures
- Ways to make magic that are not all-consuming

Recognizing the True Enemy

When Frenel and I celebrated our first Christmas as a couple, I was shocked that this man carried on life just like it was any other season. There were no decorations, no tree, no traditions or nostalgic memories he was trying to recreate. After nearly going over to spread some Christmas spirit all over his apartment for him, we ended up having several conversations about media, consumerism, and how things are in Western cultures compared to elsewhere in the world.

Frenel has lived in countless countries all over Europe and Africa. He pointed out that when you've lived around the world, you learn that there are many ways you can celebrate a special day. He also expressed the way that marketing and consumerism feed into ideals about what holidays need to look like.

He's not wrong. Over the past twenty years, holiday spending in the US has more than doubled.[1] This isn't by accident—it is fueled by consumerism. The average American takes in between four to ten thousand advertisements in a day.[2]

Why am I telling you this? Because the purpose of advertisements is to make you feel like you lack something and sell you their product as a solution. As a one-off, that may not make much of a difference . . . but ad after ad after ad begins to send a message that you are not good enough, that you need to be doing more, buying more, and filling your home with more.

I truly believe this plays a big part in the paralysis parents can feel when selecting baby gear—choosing which bottle or crib or bassinet to buy (or any of the other hundreds of items we end up purchasing for baby). Every product sales page, every ad, tells you that your baby will not sleep or eat without this product, or that you will not be able to do your job if you don't have the newest and greatest thing.

This messaging seeps into our holidays, vacations, and day-to-day life. As a result, there is a whole branch of study on media literacy. To be aware and able to critically evaluate the messages you receive from the media is a skill, just like any of the others we've discussed in this book. And it's a skill that is very valuable for moms to have in their pockets. Why? Women are constantly targeted by the media about motherhood, parenting, their body image, their home, and more. These "aspirational" ads are often what subconsciously set the bar or expectations we hold for ourselves, even though they are often unrealistic and unattainable.

Part of being able to create present, authentic memories and fun with your children is being able to tune in to your values and what really makes you feel joy, rather than trying to emulate what we are told should bring us joy.

To truly uncover our own values and stay true to them, we must cut through social messaging. It is important to be able to critically evaluate the messages we are seeing in Hollywood, advertisements, and on our favorite shows.

When you see an advertisement for a fun family vacation where everyone is smiling and happy, looking carefree with no problems in sight, it's easy to get caught up in the message. But the Center for Media Literacy encourages us to ask ourselves:

- Who created this message?
- What creative techniques are used to attract my attention?
- How might different people understand this message differently than me?
- What values, lifestyles, and points of view are represented in, or omitted from, this message?
- Why is this message being sent?[3]

When we can see a message and think critically about it, who created it, and what they are trying to achieve, we can begin to see that we are in fact not flawed or lacking. It isn't that we aren't doing enough—it's that somebody is trying to sell us a product by influencing our narrative or thought process.

It is important to stay grounded in our values. I want you to know that you are enough, your parenting is enough, and whatever you provide for your children is enough. To make lasting memories, you don't need to buy into the messaging that more is more.

Curating Your Social Feeds

Much like media literacy, a healthy use of social media requires a deeper look at what we see. In many ways, social media can be even more influential than advertisements. Messages hit differently when we see them coming from family or people we look up to.

Social media often leaves us spiraling into comparison. I can recall countless times being trapped at home with three young children while Frenel worked in the city. I would sit around scrolling through social media, seeing all my friends out with their kids, having new experiences, traveling, etc. Meanwhile, I was literally trying to make it from one nap time to the next.

I felt like a failure. I felt like I wasn't doing enough for my kids. And I felt pressure to go out and try to keep up, even when I was barely surviving at home.

I honestly think it is a form of self-torture to continue to subject yourself to things on your social media feed that make you feel less about yourself. Here are some practical things to try if you find that social media causes you to spiral into negative self-talk and comparison:

Prune your social feeds

You don't have to unfollow or unfriend people if you don't want to, but you can still curate your feed based on your needs. After all, the other person likely doesn't mean any harm. Your feelings are more about you and where you are at.

For example, I had a good friend who used to constantly post her successful workout for the day. I, on the other hand, was struggling with task initiation. Just getting up in the morning and taking care of the basics for myself and three children felt overwhelming. And every time I saw her workout post, I felt awful. It wasn't about her—it was about my own experience and my mental health.

If you find yourself comparing to someone or feeling bad when seeing their posts, unfollow or mute their posts for a while.

Turn off your notifications

Just like advertising agencies, social media platforms have a goal—to keep you engaged. Notifications are designed to pull you in. I often would find myself checking a notification on my phone and being sucked right into scrolling. The best thing I've done for my mental health is turning off notifications. This allows you to choose when you want to scroll rather than letting the apps decide for you.

Mute ads

Commercials and advertisements are created to sell you not just a product, but an idea that you *need* their products to be the mom or person you want to be. This can often play into expectations, stereotypes, and mom guilt. Silence ads on television and social media to turn down this noise.

Set a timer

How 10:00 pm can suddenly become 1:00 am while scrolling TikTok, I'll never know. I love TikTok, and I'm not planning to give it up anytime soon—sometimes after a whole day of momming, it is nice to have a mindless scroll and be entertained by your feed.

However, if you feel like when you are scrolling you end up feeling crappy about yourself or filled with self-doubt, there need to be some limits in place. Maybe you set a timer to scroll for thirty minutes or for fifteen—whatever gives you a break without impacting your mental health. Setting these types of limits can be a protective form of self-care.

Scroll mindfully

Break out of the mindless scroll. Check in after each video or every few minutes to do a mind and body scan to see how you are feeling. What messages have you taken in or what have you thought about yourself while scrolling for the past five minutes?

Taking the time to evaluate the messages we are internalizing based on what we are ingesting on social media is important and a way of caring for yourself.

Weighing "Shoulds" Against Our Values

When you can critically evaluate messages and recognize expectations or "shoulds" that someone is trying to place on you, you can stop them in their tracks and weigh them against your values.

For example, I find that there is so much messaging and pressure to have your children in a bajillion activities or you are doing them some kind of injustice. We had a brief break from this messaging during the pandemic, but it came back full force as things opened up. In fact, it felt like everyone began to socialize and do activities to make up for lost time. It is me—I am everyone. We signed two of our three boys up for hockey . . . and I regretted it from the first weekend in. Little did we know that games and practices would be at 7:00 am or 8:00 am BOTH Saturday and Sunday mornings . . . and at different arenas for each boy, leaving my husband and I frantically going in different directions all weekend.

Now, if I am describing your weekend schedule and you actually *like* it (and I know many of you do), all the power to you. I know hockey families here that are all about this life. They love it. It meshes with their values and they prioritize it as a result. But that is not us.

What we found is that our kids enjoyed it at first . . . and then it became pulling teeth to get anyone up and motivated to go. It wasn't long before it became a crummy way to spend our weekends. It didn't align with the slowness or tone of the house Frenel and I aim to foster.

It was important for us to recognize that. It doesn't mean that we are going to scrap activities altogether—it simply means that we are going to weigh the commitment and culture of the activities we choose against our lifestyle and values. Knowing our values helps us to know what we do and do not want, so that we can make decisions that feel true to ourselves. If you are hazy about what your values are, revisit chapter 3 for a refresh.

Establishing a Rhythm to Vacations and Adventures

As someone who gets very bored with the day-to-day, I often find myself wanting to plan spontaneous adventures or getting grand ideas for trips or experiences that I want to execute quickly. But this is neither practical nor financially responsible most of the time. It can be helpful to have a routine or structure to your planned vacation or leisure time so that you have something in the pipeline to look forward to.

For example, sitting down to carve out the various details and put a loose adventure or vacation plan in place for a set number of times per quarter or year can help you to feel hopeful while providing some predictability. If this is something that feels right to you, here are some questions to start the ball rolling on this conversation:

- How many weeks of paid vacation do we have as a family this year?

- How are we going to spend those weeks? (Save some for childcare days? Reserve them for vacation?)

- What is our annual budget for vacations/experiences?

- Do we want to spend this budget on one big experience or break it down into four smaller experiences—one per quarter?

- What are some day-trip adventures we would like to do this year or quarter and what is the cost?

- What is the rhythm to our current childcare? Do we need to factor closures or spring or summer breaks into our planning?

- Who is going to take charge on the planning, or how will the research and tasks be divided? Will we rotate and take turns, share in the planning and execution?

This doesn't mean you will create a set-in-stone plan after one conversation. But it can help you pencil in some loose plans so that when you feel an impulse to book something or create fun out of guilt or comparison, there are some guardrails in place.

I also want to take a moment here to acknowledge the financial and socioeconomic privilege involved in being able to travel and take vacations. If you can take one family vacation a year, let alone several, you likely experience some level of financial privilege that not everybody has. There are many families out there who can't afford to pop out for a weekend every quarter or create big family trips. I want you to remember that quality time with the family doesn't have to include big getaways. Which leads me to my next tip . . .

Ways to Make Magic That Are Not All-Consuming

Maybe you don't have a budget for vacations or adventures. Maybe you are trying to make ends meet. It can be hard if you feel like you "should" be doing more but you simply don't have the financial means to. But creating lasting memories with our children is not linked to spending money—this is a belief that we must unravel.

Memories are joy-filled moments that make a lasting impression in our child's mind. One of my favorite memories as a kid was a "pageant birthday" my mom threw for me. She had some of my friends over, allowed us each to choose a dress from her closet, set up a curtain from my room, and treated the hallway as a runway. We each got a prize (a rolled-up piece of paper) and it was a ridiculous amount of fun.

Traditions, memories, and fun are not inherently linked to spending, and they are also not meant to be carried by only you. Grandparents, family friends, and partners can help share in this load. I recall making bread and baking with my grandmother as a kid—some of my fondest summer break memories.

Doing a mutually enjoyable activity with someone you care about is the perfect place to start. Here are some activities that come to mind (meant to spark some ideas, not to place expectations). Share this list with support people around you who can share in this load:

- Baking
- Cooking
- Creating
  - Arts & crafts
  - Music
- Unique moments
  - Fort-building
  - Sleepovers
  - Campouts in the living room

- Dress-up dinners or parties

- Yes days—days where you let the kids plan the play or activities and you say yes (I put limits on these . . . it is about activities together, not buying items, or allowing them to be the parent. They can plan the day but within realistic parameters.)

- Picnics

These activities are all fun ways to create special memories. But memories are also in the little consistent things you do regularly and in the ways you show up. The tuck-ins at bedtime, the snuggles, the safety and relationship you have built—those things get internalized as well and carry more weight than a one-off special experience.

IF YOU ONLY REMEMBER ONE THING

Core memories can be unlocked without spending money, buying flashy things, or taking big vacations. It is often the little things, the consistent showing up, that matters more for your child.

IF YOU ONLY DO ONE THING

Start weighing the "shoulds" that you are holding onto against your values. You don't have to keep up with social media friends or influencers, or with ideas of motherhood that don't fit what truly matters to you. (Revisit page 239 for more on the "shoulds" versus your values.)

THE INVISIBLE LOAD OF MANAGING
YOUR MENTAL HEALTH

Noticing and anticipating your triggers

Carrying the weight of childhood wounds

Practicing self-compassion and self-reflection

Researching therapists

Navigating therapy and medications

Managing guilt and worry

Parenting while feeling overwhelmed

Navigating anxiety and intrusive thoughts

Setting boundaries

Practicing real self-care

Advocating for your own needs

Coping with the pressure to break cycles

9

MANAGING YOUR
MENTAL HEALTH

Before becoming a mother, I put a tremendous amount of work into my own self-development and healing. I understood my emotions, I was able to set healthy boundaries, and I learned how to build interdependent relationships. I knew how to communicate and rarely lost my cool or raised my voice. And I thought that would all carry right into motherhood, without question.

Here I was setting up expectations for myself without ever spending a single lived moment in the role of a parent. Once I was on the job, though, things changed. Motherhood has a unique way of bringing up our past through a different set of eyes — the fresh eyes of a new parent who often can't understand how our own wounds happened or needs went unmet.

Emotional baggage I thought had been dealt with came bubbling to the surface. Pain and resentment that I thought had been worked through suddenly felt raw, fresh, and new. I found myself grappling with wounds from my childhood that I thought had been put to rest.

At the time, I wondered what was wrong with me. I had no idea that this is a common part of the journey for many as they adjust to their new role as parents. We often don't realize how much having a baby changes not just our lives but our *identities*.

The transition into motherhood, known as matrescence, can come with a lot of big (very valid) feelings. It is a reforming of who you are. The process includes:

- Coping with mixed feelings about your role and grief over the loss of your old life

- Reconciling your ideals and expectations of motherhood with the reality of the role

- Navigating being a "good mother" and what it means to do things "right"

- Learning how to juggle all the responsibilities of your new role (and determining which to let go of)

- Confronting wounds arising from your upbringing as you raise your child

Online, you often see parenting tips about how to help with your child's big feelings—but what about our big feelings? How about learning to regulate myself while simultaneously trying to teach these skills to my children? That's what I really needed.

I knew motherhood would change me. But I thought those changes would be centered around priorities and activities. I had no idea that motherhood would rock me to my core, completely changing the way I viewed myself and my own emotions.

There have been times when I felt like I couldn't recognize myself. Who was this person who was so easily triggered? Who was this person who struggled to cope with emotions that she had just finally learned how to control? Who was this person who clenched her jaw, full of anger? Who was this person who wondered day after day if she was failing in her most important role?

Not only was I coping with the Mother Load, struggling with my own emotional baggage and wounds while trying to learn the hardest, highest-stakes job I had ever had, but I was also coping with sleep deprivation, undiagnosed postpartum depression, and overstimulation—all of which created a recipe for a full emotional breakdown.

Motherhood brought up a lot that I wasn't expecting—childhood wounds that I thought were long-resolved and buried. Pain as I grieved what I hadn't had. Postpartum depression that I didn't recognize until my breakdown/breakthrough. And much to my surprise, an absolute inability to continue with my path of perfectionism. I could barely initiate tasks. I forgot about things I intended to do. I would get so overwhelmed by the noise and stress that I wanted to hide in a dark closet, alone without all the chaos. I found myself struggling with time management even more than I ever had before (which I wasn't aware was possible).

> I had no idea motherhood would rock me to my core, completely changing the way I viewed myself and my own emotions.

Part of that struggle was certainly the depression. But what I didn't realize for many years was that there was even *more* going on.

It wasn't until I was having one of my boys evaluated for ADHD that it finally clicked—I was also coping with it. Statistically, there was a 41 percent chance that I also had ADHD if one of my children had it.[1] It took some time to piece the puzzle together that this was a cornerstone of many of my struggles with the Mother Load.

In retrospect, ADHD wasn't just an additional struggle—it might have contributed to my postpartum depression. Undiagnosed and untreated ADHD is considered a risk factor for anxiety and depression.[2] And, just like seeking help for postpartum depression opened my eyes to a new path in motherhood, seeking help for ADHD opened the world up for me. I saw an almost immediate change in task initiation, my ability to handle overstimulation, and my tolerance for difficult situations. I was able to show up in an entirely different way, in my business, in my home, and in my life in general.

But one of the biggest differences was my ability to have compassion for myself. I'd spent years trying to shame or blame myself into just *being better.* Into just doing what I had to do. Into just not procrastinating. Into just handling everything the way other people seemed to be able to.

I hear from moms every day who do the same—whether they're neurodivergent, struggling with postpartum mood concerns, or generally overwhelmed and burnt out from the sheer weight of the Mother Load. We're often terrible at determining whether our experience is "normal" or a sign of something a little bit more. And because we are carrying messages about what we *should* do as "good moms," we end up putting blame on ourselves. We somehow believe if we just beat ourselves up enough, we can compartmentalize our mental health and become the moms we want to be. But we can't bully ourselves out of mental health struggles. We have to meet ourselves where we need to be met.

If you had a broken arm, you wouldn't just try to skate through life without going to the doctor and getting a cast or a sling—and you certainly wouldn't tell yourself you were failing if your pain kept you from functioning at full capacity. So, when it comes to mental health, why would we treat it any differently?

Each of you out there reading this book is in a different boat. Some of you are struggling with depression or anxiety. Some of you are neurodivergent. Some of you are carrying childhood trauma, unhealed wounds, and generational cycles that you want to break away from. Some of you are simply crumbling under an unfair weight of emotional and mental labor.

No matter where you are, I want you to know that it isn't your fault. Your mental health matters. Your needs matter. And taking care of yourself matters, whether that means seeking therapy, starting on medication, or just using this book to alleviate some of the immediate pressure of the Mother Load so that you can make space to do the work in *this* chapter (which in turn will lay the foundation to truly release the load).

Every load that I have covered so far in this book matters—and every load has mental health components. But the real weight of the Mother Load culminates here—the pressure, the worries, the guilt, the shame, the struggle to meet our own needs or break the patterns that have been passed down to us.

Becoming a mom doesn't mean we don't experience a wide range of emotions. It doesn't mean that we will never struggle to stay peaceful and calm. It doesn't mean we will never struggle with our mental health. It doesn't mean not having negative emotions, or experiencing mom rage or overstimulation. It doesn't mean we will never repeat patterns based on what was modeled for us. It doesn't mean we get it right all the time. It means that we have done the work and learned the skills to help us manage those situations in a healthier way.

The truth is that our feet are never put to the fire like they are in motherhood. At no other time in our lives are we as likely to sacrifice our own needs, to carry such an immense emotional and mental load, and to hold ourselves to such high standards of perfection with such a high-stakes mindset. And many of us didn't grow up with parents who acknowledged, or even understood, emotional needs (through no fault of their own—they likely didn't have these skills or tools either). This means that not only are we thrust into a highly emotional situation without our needs being met, but we're doing it without the skills that we actually need.

> The Mother Load culminates here—the pressure, worries, guilt, shame, and struggle to meet our needs or break patterns passed down to us.

There is a massive emotional and psychological load here: navigating our own mental health struggles or needs, processing trauma, regulating our emotions, teaching ourselves skills we didn't learn when we were younger. This *is* labor—time-consuming and energy-consuming labor.

But it is labor that matters, for each of us. And it is labor that we deserve to devote ourselves to—because it is labor that creates the path for releasing the Mother Load.

THE LOAD OF CARING FOR OUR MENTAL HEALTH

The adjustment to motherhood, the matrescence we go through, can feel like a free fall into a dark and lonely pit. We're experiencing massive shifts, not just in our priorities and our relationships, but in our identity. Overnight, it feels like we lose who we are and become somebody different. There is often grief about losing our old life, frustration at the uncertainty in our new role, and disappointment at the clash between expectations and reality (for more about the postpartum adjustment period, you can refer back to page 111).

New parents are at high risk of developing postpartum depression and anxiety. They might carry the weight of those mental health struggles and the symptoms that go with them. They also likely must carry out the emotional labor of monitoring those symptoms and deciding whether they are normal post-baby experiences or signs of needing help. Then, if they do decide they need help, they carry even more labor—seeking out therapists and doctors, deciding whether to take medication, following a treatment plan, and trying to advocate for their own needs. Even if parents don't develop depression or anxiety, they still carry mental health labor, both in and out of stressful moments.

As we move through these loads, it's important to remember that this labor is different from the others. Because this load exists within ourselves, there is no handing this labor off. We can't pass our own emotional regulation to our partner.

So, even more than in the other loads in this book, most of the releasing here comes from within as well. We need to understand that if we want to reduce the Mother Load, we can't neglect our mental health. What we can do is learn the skills before a crisis so that we can put them into play and manage our mental health, freeing up our capacity to do the rest of the work that goes into releasing the Mother Load.

In our day-to-day moments, we often find ourselves struggling to take care of immediate needs and navigate stress, worries, and emotional self-regulation. Daily labor of mental health care includes noticing stress signs in our body or indicators of anxiety, worry, overstimulation, or anger in motherhood. We navigate shame and guilt, anticipate our stressors and triggers, and anticipate when we need to take a break or cool off.

We are all at different places on our mental health and self-development journey. Where you are on that path will dictate what the anticipation of needs looks like. Early in the journey, this often involves acknowledging and accepting the need to do this internal work. It evolves into noticing your own signs and symptoms that your needs aren't being met (rage, irritability, stress signs, physiological changes such as clenched jaws, tightened stomachs, and other physiological signs of anger, stress, or distress).

At first, we might only notice that we are angry or raising our voices. We often need to learn to dig beneath the surface. This involves getting attuned to our body and our indicators—such as heart racing, clenching jaws, stomach tension. It takes a great deal of noticing to be able to manage our mental health daily. As we develop more awareness and understanding, we practice mindfulness, work on our awareness, and check in with ourselves often during this stage.

We also anticipate the things that contribute to our emotional state, like sleep deprivation, lack of a break, hunger, or stress due to deadlines or to-dos. We might notice intrusive thoughts of harm coming to our children, or other signs of anxiety, such as a racing heart or mind.

It's also important to note that many of us have not been trained to do this labor. Regulating our own emotions can be extremely difficult—especially when we come from unhealthy patterns or family dynamics. If what was modeled for us was yelling or conflict avoidance, we will often default to that, especially when we are stressed out or overwhelmed. Working through that requires a significant amount of emotional labor—but even though it feels daunting, it is worth it.

Another key component of prioritizing our mental health is the embodiment of true self-care—and when I say "self-care," I don't mean bath bombs and massages and bubble baths. There's nothing wrong with those things. However, when we tell moms it's their job to practice self-care and relaxation, we often add labor to their plates—labor that essentially serves as a band-aid. It might feel nice to take a bubble bath, but if the true problem is overwhelm, postpartum depression, or a critical inner voice, that relaxing bubble bath won't feel much like self-care when we realize we're still critical of ourselves there too. True self-care is working within, comprehensively prioritizing your own mental health, and learning to be kind and compassionate with yourself. Until we do that, no amount of massages or candles will truly help.

Dr. Pooja Lakshmin, author of *Real Self-Care*, joined me on episode 164 of *The Momwell Podcast* to discuss what self-care truly is.

The wellness industry has taken a vital topic and turned it into bubble baths and pedicures. But Dr. Pooja explained that real self-care is less about the methods we use and more about principles to live by—it's a commitment to ourselves to meet our needs.[3]

There's nothing wrong with bubble baths or massages (and I absolutely support you carving out time for those things), but the real self-care is:

- Putting your needs on an equal playing field
- Protecting your time
- Advocating for yourself
- Setting boundaries
- Giving yourself permission to take time for yourself

Personally, I think that mothers struggle with self-care because they feel unworthy and guilty for taking it. Moms often feel like taking the steps to prioritize their needs so they can go for dinner with a friend or routinely get to the gym is centering their needs above those in their family. They are used to sacrificing their needs for others—so even the smallest shifts toward their own needs can feel selfish. They end up getting visited by the mom-guilt surveillance crew when they try. One way I want you to challenge this unworthiness narrative is to ask yourself if you would carve out or protect the time for your partner or child to do the same task.

If your partner was struggling with their mental or physical health and wanted to go to the gym once a week, would you encourage them to? If your child was passionate about music and wanted to attend piano lessons, would you help figure out the logistics?

So . . . why not you? Embracing acts of self-care is not selfish. It is simply treating yourself the way you would treat the rest of your family.

NAVIGATING RELATIONSHIP DYNAMICS

We often experience shifts in our relationships (romantic, social, and familial) after we become moms, which can impact our mental health as well. We've likely not had to set such a volume of boundaries or build the level of communication skills that become necessary after these relationship shifts. This brings new skills to attain and new emotional challenges that we must overcome. Without those skills, resentment can surface, bringing even more emotional labor that we must unpack and work through.

This labor might include noticing conflict patterns or areas of resentment, paying attention to what's going on below the surface when we react negatively to a partner or family member, identifying triggers, and determining where we feel our needs are not being met. We might research relationship counselors or online courses to help us work through resentment, intimacy barriers, or other relationship difficulties. We might also create plans for regular check-ins, date nights, family time, or friend outings.

If we struggle with communication, we might have to read articles or listen to podcasts on communication skills and healthy conflict. These are often big, intense skills to develop, especially if we didn't have a positive model of this in our lives. Because many of us haven't built these skills or developed these muscles, we sometimes struggle to communicate our needs. Many of us didn't grow up being taught healthy boundary setting. We weren't told it was okay to advocate for what we needed. In fact, we were often told the opposite (to "respect" our elders or to sacrifice our own needs to please those around us).

Once we become moms, the need for boundaries becomes so much more obvious. We often learn to set boundaries both within partnerships and in other relationships. Family members (or even complete strangers) might tell us how to parent or interject their values onto us. Part of managing our own mental health becomes learning how to set boundaries, stick to them, and push for our own needs to be met (more on this in the skills section of this chapter).

BREAKING CYCLES

Motherhood has a way of stirring up old trauma and pain from a different vantage point. When you enter motherhood and see your childhood through the lens of a parent, it hits differently.

New moms often find themselves grappling with old wounds, trauma, and emotional baggage. They revisit their relationships with their own parents and the way they were brought up. Sometimes, these wounds have been buried for decades, only to rise and cause pain after becoming a mom. They might suddenly feel sadness, grief, anger, or resentment that has long been buried toward their parents for the way they were raised or for tough upbringing experiences. Learning how to process and move through those emotions takes a great deal of invisible labor.

Breaking cycles often involves anticipating our own triggers and patterns—noticing what behaviors result in mom rage or stress and tuning in to why we feel that way. It requires recognizing when we feel angry *before* we get to the point of losing our cool, which involves tuning in to our body's physiological signs and staying calm in stressful moments. Getting curious about your own patterns requires a great deal of courage. You might face pain, trauma, and wounds in this process. But understanding our past helps us show up as the parents we want to be.

If we want to break cycles, we often must look inward for the *why* and confront our childhood wounds. This can be particularly painful work, and it often takes years to fully process. When trying to be a cycle-breaker, self-compassion is important. When you have spent your entire life experiencing certain family patterns, they are very likely to be your default, even if you consciously try to break away from them—especially when you are sleep-deprived, stressed out, or overwhelmed.

Forming new patterns requires encountering resistance. Think of it as standing in a cornfield. We have been walking a path that is well-worn—the default path that is ingrained in our brains. As we learn and practice new skills, we form new pathways and rewire our brain, breaking patterns and cycles. This ability to change our brain patterns is called neuroplasticity. It is difficult to push through the corn, to create a new way forward. But it will get easier over time.

It is also important to remember that breaking unhelpful patterns through our parenting doesn't mean we will never experience negative emotions. It means that we have done the work and learned the skills to help us manage those situations in a healthier way. The amount of anger I've felt in tough parenting moments has surprised me at times, but how I view that anger and how I manage it are what breaks cycles.

MENTAL HEALTH AND THE INVISIBLE LOAD

As we look at this emotional labor within ourselves, it's important to understand how tied it is to the invisible load.

It isn't just its own set of labor that we carry day in and day out. It also keeps us from releasing any of the rest of it. Ironically, it even interferes with our ability to show up as the moms we want to be. While we're struggling with our own emotional and mental health, it's much harder to be present and patient. The pressure we put on ourselves often causes us to overlook the work that we are doing internally—to learn these skills, to regulate ourselves, to show up in a different way. And, as we overlook it and strive for perfection, we leave ourselves with less capacity to deal with all the other loads.

This becomes a vicious cycle of perfection, pressure, shame, and then recommitting to do better tomorrow—a cycle that is excruciatingly hard to break out of.

During the postpartum period, we often put our own needs on the back burner. We cram down a granola bar in between feeding the baby instead of eating a full meal. We put off moving our body, believing there will be time for it later. And when it comes to our mental health, we try to do the same. We might avoid or withdraw from our problems, or simply never check in with ourselves and listen to our needs. But the more we neglect our mental health, the harder it becomes to function as a mom.

When we put our mental health on the back burner until we're in crisis, we make it that much harder to develop the skills we need to regulate and make changes. But if we can prioritize our mental health from the beginning (or starting today), we can learn those skills and make changes *before* a burnout or breakdown moment. We can learn to pay attention and take care of ourselves, stepping out of the cycle.

You'll notice that this chapter does not contain load maps like the others. That is because this load cannot be passed off. But that doesn't mean our support system can't share in this load. Partners or other support members can help with research, remind us of strategies and tools, and provide a sounding board as we work through our mental health. They can help us book doctor's appointments or help create systems to remember to take our medication. Just because this is internal work doesn't mean we have to do it all alone.

Mental Wellness Check-In

Let's pause and do a quick pulse check on your current mental status. It's important to monitor our mental health and seek support when something has shifted. Take a moment to answer these prompts based on how you've been feeling over the last 7-14 days:

	Never	Rarely	Sometimes	Often	Always
I feel frustrated about my motherhood role					
I find myself feeling tired or fatigued, even if I get enough quality sleep					
I experience irritability or mom rage					
I feel overwhelmed by the mental load in the home					

I feel low or cry without an obvious trigger					
I feel resentful toward my partner					
I compare myself to other moms and feel as if I don't measure up					
I find myself thinking that I am not a good mom or that my child deserves better					
I feel guilt or shame about not doing enough					
I feel like I can't cope with the pressure of motherhood					
I find it hard to complete my own daily hygiene or care tasks					
I avoid tasks or outings because they make me feel anxious					
I feel like a burden or like my family would be better off without me					
I haven't been feeling like myself					
I wonder whether I should seek mental health support					

If the majority of your answers to these statements are skewed toward "often" or "always," this is an indication that you are struggling and could use some mental health support.

Take these answers to your primary care doctor or a therapist for further discussion. You can also contact the Postpartum Support International HelpLine by calling 1-800-944-4773 or texting 800-944-4773 for English or 971-203-7773 for Spanish. (Please note that this is not an emergency line—if you are in an emergency situation, call your country's emergency line right away.)

ASSUMPTIONS THAT REINFORCE
THE LOAD WE CARRY

Mental health and motherhood are forever intertwined. Intensive mothering tells us to give and give and give of ourselves, neglecting our own needs in the process. And yet, it also tells us to be beacons of light, joy, and nurturing.

Until we confront these beliefs and put them to rest, we will never measure up to our internal expectations. When we sacrifice our own mental health, we suffer as moms and as individuals.

The best thing we can do, both for ourselves and for our children, is to develop the skills we need to stay mentally well.

Assumption 1

Assumption: Mental well-being is a destination.
Reframe: Healing and mental well-being are processes—they are ongoing and require attention, adjustment, and focus.

We often think of mental health in black-and-white terms. We're either healthy or unwell, stable or unstable. We end up dismissing concerns and symptoms because we're sure we're "fine."

But would we do the same with physical health? Would you decide that you were just "fine," so you never needed to work out, eat vegetables, or visit the doctor for a wellness check? Of course not—because we understand that physical health is not a destination.

On episode 3 of *The Momwell Podcast*, reproductive psychiatrist Dr. Kristin Lasseter pointed out that we all have mental health, just as we all have physical health. And just like our physical health, we must take care of our mental health.[4]

Mental well-being doesn't just come in "healthy" or "unhealthy." It is an ongoing process. Healing and wellness don't just happen—they take time and attention and ongoing work.

Assumption 2

Assumption: As a mom, I should automatically know what to do in high-stakes moments.

Reframe: It takes skills and practice to control and regulate emotions.

It isn't enough to just say we're "never" going to yell, scold, or lose our cool. That expectation we hold for ourselves doesn't automatically grant us the skills we need to parent in the way we want.

The commitment to breaking cycles is great—but it's just a start. It doesn't mean we will automatically know how to handle triggering situations or how to respond to our children. We need to learn self-regulation skills—and even when we do know them, we're still going to make mistakes sometimes.

Assumption 3

Assumption: Struggling with my mental health means that I am failing as a mom.

Reframe: I am human—it is normal to struggle with my mental health sometimes.

We often extend grace to others when they struggle with their mental health. We might even feel self-compassionate if we struggle at other times in our lives. And yet, when we become moms, we feel as if we are failing if we can't motivate ourselves, if we don't feel joyful all the time, or if we struggle to cope and adjust. We look at ourselves as weak if we need help.

The truth is that we all experience times when our mental health is not at its best. It's unrealistic to expect anything different in our motherhood role. Asking for help doesn't make you weak, and it doesn't make you a failure. In fact, it may be the most courageous thing you could ever do!

Assumption 4

Assumption: I've moved on from my past—it's all water under the bridge.
Reframe: The roadmap that we have been given for parenting directly draws on our past—revisiting it is inevitable.

People are often surprised at the sadness, grief, resentment, or anger that they feel toward their parents when they become moms. We're shocked to feel these mother or father wounds rise to the surface. But when we become parents, we see our experiences in childhood through a different lens. Old wounds, trauma, or simply experiences that left us feeling hurt often come up. Other times we might see situations from our own childhood in a new light, with fresh understanding or curiosity. Motherhood brings complex emotions that we must navigate.

Assumption 5

Assumption: As a mom, I can derive fulfillment by putting everyone else's needs above my own.
Reframe: I need to prioritize my own needs and my own mental health—when moms are well, our families are well.

Intensive mothering tells us that we must sacrifice everything—our time, our energy, our identity, our needs. But this is a direct line to burnout. We unintentionally create a self-fulfilling loop; we martyr ourselves, believing we will find fulfillment, but when that fulfillment doesn't come, we keep pushing harder and harder—until we're burnt out, lost, and depleted.

I'm not asking you to forsake the needs of your children. I'm not even asking you to put yourself first. But if we think of ourselves and our needs as *equal* to the rest of our family, and we value our own mental health, it creates a ripple effect. It makes us feel more fulfilled, less overwhelmed, and freer. And in turn, our children see that happiness—and learn to take care of their mental health in the process.

SKILLS AND TOOLS FOR RELEASING THIS LABOR

It might be tempting to skip over this foundational work. However, I would argue that it is absolutely essential to releasing the Mother Load. Until we take a holistic look at our mental health and understand what this work entails, we will likely continue to feel flustered, overwhelmed, and lacking capacity to do the rest of the work in this book.

In this section, we'll cover skills and tools that include:

- Putting your needs on equal ground

- Boundaries as a form of self-care

- Boundary scripts for common parenting situations

- Dealing with boundary violators

- Radical responsibility for your needs

- Tuning in to your needs

- Self-care in and out of the moment

- Communicating our needs to others

- Radical acceptance

Putting Your Needs on Equal Ground

For many moms, the idea of putting themselves first feels very selfish—it goes so forcefully against the grain of how we have been socialized to put others' needs before our own.

When we're beginning this inner work, the idea of putting ourselves first can feel like too far of a leap. It might even feel impractical, especially when you have little helpless newborns or dependent toddlers with urgent needs. The goal here isn't to center your needs above the rest of your family's (although I am very mom-centered and focused). Instead, the goal is to see and commit to your needs being *equal* to those around you. This is true self-care, which we will discuss further in a moment.

These things are of equal importance:

- Child's bath and hygiene
- Family being fed
- Child having social opportunities
- Child having hobbies/ activities
- Child attending care appointments

- Mom's showers and hygiene
- Mom being fed
- Mom having social opportunities
- Mom having hobbies/ interests
- Mom attending care appointments

None of these tasks or needs are particularly earth-shattering on their own—but when all are neglected in the name of being a good mother, the effects are felt.

I want you to understand that meeting your needs isn't selfish. It doesn't put you above your family or take away from your role—it simply puts you on an equal playing field in terms of importance. Committing to seeing your needs this way is a true act of self-care.

Boundaries as a Form of Self-Care

Many moms grew up as people-pleasers. But people-pleasing is really code for a boundaryless life. A life with no boundaries feels extremely chaotic—full of resentment, anger, and frustration at the people in our lives for not anticipating our needs or taking a hint. A boundaryless life can leave you feeling like you are at the mercy of others and that you give more to others than they give in return.

Sometimes, we don't even realize we struggle with boundaries until we enter motherhood. But once we become moms, we are often required to set boundaries more than ever before. Guests pop by unannounced, grandparents feel entitled to access their grandchildren, and people bombard you with unsolicited advice about how to parent.

That's why we start to truly feel the effects of our struggles with boundaries after becoming moms. On episode 93 of *The Momwell Podcast*, Dr.

Ashurina Ream shared that navigating parenthood with no boundaries often feels like living with a backyard that has no fence. Everyone is freely entering your property, coming into your house, questioning what you're grilling for dinner, and using your toys and equipment without asking permission. This is a recipe for resentment and frustration.[5]

Boundaries are a form of self-care because they clearly teach people what we will and will not tolerate in our interaction with them. One of the biggest worries I hear from clients when discussing boundary-setting is that others will get mad or upset with them. And, while there are cases of boundary violators who won't like our boundaries, most people like to know the rules of engagement in your relationship with them.

If you are in healthy relationships and friendships, the people in your life may be overstepping your boundaries in error, not realizing the impact it is having on you. But you can set boundaries, lay down the rules of engagement, and change the way people interact with you. It is your responsibility to set boundaries, based on your commitment to your own self-care, and your commitment to put yourself on an even playing field with your partner or your child.

So, what happens when people don't respect our boundaries? There may be times when we have boundary violators in our lives—those whom we have set a clear boundary with before, only for them to continue to repeat the behavior. These can be tricky to navigate . . . but that doesn't mean that boundaries shouldn't be set or held in these cases.

Boundary Scripts for Common Parenting Situations

Having go-to scripts can help us establish firm, clear boundaries and avoid slipping into unwanted people-pleasing patterns. Here are some helpful scripts to lean back on in common parenting situations.

When unsolicited comments come in about your parenting style
- "I understand you are coming from a place of concern, but in our family we . . ."

- "I can see how much you care, but my partner and I have decided . . ."

- "I can see how much you care. If we need your help with something, we will be sure to ask."

- "I understand that is how you parent, and it's okay to have a different approach."

When people show up with little notice or unannounced

- "It's not a good time right now. If you'd like to come for a visit, please plan with me in advance."

- "I know you're in the area . . . Thanks for thinking of us, but right now is not a good time."

- "I am home and free today, so you can visit for half an hour, but next time make sure to plan ahead because our schedule is unpredictable."

When others are telling you how to parent

- "I appreciate that this is how you approach things. It's okay for us to do things differently."

- "I can see how that works for your family and what you value. However, we approach things differently—and that's okay."

- "I understand that is how you do things. The beauty of parenting is that there are many effective approaches."

- "I can see where you're coming from, and I am glad to hear that works for you and your family."

- "There is no one right way to parent, so it is okay that we approach things differently."

When someone is doing something you don't like

- "I would appreciate if you would ask me first before doing . . ."

- "I can see you're trying to help. In our home we approach it this way . . ."

- "You see how they [insert child cue]? That means they don't like [insert boundary (to be tickled like that, to be fed that way, etc.)]."

- "I know you're trying to help, but when you [insert action], it makes me feel [insert emotion]. Next time, please [insert positive need (do this instead, call ahead, ask to do XYZ)]."

Dealing With Boundary Violators

People with healthy boundaries tend to respect and appreciate when we express things we do and don't like. They care for us, and they want to show up for us in a way that truly meets our needs. But this isn't *always* the case.

You may have others in your life who are more focused on what they want than listening to your rules of engagement. They might bulldoze over your boundary, even when you have stated it clearly and directly. These people are boundary violators—those who clearly see the line you have drawn in the sand and who choose to walk all over it.

With boundary violators, you will still need to clearly assert your boundary. You might need to parrot it many times to reinforce it. But there are other measures you can put in place for an added sense of safety and security.

For example, if your mother or mother-in-law tends to enter your home and make judgmental or harsh comments, create conflict, or make you feel uncomfortable, and you have tried boundary-setting scripts to no avail, the next step would be to create physical boundaries.

This can look like:

Meeting in a public space

This tends to ensure boundary violators will be on better behavior because there are other people around. Often outings like lunch or going to a playground have a clear and distinct meeting and departing time, not allowing the other person to overstay their welcome.

Adjusting the frequency of contact

The idea of reducing contact with family members can feel very uncomfortable. The importance of family relationships varies significantly from person to person—and there are many factors that play a role, such as culture and upbringing. Cutting off a family member entirely may feel like a non-option for some people, which I completely respect. But it doesn't have to be all-or-nothing. One thing you can do for your own mental health is adjust the frequency of your interactions with boundary violators. Just because they call during dinner doesn't mean you need to answer the phone. Just because they text you doesn't mean you need to immediately text back. You can set a frequency of interaction with people in your life that you can manage mentally and emotionally.

When I bring this up with clients, they often express concern that reducing contact would upset the other person. If the boundary violator in your life is a parent or close family member, you might have been made to feel responsible for their emotions and happiness growing up. But if an adult cannot respect your boundaries while interacting with you, it is perfectly acceptable for you to protect yourself. They do not deserve to bulldoze down the door at the cost of your mental and emotional health. Working through how to set and hold these boundaries is a cornerstone of emotional well-being.

Tuning in to your values

I had a boundary violator in my life, and it was one of the most tumultuous and damaging relationships I've ever experienced. But at the end of the day, this person was a close family member—and I didn't want to have the regret of cutting them off completely or not allowing them to see my children. After really stepping back, tuning in to my values, and determining what was important to me, I decided to visit this person on major holidays a few times a year. This allowed them to be a part of major milestones and celebrations, while also shielding me from the day-to-day conflict and pain that comes from allowing a boundary violator in.

Ultimately, you are the advocate of your needs and boundaries and are responsible for ensuring they are clearly stated and known to those around you when necessary. After you have communicated and reiterated the boundary a couple of times, if the person doesn't seem to be getting it or doesn't seem interested in understanding your perspective, it may be time to up the boundaries and buffers you have in place.

Radical Responsibility for Your Needs

So many of us didn't get what we needed when we were children. Saying that doesn't mean we hate our parents or are being disrespectful. It doesn't mean we blame them. We can acknowledge the fact that we had unmet needs in childhood and still understand that our parents did the best they could. That doesn't change the fact that when our emotional needs were unmet, we experienced real pain—pain that often stays with us and impacts all our relationships in the future.

When this happens, we can end up with a hole that we want to be filled. We want someone to truly see us. We want someone to take care of us. We want someone to anticipate our needs and fulfill them. But what we often do is expect our partner to step into that role. We want them to anticipate our needs and fulfill them because that would make us feel loved.

I can totally relate—I had been strong and cared for myself and everyone around me from such a young age that I wanted to be cared for and loved the same way in return. But lean in for a second—I'm going to get real here—it is *not* your partner's responsibility to care for you in the ways you weren't cared for.

Should they care for you and care about your needs? Yes. But are your needs theirs to take responsibility for, filling a void of childhood wounds? In the most loving way, no.

In the book *Needy*, Mara Glatzel describes the art of taking "radical responsibility" for your needs. She points out that *you* are the steward of your needs. You are the only one who knows what you need, and therefore, it is up to you to advocate for yourself.[6]

When little you with unmet needs becomes adult you with unmet needs, it is tempting to look to others around you to fill them. But adult you is now responsible for little you, and you have the opportunity to be the parent to yourself that you needed when you were younger. To anticipate and identify your needs—and to ensure that they are met.

That's not to say that your partner gets to just do their thing without any consideration of your needs or that they don't have some responsibility in the relationship—just that they can't realistically *anticipate* your individual needs. You are the one who is responsible for identifying your own needs. You are the one responsible for advocating for your needs out loud. And you are the one responsible for setting the boundaries that will help those needs get met.

Tuning In to Your Needs

We often have a romanticized idea that our partner or those in our life should "know us" and should know what we need. But if there is something that I have learned working with countless moms—WE DON'T EVEN KNOW WHAT WE NEED. When our needs have been pushed to the back burner for so long, we lose touch with ourselves—needs included. If we want our partner, or anyone else, to understand our needs, we first need to understand them ourselves.

In the book *Nonviolent Communication*, Marshall Rosenberg wrote that "judgments of others are alienated expressions of our unmet needs."[7] When you find yourself being critical of your partner or blaming them because you feel that your needs aren't being met, first pause and seek to understand what the need is. Here are some statements you might find yourself saying and ways to tune in to your needs:

"You never come home on time!"

Maybe you need a break or to feel that your time is respected or to feel prioritized.

"You never help around the house."

You are carrying too much and need more hands.

"You're always on your phone."

You want time and connection.

If your toddler was experiencing a meltdown, you would likely stop and think about their unmet needs that might be contributing. And yet, we often don't do that with *ourselves*. Practice using your emotions as clues to your needs.

Another way to tune in to your needs is to briefly stop and check in with yourself. This might look like:

- Mindfully focusing on your stomach, asking yourself whether you're hungry or thirsty

- Noticing the emotional lump in your throat you've been trying to hold back and acknowledging it's there

- Scanning your senses and realizing that there is way too much noise in the room

- Checking in with your body and realizing you are clenching your jaw or that your shoulders are tense

The reality is that many of us have been taught to disconnect from and ignore our needs. Society has conditioned us to ignore when we are hungry for the sake of a diet. Many of us have learned to doubt or minimize our emotions because our parents didn't have the skills to help manage them. And motherhood tells us that our needs don't matter.

But your needs *do* matter. They matter because you matter. They matter because you are setting an example for your children. And they matter because you are a cycle-breaker. A commitment to real self-care is seeing your needs as equal to others, which then allows you to become curious, explore, and ask yourself what it is that you need.

Self-Care (In and Out of the Moment)

As mentioned earlier in this chapter, real self-care isn't about a massage or a pedicure or even a break here and there. Real self-care is about diving deeper into our needs and creating the shifts in our lives that allow those needs to be met. I'm not going to tell you that you need a girl's night out or a bubble bath every day. Maybe that's helpful for you—and if so, that's great! But I am focused more on reframing the very concepts you believe about how you care (or don't care) for yourself. This includes your perceptions around when it's necessary, or even okay, to ask for help.

Asking for help

There are several contributing factors to why we struggle to ask for help in our motherhood role:

- Societally, we are told we can be and do it all (and that we should be able to do it with ease).

- We often see other people's curated social media highlight reels. They don't appear to be struggling. They look like they can always keep up. So we often compare ourselves, feeling as if there is something wrong with us.

- In many ways, asking for help feels like we are admitting we are failing in our most important role.

- When we've opened up in the past, we might have been met with a minimizing or invalidating response.

Those factors are primarily external. But there are also some other boundary-related reasons that we struggle to ask for help:

- If we have porous or overly flexible boundaries, we may struggle to ask for help because we don't want to be a burden to others. We might feel uncomfortable being assertive enough to communicate our needs.

- On the other hand, if we have overly rigid boundaries and wall others out as a way of keeping ourselves safe, we may develop a strong distrust in others and not want to admit what we are going through.

Whatever the reason that has prevented you from asking for help, you need to figure that shit out and move past it. Remember—if you have made a commitment to real self-care and taking care of yourself the same way you would take care of others, this also includes asking for help.

If your child was at school and needed support from their teacher, would you advise them to swallow their need and sit in class so they don't disturb anyone? If they were having a hard day, would you advise them to put on a smile and act like everything is fine? Of course not.

Learning to ask for help from others and communicate your needs is an act of self-care. It is a form of self-advocacy that will ensure your needs get met. As big you, you are your parent now. Taking radical responsibility means ensuring your needs get met. You need to begin to parent yourself the way you parent your children and advocate for what you need.

Communicating Our Needs to Others

Being in tune with yourself and having a clear understanding of what you need is more than half the battle. From there, there are many ways that you can communicate this to others in your life:

- You can revisit the red vs. green light conversation tips on page 120.
- You can use the soft conversation starters on page 122.
- Or you can use an old faithful "I" statement. It goes like this:

    "I feel [insert emotion] when [insert event, behavior, etc.] because [state outcome of how it impacts you]. Could you help me by [state clear positive need]? I will [list ways you're taking responsibility and helping the situation, or yourself, etc.]."

    Examples:

    "I feel resentful when I am the only one getting up at night. Could you help me by taking the first wake-up tonight so I can get some sleep? I will try to get better at communicating what I need from you sooner."

"I feel frustrated when you leave the dishes in the sink overnight because when I get up to make the kids breakfast, I don't have access to it. Could you please clear the sink so I can get breakfast?" (Then maybe you proceed to troubleshoot as a team a way to keep the sink functional even if pots sit for a day.)

"I feel like I haven't been myself lately because I am having thoughts that feel unlike me. Could you help me book an appointment with my doctor to discuss whether this is normal?"

Radical Acceptance

In therapy, there is a concept called radical acceptance; the premise is that painful or difficult experiences are turned into prolonged suffering based on how we cope or deal with them. Learning this skill can help us work through the Mother Load by accepting what we can't change so we can focus on what we can.

When we feel pain, we react and respond in a number of ways. We may avoid, numb, binge, keep ourselves busy, or try to control situations around us. But none of these reactions are looking to understand the pain itself in order to process or move through it—they are knee-jerk reactions to alleviate our distress as quickly as possible. These default patterns or ways of coping often actually prolong our distress.

But there is a way to reduce the distress—radical acceptance. Radical acceptance sees pain as a part of life that cannot be avoided. But how we handle our pain is what impacts our level of suffering. So much of our distress and suffering in life has to do with how we handle painful situations. We try to outrun the pain, but it takes a stronger hold. Instead, we can accept that the situation is hard and painful so that we can problem-solve productively.

A key indicator that we're wrestling with our reality rather than accepting it is saying or thinking things like:

- "It shouldn't be this way."

- "It shouldn't be this hard."

- "They should be sleeping by now."

- "I should have this figured out by now."

Talking about the way things "should" or "should not" be means that our expectations for the situation are not in alignment with the reality of what we are facing. This misalignment gets in the way of processing our pain, unintentionally prolonging our suffering.

IF YOU ONLY REMEMBER ONE THING

Taking care of your own needs doesn't mean you are selfish or overlooking your child's needs. In fact, meeting your own needs *is* prioritizing your child's needs and is an essential part of being a parent. The best thing you can do for your child is to take care of your own mental health.

IF YOU ONLY DO ONE THING

Commit to radical responsibility for your own needs. You are the person most equipped to understand your own needs. You are the only one who can advocate for those needs. And you are the steward to ensure that your needs are met. Break away from the idea that other people should anticipate those needs, and start communicating them out loud.

CONCLUSION

By now it's no secret that entering motherhood rocked me to my core. What I thought was going to fulfill me almost broke me. And that has nothing to do with my children—whom I absolutely adore. I love being a mom. And yet "motherhood," the construct, cost me so much. It felt like a part of me died.

It cost me my passions. It cost me my identity. It cost me my talents, my interests, my values, and my needs. I spent so much time, energy, and effort chasing the perfect mother myth that I lost out on moments that could have been so different, so *still*, and so true to who I was.

Part of the difficulty was the postpartum period and the wild ride that it always is. And part of it was my neurodivergence. Those pieces would have been there no matter what. But I can't help but wonder what those early days might have looked like if I focused less on what I *thought* it should be and more on what mattered to me, to my family.

I don't want to dwell on those moments that I missed. I spend plenty of time now living in the moment and connecting with my children in a way that doesn't leave me feeling guilty. But if I could give myself a gift in those early days, it wouldn't be more baby gear or a cute onesie, or even more sleep (although, let's be honest, that's definitely what I wanted and needed at the time).

It would be permission.

Permission to tune in to my values.

Permission to let go of all the noise.

Permission to have self-compassion.

Permission to turn gender norms on their heads.

Permission to set boundaries.

Permission to give intensive mothering a well-deserved middle finger.

Permission to reclaim parts of myself while I became something new.

Permission to release the Mother Load.

And permission to find something for myself beyond motherhood.

That's the gift that I hope to give you now. I want you to know that you matter—not just as a side accessory to your children, but as a whole human being—one who is many things, only one of which is a mother.

You have gifts to give the world. Mothering may be a big part of that—I know that it is for me. But it isn't everything.

You have value to share with the world. You have the ability to make an impact—on your family and those around you, and beyond, if you choose.

I hope you give yourself permission to release the Mother Load and be *all* of who you are.

Growing in Our Beliefs

On page 57, we did an exercise to help us identify our own underlying beliefs about motherhood, our role, and what it means to be a "good mom."

It's time to reflect on our journey together and how your beliefs have evolved. Take a minute to complete the following sentences based on your perspective *now*:

- Good moms . . .

- Moms should . . .

- I am . . .

- My partner is . . .

- My family should . . .

- My needs . . .

- I should be able to . . .

- The house should be . . .

- The food my kids eat should be . . .

- Organizing my kids' schedules should be . . .

- I know I'm a good mom when . . .

Look back over your responses from page 57 and compare them with your answers now. How have your beliefs evolved? Have you reframed some unhelpful beliefs into something more empowering? How does that make you feel? Do you feel freer? More confident? Less pressured?

I encourage you to revisit these beliefs from time to time. If you find yourself sliding backward into old belief patterns or wondering if you're failing, come back to this exercise. You are enough. You are not failing. You and your needs matter.

FROM BREAKDOWN TO BREAKTHROUGH

When I had my rage breakdown, I'd hit my breaking point. The stress and tension that I was under caused the facade of perfection I was trying to achieve to come crashing down. What was the most difficult thing I had ever experienced finally gave way as I began to accept my own imperfections and see that the problem wasn't me—it was the perfect mother myth I was trying to chase.

> Motherhood isn't hard because you are failing to manage it correctly—it is hard because the pressure we face as women and mothers is unrealistic.

The problem isn't me, and the problem isn't you. Motherhood isn't hard because you are failing to manage it correctly—it is hard because the pressure we face as women and mothers is unrealistic.

I accepted that I needed help, I got on medication for postpartum depression and anxiety, and the clouds in the sky finally began to part.

You might not be able to see the sun right now. I want you to know that I *see* you. Your struggle is valid. And, just like me, a breakthrough is waiting to happen for you.

If you are in the struggle right now, or if you start down the path to releasing the Mother Load but find yourself picking it back up, take these reminders with you:

- Motherhood does not require perfection.
- My children benefit from having a healthy, happy mom.
- My needs are just as valid as everyone else's in the family.
- My worth in motherhood is not measured by how much labor I do.

- It isn't selfish to care for my own needs.

- Mental health *is* health.

- I cannot realistically do and be it all for my children—and that's okay.

- I can choose the path of ease.

- Social expectations don't have to define motherhood for me.

- My values are my roadmap in motherhood.

Discovering Your "Why"

The work in this book doesn't happen in one day or one sitting. It isn't a magical button. It isn't a quick fix. You will likely struggle. There might be times you want to quit. There might be times you want to take certain loads back. There might be times when you want to people-please or succumb to the perfect mother myth. There might be times when the doubts are hard to silence.

When times get tough, it is important to remember WHY you've committed to doing this work. Perhaps it is to have less stress and more peace. Or maybe it is to feel less guilt and experience more confidence. It could be to carry less so you can enjoy motherhood more. Either way, your why is what will keep you going and committed to this work. With one small step in front of the other, before you know it, you'll look back and realize that you're miles from where you began.

Finding your why can also be linked to your passions and desires— the hopes and dreams you have for yourself beyond survival. Maybe that is intimidating to dream about, but my hope is that through releasing some of the load, you will reclaim parts of yourself that are allowed to dream.

I encourage you to ask yourself these questions to help identify your why:

- What is it that you are hoping to gain back into your life by doing this work? (This might be freedom to explore your interests, less resentment toward your partner, or time to just *breathe*.)

- How do you want to *feel* as you do this work? (Seen? Acknowledged? Valued?)

- What is your life lacking because of the Mother Load? (Freedom? Spontaneity? Adventure? Mental peace?)

- What would you want for other moms who are coping with this load? Would you encourage them to release it?

- If you didn't carry so much of this weight, what would your life look like? (Feel free to explore this in detail. Would you read that book that has been sitting on your shelf for months? Would you enjoy your time with your kids more, not worrying as much about the other to-dos? Would you prioritize sleep and rest? Go back to school? Start a business?)

Use those answers to form your why. I encourage you to write it down. Take it to heart. Remember it.

Change isn't easy. But it is worth it.

THE THREE "RADICALS" TO REMEMBER

In this book, we have already discussed radical acceptance and radical responsibility for your needs. I'd like to leave you with a third radical to remember—*radical self-compassion.*

Webster defines compassion as a "sympathetic consciousness of others' distress together with a desire to alleviate it."[1] As women, we have been socialized into this role of caring for others and tending to their needs, so I know we have it in us to take those skills and apply them to ourselves.

Self-compassion is empathizing with our own distress, and a desire to want to soothe it or help make it better. It's easy to try to blame—whether that blame falls to ourselves or to others. It's sometimes harder to offer compassion.

When you find yourself criticizing or judging your own actions, lean back on these statements:

- I am human and it is okay that I am imperfect or make mistakes.

- My needs are important and deserve to be met.

- I am worth speaking kindly to.

- I forgive myself for my mistakes.

- My emotions are meant to help me, not harm me.

- How I feel in this moment is valid.

- I am not a bad person—I made a bad choice.

- My imperfections allow me to model repair and self-development to my child.

- I deserve to mother according my values.

- I am allowed to have an identity outside of motherhood.

- I recognize I am having a hard time right now.

As you move forward with this work, I want you to lean back on these three "radicals."

When you hit a wall, they can guide you forward. If you find yourself struggling to release, or slipping back into old patterns, or worrying about social expectations or the needs of others, follow these steps:

Step 1: Radical Self-Acceptance

Instead of pushing back against your situation or your phase of life, allow yourself to accept where you are. You are a mom. You want what is best for your kids. You are in a phase of life that can be tough. There are things you won't be able to release—especially if you don't have a willing partner or a support system in place. But there are also plenty of things you *can* release.

Step 2: Radical Responsibility for Your Needs

It might feel like putting your needs behind everyone else's is the right thing to do. But there's a saying, "If you don't make time for your wellness, you'll be forced to make time for your illness." This isn't just true of physical health but of mental health as well. When we put our emotional and mental needs on the back burner, we're setting ourselves on the path to burnout—or worse.

Resist the urge to put your needs on the back burner. If you are feeling overwhelmed, overstimulated, or burnt out, don't ignore that. It's time to advocate for yourself, out loud. What do you need? Time to yourself? A creative outlet? Helping hands? Think about what you can do for yourself, as well as ways you can ask others to help to ensure your needs get met—physically, mentally, and emotionally.

Step 3: Radical Self-Compassion

You are not being too sensitive. You are not being overdramatic. You are not overreacting. You are not failing. Motherhood as a social construct is failing *you*. Give yourself compassion for your struggles. Validate that it's okay if the Mother Load is hard to handle. Acknowledge that it's also okay if you find it difficult to release it. The more that we practice tuning in to our values, letting go of expectations, and choosing a path that feels right for us, the easier it will become. In the meantime, we all deserve patience, grace, and compassion.

Practicing these three "radicals" will help you ward off the mom-guilt surveillance crew. It will help you keep unwanted and unhelpful messages from entering back into your mental filing cabinet. And it will help keep you on the path you are creating based on your values.

The Mother Load can be released—and you deserve to let go of the weight.

WHAT COMES NEXT?

Those of you reading this book come from all walks of life. Different races, different cultures, different sexual orientations, different upbringings. But you are all here because you are ready to shed the load you're carrying.

I am going to let you in on a little secret. It might feel a little scary.

Letting go of this load is going to leave you with capacity that you are not used to if you've been consumed by the weight. That capacity might feel uncomfortable at first. On episode 157 of *The Momwell Podcast*, Kate McReynolds and I discussed how to decide whether or not to expand our family. As we chatted, I brought up that I have seen a trend with my clients—when they move past the postpartum phase or begin to carve some capacity for themselves, the knee-jerk reaction is often to fill that space with another baby.[2]

Now, I am certainly not saying that you shouldn't use that capacity to add another baby if you want to! What I am saying is that sometimes we turn to having another baby to fill a void. Sometimes we choose to expand the family because our identity is so wrapped up in motherhood that we can't picture anything else.

As you regain capacity by releasing the Mother Load, I urge you to take a step back and pause. When you come out of the fog and start to breathe again, I want you to consciously ask yourself, what else do *you want* to fill this space with?

You will have accomplished something big, powerful, and important. You defined motherhood for yourself.

You modeled for your children that you can be a parent without losing yourself.

And you allowed yourself to dream beyond just one role.

That is the problem with motherhood, the construct. It is currently boxing moms into a role that they didn't choose for themselves.

Your dreams don't have to die with motherhood. It doesn't have to be a cage . . .

But it doesn't have to be that way. Your dreams don't have to die with motherhood. It doesn't have to be a cage; it can be the vessel for discovering a new you—a you who is part who you used to be, part who you are now, and part whoever you want to make yourself.

I want you to think about what you want from the freedom you will gain. Ask yourself these questions:

- What is something that you feel you've had to give up because of motherhood?

- If time wasn't an issue, what would you spend your time doing?

- What is something that lights you up that you wish you could do more of?

- What are your interests, hobbies, or talents? Or if those have been gone for so long that they feel foreign, what have you always been drawn to that you want to try?

- What could you spend hours doing or talking about?

- When you imagine yourself ten years from now, what do you see yourself doing?

Whether you want to learn a new skill, return to work, travel, or go back to school, your desires are valid, and by slowly practicing releasing the load, you begin to regain parts of yourself again. My hope is that you have learned some skills to release the load so that you have the capacity to find yourself again—to reignite passions and dreams that you thought had died when you began to put everyone else's needs first.

Most of all, I hope that you have given yourself permission to move forward in a way that aligns with your own values. You get to fill your cup in the way you want now. The Mother Load, the perfect mother myth, intensive mothering, and whatever else is in your filing cabinet that you don't need doesn't get to shape what you do anymore.

When you start to doubt the work you are doing (and trust me, there will be times when you do), remember this:

You deserve to take up space.

You deserve to have your needs met.

You deserve to have an identity outside of being a mother.

You deserve to be seen, recognized, and validated.

You deserve leisure time to breathe, to find yourself, and to just . . . *be*.

You deserve time to create.

You deserve time to become not just the mother, but the person you want to be.

ACKNOWLEDGMENTS

Writing a book has been an awe-inspiring, enlightening, eye-opening experience. And, just like motherhood, it becomes easier when you have a village to support you every step of the way.

I'd first like to thank Little Erica. Who the heck would have thought we would make it here? You would be so proud of where we end up. Your scrappy resilience and ability to face a challenge head-on are the reason we are here today. I know that it hasn't always been easy. The healing you've had to do, the limiting beliefs you've had to overcome, and the permission you've had to give yourself to take up space and dream big are the foundation of not just this book, but of our beautiful family, of Momwell, and of the impact we are having on moms everywhere. You've worked hard for this. I'm proud of you—of every mistake you made and every obstacle you overcame. You are deserving of every good thing that comes your way.

Frenel, I wouldn't be here without you. The scrappy, fiercely fiery, independent part of me still thinks that I would, but in reality, the secure and strong bond you built with me and the safe space you provided for me to heal and truly find myself have made this possible. Thank you for building such a bond with me, and for providing me the safe space I needed to heal and truly find myself. I have the utmost respect for you—I have never met such an intelligent, loyal, dedicated, and overall solid person. The belief and confidence you have in me always keep me going when I doubt myself. Thank you for being open to growing and changing with me as we've navigated parenthood and challenged social norms—you've been the dad handling pick-up and drop-off, taking the kids to doctor's appointments, doing the grocery shopping, and so much more, so that I could build a company, write this book, and accomplish everything I set my mind to. Most of all, thank you for being an example to our three boys who will truly see a home with equal partners, who will watch both of their parents do amazing things while still providing a loving, caring home.

To my boys—being the mother to three wild boys is nothing I had ever imagined or planned for, but it is the most amazing gift I've been given. You are my inspiration in life—to develop and care for myself, to make the world a better place.

To my oldest—I love your creativity and the way you see the world. Your gentle nature paired with your curiosity help keep me grounded and remind me of what is important. Thanks for always being my cheer-leader and sharing in (and matching) my excitement level.

To my middle—your fire and determination are going to take you amazing places. You match my need for adventure and I can't wait to see where it takes us.

To my youngest—your empathy and thoughtfulness are so enduring. The care you show for others paired with your playful spirit make you light up every room.

Experiencing the world through all of your eyes has caused me to slow down, be more mindful, appreciate the simplicity and return to my values and what is truly important. Watching you grow and loving you so deeply has also taught me to accept and appreciate those parts of myself. As I always tell each of you, I am so honored and happy to be your mom.

I also want to thank my parents. Becoming a parent myself has given me a new perspective on my own upbringing and helped me to understand you both in a different way. Mom and Dad, I want to thank you for all that you did to raise my brother and me. You both strived to parent differently than your own parents and made many sacrifices to put us first.

Mom, I am especially grateful for your support during the writing of this book. Your willingness to help, whether it was delivering a holiday meal or putting together a last-minute birthday celebration, made all the difference. Your love and encouragement have meant the world to me—thank you for everything.

This book wouldn't be possible without my agent and editorial team.

Carly Watters, my agent—thank you for seeing a book in me before I even saw one in myself! Your wisdom and knowledge throughout this process have been invaluable.

Zoe Maslow, editor at Appetite by Penguin Random House, thank you for your excitement for this book. I'm grateful to you for reminding me that I have the ability to change the world. Your words to me are framed in my office and forever etched in my brain.

Diana Ventimiglia, editor at Sounds True, thank you for your enthusiasm and encouragement in moments of doubt or overwhelm along the way. You've been such a reassuring voice in this process.

Cassie Nguyen, you are such an important part of my team and this book. You worked tirelessly to help me shape and refine my ideas, and your expertise and insight were instrumental in bringing this book to life. Your guidance and support have made this book a reality.

Thank you to the entire team at Penguin Random House and Sounds True for bringing this book to life and understanding how important this work is.

Last, but not least, to my clients and community of moms. Your stories have been my inspiration. Thank you for sharing your lives and your experiences with me. You've let me into places in your lives where no one else is allowed to enter. The insights I have learned from working with you can be found throughout the pages of this book. I want each of you to know that you deserve better. A better motherhood experience. Better support. Better care. I hope that this book shifts the narrative around motherhood, even just a little, to allow for you to make space to prioritize and rediscover yourselves.

NOTES

INTRODUCTION

1. Miriam Liss et al., "Development and Validation of a Quantitative Measure of Intensive Parenting Attitudes," *Journal of Child and Family Studies* 22, no. 5 (2013): 621–36, doi.org/10.1007/s10826-012-9616-y.

2. Kathryn M. Rizzo, Holly H. Schiffrin, and Miriam Liss, "Insight into the Parenthood Paradox: Mental Health Outcomes of Intensive Mothering," *Journal of Child and Family Studies* 22, no. 5 (2013): 614–20, doi.org/10.1007/s10826-012-9615-z.

3. Liz Dean, Brendan Churchill, and Leah Ruppanner, "The Mental Load: Building a Deeper Theoretical Understanding of How Cognitive and Emotional Labor Over*load* Women and Mothers," *Community, Work & Family* 25, no. 1 (2022): 13–29, doi.org/10.1080/13668803.2021.2002813.

4. Alison Daminger, "The Cognitive Dimension of Household Labor," *American Sociological Review* 84, no. 4 (2019): 609–33, doi.org/10.1177/0003122419859007.

5. Ruth Igielnik, "A Rising Share of Working Parents in the U.S. Say It's Been Difficult to Handle Child Care During the Pandemic," Pew Research Center, January 26, 2021, pewresearch.org/fact-tank/2021/01/26/a-rising-share-of-working-parents-in-the-u-s-say-its-been-difficult-to-handle-child-care-during-the-pandemic/.

6. Kim Parker and Juliana Menasce Horowitz, "Majority of Workers Who Quit a Job in 2021 Cite Low Pay, No Opportunities for Advancement, Feeling Disrespected," Pew Research Center, March 9, 2022, pewresearch.org/short-reads/2022/03/09/majority-of-workers-who-quit-a-job-in-2021-cite-low-pay-no-opportunities-for-advancement-feeling-disrespected/.

7. Jessica McCrory Calarco et al., "'Let's Not Pretend It's Fun': How COVID-19-Related School and Childcare Closures are Damaging Mothers' Well-Being," SocArXiv, October 4, 2022, doi.org/10.31235/osf.io/jyvk4.

8. Clayton J. Shuman et al., "Postpartum Depression and Associated Risk Factors During the COVID-19 Pandemic," *BMC Research Notes* 15, no. 102 (2022): doi.org/10.1186/s13104-022-05991-8.

9. Ana Sandoiu, "Postpartum Depression in Women of Color: 'More Work Needs to Be Done,'" Medical News Today, July 17, 2020, medicalnewstoday.com/articles/postpartum-depression-in-women -of-color-more-work-needs-to-be-done/.

10. Shawna J. Lee and Kaitlin P. Ward, "Stress and Parenting During the Coronavirus Pandemic: A Research Brief," Parenting in Context Research Lab (Ann Arbor, MI: University of Michigan, 2020), parentingincontext .org/uploads/8/1/3/1/81318622/research_brief_stress_and_parenting _during_the_coronavirus_pandemic_final.pdf.

11. Lisa K. Forbes, Courtney Donovan, and Margaret R. Lamar, "Differences in Intensive Parenting Attitudes and Gender Norms Among U.S. Mothers," *The Family Journal* 28, no. 1 (2020): 63–71, doi.org /10.1177/1066480719893964.

12. Maaike van der Vleuten, Eva Jaspers, and Tanja van der Lippe, "Same-Sex Couples' Division of Labor from a Cross-National Perspective," *Journal of GLBT Family Studies* 17, no. 2 (2021): 150– 67, doi.org/10.1080/1550428X.2020.1862012.

13. Sharon Hays, *The Cultural Contradictions of Motherhood* (New Haven, CT: Yale University Press, 1998), 49–50.

CHAPTER 1: THE BIRTH OF THE INVISIBLE LOAD

1. Erica Djossa, "129: Recovering from Motherhood Burnout with Licensed Therapist Erin Spahr," July 12, 2022, in *The Momwell Podcast*, podcast, MP3 audio, 53:31, momwell.com/listen.

2. Alison Daminger, "The Cognitive Dimension of Household Labor," *American Sociological Review* 84, no. 4 (2019): 609–33, doi.org/10 .1177/0003122419859007.

3. Daminger, "The Cognitive Dimension of Household Labor."
4. Lindsey G. Robertson et al., "Mothers and Mental Labor: A Phenomenological Focus Group Study of Family-Related Thinking Work," *Psychology of Women Quarterly* 43, no. 2 (2019): 184–200, doi.org /10.1177/0361684319825581.
5. Daminger, "The Cognitive Dimension of Household Labor."
6. Daminger, "The Cognitive Dimension of Household Labor."
7. Kate Mangino, *Equal Partners: Improving Gender Equality at Home* (New York: St. Martin's Press, 2022).
8. Mangino, *Equal Partners*, 55–7.
9. Petra Bueskens, *Modern Motherhood and Women's Dual Identities: Rewriting the Sexual Contract* (New York: Routledge, 2018).
10. Karl A. Ericsson, Ralf T. Krampe, and Clemens Tesch-Römer, "The Role of Deliberate Practice in the Acquisition of Expert Performance," *Psychological Review* 100, no. 3 (July 1993), 363–406, doi .org/10.1037/0033-295X.100.3.363.
11. "FMLA Frequently Asked Questions," US Department of Labor, accessed March 31, 2023, dol.gov/agencies/whd/fmla/faq.
12. Sharon Lerner, "The Real War on Families: Why the U.S. Needs Paid Leave Now," *In These Times*, August 18, 2015, inthesetimes .com/article/the-real-war-on-families.
13. Lerner, "The Real War on Families."
14. Janet Shibley Hyde et al., "Maternity Leave and Women's Mental Health," *Psychology of Women Quarterly*, 19, no. 2 (1995), 257–285, doi.org/10.1111/j.1471-6402.1995.tb00291.x.
15. Zoe Aitken et al., "The Maternal Health Outcomes of Paid Maternity Leave: A Systematic Review," *Social Science & Medicine* 130 (April 2015): 32–41, doi.org/10.1016/j.socscimed.2015.02.001.
16. Hyde et al., "Maternity Leave and Women's Mental Health."
17. Erin M. Rehel, "When Dad Stays Home Too," *Gender & Society* 28, no. 1 (2014): 110–32, doi.org/10.1177/0891243213503900.
18. Mareike Bünning, "What Happens after the 'Daddy Months'? Fathers' Involvement in Paid Work, Childcare, and Housework after

Taking Parental Leave in Germany," *European Sociological Review* 31, no. 6 (December 2015): 738–48, doi.org/10.1093/esr/jcv072.

19. Bünning, "What Happens after the 'Daddy Months'?"

20. "Family Matters: Parental Leaves in Canada," Statistics Canada, last modified February 10, 2021, accessed March 31, 2023, www150 .statcan.gc.ca/n1/pub/11-627-m/11-627-m2020048-eng.htm.

21. "Why Parental Leave for Fathers Is So Important for Working Families," US Department of Labor policy brief, 2012, accessed March 31, 2023, dol.gov/sites/dolgov/files/OASP/Paternity-Leave.pdf.

22. "Why Parental Leave for Fathers Is So Important for Working Families."

23. Scott Coltrane et al., "Fathers and the Flexibility Stigma," *Journal of Social Issues* 69, no. 2 (2013): 279–302, doi.org/10.1111/josi.12015.

24. Erica Djossa, "177: The Invisible Load of Fatherhood with Dr. Singley, Psychologist and Director of The Center for Men's Excellence," February 2, 2023, in *The Momwell Podcast*, podcast, MP3 audio, 57:22, momwell.com/listen.

CHAPTER 2: THE BELIEFS THAT SHAPE THE LOAD WE CARRY

1. Lisa K. Forbes, Courtney Donovan, and Margaret R. Lamar, "Differences in Intensive Parenting Attitudes and Gender Norms Among U.S. Mothers," *The Family Journal* 28, no. 1 (2020): 63–71, doi.org /10.1177/1066480719893964.

2. Clayton J. Shuman et. al., "Postpartum Depression and Associated Risk Factors During the COVID-19 Pandemic," *BMC Research Notes* 15, no. 102 (2022): doi.org/10.1186/s13104-022-05991-8.

3. Kathryn M. Rizzo, Holly H. Schiffrin, and Miriam Liss, "Insight into the Parenthood Paradox: Mental Health Outcomes of Intensive Mothering," *Journal of Child and Family Studies* 22, no. 5 (2013): 614–20, doi.org/10.1007/s10826-012-9615-z.

4. Sophie Brock, "Motherhood Studies Practitioner Certification," online course, drsophiebrock.com/motherhoodstudies.

5. Miriam Liss et al., "Development and Validation of a Quantitative Measure of Intensive Parenting Attitudes," *Journal of Child and Family Studies* 22, no. 5 (2013): 621–36, doi.org/10.1007/s10826 -012-9616-y.

6. Rizzo, Schiffrin, and Liss, "Insight into the Parenthood Paradox."

7. Sharon Hays, *The Cultural Contradictions of Motherhood* (New Haven, CT: Yale University Press, 1998), 21.

8. Sophie Brock, "Motherhood Studies Practitioner Certification," online course, drsophiebrock.com/motherhoodstudies.

9. Rizzo, Schiffrin, and Liss, "Insight into the Parenthood Paradox."

CHAPTER 3: VALUES AS YOUR MOTHERHOOD ROADMAP

1. Erica Djossa, "106: Discover Your Personal Core Values with Licensed Marriage and Family Therapist Dr. Cassidy Freitas," February 2, 2022, in *The Momwell Podcast*, podcast, MP3 audio, 1:04:37, momwell.com/listen.

2. Djossa, "106: Discover Your Personal Core Values."

CHAPTER 4: THE DEFAULT CAREGIVER

1. Kate Manne, *Entitled: How Male Privilege Hurts Women* (New York: Penguin Random House, 2021), 127.

2. Janette Dill and Mignon Duffy, "Structural Racism and Black Women's Employment in the U.S. Health Care Sector," *Health Affairs* 41, no. 2 (February 2022): 265–72, doi.org/10.1377/hlthaff.2021 .01400.

3. Arlie Russell Hochschild with Anne Machung, *The Second Shift: Working Families and the Revolution at Home*, rev. ed. (New York: Penguin, 2012).

4. Joanna Syrda, "Gendered Housework: Spousal Relative Income, Parenthood and Traditional Gender Identity Norms," *Work, Employment and Society* 37, no. 3 (2023): 794–813, doi.org/10 .1177/09500170211069780.

5. Usha Ranji and Alina Salganicoff, "Balancing on Shaky Ground: Women, Work, and Family Health," Henry J. Kaiser Family Foundation, October 2014, files.kff.org/attachment/balancing-on-shaky-ground-women-work-and-family-health-data-note.

6. Sarah Jane Glynn, "An Unequal Division of Labor," Center for American Progress, May 18, 2018, americanprogress.org/article/unequal-division-labor/.

7. Sharon Radzyminski and Lynn Clark Callister, "Mother's Beliefs, Attitudes, and Decision Making Related to Infant Feeding Choices," *The Journal of Perinatal Education* 25, no. 1 (2016): 18–28, doi.org/10.1891/1058-1243.25.1.18.

8. Michele L. Okun, "Sleep and Postpartum Depression," *Current Opinion in Psychiatry* 28, no. 6 (November 2018): 490–96, doi.org/10.1097/YCO.0000000000000206.

9. Patricia Armstrong, "Bloom's Taxonomy," Vanderbilt University Center for Teaching, accessed April 17, 2023, cft.vanderbilt.edu/guides-sub-pages/blooms-taxonomy/.

10. Erica Djossa, "143: Returning to Work After Maternity Leave with Dr. Cassidy Freitas, Marriage and Family Therapist," October 19, 2022, in *The Momwell Podcast*, podcast, MP3 audio, 54:21, momwell.com/listen.

11. Alyson Fearnley Shapiro, John M. Gottman, and Sybil Carrère, "The Baby and the Marriage: Identifying Factors that Buffer against Decline in Marital Satisfaction after the First Baby Arrives," *Journal of Family Psychology* 14, no. 1 (2000): 59–70, doi.org/10.1037//0893-3200.14.1.59.

12. Maryam Ghaedrahmati et al., "Postpartum Depression Risk Factors: A Narrative Review," *Journal of Education and Health Promotion* 6 (2017): 60.

13. Erica Djossa, "141: Protecting Maternal Sleep with Dr. Nicole Leistikow, Reproductive Psychiatrist and Psychotherapist," October 5, 2022, in *The Momwell Podcast*, podcast, MP3 audio, 1:02:30, momwell.com/listen.

14. Samantha Meltzer-Brody et al., "Brexanolone Injection in Post-Partum Depression," *Lancet* 392, no. 10152 (September 2018): 1058–70, doi.org/10.1016/S0140-6736(18)31551-4.

15. V. Cheung et al., "The Effect of Sleep Deprivation and Disruption on DNA Damage and Health of Doctors," *Anaesthesia* 74, no. 4 (April 2019): 434–40. doi.org/10.1111/anae.14533.

16. Nicole Leistikow et al., "Prescribing Sleep: An Overlooked Treatment for Postpartum Depression," *Biological Psychiatry* 92, no. 3 (August 2022): e13–e15, doi.org/10.1016/j.biopsych.2022.03.006.

17. Djossa, "141: Protecting Maternal Sleep."

18. John Gottman, "The 6 Things that Predict Divorce," *The Gottman Relationship Blog*, The Gottman Institute, October 10, 2014, gottman.com/blog/the-6-things-that-predict-divorce/.

19. Ellie Lisitsa, "How to Fight Smarter: Soften Your Start-Up," *The Gottman Relationship Blog*, The Gottman Institute, March 15, 2013, gottman.com/blog/softening-startup/; Ellie Lisitsa, "The Four Horsemen: Defensiveness," *The Gottman Relationship Blog*, The Gottman Institute, May 6, 2013, gottman.com/blog/the-four-horsemen-defensiveness/.

CHAPTER 5: FEEDING THE HOUSEHOLD

1. Erica Djossa, "069: The Perfect Mother Myth with Sociologist Dr. Sophie Brock," May 19, 2021, in *The Momwell Podcast*, podcast, MP3 Audio, 58:38, momwell.com/listen.

2. "Just 6% of the World's Top Restaurants Are Led by Women, Study Finds," *Restaurant*, last updated July 20, 2022, restaurantonline.co.uk/Article/2022/07/20/Just-6-of-the-world-s-top-restaurants-are-led-by-women-study-by-Chef-s-Pencil-shows.

3. Jennifer S. Savage, Jennifer Orlet Fisher, and Leann L. Birch, "Parental Influence on Eating Behavior: Conception to Adolescence," *Journal of Law, Medicine & Ethics* 35, no. 1 (2007): 22–34, doi.org/10.1111/j.1748-720X.2007.00111.x.

4. Ellyn M. Satter, "Ellyn Satter's Division of Responsibility in Feeding," Ellyn Satter Institute, August 2015, accessed June 7, 2023,

ellynsatterinstitute.org/wp-content/uploads/2015/08/ELLYN
-SATTER%E2%80%99S-DIVISION-OF-RESPONSIBILITY-IN
-FEEDING.pdf.

5. Erica Djossa, "079: When Treatment Becomes Trauma with Clinical Psychologist Dr. Quincee Gideon," July 28, 2021, in *The Momwell Podcast*, podcast, MP3 audio, 1:00:07, momwell.com/listen.

6. Diane L. Putnick et al., "Trajectories of Maternal Postpartum Depressive Symptoms," *Pediatrics* 146, no. 5 (November 2020): e20200857, doi.org/10.1542/peds.2020-0857.

7. Savage et al., "Parental Influence on Eating Behavior."

CHAPTER 6: THE KEEPER OF THE HOUSE

1. Kate Mangino, *Equal Partners: Improving Gender Equality at Home* (New York: St. Martin's Press, 2022), 86–88.

2. Lucy Westcott, "Girls Spend 40 Percent More Time on Chores than Boys Around the World," *Newsweek*, October 7, 2016, newsweek .com/girls-chores-40-percent-unicef-boys-507374.

3. KC Davis, *How to Keep House While Drowning: A Gentle Approach to Cleaning and Organizing* (New York: Simon Element, 2022), 37–9.

4. Erica Djossa, "136: Why Does a Messy House Give Me Anxiety? With KC Davis, @domesticblisters on TikTok and Founder of Struggle Care," August 31, 2020, *The Momwell Podcast*, podcast, MP3 audio, 55:53, momwell.com/listen.

5. Djossa, "136: Why Does a Messy House Give Me Anxiety?"

6. Djossa, "136: Why Does a Messy House Give Me Anxiety?"

7. Djossa, "136: Why Does a Messy House Give Me Anxiety?"

CHAPTER 7: THE SCHEDULER

1. Eve Rodsky, *Fair Play: A Game-Changing Solution for When You Have Too Much to Do (and More Life to Live)* (London: Quercus, 2021), 54–5.

2. Rodsky, *Fair Play*, 57–77.

3. *Merriam Webster*, s.v. "executive function," accessed April 17, 2023, merriam-webster.com/dictionary/executive%20function#:~:text=

%3A%20the%20group%20of%20complex%20mental,required %20for%20goal%2Ddirected%20behavior.

4. Kim Elsesser, "Moms Cut Work Hours Four Times More Than Dads During Pandemic," *Forbes*, July 17, 2020, forbes.com/sites /kimelsesser/2020/07/17/moms-cut-work-hours-four-times-more -than-dads-during-pandemic/?sh=225ceff149ca.
5. Brie Weiler Reynolds, "Lack of Flexible Work Keeps Moms from Staying in Workforce," FlexJobs, accessed April 17, 2023, flexjobs .com/blog/post/survey-flexible-work-moms/.
6. Katherine Schaeffer, "Working Moms in the U.S. Have Faced Challenges on Multiple Fronts during the Pandemic," Pew Research Center, May 6, 2022, pewresearch.org/fact-tank/2022/05/06/working -moms-in-the-u-s-have-faced-challenges-on-multiple-fronts-during -the-pandemic/.
7. Misty L. Heggeness et al., "Moms, Work and the Pandemic," United States Census Bureau, March 3, 2021, census.gov/library/stories /2021/03/moms-work-and-the-pandemic.html.
8. Erica Djossa, "127: Unpacking Gender Norms Part 1: Understand-ing the Connection to the Invisible Load with Gender Expert Kate Mangino," June 29, 2022, in *The Momwell Podcast*, podcast, MP3 audio, 48:49, momwell.com/listen.

CHAPTER 8: THE CREATOR OF FUN

1. Tugba Sabanoglu, "Holiday Retail Sales in the United States from 2002 to 2022," Statista, November 14, 2022, statista.com/statistics /243439/holiday-retail-sales-in-the-united-states/&sa=D&source= docs&ust=1680055012363332&usg=AOvVaw2g76VaO1xxGxw _p55ixmCO.
2. Jack Flynn, "35+ Amazing Advertising Statistics [2023]: Data + Trends," Zippia, January 16, 2023, zippia.com/advice/advertising -statistics/#:~:text=How%20many%20ads%20does%20a.
3. "Five Key Questions of Media Literacy," Center for Media Literacy, 2005, medialit.org/sites/default/files/14B_CCKQPoster+5essays.pdf.

CHAPTER 9: MANAGING YOUR MENTAL HEALTH

1. Martina Starck, Julia Grünwald, and Angelika A. Schlarb, "Occurrence of ADHD in Parents of ADHD Children in a Clinical Sample," *Neuropsychiatric Disease and Treatment* 12 (2016): 581–88, doi.org /10.2147/NDT.S100238.

2. Mira Elise Glaser Holthe and Eva Langvik, "The Strives, Struggles, and Successes of Women Diagnosed with ADHD as Adults," *SAGE Open* 7, no. 1 (2017), doi.org/10.1177/2158244017701799.

3. Erica Djossa, "164: Real Self-Care for Moms with Dr. Pooja Lakshmin, Psychiatrist," March 14, 2023, in *The Momwell Podcast*, podcast MP3 audio, 50:07, momwell.com/listen.

4. Erica Djossa, "003: Are Psychiatric Medications an Option While Pregnant or Nursing? with Reproductive Psychologist Dr. Kristin Lasseter," September 20, 2019, in *The Momwell Podcast*, podcast, MP3 audio, 49:01, momwell.com/listen.

5. Erica Djossa, "093: Setting Boundaries with Moms and Mothers-in-Law with @psychedmommy Dr. Ashurina Ream," November 3, 2021, in *The Momwell Podcast*, podcast MP3 audio, 57:24, momwell .com/listen.

6. Mara Glatzel, *Needy: How to Advocate for Your Needs and Claim Your Sovereignty* (Boulder, CO: Sounds True, 2023).

7. Marshall Rosenberg, *Nonviolent Communication: A Language of Life: Life-Changing Tools for Healthy Relationships* (Encinitas, CA: Puddle-Dancer Press, 2015).

CONCLUSION

1. *Merriam Webster*, s.v. "compassion," accessed April 17, 2023, merriam -webster.com/dictionary/compassion.

2. Erica Djossa, "157: Should I Have Another Baby? with Kate McReynolds, Mental Health Counselor," August 17, 2022, in *The Momwell Podcast*, podcast, MP3 audio, 51:58, momwell.com/listen.

ABOUT THE AUTHOR

Erica Djossa is the CEO and founder of Momwell, and a registered psychotherapist specializing in maternal mental health with over a decade of experience. As a mother of three rambunctious young boys, Erica understands first hand the challenges of motherhood. Perfectionism, pressure, and loss of identity fueled her battle with postpartum depression, and she realized how difficult it is to seek care. She founded *Happy as a Mother*, which has now evolved into *Momwell*, to provide mom-centered virtual therapy and mental health services for moms at every stage of their motherhood journey.

Erica is also a regular media contributor. She has been featured in *Time* magazine, *The Toronto Star*, *Cityline*, *Breakfast Television*, Scary Mommy, Medium, PopSugar, and Romper. Her graphics have been shared by celebrities like Snoop Dogg, Ashley Graham, Nia Long, Hilaria Baldwin, Christy Turlington, and Adrienne Bosh.

Erica is passionate about inclusive, accessible maternal mental healthcare, advocacy for women, and redefining the expectations of motherhood. She believes that moms everywhere should be able to define the role for themselves, retain their identities in motherhood, and break away from patterns of gender norms, unrealistic pressures, and socialized expectations.

ABOUT SOUNDS TRUE

Sounds True was founded in 1985 by Tami Simon with a clear mission: to disseminate spiritual wisdom. Since starting out as a project with one woman and her tape recorder, we have grown into a multimedia publishing company with a catalog of more than 3,000 titles by some of the leading teachers and visionaries of our time, and an ever-expanding family of beloved customers from across the world.

In more than three decades of evolution, Sounds True has maintained our focus on our overriding purpose and mission: to wake up the world. We offer books, audio programs, online learning experiences, and in-person events to support your personal growth and awakening, and to unlock our greatest human capacities to love and serve.

At SoundsTrue.com you'll find a wealth of resources to enrich your journey, including our weekly *Insights at the Edge* podcast, free downloads, and information about our nonprofit Sounds True Foundation, where we strive to remove financial barriers to the materials we publish through scholarships and donations worldwide.

To learn more, please visit SoundsTrue.com/freegifts or call us toll-free at 800.333.9185.

Together, we can wake up the world.

sounds true

WAKING UP THE WORLD

THE DEVIL
BEHIND
THE BADGE

THE DEVIL
BEHIND
THE BADGE

======

THE HORRIFYING TWELVE DAYS
OF THE BORDER PATROL
SERIAL KILLER

RICK JERVIS

DEYST.

An Imprint of WILLIAM MORROW

Photograph credits: Page vii: (*top left*) Courtesy of the family of Melissa Ramirez; (*top right*) Courtesy of the family of Claudine Anne Luera; (*bottom left*) Courtesy of the family of Guiselda Alicia Cantu; (*bottom right*) Courtesy of the family of Janelle Ortiz; page xiii: Webb County Sheriff's Office.

HarperCollins books may be purchased for educational, business, or sales promotional use. For information, please email the Special Markets Department at SPsales@harper collins.com.

FIRST EDITION

Designed by Jennifer Chung
Map design by Mike Hall

Library of Congress Cataloging-in-Publication Data has been applied for.

ISBN 978-0-06-296296-6

24 25 26 27 28 LBC 5 4 3 2 1

FOR ELENA

He said that men believe the blood of the slain to be of no consequence but that the wolf knows better.

—CORMAC MCCARTHY, *THE CROSSING*

For such men are false apostles, deceitful workmen, disguising themselves as apostles of Christ. And no wonder, for even Satan disguises himself as an angel of light.

—2 CORINTHIANS 11:13–14

Melissa Ramirez

Claudine Anne Luera

Guiselda "Chelly" Alicia Cantu

Janelle Ortiz

This narrative contains depictions of sexual assault, substance abuse disorder, and murder that may be triggering or disturbing for some people.

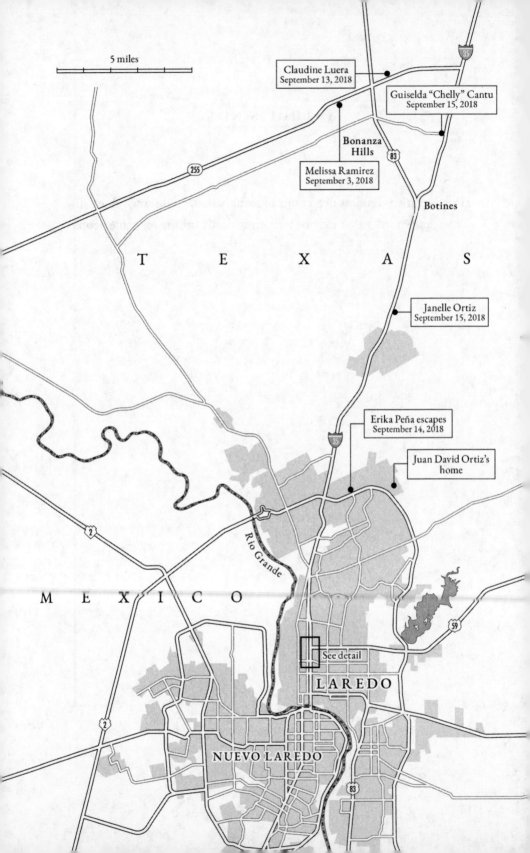

5 miles

Claudine Luera
September 13, 2018

Guiselda "Chelly" Cantu
September 15, 2018

Bonanza
Hills

Melissa Ramirez
September 3, 2018

Botines

T E X A S

Janelle Ortiz
September 15, 2018

Erika Peña escapes
September 14, 2018

Juan David Ortiz's
home

Río Grande

M E X I C O

See detail

LAREDO

NUEVO LAREDO

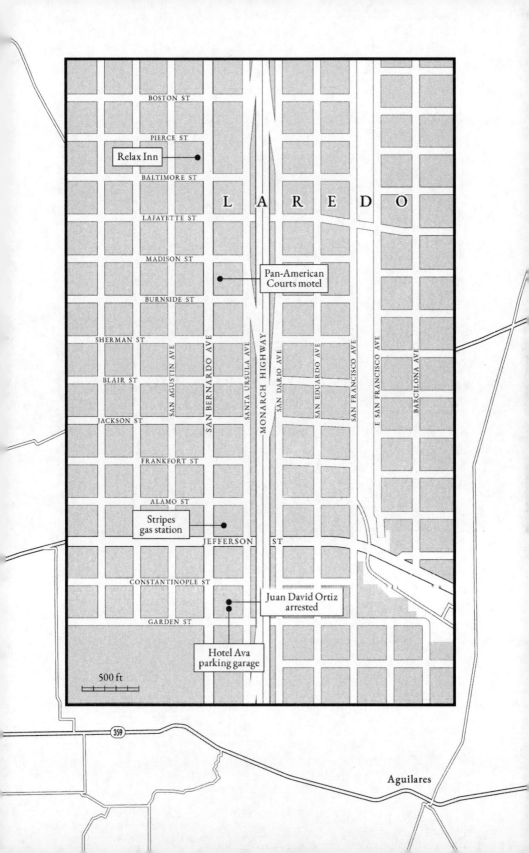

Juan David Ortiz,
early in his Border Patrol career

Erika Peña emerged from behind the Valero gas station in north Laredo, shirtless and terrified, her eyes scanning the dark lot for help.

She took staccato gulps of air, trying to wrangle her breath. Her heart hammered in her chest. Cortisol and adrenaline coursed through her bloodstream, colliding with morphine molecules from a recent heroin high. She kept walking, deciphering her next move.

It was an average Friday evening at the Valero off Bob Bullock Loop. Customers pumped gas; others strolled toward the Circle K convenience store for sodas or cigarettes. A few surely stole a glance at the panicked woman in ripped white jeans and a pink bra, though no one said anything. In Laredo, stranger things have emerged from gas station shadows.

Erika's mind reeled. Images, just a few moments old, turned in her mind as if from a dream. The familiar face. The white truck. Melissa. Claudine. David. His dead-eyed glare as he pulled out the gun and pointed it at her chest. The muzzle of the black weapon inches from her heart. Her impulse to go. *Go!* A struggle. His grip. The blouse being ripped off her back. Jumping out of the truck. Screaming. Running. *Go!*

Panting in front of the Circle K, she struggled with what to do next. Someone pointed her to pump number four, where a Texas Department of Public Safety state trooper filled his black Chevy Tahoe patrol unit with gas. Normally, Erika would head in the other direction from law enforcement officers; her lifestyle and livelihood didn't mix well with them. But at that moment, the red-and-blue lights looked like salvation itself. She walked fast across the gas station and approached the trooper.

"Help me! *Help me!*" Her story poured from her in a torrent: the truck, the gun, the escape.

Trooper Francisco Hernandez urged Erika to calm down. A thirteen-year veteran of the force, Hernandez was used to seeing people in states of distress. Usually the calmer he remained, the calmer they got. He asked if she needed medical attention; no, she said. To the lesser trained, a wild-eyed woman dressed in just a bra and telling a story involving a gunman would be cause to start slowly stepping away or to call in mental health professionals. Instead, Hernandez listened. Intently.

Suddenly, something Erika said clicked—a small detail in the current of words. Somehow, Erika had stumbled onto one of a dozen or so law enforcement officers in Webb County who knew precisely what to do with the information she was sharing.

"Sit tight," Hernandez told Erika. He positioned her by his SUV's driver's-side door, then glanced around the gas station to make sure the gunman wasn't still hunting her. After waiting nearly twenty minutes for Laredo police, he texted E. J. Salinas, a Texas Ranger special investigator who had been working a double murder case in Laredo that, for nearly two weeks, had stumped him and the entire Criminal Investigation Division at the Webb County Sheriff's Office.

Five minutes later, Salinas called him.

"Tengo una girl," Hernandez told the ranger in Spanglish, "who escaped from a guy who pointed a gun at her."

"Bring her in," Salinas replied.

====

FOUR WEEKS EARLIER, ON THE AFTERNOON OF AUGUST 17, 2018, Melissa Ramirez had been edgier than usual. Her sister-in-law, Gracie Perez, convinced her to accompany her across the international bridge into Nuevo Laredo, Mexico, to buy a tube of clotrimazole ointment for a rash that had bubbled across the neck of Gracie's two-year-old daughter.

Melissa, twenty-nine, didn't like Nuevo Laredo and rarely ventured there. She was born in Laredo, Texas, a city perched on the international boundary between Texas and Mexico, where nearly everyone spoke Spanish, where shop signs offered barbacoa tacos, seguros de auto, and muffler repair, and where most people had a tía or primo living across the Rio Grande in Nuevo Laredo. Even though Laredo and Nuevo Laredo were closely aligned, separated only by a four-hundred-foot-long bridge over a bend in the Rio Grande, Melissa feared the drug cartels and hit men who prowled the Mexican side. In her twenty-nine years, Melissa had only ventured across the bridge into Mexico a half dozen times.

But Gracie was insistent. The ointment was cheaper in Mexico than in the United States and could be bought without a prescription and with fewer questions. She didn't want to cross over alone.

Melissa was close to her sister-in-law. The two had gotten pregnant within a few years of each other as teenagers, had attended the same high school, shared a similar dry sense of humor, and both adored Melissa's younger brother, Cesar Ramirez, Gracie's husband. Melissa loved Gracie and would do anything for her. After a few pleading phone calls, Melissa relented and agreed to go with her into Mexico.

When Gracie picked her up at a friend's home near downtown Laredo, Melissa had just polished off a twenty-four-ounce can of Four Loko malt liquor beer, which packs the alcoholic punch of several smaller beers. Melissa drank, but it was rare to see her this inebriated. Standing five feet eight inches and barely 120 pounds, it didn't take much to wobble her, and here she was buzzed, moving with that cocky gait Gracie had seen before. Melissa slid into Gracie's car and giggled and rambled from one topic to the next, her speech choppy and slurry, her eyes rheumy. Melissa's straight, shoulder-length hair was so inky black it sometimes shaded blue. Her eyes were round and liquid black and squinted when she laughed, which was often. She had high, rounded cheekbones and smooth pearly white skin, fairer than the darker Indigenous Mexican features of other Latinas in Laredo. A natural beauty glinted through, veiled by years of substance and physical abuse to her body.

Gracie drove past strip malls anchored by H-E-B supermarkets and AutoZone stores, past two Taco Palenques and Los Jacales Mexican Restaurant. Despite the blistering heat of the tail end of a South Texas summer, with temperatures still in triple digits, Laredo bustled with shoppers, street vendors selling cacahuates in white paper cones, green-uniformed Border Patrol agents rumbling down avenues in white Ford

Explorers, and residents busily driving to and from work. Rent-a-tire shops crowded next to taquerías, cell phone repair stores, and Valero gas stations.

As Gracie and Melissa neared the border, the scent of warm conchas and pan dulce wafted from Mexican bakeries and mingled with the smell of grease from tire shops.

Gracie pointed her car down San Agustin Avenue, toward the signs for "International Bridge #2," on the northern bank of the Rio Grande, and parked in a lot behind the Outlet Shoppes at Laredo, a cluster of Banana Republic, Abercrombie & Fitch, and Nike stores that overlooked Mexico. Then she and Melissa walked across the bridge, glancing down at the green-brown river churning beneath them, and into Nuevo Laredo Melissa was jittery. Her eyes danced over the people around her, a habit acquired from long nights on streets lurking with danger. For the past decade, Melissa had been living, working, and surviving on the streets of Laredo. She offered quick sexual acts to truckers and drifters when she needed money and rarely kept enough of it for hot meals or new clothes. Most of her earnings fed a consuming crack cocaine and amphetamine habit.

They walked to a pharmacy a block from the bridge and bought the clotrimazole. The whole venture took thirty minutes. As they joined the line of people making their way back across the bridge into the United States, Melissa realized she had forgotten her ID. She was a U.S. citizen but had never owned a passport. She'd had several driver's licenses over the years but kept losing them, and her mother kept her birth certificate—the sole document proving her existence—safely in a drawer in her bedroom, fearing she'd lose that, too. As Melissa and Gracie waited their turn with U.S. Customs and Border Protection, Melissa glared at the line of Mexicans waiting to enter the United States and the CBP guards checking passports. "They're staring at me," she told Gracie. "Everyone's staring at me."

Gracie assured her no one was looking at her and urged her to play it cool. She was used to bouts of paranoia from Melissa and knew the best way to defuse them was to keep calm herself. When it was their turn at the counter, Melissa explained her situation to the CBP agent: U.S. citizen, no ID. The border agent punched her name into a computer and asked why she didn't have an ID. Melissa said it was because her mom didn't trust her. The conversation escalated. "I am a U.S. citizen," Melissa said, anger injected into every syllable. Gracie tensed. She knew from past experiences how quickly Melissa's temper could flare. When the agent asked her to sign her name on a form, Melissa wrote it out in mocking, oversized letters. He waved them through.

Gracie had grown used to Melissa's emotional turbulence. She had seen it get her into fights, first in their high school days and then on city streets. Once, Melissa and Gracie were stuck in traffic near San Bernardo Avenue in central Laredo, and Melissa had gotten into a yelling match with another driver who refused to let them merge into a turn lane. Melissa had sprung out of the car and jumped on the stunned motorist's hood, yelling obscenities. The driver had rolled up her window.

Back on the U.S. side, Gracie drove Melissa to her mother's two-bedroom trailer home on Margarita Lane in Rio Bravo, a small, dusty colonia fourteen miles south of Laredo that sits directly on the Rio Grande. Broken toys and a trampoline sat in the side yard. Her mother, Cristina Benavides, had cared for Melissa's two children, Allan, four, and Cristina, seven, ever since the drugs took hold of Melissa and child welfare workers threatened to take them away.

Inside the trailer, Melissa had a tickle fight with Allan, poked through the refrigerator, and teased her mom about her clunky Chinese-made ZTE smartphone. Her kids always brightened Melissa's mood. Suddenly, a gloom settled into her. She walked over to a rosary Cristina kept draped over an open Bible on a small table by the kitchen, mumbled a few verses, and made the sign of the cross. *En el nombre del Padre y del Hijo y del Espíritu Santo. Amen.*

Cristina eyed her daughter curiously. Melissa was raised Catholic but rarely went to church and wasn't outwardly religious. There were no crucifixes or gold-plated santos dangling from chains around her neck, like other Laredo women her age had, and she rarely talked about Jesus or heaven. Curious and troubled, Cristina grabbed her smartphone and began filming her daughter.

"Who do you think you are, La Gordiloca?" Melissa told her, referring to the nickname of Laredo's popular renegade citizen journalist. Then Melissa stopped smiling and a darkness draped her face. She slumped into an overstuffed recliner and hushed the room. "Me van a matar," Melissa told her mom and Gracie. "Así es como me matarán," she continued, bowing her head slightly and pointing two fingers at her right temple.

Cristina told her to hush.

"Listen to me," Melissa said. "In less than a month, I'll be dead."

Cristina winced at the words. Gracie was equally unnerved. Melissa was known to act silly and have mercurial mood changes, but this felt different. It was too matter-of-fact, too sincere. Cristina grew worried. It wasn't the first time her daughter had seemingly peeked into the future. As a young girl, she once predicted an empty lot in their neighborhood would soon become a convenience store. A few weeks later, workers broke ground on the store. She would also randomly find long-lost trinkets around the house: her mother's watch, a missing sock, a toy. Likely just coincidences, but Cristina placed credence into those things; the ability to see into the void—el mundo espiritual—was a very real thing, as far as she was concerned, and not something easily dismissed.

For Cristina, Melissa's words that afternoon arrived after more than a decade of worrying about, fighting, badgering, caring for, reprimanding, and coddling her daughter, as Melissa bounced between therapists, rehab centers, and the streets of Laredo. Cristina knew what her daughter did on the streets, how she leased her body to strangers for money, and of the sickness that made her dependent on drugs. Crack cocaine, pills, and weeklong binges had hardened her daughter; Cristina longed for the soft, giggly baby she once bounced on her knee and wondered where that child had gone.

Over the years, Melissa had come home with fat lips and purpled eyes from scrapes with clients and fellow sex workers. She came home limping, the soles of her feet raw and bloodied from walking for miles in chancletas or, when those were sold or stolen, barefooted. Far more worrying to Cristina were the long stretches when Melissa didn't appear at all. Weeks at a time of nothingness. No phone calls assuring her mom she was all right and no phone for Cristina to call—Melissa had long ago sold her only cell phone for drug money. In those stretches when she wouldn't hear from her daughter, Cristina's mind would spin with the worst possible scenarios: she was sprawled and overdosed on a motel room floor; she was lying unconscious in a hospital, unidentified; a medical examiner somewhere was tagging her toe.

She would spend long, sleepless nights rubbing her rosary beads and scanning her daughter's Facebook page for clues of her whereabouts. Her daughter's life was like a hazy, jagged dream, interrupted by periods when Melissa would suddenly appear at her trailer door, bruised, tired, and hungry but alive—and the haze would sharpen into focus, if only for a few days. Cristina wanted her daughter off the streets, told her so relentlessly, but when she showed up at home, in whatever condition, Cristina kicked into mother mode: bandaging her swollen feet, drawing a hot shower, cooking up vats of rice and picadillo, Melissa's favorite. Each time Melissa appeared, hope yawned in Cristina that her family could return to what it was, that Melissa would stay for good this time.

Melissa never openly talked to her mother about what she did to survive on the streets, but she never concealed it from her, either. Laredo and Rio Bravo were small enough and close enough to each other that word rippled back to Cristina through concerned friends who had seen Melissa along San Bernardo Avenue, climbing into strangers' cars. Cristina knew that Melissa had been with truck drivers, migrant workers, businessmen. She knew that she slept with ranchers and the occasional off-duty law enforcement officer.

Now, Melissa was in her living room, adding a new dimension of dread to Cristina's life. The specificity with which her daughter described her imminent death unnerved her.

"Cállate," Cristina hushed her with a nervous half laugh. "Your kids will hear."

Melissa looked up at her mom, her eyes calm and dark. "Pay attention," she said. "I'm not kidding."

An hour later, Gracie drove Melissa back to San Bernardo Avenue in Laredo, a ten-minute drive from Rio Bravo. Melissa urged Gracie to hang out with her. "Vamos a porriar," she told her. "Let's have a drink. You may not see me again."

Melissa made Gracie go through a drive-through liquor store on San Bernardo, and they bought two more tall Four Lokos. Gracie pulled into the parking lot of a small park, and the two sat and sipped the beers and chatted as kids clambered up jungle gyms nearby. Melissa talked about her five kids—two living with her mom, three others in state custody with foster or adopted families. She loved all her kids, she told Gracie, but she needed to regain stability in order to see them again.

Melissa asked Gracie for her cell phone and dialed the number of a caseworker with Texas Child Protective Services who had been working her custody cases. There was still one child, ten-month-old Angel, Melissa hoped to regain custody of. Her plan was for her mom to take him temporarily until Melissa could get off the streets, get off drugs, find an apartment, and get a job. In the soft dusk light by the park, the effects of the strong beer swirling through her, the prospect seemed reachable to Melissa. She could turn her life around, she told Gracie. She could be a better person. A better mom.

The caseworker answered Melissa's call and got to the point: forget it, he told her that day. The child would remain in state custody and be adopted out. Melissa had missed too many court hearings, failed too many drug tests. She had lost all rights to her son.

Melissa clicked off the call and sobbed. The two hugged, and Melissa asked Gracie again if she would stay with her that evening. They could do whatever she wanted, Melissa said; she just didn't want to be alone. Gracie knew Melissa's destructive lifestyle repelled most people around her, family included, but she also knew this softer side to Melissa. She knew the Melissa who brought her plates of fresh enchiladas when she was pregnant with Carolynn, when Gracie's own family had shunned her for getting pregnant during her junior year in high school.

She knew the Melissa who listened patiently and openly during marathon late-night chats, when she told Melissa how terrified she was of having a baby, and how Melissa had hushed her and promised that they were in this together. Always. Gracie loved her sister-in-law and wanted to be there for her. But it was getting late, and she had her own family to attend to. She needed to go.

Dusk shaded to night, and San Bernardo's streetlights blinked on. Gracie drove down the four-lane avenue under their warm glare as trucks rumbled by. She stopped at Loma Alta Motel, a whitewashed two-story, U-shaped building and one of the cheaper motels on the strip, a magnet for prostitutes and johns and the perpetual violence and pain that trailed them. Some of the female sex workers who lived there were emerging from rooms, readying for a night on the streets.

Gracie watched as Melissa slowly got out of the car. She waved goodbye, turned toward Loma Alta, and vanished into one of its rooms.

PART 1

CHAPTER 1

Pat and Nora Roth drove north along Highway 83 in the rented Penske moving truck from McAllen to Laredo, marveling at how the landscape morphed from the green lushness of the Rio Grande Valley to the arid thornscrub ecoregion of Laredo.

It was the summer of 2014, and Pat had just accepted a job as an executive at a Laredo-area roofing company. Pat, fifty, of Adkins, Texas, and Nora, twenty-eight, of Michoacán, Mexico, had met a year earlier at a McAllen nightclub, and despite the age difference and the fact that Pat spoke next to nothing of Nora's native Spanish, the pair had started dating immediately. Communicating mostly through the Google Translate app on Pat's phone, they had moved in together. Soon after, they had been married. The move to Laredo was the first big step in their new life together.

Savannas of flat scrubland and honey mesquite trees stretched to the horizon and shone white under the glare of the sun as Pat piloted the Penske northwest along the border. The flat land was layered in prickly pear cacti and the gray thornbushes known as chaparral. Plants around Laredo are either heavily armed or toxic or both and able to defend themselves not unlike its earliest Spanish settlers, who found ways to survive through drought, famine, oppressive heat, and raiding Comanches and Lipan Apaches. The vast sky turned a grayish white in the summer heat as they approached Laredo, a few miles east of the Chihuahuan Desert. The heat pressed in like a vise, spiking to triple digits and challenging the Penske's whining air-conditioning.

═══

Take a Greyhound bus from San Antonio to Monterrey, Mexico, and doze off midway, and you'll wake up as the bus pulls into Laredo's Jarvis Plaza. Stroll a few blocks south to San Agustín Plaza, and it's hard to discern whether you're still in the United States or have crossed into Mexico. Spanish signs dominate the landscape, heralding "Ventas Especiales" or "Almuerzo Caliente." The rhythmic cadence of Spanish drifts from the lips of pedestrians, as they cradle duffel bags crammed with baby clothes, blenders, DVD players, quinceañera dresses, and shiny new soccer balls, awaiting rides back to Mexico. The cobblestone streets and copper statues of the plaza are reminiscent of those in Mexico City or Guadalajara. The Spanish Revival architecture of La Posada Hotel could be equally at home in Puebla or San Miguel de Allende, and the soaring clock tower of San Agustín Cathedral, which traces its beginnings to 1755, could be easily confused for the one in Zacatecas or Cuernavaca.

Other U.S. border towns are similarly influenced by their southern neighbor, but few have that influence so deeply entrenched in their culture, traditions, and language. Listen to two native Laredoans talk and it's not uncommon to hear the conversation swerve continually and effortlessly between English and Spanish. A customer at a used car lot may ask the owner, "Oye, guey, do you have a white troca que tenga un radio that works well?" The owner may answer, "Sí, patrón, we have a nice troca para que veas in the back lot." Each understands the other perfectly. The worker behind the counter at Taco Palenque may ask the customer with combed-back jet-black hair and dark eyes, ";Quieres probar el especial de hoy?" while turning to the Anglo businessman next to him and asking with a smile, "How may I help you today?"

Pat didn't speak or understand more than a few passing words in Spanish. Still, he was charmed by Laredo's sights, sounds, and smells.

As they entered the city, they passed signs for International Bridge 2, the southern terminus of the 1,568-mile-long Interstate 35, which begins in Duluth, Minnesota, to the north and ends at the Laredo–Nuevo Laredo border. They drove west on Hidalgo Street, then south, past the Biomat USA plasma center and the Border Heritage Museum, over cobblestone roads and into San Agustín Plaza. At the plaza's southern edge, La Posada Hotel's wrought-iron balconies, ceramic red-tile roof, and seven flags flapping above the front entrance reminded passersby of the seven entities under which Laredo has been ruled. The plaza emanated history—and for generations bore silent witness to Laredo's tumultuous past.

=====

SINCE DON TOMÁS SÁNCHEZ FIRST FOUNDED THIS VILLAGE IN the sharp bend of the Rio Grande in the name of the Spanish Crown in 1755, Laredo has seen its share of violence and vice. In April 1790, a band of Lipan Apaches overran the town, captured the military garrison's powder magazine, and blew it up, nearly ending Laredo's existence before it had begun. As the town's defenders retreated to their homes, the Natives seized San Agustín Plaza and, throughout the night, celebrated, terrifying the Spanish settlers with singing, yelling, and the loud clatter of drums. At first light, the Natives withdrew, ending the first battle of Laredo and leaving residents stunned and horrified.

By the 1830s, the arid region around Laredo remained part of Mexico but was caught in the middle between rebel Texans and Mexican generals. In the winter of 1836, General Antonio López de Santa Anna marched six thousand Mexican infantrymen up from Saltillo, Mexico, and across the Rio Grande near what today is Eagle Pass, Texas, about one hundred miles upriver from Laredo, en route to the Alamo Mission in San Antonio to face off against James Bowie, David Crockett, and the rest of the doomed rebels.

Four years later, Laredo hosted its own revolution. Shortly after Texas staked its independence from Mexico, Laredo became the seat of the Republic of the Rio Grande, declaring itself an independent nation. The breakaway republic, which included three northern Mexican states, consisted mostly of disgruntled rancheros angered by Santa Anna's seizure of power in Mexico City. It reigned for just 294 days, until centralist Mexican forces crushed the republic's fledgling army.

The rebellion, albeit short-lived, awarded Laredo the distinction of being the only Texas city ruled under seven flags: Spain, France, Mexico, the Republic of Texas, the Republic of the Rio Grande, the Confederacy, and the United States.

The 1848 Treaty of Guadalupe Hidalgo, which ended the Mexican-American War, split the city along the Rio Grande, creating Laredo to its north and Nuevo Laredo to its south. Laredo's designation as a U.S. city didn't stop Laredoans from treating the two sides as one sprawling city, crossing constantly back and forth. Nor did it stem its lawlessness. Laredo's remote location—it was a two-week oxcart journey over harsh terrain and through Native territory to San Antonio, the nearest U.S. city—made it an ideal place for rebels, revolutionaries, smugglers, and bandidos to avoid the legal reach of Mexico City or Austin. The border town's searing heat, proximity to Mexico, and undercurrent of danger spawned a state of lawlessness rivaling any frontier outpost. Hooves and carriage wheels kicked up clouds of dust that powdered the town and clogged lungs. Native Americans routinely attacked the ranches around Laredo, and smugglers, sneaking animal hides or precious gems across the U.S.-Mexico line, often shot it out with constables or customs agents on city streets. Saloons throughout town fueled the violence with cheap whiskey. In 1854, a writer identifying themself as "Texas" described Laredo life in a dispatch to the *New York Times,* reporting repeated Indian attacks, public debauchery, and bloody street clashes. "Everything is in a state of siege," they wrote. "The fact is, bad people sell bad brandy which drives bad men mad, and they devour each other . . . The climate is choleric. When a man has to undergo three hours a day of temperatures of 115 degrees even in the shade . . . with an atmosphere filled with clouds of the fine dust, he is apt to grow 'hot.'"

=====

OVER THE DECADES, LAREDO SLOWLY EVOLVED AWAY FROM ITS outlaw past. Today, more than fifteen thousand trucks cross the border through Laredo each day, making it the busiest inland port along the

U.S.-Mexico border, and carry nearly $300 billion worth of goods each year, or more than half of all U.S.-Mexico trade. Despite the constant bloody turf wars of drug cartels across the Rio Grande in Mexico, violent crime remains low in Laredo, with only a dozen or so homicides a year in a city of 260,000, making it one of the safer cities in Texas. Each morning, thousands of Mexicans from Nuevo Laredo stream through the port of entry, flashing their laminated border crossing cards to come to Laredo to shop, study at Texas A&M International University, visit family, or, even though they often lack official permission, work at the city's many hotels, restaurants, and stores. The two sides share a common language, culture, and, often, family. It's not uncommon for a couple to get married in Laredo and have their wedding reception in Nuevo Laredo, or vice versa.

Each February, the city bursts with carnival rides and parades in celebration of George Washington's birthday, a gathering that culminates with two youngsters dressed in antebellum American costumes meeting on the bridge over the Rio Grande and embracing a young couple dressed in similarly historic Mexican garb. It's a singular Laredo event dating back to the 1890s celebrating its unique perch on the border.

Despite Laredo's relatively low murder rate, the city's location on the border, with global drug rings smuggling millions of dollars' worth of contraband and people past border agents each year, means illicit drugs—and the criminality they draw—are never too far off.

———

PAT FELT THE TUG OF LAREDO'S HISTORY AS HE DROVE THE PENske truck through central Laredo and out to the northern stretches of town, toward a house he had rented with Nora. The two settled into their new home as Pat spent his first six months working as vice president for the roofing company before stumbling onto a new opportunity: his company had done a complete re-roof of the Relax Inn, a thirty-room, two-story 1970s-era motel on San Bernardo Avenue a few miles north of downtown. The motel's owner asked Pat to manage the property, in exchange for living rent-free in the one-bedroom apartment adjacent to the lobby. Pat could save some money, launch his own roofing company, and employ Nora to run the front desk. They snatched up the offer and moved into the Relax Inn.

The motel's small lobby had a counter, a stained Mr. Coffee coffeemaker, and a round clock hanging on a wall next to a picture of Nuestra Señora de Guadalupe, Mexico's patron saint. A cracked bulletproof window faced the parking lot and had a slot at the bottom where customers slid keys or cash. A sticker taped to the window warned that the property was under surveillance, and, under it, a letterboard alerted customers, in English and Spanish, "Cash Only" and "We Do Not Lend Phone."

From the lobby's east window, Pat looked out on San Bernardo Avenue, a four-mile stretch of Mexican import shops, drive-through liquor stores, taco stands, and $30-a-night motels. By day, tourists—some from Monterrey, others from Austin or Dallas—perused the rows of earthenware plates, lawn decor, and hand-carved benches in the import shops or lunched on parrilladas at the elegant Palenque Grill. By night, the avenue populated with sex workers, drug pushers, addicts, and undercover vice squads. Other motels on the strip, like the Pan-American Courts, Loma Alta Motel, and Hotel Plaza Laredo, also offered $30- or $40-a-night rooms, and the sex trade thrived within their walls. Some of the sex workers lived at the Relax Inn, paying their nightly rent in crumpled ten- and twenty-dollar bills; others used it strictly for transactional purposes. Rooms at the Relax Inn had stained dark green carpeting, green drapes, and patches covering holes on the ceiling and walls, some flaking down like white tongues. A single air-conditioning unit in the corner of the room had to be turned on in advance. Television remotes were kept behind the counter in the lobby and handed only to customers who paid a $20 deposit at check-in. Mattresses were firm and pillows thin and lumpy. Roaches sometimes darted across the carpeted floor; other times rodents scampered behind furniture.

The Relax Inn's cheap rent made it the ideal setting for victims of substance abuse disorders and weekend binges. Drug dealers in cars with temporary tags drove into the motel's parking lot, where they exchanged baggies for cash. After customers checked out, rooms were littered with small plastic bags dusted with heroin or cocaine residue, dirty syringes, and bloodstained bedsheets. Maids wore rubber gloves and changed sheets with an abundance of caution so as not to accidentally poke themselves with discarded needles. One day, shortly after taking over the Relax Inn, Pat discovered a man in his early twenties slumped on the sidewalk just outside the property, his eyes rolled back in his head. Paramedics arrived, pumped the man's stomach, and ferried him away.

It soon dawned on Pat that the opportunity he'd enthusiastically accepted came with daily brushes with Laredo's criminal underworld. "I didn't know what I was walking myself into," Pat said later. "I've seen things there that just blow my mind."

One repeat customer always requested the same room—room 101—for one night, checked out the next morning, then reappeared two nights later. Always paid cash. On the night between his visits, another man would request the same room for one night. Growing suspicious, Pat searched the room and discovered a plate-sized hole behind the bed's headboard. The first man had been leaving drugs in the hole, to be retrieved by the second man. He posted pictures of both men in the lobby and barred them from the premises.

The flow of cash, drugs, and addiction stretched well beyond the confines of the Relax Inn and pulsed up and down San Bernardo, just as it had for generations.

═══

KNOWN AS THE PAN-AMERICAN HIGHWAY IN THE 1800S, THE avenue was the final southern leg of the 157-mile road linking Laredo with San Antonio. At a time when it took more than a week to travel between the two cities using horse-drawn carriages, the road connecting them became a well-heeled highway for all shades of travelers looking for adventure. Laredo was the country's southernmost outpost.

Throughout the nineteenth century, the stretch of the Pan-American

Highway that ran through Laredo teemed with adventurers, Mexican merchants, con men, bandidos, ranch hands, rum runners, tequileros, Texas lawmen, and fugitives. Bordellos sprouted up along the corridor to serve the newcomers, as well as saloons and mezcal bars friendly to prostitutes. Money and booze flowed freely into the twentieth century as the avenue, now renamed San Bernardo, became the ideal setting for the city's entrepreneurial sex workers and madams. Prostitutes from Nuevo Laredo flocked to the new action on San Bernardo Avenue. Mexican, Anglo, and African American sex workers loitered in the avenue's roadhouses and bordellos, fraternizing with drunken tourists and rowdy locals.

The lascivious activity grew so rampant that, in July 1937, a group of concerned San Bernardo citizens petitioned city leaders to bring an end to it. "Protests from residents of the vicinity of a roadhouse and other notorious resorts that are constantly infested by bawdy women, drunken men and immoral sights that are to be witnessed, together with the use of language and yelling that would shame anyone, have come to the council," a front-page story in the *Laredo Times* read. Later that month, the *Laredo Times* ran another front-page article complaining of police inaction, with the headline: "Prostitutes Still Welcome Laredo Visitors." Even as detectives targeted the bordellos and saloons catering to the sex trade, not all Laredoans supported the vice raids. "Your attack on the San Bernardo Ave., courtesans and groggeries is below par for the press of 1937," one *Laredo Times* reader complained in a letter to the editor. "Prostitution thrives in Laredo, even under most unfavorable conditions. It has always thrived and always will."

By the 1970s and '80s, the bordellos were gone, but San Bernardo Avenue's reputation as the place for action in the city remained. High schoolers showed off tricked-out Mustangs and Corvettes down the strip, Tejano music and hip-hop pouring from their speakers. A theater showing pornographic movies opened for a while on the avenue, then closed. Drive-through liquor stores sold beer to minors, while scantily clad female employees offered customers quick sex acts for money along with their booze purchases. The strip became known by its Spanish-sounding nickname, "Sanber" (pronounced with a roll of the final *r*: *SAHN-berr*).

Police squads eventually cracked down on underage drinking and the rampant drug deals along San Bernardo but struggled to slow prostitution. Entrenched in the strip for more than 150 years, sex work continued on side streets, behind gas stations, and within the avenue's clusters of cheap motels. Beginning around the 1970s, another factor bolstered the sex trade along San Bernardo: black tar heroin. Grown in the mountains of southwest Mexico, Laredo's black tar heroin, known locally as "chiva," was sold as tiny black goo balls ("big as a booger," as one Laredo police investigator described it) wrapped in aluminum foil or in the cut-out corners of plastic sandwich bags for as little as $10 a hit. Heroin swept through Laredo with the startling punch of a rogue wave. The Houston division of the U.S. Drug Enforcement Administration, which covers a swath of South Texas stretching from Brownsville to Del Rio along the border and north to Waco, saw heroin seizures in its area soar, from 198 kilos in fiscal year 2016 to 535 kilos in fiscal year 2019. The border often bore the brunt of the scourge. Overdose deaths in Laredo, fueled mainly by heroin mixed with fentanyl, nearly doubled from 22 in 2014 to 43 in 2017—or around 17 per 100,000 residents, significantly higher than Texas's overdose death rate.

Young women—some just out of high school—turned to sex work to finance their growing heroin habits. They clustered along the avenue, picking up johns at bus stops, and used their earnings to buy foils of chiva and get high at "trap houses" so named because once you started visiting them, it was hard to stop.

Ridding Laredo of its heroin and sex worker scourge became a thorny challenge for police. More so than with other drugs, informants were particularly hard to flip, since they feared being cut off from their habit and facing dreaded heroin withdrawal. Nearly all the dozen or so prostitutes Laredo police vice squads routinely picked up along San Bernardo were working to fund heroin habits. The illicit activity became so prevalent along the San Bernardo corridor that the department, in 2018, landed a federal grant to help with monitoring and enforcement. Money

from Operation Stonegarden, a federal initiative to promote cooperation between local and federal agencies, allowed Laredo police to install
surveillance cameras along the strip and help train and fund undercover
sting operations. The beefed-up surveillance led to dozens of arrests and
shuttered trap houses in the area. But as soon as one closed, a new one
popped up. The same sex workers were arrested repeatedly. A few days
or weeks later, they would be released from jail for lack of evidence or
witnesses.

Back on the street, the sex workers—like they had for generations
before them—gravitated to San Bernardo Avenue and, more specifically,
the Relax Inn.

———

PAT AND NORA DECIDED TO THWART ILLICIT ACTIVITY AT THE
Relax Inn, even if it cost them customers. Pat invited Laredo police
detectives to set up undercover sting operations at the motel, including
sweeping the property with drug-sniffing dogs. Nora, who ran the front
desk with a photographic memory and steely determination, refused
rooms to those she recognized as repeat offenders. She and Pat raised
rates from $55 to $75 a night and required a $30 deposit. Some clients
threatened her when denied a room, but most drifted away, looking for
an easier route to drugs and a clean bed.

Business sagged, but the place quieted. Police cruisers routinely took
laps through the motel parking lot, aiming spotlights into parked cars.
Word spread along San Bernardo Avenue that the Relax Inn was no longer a safe haven for partying or drugs. The clientele shifted from johns
and drug users to truck drivers, day laborers, and shoppers from Mexico.

Pat and Nora agreed on another rule that nearly crippled their
business: no prostitutes or prostitution anywhere on the property. The
activity was too risky and almost always led to hard-core drug use and
volatile personalities. They ran sex workers off their lot and posted
pictures of those who kept returning, to alert workers not to rent them
rooms.

They made an exception, however, for four women: Claudine, Chelly, Janelle, and Melissa, who had been frequenting the Relax Inn as sex workers on and off for the better part of five years. Pat saw them repeatedly lead clients into rooms for an hour or so at a time. He knew what they were up to. But these women were different. They respected the property, paid in cash, and displayed a sense of humor and humanity that struck a chord with Pat. Behind the crushed vein scars and scabbed skin, behind the tough personas and occasional angry outbursts, Pat saw glimpses of loyalty and love and humor that set the four women apart. He let them stay.

The four women hung out with one another constantly, sometimes sharing rooms. Chelly had scarred, pus-filled boils on her legs, revealing decades of drug injection, but she always paid on time, even when business was slow. Janelle, a sassy transgender woman, and her brother, Ezekiel, would sweep the driveway if they were short on rent money and make Pat laugh with off-color jokes. Claudine was older than the others and spoke with a fluency and education few other women on the avenue possessed. Melissa had trouble controlling her barbed disposition but was kept in line by her friends and generally friendly with Pat and Nora. When not making trouble, Melissa was funny and generous, sharing what little money or food she may have scored that day. Pat called Janelle "Double-G" (for the false bosom she propped under her T-shirt); Ezekiel was "EZ."

Chelly was the hardest worker, walking the avenue every day, rain or shine, always scraping enough money together for a room. She stayed in room 207 for weeks or months at a time, with a boyfriend who doubled as a bodyguard. When other women on the strip ran out of money and didn't have a place to stay, Chelly would open her door and let them sleep on a comforter on the floor or take a quick shower. Her room was constantly buzzing with people and activity. She would rent out her room to other girls on the avenue, allowing them to take customers there and taking a $5 cut from the transaction.

Other times, when Chelly was not around and Melissa or Janelle needed a room, Pat would open one of his recently vacated rooms and let them take a nap on the unmade bed or use the shower. Whenever he made brisket or chicken wings on the charcoal grill in his apartment's small, walled-off patio, the women would drift over—some hadn't eaten in days—and he would feed them. They became less like customers, more like younger, albeit reckless, sisters.

In exchange, the women kept the Relax Inn safe. They knew who the troublemakers were and warned them to steer clear of the property. They confided in Pat and rarely hid how they made their money. "They would show me where they would get their drugs, they would tell me everything," Pat said. "At the end of the day, they were just crying out for help."

Farther down San Bernardo, as dusk fell, other sex workers fanned out along the four-lane avenue and drifted in and out of hotels like the Loma Alta and Hotel Plaza, making enough money for one more crack hit or pinch of chiva. Some were trying to erase memories of grade school rapes; others were quieting brains revved by bipolar or other disorders. For Melissa Ramirez, the crack cocaine she smoked out of a small glass pipe she tucked away in her bra helped blur bad memories.

==

AFTER THE DAY SHE WENT TO MEXICO WITH HER SISTER-IN-LAW in August 2018, Melissa mostly vanished from her family's life. Gracie and Melissa's mom, Cristina, heard from her only occasionally, and her friends along the strip saw her sporadically, usually when flagging down customers along San Bernardo. She drifted from hotel to hotel, spending days sharing a pipe with others in an empty lot on San Agustin Avenue. By the end of August, Melissa had smoked through the little money she had. She had no place to stay and no money for a hotel room. Even Pat at the Relax Inn could no longer shelter her because of her relentless lack of funds. Barefoot and homeless, carrying a small plastic bag filled with a few personal items, Melissa limped down San Bernardo Avenue. She needed a miracle.

Then she ran into an old friend.

CHAPTER 2

Emily Varela, twenty-six, saw Melissa Ramirez hobbling along San Bernardo Avenue in late August 2018, her feet bloodied and blistered. She offered to let Melissa stay with her in her small second-floor room at the Pan-American Courts, three blocks down from the Relax Inn.

Melissa and Emily had been friends for years, long before Emily was Emily, back when she was still Emilio, being bullied at school and struggling with her sexual and gender identity. Relieved, Melissa accepted her friend's offer.

Inside the room at the Pan-American, Emily pushed aside mounds of T-shirts, bras, shoes, empty bags of Flamin' Hot Cheetos, and discarded cigarette packs and pulled in a used love seat next to the room's bare mattress for Melissa. Jeans, shirts, Subway sandwich wrappers, and Styrofoam gas station soda cups littered the stained blue-carpeted floor. Dingy blue curtains hung over the only window, which was covered with tinfoil. Four wigs, including a short hot-pink one and a long, flowing black one, dangled on the back of a folding chair. Emily peeled off the wig on her head and propped it with the others.

Emily knew she was taking a risk bringing in her old friend. She had been recently released from Webb County Jail, where she had spent four months on drug possession charges, and a parole officer was paying her unannounced visits at the Pan-American. She had managed to wean herself off a crack cocaine habit while in jail and was hoping to stay clean. Any hint of the drug could land her back in jail. The manager of the Pan-American could also notice the smell and kick them both out of the motel—the one place on the strip that had welcomed Emily and that she could afford. She knew her friend's wild streak and penchant for getting high. She gave Melissa an ultimatum: no drugs in the room or anywhere on the motel premises. Melissa agreed.

The two picked up where their friendship had left off years earlier. They slept, worked the streets at night, and reminisced about growing up in Laredo.

=====

MELISSA RAMIREZ GREW UP IN RIO BRAVO, THE THIRD OF FOUR children born to Cristina Benavides, a Nuevo Laredo native who had lived in Laredo and its surroundings for most of her adult life. By the time Cristina gave birth to Melissa, she already had two other children: Carlos, who was seven at the time of Melissa's birth, and Erika, who was three. Cristina loved all her children but *adored* Melissa, or "Meli," as she called her. She was enamored by her daughter's dark full-moon eyes, her long lashes, her smooth, porcelain skin.

The children's father, Juan Ramirez, also from Nuevo Laredo, was a drifter and day laborer who flitted between Mexico and the United States and in and out of prison. By the time Cristina's fourth child, Cesar, was born in 1997, he was gone for good. Cristina moved herself and her children into her mother Olga's four-bedroom home on Margarita Lane in Rio Bravo, a grouping of low-slung concrete cylinder homes and brown lawns torched by the South Texas sun. Plastic flamingos and porcelain Virgen de Guadalupe statuettes dotted front lawns. As Cristina worked odd jobs, Olga became the kids' main caretaker.

Melissa called her grandmother "mamiabuela," an endearing confluence of the Spanish words for "mother" and "grandmother." As a toddler, Melissa flashed violent tantrums and had a penchant for drama, sometimes crying and screaming for more than an hour if she didn't get her way. Olga would simply roll her eyes and let her cry it out.

When summer muscled in, the Ramirez children filled a bucket with balloons and had water balloon fights in the front yard or chased el heladero down the street. Melissa became inseparable from Cesar, whom she affectionately called "Gordo." The two would watch horror movies like *Halloween* and *A Nightmare on Elm Street* on cable TV or stroll through the nearby Blockbuster store together. At dusk, they would hunt for crickets in the yard's high grass or cut through empty lots to the nearby food mart for Flamin' Hot Cheetos and sodas, using pocket change given to them by their abuela. Melissa bought pickles out of a jar on the counter, sliced them up, and ate them with her spicy chips.

Melissa became fiercely protective of her younger brother. One day, as Cesar walked home from his elementary school, he ran up against a group of older boys. The boys threw rocks at him, and Cesar ran all the way home in tears. Seeing her brother's distraught state, Melissa grabbed a hammer from her grandmother's cabinet and marched Cesar back to where the kids were.

"If any one of you touches him," she warned them, waving the hammer, "I'll smash your heads in."

Cesar was left alone after that.

Daisy Hernandez, Melissa's friend who lived next door, remembered her as generous and funny. Each time the ice cream truck clamored down the street, Melissa pulled out a few extra dollars to treat her neighbors. As middle schoolers, Melissa and Daisy caught rides to Mall del Norte in Laredo together, buying underwear or discounted shoes at Ross, or spent nights gossiping at the fence separating their homes.

Cristina doted on her daughter. When Melissa expressed an interest in music, her mother bought her a secondhand accordion. Melissa spent hours teaching herself how to play songs by Ramón Ayala and other norteño musicians. At night, she held noisy concerts for her family, squeezing the old instrument and singing, often to the chagrin of neighbors.

By most accounts, Melissa had a fun, carefree adolescence.

That changed one night when she was twelve years old and went to a sleepover at a friend's house in Rio Bravo. That evening, the friend's thirty-year-old brother crept into her room and sexually assaulted her. Perhaps it was the trauma, the crushing stigma of such an event, or the confusion of the incident to a preteen girl, but Melissa rarely talked about that night. Her mother didn't know. Her brother Cesar also claimed to know nothing about it. She confided in her older sister, Erika, and only a few close friends, Emily and Gracie among them. Regardless of whom she told, Melissa changed after that night.

Soon after, her life began to spiral, most noticeably at school. During the 2001–2002 school year, her record at Salvador Garcia Middle School was riddled with disciplinary complaints: "inappropriate conduct," "verbal conduct," "foul language," "insubordinate/defiant of authority," "calling student bitch," "disruptive & abusive behavior"—eight total write-ups in one year, leading to seven in-school suspensions.

At home, friends and family members noticed Melissa's mercurial mood swings: laughing relentlessly one second, angrily yelling the next. A few minutes later, she'd be smiling again. Melissa started hanging with friends and returning home at two or three in the morning. Sometimes, she'd stumble home two days later. Through parents of friends, Cristina learned that her daughter was experimenting with pills, mainly Xanax. Any protest by Cristina would end in shouting matches with her daughter.

Melissa grew closer with her neighbor across the street, Vanessa Navarro, who was roughly her same age. They skipped school together, got buzzed sipping tiny airplane bottles of Smirnoff vodka pilfered from Vanessa's parents' dresser drawers, and spoke long into the night about music, boys, and, increasingly for Melissa, girls.

Melissa didn't broadcast her growing attraction to girls, but it wasn't much of a secret, either. Her bedroom walls were plastered with posters of the scantily dressed female stars of *Rebelde*, a popular Mexican telenovela, and actress Catherine Zeta-Jones, her biggest celebrity crush. At Salvador Garcia Middle School, she developed attractions to female classmates and teachers, for which she was teased incessantly by classmates. They called her "lesbiana," provoking hallway fistfights.

At Lyndon B. Johnson High School, visits to the principal's office became the norm. One day, in Melissa's junior year, Cristina received a call from a school counselor: she needed to pick up Melissa right away. When she got there, school officials showed Cristina angry red welts along Melissa's forearms and scratches on her face—all self-inflicted.

Cristina needed to seek help for her daughter or Texas Child Protective Services would take her away, they told her.

Cristina drove her daughter to a psychiatrist in Laredo. She was deeply disturbed by Melissa's self-mutilation but hopeful a professional could help fix what was broken in her. The psychiatrist gave Melissa a series of tests, diagnosed her as bipolar, and prescribed half a Xanax a day. Cristina was perplexed. "I took her to the doctor to get her help and off drugs, and the one thing I didn't want her to have anymore, he prescribes," she said later.

===

AROUND THIS TIME, MELISSA MET EMILIO VARELA AT VANESSA'S house. He lived nearby and was quiet and sweet and possessed an endearing lack of confidence. She, in turn, was loud, funny, and full of boundless energy. They were both viewed as outcasts by their peers at school. They gelled instantly. In late-night chat sessions in Vanessa's house, Emilio confided to Melissa his sexual and gender identity struggles and how he had contemplated taking his own life. He told her how butterflies fluttered in his stomach when he was around other boys and how he secretly tried on his sister's clothes when no one was around.

Melissa, three years older than Emilio, smiled patiently. "This is how happiness works," she told Emilio at the time. "Just laugh when you feel those butterflies. You feel them because you're gay." She repeated it, for emphasis. "You're gay." And that was okay.

Emilio felt a weight suddenly dissolve off his shoulders. Slowly, he began pulling on tight dresses and wigs and wearing them first around the house and later to school, despite the derision and abuse it drew from classmates. His mother didn't understand it and his sisters found it bizarre. He was laughed at and bullied and shoved out of the girls' bathroom at school. But he persisted. He insisted everyone call her Emily.

Melissa delighted in Emily's transformation and encouraged her to wear tighter dresses and heels. Melissa began dating an older man, thirty years her senior, who bought her a used Ford Mustang convertible. She would drive Emily to downtown Laredo's gay clubs, like Chelsea's and Zebra's, or over the bridge into Nuevo Laredo and to Boys' Town, the city's walled red-light district. Melissa would flirt with the pretty girls; Emily would ogle the cute men. At a club called Vito's, Melissa introduced Emily to her first boyfriend, literally shoving her toward him.

"She was my gay mother," Emily said later. "She would teach me a lot of things I knew were inside of me."

Melissa introduced her to other things as well. By high school, Melissa had elevated her drug use to crack cocaine. One day, she pulled out a glass pipe and showed Emily how the small white rocks cooked in the pipe's valve, how the acidic smoke stung the lungs and flooded the bloodstream, wrapping the mind in a dizzying, warm gauze. Emily grew accustomed to Melissa's mood swings and how her friend often talked to herself, sometimes in low, hushed whispers, other times aloud, as if someone else were next to them. When asked about it, Melissa would laugh it off.

As they approached their twenties, both Melissa and Emily were high school dropouts with growing drug addictions and no employable skills. One day, Melissa picked up Emily in her Mustang. "Come on, we're going to make some money," she told her friend.

She drove them to a truck stop on Santa Maria Avenue, three miles north of downtown Laredo, and parked the car. Emily nervously watched as Melissa walked over to a parked truck, chatted with the driver, and disappeared into his cab. She emerged a few minutes later, a crumpled twenty-dollar bill in her fist. Melissa drove Emily around Laredo—Santa Maria Avenue, San Agustin, San Bernardo—turning quick tricks for cash. She taught her friend the going rates: $20 for oral sex, $40 to $60 if they wanted to do more. If the client seemed generous or well-off, she'd convince him to rent a room along San Bernardo. The room rentals were the big score: more money, all-night partying, a shower, and, eventually, a bed on which to sleep it all off. Soon, Emily was following in her friend's footsteps.

===

MELISSA SPIRALED DEEPER AND DEEPER INTO STREET LIFE, crashing on friends' couches or in hotel rooms with clients. When Emily was arrested in 2016 on drug possession charges and ordered into drug rehab as part of her sentencing, the two drifted apart. Melissa kept hustling. She was in and out of jail—four trips to Webb County Jail in eight years on prostitution and drug possession charges—and in and out of court-ordered drug rehab. The treatment never stuck: as soon as she left rehab, she'd find her friends and pull out her glass pipe.

Though she favored women, Melissa also went through a string of boyfriends. From age fifteen through twenty-eight, she had five children with at least three different men. Each time, Child Protective Services appeared at the hospital's maternity ward to take the baby into state custody. Her record was too riddled with missed court appearances and failed drug tests. Her mother managed to convince the state to allow her to keep two: Cristina and Allan, siblings four years apart. She became their main guardian.

After an arrest on assault and drug charges, Melissa lost the Mustang. A few days each month, Melissa would scrape together the $1.50 bus fare and take the El Aguila Rural Transit bus from downtown Laredo to Rio Bravo. Her mom, then living in a three-bedroom trailer home farther up the street on Margarita Lane with her new boyfriend, Martin, shuddered at how her daughter had changed: she was thinner, her skin coarser, her hair knotted and unkempt.

Cristina Benavides both feared and cherished having Melissa home. She loathed the toll the streets were taking on her daughter, but seeing her—even shoeless and beat up—was far better than not knowing her whereabouts. In her mom's trailer, Melissa would take long, hot showers while Cristina cooked her picadillo—ground beef spiced with chili peppers, onions, and tomato sauce. She would eat, then collapse on the couch, sleeping until the next day. Cristina pleaded with her daughter to stay and get help. Melissa would stay for several days, play with her children, then vanish again.

Melissa would also emerge from time to time at her brother Cesar's apartment in south Laredo. It was a small rental where Cesar lived with his wife, Gracie, and their four-year-old daughter, Carolynn. Melissa would stay a few days, sleep on the couch, babysit Carolynn or cook batches of scrambled eggs mixed with diced hot dogs. She still called Cesar "Gordo," and the two would go to the dollar movie theater on Santa Maria Avenue to watch *Alice in Wonderland* with Johnny Depp or the latest slasher movie.

Each time, Cesar urged his sister to spend a few more weeks with them. She could help them with Carolynn, wean herself off drugs, leave the streets behind, he told her. Each time, Melissa would stay a few days, then vanish.

On San Bernardo Avenue, Melissa had a hard time keeping friends. Her combative personality and mood swings repelled many of the other sex workers on the strip. But three of them—Claudine, Chelly, and Janelle—seemed to have a higher tolerance for her, and she stuck with them. The four became good friends, staying mostly at the Relax Inn.

Claudine saw through Melissa's tough-girl veneer to something more vulnerable underneath; she considered her a little sister. Chelly and Janelle would clash with Melissa—verbally and at times physically—but ultimately took care of her, helping her find another crack rock when she was broke and struggling with withdrawals or fight off an aggressive john. Miles and worlds away from their actual relatives, the four became a family.

At the Relax Inn, they would emerge from their rooms, strung out or hungry from a multiday party, and chat with Nora in Spanish in the motel's small lobby. Nora had less patience for Melissa's brashness and ordered her off the premises several times. Pat would intervene, soothing Nora and counseling Melissa, then buying her a taco and allowing her back in. Beyond Melissa's dark moods, Pat saw a frightened girl, roiled by mental instability and pleading for help.

Melissa partied hard; she climbed into truck cabs when she needed cash and spent the money almost immediately on a few crack rocks. That pattern changed, somewhat, with the birth of her son Angel in 2017. The cherubic baby with long lashes pulled at Melissa's heart with renewed intensity. State officials took Angel immediately into custody, but this one, she told family and friends, she was determined to win back. CPS allowed her occasional supervised visits with Angel, who was in foster care, as long as she didn't show up to the visits stoned. In a blurry cell phone video taken during one of those visits in the summer of 2018, Melissa and Cristina sit with Angel in a small government visiting room with tiny chairs. Baby toys litter a brightly colored rubber play mattress. Cristina coos over the small child, who happily kicks his chubby legs. Melissa had failed an earlier drug test so wasn't allowed to touch the baby. In the video, she sits motionless and wordless, staring somberly at her son, hands at her sides, head cocked slightly, as the baby reaches for toys.

She would leave her visits with Angel with conflicting emotions: a powerful desire to clean up and win back her baby colliding with an urge to run back to her pipe and erase the pain.

On the streets, Melissa's paranoia mounted. Vanessa Rodriguez, twenty-eight, often partied with Melissa at mutual friends' homes or at her house with her husband, Hector Leya. One night, in August 2018, at around 2:00 a.m., the three were smoking crack and hanging out at Hector and Vanessa's house in Laredo. Melissa was in the kitchen by herself when Hector heard a commotion. He found Melissa on the floor, her knees pressed to her chest, clutching a large kitchen knife.

"Why the knife?" Hector asked.

"They're coming to kill me," she replied.

Hector and Vanessa calmed her and carefully extracted the knife from her hands.

By the summer of 2018, Melissa's mood swings had morphed into moroseness. She was perpetually broke and Pat could no longer let her stay at the Relax Inn. As much as he had tried to rein her in and keep her under his watch, her debts had piled up, and he had to send Melissa on her way. No cash, no room, no more excuses.

Bumping into Emily on San Bernardo was a godsend. At least now Melissa had a roof over her head. Her mood improved. And she found a new boyfriend. To anyone who would listen, Melissa boasted about the new man she was seeing. He was older, with a shiny new truck and a ranch, and was "taking care of her." For sex workers on San Bernardo Avenue, it was the equivalent of the holy grail: a repeat customer, married to another woman, who wouldn't pester her too much, paid steadily, and showered her with gifts, making her his sancha.

On the morning of August 31, 2018, while living at the Pan-American Courts with Emily, Melissa called her mom to tell her she would pay her a visit later that day and would bring dinner. Cristina was buoyant, and not just from receiving a rare phone call from her daughter; it was also encouraging that Melissa was bringing food—a sign, however tenuous, of stability and extra income in her daughter's life and that she was still interested in eating, despite the drugs that so often erased her appetite. Cristina tidied up the trailer home, laying out three new blouses on her daughter's bed that she had bought for her.

Melissa arrived at the Rio Bravo trailer at around 2:00 p.m., went straight to the kitchen, and set down a small pepperoni pizza from Domino's, a footlong turkey sub from Subway, a large soft drink, and a bag of Lay's potato chips. Cristina hugged her child. The Subway turkey sub was her favorite. "Gracias, mi'ja," she told her.

Melissa went to her former bedroom to change clothes and iron her long black hair.

"Tell my friend to come in," she yelled from her room.

Cristina hadn't noticed anyone with her daughter. She peered out the window and saw a middle-aged Hispanic man in jeans and cowboy boots, leaning against the fence. He had a thin build, wore a dark baseball cap pulled tight on his head, and had a closely cropped salt-and-pepper beard. Cristina's danger senses tingled.

"Why do you want me to do that?" she said. "I don't know him."

"Mamá, he'll leave, and you're not going to drive me back to Laredo. Ask him in."

Cristina looked at the man again. Something about him didn't sit right with her.

"I'm not telling him anything," she said.

Melissa sighed, stomped to the front door, and called out to the man, waving him inside. Wordlessly, he came in and sat on the couch. Uncomfortable silence filled the small trailer, punctuated only by Melissa's rustling in the bedroom. He stared over at Melissa, who was slightly visible down the hall. Cristina found it strange that he wouldn't introduce himself or even acknowledge her; it was stranger still that he appeared to be twice Melissa's age. She didn't like the way he stared at her daughter.

"¿Cómo se llama usted?" Cristina asked, finally breaking the silence.

"David Garza,"* he said.

"¿Y cuántos años tiene usted?"

"Cincuenticuatro."

"Usted es muy mayor para ella," Cristina said, her voice tightening.

The man shrugged. "What can we do? She's old enough," he answered in English.

Melissa emerged from her bedroom wearing black shorts and a new olive-green tank top her mom had bought her. Her hair was freshly ironed, and black eyeliner etched her dark eyes. Cristina smiled at her. Through all the rough days, her daughter still looked stunning.

Melissa pulled a slice of pizza out of the box, dipped it in ranch dressing, and took a bite. She turned to the man on the couch.

"Ready?"

The three of them walked outside into the stiffening late summer heat, and Melissa and her escort climbed into the man's large black pickup truck. She rolled down her window and waved goodbye to her mom.

"Meli, llámame," Cristina told her. "Please don't forget to call me. God bless you. Be careful, please."

"Sí, Mamá," Melissa said, smiling.

The truck rumbled off and disappeared down the street.

Later that evening, at around 6:00 p.m., Melissa called to tell her mom David had dropped her off at the Pan-American Courts. She was calling from Emily's phone. Melissa hadn't had a cell phone in months and relied on friends to make calls.

---

* A pseudonym.

She told her mom to jot down a phone number for her. It was David's number, she told her. Her mother kept many of Melissa's contacts for her. Cristina entered the number in her phone and punched in his name. Next to it, she wrote: "(Meli)."

"Everything's fine," Melissa told her mom. "He even told me not to go out tonight."

Cristina's mood lightened. She was happy her daughter wouldn't be on the streets, at least for one night. But another thought lingered in her mind, twisting there like a spur: *Why* would he tell her that?

———

A WARM, PELTING RAIN FELL ON THE MORNING OF MONDAY, September 3. It was Labor Day and schools were closed. Melissa's children Cristina and Allan were home with their grandmother watching TV cartoons. At around 10:00 a.m., Cristina dressed her grandchildren and drove everyone to the nearby H-E-B supermarket on Highway 83 to pick up a few things for dinner. As she pulled into the parking lot, rain hit the windshield and Cristina's mood darkened. Melissa's absence was consuming her more so than usual.

Several days had passed without word from her daughter. It was normal for days, sometimes weeks, to go by without a call from Melissa. But she couldn't shake the image of her daughter with that man. Something didn't sit right.

Worried thoughts spun through her mind: Was she okay? Was she getting enough to eat? Was she still with that man? She kept her darker concerns buried deeper in her subconscious. She couldn't deal with thoughts like those, of Melissa getting seriously hurt. They were too barbed, too consuming.

Suddenly, her face brightened with a thought.

"Let's go watch a movie!" she told her grandchildren. "Let's go find Meli and watch a movie."

Cristina and Allan squealed with delight. "Which one?" her granddaughter asked.

"I don't know," Cristina said. "We'll see what's playing when we get there."

She struck an agreement with the children: If they found Melissa, they'd all go to the movies together. If they didn't, they'd just return home. Everyone agreed.

"¡Órale!" said the younger Cristina, giddy for the impromptu adventure.

Cristina steered the Nissan out of the H-E-B parking lot and drove west on Highway 83 toward downtown Laredo. She turned right on San Bernardo Avenue, then drove north among the motels there, searching for her daughter. With Melissa lacking a cell phone, this was how Cristina often located her: driving around San Bernardo until her daughter or one of her friends appeared. As always, Cristina harbored thoughts that, if she could just locate her daughter, this might be the trip that convinced her to get off the street. They would watch a movie, like a real family, and she'd fill with just enough love to come home and leave the streets behind. For good.

Cristina drove up San Bernardo, down San Agustin, and made the loop again. On her second lap down San Agustin, she spotted Claudine. She had met her once before and knew she was friends with her daughter. She pulled the Nissan over and rolled down her window.

"¡Hola!" she called out. "¿Has visto a Melissa?"

Claudine came over to the car. She was thin and handsome, with long, straight sandy hair and cornflower-blue eyes. She was wearing a tight dress and high heels. She looked older than the other girls on the avenue but generally more attractive. Melissa's daughter commented on how pretty the woman's hair was. Claudine smiled.

Sorry, she said. She hadn't seen Melissa in days. Cristina's face crinkled with concern.

"Please, if you see her, tell her to call me. I'm her mom."

"Yes, I remember you," Claudine said.

They waved goodbye, and Cristina pulled away. She continued driving, up along San Bernardo, down San Agustin, then up again, scanning the parking lots of the Pan-American Courts, Siesta Motel, and

Relax Inn. She checked the Burger King inside the Exxon gas station on the corner of San Bernardo and Lafayette Street, where she had lunched with her daughter a few weeks earlier, as well as the Taco Mais outdoor taco stand, Danny's Restaurant, and Charlie's Corona Bar & Grill. No sign of Melissa.

"Lo siento," she told her grandkids.

She pointed the Nissan back toward Rio Bravo, and they drove home in silence.

CHAPTER 3

At fifty-one years old, Mary Haynes, known as "Big Mary" to the other women and clients for her large stature, was one of the older sex workers on the avenue—and one of its more experienced. She dished out advice to younger girls from her two decades on the avenue, including how to spot an undercover police sting ("Assume any new prostitute on the avenue is an undercover officer") and how to defuse a violent situation with a client. In her twenty years selling sex on San Bernardo, she had never once been stabbed or shot at. She'd only been arrested four times in two decades. But she knew plenty of girls who had fared far worse. One woman was stabbed in the head by a client; another was stabbed eleven times but lived. Even she was not completely immune: Big Mary was raped once by a potential john. She later led police to the man, a repeat customer, and he was arrested and sent to prison for thirty years.

When she first met Melissa Ramirez, Big Mary thought she was the type of person who could get herself into real trouble on the streets. She was also struck by how youthful she looked. She took an immediate liking to her, and the two became close, partying together and sharing clients.

In the early evening of September 2, 2018, Big Mary called Melissa via Facebook Messenger. She was having a profitable day and offered to rent them a hotel room for the night. She still had a few more "interviews"—what Big Mary called meetings with clients—but they would reconnect later.

"Hey, I'm going to get us a room," she told Melissa. "Let's meet up later."

"Okay, I'll be ready," Melissa told her.

The two hung up.

A few hours later, Big Mary called Melissa again. Once, twice, three times. No answer. The green dot on Melissa's Facebook Messenger profile indicated she was still logged in. But, still, no answer.

=====

EMILY VARELA WAS STARTING TO REGRET TAKING IN MELISSA.

In the two weeks since she allowed her good friend to stay with her at the Pan-American Courts on San Bernardo, Melissa hadn't contributed a dime to rent. She rarely left the small room, taking naps on the only mattress, and seldom showered, cleaning up only when her boyfriend was coming to pick her up. He was an older guy with a pickup truck. For reasons she didn't fully understand, he creeped Emily out. And as Emily was trying to stay clean, Melissa would routinely arrive home high on crack or amphetamines.

She hadn't expected Melissa to suddenly turn her life around, but she was hoping she would do . . . something.

Around 2:00 a.m. on Monday, September 3, Emily returned home from a long night of turning tricks, tired and feet throbbing, but with a fistful of crumpled tens and twenties in her bra. She unlocked the door to her room. Melissa, fully dressed, slept on the mattress in the middle of the small room, snoring softly. The familiar burnt-plastic smell of freebased crack rocks wafted through the air. Emily grew enraged.

She loved Melissa. But she couldn't afford to get kicked out of the Pan-American and she definitely did not want to go back to jail. Melissa had broken the one rule she had imposed: no drugs in the room. She had tried to be patient with her friend. But enough was enough.

She shook Melissa awake.

"I don't want you here," Emily told her friend. "Go make some money. Go do *something*. Just leave."

Melissa staggered to the bathroom. She patted down her hair with water from the sink and applied some eyeliner. Then she pulled on sandals, grabbed a small pocketknife she always carried with her, and, without muttering a word, shuffled out into the humid Laredo night.

═══

SAN BERNARDO AVENUE WAS QUIET AND WET IN THE EARLY-morning hours of September 3. Under a light rain, Melissa wandered along the strip, likely trying to puzzle out where to sleep that night or how to score her next crack hit. The sky was black and starless, dawn still five hours away.

Sometime after 2:00 a.m., a white 2015 Dodge Ram 2500 pickup truck pulled over on San Bernardo Avenue. The driver swung open the passenger-side door and Melissa hopped inside. The truck drove off into the night.

═══

TEN HOURS LATER, AT AROUND NOON, A PASSERBY INSPECTING ranches for sale in a rural stretch of northwest Webb County, twelve miles north of Laredo, spotted something clumped in the grass alongside the gravel road. As he pulled to a stop, he saw the contours of a body. A woman in black shorts and an olive-green tank top, shoeless with black socks on, lay facedown in the brush just off the intersection of Jefferies Road and State Highway 255. Her stockinged toes still touched the gravel path, as if she had fallen face-first into the thornbush. She wasn't moving. The motorist called police and alerted nearby neighbors, who called John Chamberlain, the owner of the ranch where the body lay.

Just then, Rene Arce, an off-duty seven-year veteran of the Laredo Police Department, drove his thirteen-year-old stepdaughter and three-year-old son in his black Dodge Ram on Jefferies Road. The three were enjoying a lazy Labor Day drive, while his wife, Tanya Arce, ran errands in town. Arce was scouting for land on which to build a home for his growing family and enjoying some rare downtime with his kids. The drive took him north on Jefferies Road and past State Highway 255. When he saw Chamberlain's truck blocking the road up ahead, he turned the truck around and decided to loop back on Jefferies Road, stopping briefly to let his stepdaughter and son enjoy a few horses neighing and grazing at the fence line of the Chamberlain Ranch. When his wife called them back for lunch, he drove off.

It was an innocuous Laredo outing. But to the neighbors and Chamberlain—the image of a stiffening body still fresh in their mind—it was suspicious. They hopped in their car and circled around Jefferies Road, drove up behind the black truck on State Highway 255, and snapped pictures of the license plate with their cell phones. A short time later, a Webb County sheriff's deputy arrived at the scene. The body was stretched out prone in a tangle of blue-green thornbush. Her left arm was folded under her, her left hand clutching a yellow bag of peanut M&M's. Her right arm was bent next to her. Blood congealed in a small, round hole on the right side of her jaw, and two small, circular dark red wounds punctured her neck, just under her right ear. Dark blood thickened in a leech-sized hole in her right wrist, just below the base of her palm. A large puddle of crimson blood bloomed near her head and seeped into the dirt around her. Her face was streaked with dried blood. Near the body, there was a small plastic baggie containing several crack cocaine rocks. Her eyes were half open. She had been shot three times at close range. Her face swelled from the trauma it had recently received. Shell casings were found nearby in the thornbush. As Webb County sheriff's deputies arrived, Chamberlain told them about the suspicious truck that had U-turned and sped off. He showed them the license plate number.

This wasn't a hit-and-run or a border crosser dying of exposure. This had much darker undertones. The deputies radioed in the body and plate number.

=====

CAPTAIN FEDERICO CALDERON, HEAD OF THE WEBB COUNTY Sheriff's Office Criminal Investigation Division, was home enjoying Labor Day off when he received a call from a deputy about a body on Jefferies Road. As supervisor of investigators, Calderon often fielded calls from detectives asking for advice or help planning out next steps.

But as the deputy described the victim and the scene, Calderon realized this one was different.

Tall and heavyset, with small, smiling eyes set in a round, boyish face, the soft-spoken Calderon was unique within the sheriff's office in that he was popular among both the rank-and-file and top brass. His father was a business owner from Nuevo Laredo, and his mom, a government worker from Laredo; Calderon embodied the Nuevo Laredo–Laredo symbiosis, easily fluent in both English and Spanish. He had studied technology at Texas A&M International University and thought he would pursue a career in that field. But after college, he landed a job with the district attorney's office, and the county prosecutor offered to send him to the police academy. He graduated and started working for the Webb County Sheriff's Office, rising from sergeant to lieutenant to captain. He supervised the cybercrime division and became president of the Webb County Deputy Sheriffs Association, the local union. Smart and persuasive, wielding respect he had garnered over the years from Sheriff Martin Cuellar, Calderon negotiated contracts for higher salaries and better working conditions for his coworkers. "You have to have a special kind of character to bring both those sides together," coworker Lieutenant Joe Peña said. "He did it very well."

Assigned to lead the Criminal Investigation Division in 2015, Calderon oversaw everything from home robberies and sexual assaults to gang-related violence and safe houses used by smugglers. Deaths often included migrants hit by passing trucks or dying in Laredo's triple-digit heat and suicides. Murders were less common.

As the deputy described the scene on Jefferies Road—the victim's wounds, the shell casings, the suspicious truck—Calderon realized he should see this one for himself. He grabbed his gear and drove out to the scene. When he arrived, Sheriff Cuellar and other deputy sheriffs were already there. Calderon examined the body and jotted down notes from the investigators. Cuellar pulled him aside: something about this one felt strange. He wanted him personally leading the case. Calderon agreed.

A few minutes later, Texas Ranger Ernesto "E. J." Salinas arrived at the scene. Medium height and clean-shaven, Salinas, 49, was barrel-chested and had a military crew cut that ran high to a small patch of silvery dark hair, which was perpetually covered by a white Stetson hat. He was in his usual uniform of starched white shirt and beige tie, pressed beige slacks and ostrich skin cowboy boots. His eyes creased down at the outer edges, and his face was framed by a hard chin and perma-wrinkled brow, weighed down by years of investigating bullet-ripped bodies and miscreants along the border. He spoke in measured, low tones weighted with authority with a hint of a Spanish accent, like a Latino drill sergeant. As a Texas Ranger, he was elite among the borderlands' criminal investigators.

Though there are more than 80,000 law enforcement officers across Texas, only about 160 of them call themselves Texas Rangers. Each year more than a thousand applicants try to land one of the handful of coveted slots, if or when one becomes available, and become rangers, who have been defending lives and property in Texas since 1823. Today, the Texas Ranger unit is a division of the Texas Department of Public Safety, alongside state troopers and driver's license officials, and focuses almost entirely on major criminal investigations and border intelligence. Rangers need to have eight years of experience with a law enforcement agency and be employed by DPS before even applying. If chosen, after a thorough criminal and personal background check, the ranger is assigned to one of six "companies" across the state. Salinas was a criminal investigator in Company D, a twenty-six-county region stretching 425 miles along the U.S.-Mexico border from Texas's southernmost city, Brownsville, northwest to Val Verde County. When taking over a case, the ranger brought not just expertise and specialized training but the substantial resources of the State of Texas, including the nearly $2 billion annual budget of the Texas Department of Public Safety.

Salinas grew up on a ranch near Oilton, Texas, a town of 170 souls thirty miles east of Laredo. His father, Ernesto Juvenito Salinas, was the county's elected justice of the peace and Salinas grew accustomed to residents rapping on their ranch house door any hour of the day and night to ask for help with a disabled truck or report a dead body. That rural sense of public service and law enforcement permeated young Salinas. At age six, he'd survey the cars parked outside his father's grocery store/gas station and jot down their license plate numbers. If someone robbed his daddy's store, he told customers, he'd know where to find them.

After high school, Salinas worked for a few years as a roughneck on oil rigs in South Texas before going to college and getting a job with the Webb County Sheriff's Office. It took him four tries to finally, in 1997, land a position as a state trooper with DPS, then another fourteen years before being promoted to ranger in 2011. He worked first in the Laredo Joint Operations Intelligence Center in charge of border security issues, then transferred to the Texas Ranger field office as a criminal investigator. Better trained, with deeper pockets and access to myriad state databases, rangers are routinely called out to help on murder investigations, especially along the border, bringing more resources and expertise to smaller jurisdictions and sheriff's departments.

Calderon had worked with Salinas on past cases, including sexual assaults and a number of child abuse cases. The two greeted each other, and Calderon filled him in on what they'd found so far. Nearby, county CID investigators photographed the body and the scene and bagged evidence. Three shell casings, all from a .40-caliber handgun, were collected and deposited into clear plastic evidence bags.

Calderon recognized the .40-caliber shell casings. They were for jacketed hollow points—the bullet of choice among law enforcement departments—which mushroomed on impact, causing a larger diameter of damage. Police departments favored them because they didn't pass through bodies and injure anyone beyond the intended target. And they caused maximum damage as they expanded and tore through bones and organs.

Detectives also collected the small plastic baggie filled with crack rocks and the M&M's bag, dropped them into evidence bags, and labeled them. Salinas squatted next to the victim and studied the wounds. The one on the woman's right wrist, he noted, was a defensive scar from trying to shield her face from the bullets. In her final moments, she had tried to deflect her death. Something else caught his eye: the victim had on black socks and no shoes. Salinas knew that area well and had grown up on similar ranches. Anyone living out there wore cowboy boots. The victim was not from around there—nor, he assumed, was the gunman. He also noticed the victim had scrawled a phone number in pen on her left thigh, and took note of the number.

Salinas took his own photos of the scene. He spray-painted circles around evidence in the field, alerting technicians to their location. Then he and Calderon left to investigate their first lead: the mysterious black truck.

=====

ARCE HAD RETURNED HOME WITH HIS CHILDREN WHEN HE RE-ceived a call from a buddy at Laredo PD: his truck was being sought in connection to the body found on Jefferies Road. Alarm and confusion billowed in his mind. He remembered driving up to the police cars earlier that day. He picked up his phone and called the watch commander on duty at the Laredo Police Department, explained what had happened, and asked what he should do. The commander told him he would get back to him and that he should "stand by." A few minutes later, Arce's stepdaughter received a call from a neighborhood friend: their street was lined with armed police officers, who were circling the Arce home. Tanya Arce, her three-year-old son on her hip, opened the garage door to flag down a police officer and clear up the misunderstanding.

Outside, Webb County sheriff's deputies and Laredo police officers, dressed in body armor and Kevlar helmets, assault rifles at the ready, closed in on the couple. They ordered them to kneel and cuffed Rene and Tanya Arce on their front lawn. The pair was driven to a sheriff's substation on Highway 59 for questioning. They were told they were being questioned for a case being investigated by the FBI and Texas Rangers. There was no search warrant. They were never read their Miranda rights.

Rene Arce, a law enforcement officer with a clean record, agreed to cooperate. Calderon and Salinas questioned Rene and Tanya. Rene explained how he had driven his stepdaughter and son down Jefferies Road earlier that day, how he had turned around when he saw the road blocked. He allowed them to check his phone. The investigators wanted to know if he was having an affair with any women and why he had not called in the discovery of the body. No, he was not having any affairs, he told them. And he never saw the body; he hadn't gotten close enough.

After nearly five hours of questioning, the couple was released and deputies drove them back to their home. Rene Arce's personal guns were confiscated, and he was placed on administrative leave until further notice.

Arce wasn't completely ruled out, but by the end of the day, investigators realized they had the wrong person. Arce was not a suspect. News of the raid on his home nonetheless leaked out into the city via La Gordiloca, a rogue local muckraker. La Gordiloca—or "crazy, fat woman" in Spanish, whose real name is Priscilla Villarreal—had heard of the raid through a Laredo police source and shared it with her more than eighty thousand Facebook followers. La Gordiloca had created a loyal online following by cruising Laredo streets in her 1998 Dodge pickup and reporting on car crashes, drug raids, homicides, and other nocturnal crimes via Facebook live streams laced with Spanish profanity and street lingo. "¿Qué rollo?" she often asked at the start of a nighttime shift, prompting streams of heart emojis from audience members watching live. Villarreal, a tenth grade dropout with a shaved head and spackled with tattoos, rolled up to crime scenes or reported on tips fed to her from sources within Laredo PD, often beating out local media to stories. In one of those scoops, she reported on a former Laredo police investigator who resigned after he was caught skimming gambling proceeds from raids on slot machine casinos. Her posts appeared days before any other media had the story.

But her quick-to-report style and loose sourcing tactics drew trouble. In 2017, she posted allegations of abuse at a local childcare center ("Teenagers having babies!") that proved unfounded. The center sued for defamation and won a $300,000 judgment after she failed to appear in court; Villarreal appealed that ruling. Later that year, Laredo police arrested her and charged her with misuse of information after she reported on the suicide of a U.S. Customs and Border Protection supervisor, whose name she published. That case was dismissed, and Villarreal sued the police department in a case that reached the Fifth Circuit Court of Appeals.[*]

The raid on the Arce home was prime Gordiloca fodder: salacious, dramatic, and involving a law enforcement official. Villarreal went live, informing followers, "It is being said but NOT CONFIRMED that a Laredo Police department officer has been or will be detained at any moment. Authorities are at a home located inside La Cuesta Subdivision this is in the North Side of Laredo." The next day, she posted an update with more details on the raid: "Authorities surrounded a home yesterday that is said to be of a Laredo Police Officer by the last name ARCE In north Laredo at La Cuesta Subdivision. It is being said the officer was taken in for questioning a [sic] released hours later." Pictures of the Arces' home and their vehicles also circulated on social media.

Calderon reminded himself of the bad information that could often circulate in Laredo involving crimes. Running down leads like Arce, which proved baseless, was a necessary though less than pleasant part of the job.

Later that day, a Webb County sheriff's deputy who had worked at the county jail recognized the face of the victim from a photo taken at the crime scene. The medical examiner also ran the victim's fingerprints through a Webb County police database and confirmed that the young woman found slain on the side of Jefferies Road was Melissa Ramirez.

[*] In a narrow decision in January 2024, the Fifth Circuit Court of Appeals ruled against Villarreal, saying the city and county officials she was suing have "qualified immunity." In a Facebook post shortly after the ruling, Villarreal vowed to take the case to the U.S. Supreme Court.

CHAPTER 4

Cristina Benavides was tired and groggy. She hadn't slept much the night before because Allan had a cough; she had kept him home from day care, and he was sleeping in Melissa's bedroom. A deepening worry had spread inside her about her daughter's whereabouts. She was used to Melissa dating older men, but this man had frightened her. She tried to push the thoughts out of her mind.

Cristina was washing dishes in the kitchen at around 2:00 p.m. on September 4 when Mia, the tiny Chihuahua they kept on a leash outside, began barking. She peered out the window. Two detectives from the Webb County Sheriff's Office, badges dangling on chains around their necks, stood by her fence.

Melissa was in trouble again, Cristina thought. What was it this time? Another drug arrest? Did she assault someone? Darker thoughts bubbled up. Her heart leaped into her throat.

Cristina came outside but stayed on her front steps.

"How can I help you?" she called out.

"Does Melissa Ramirez live here?" one of the deputies said.

Cristina went back inside, pulled on her sandals, and scooped up Allan, who had awakened with Mia's barking. She walked over to the fence.

The men asked again if Melissa lived there.

"She's not here right now," Cristina said.

The detectives looked at each other uncomfortably.

"We're conducting an investigation. We need you to come down to the sheriff's office."

Fear spiked through Cristina.

"I can't. My car doesn't work," she lied. "Plus, I have him"—she nodded toward Allan—"and another girl on her way home soon from school."

"We need to talk to you. Can you open the gate?" one of the men said.

"About what?" Cristina's voice began to quaver. "What did Melissa do?"

"Listen," he said. "We found your daughter." He paused. "She's dead."

"¿Cómo?" Cristina heard herself say. But the voice sounded small and far away, as if spoken by someone else.

She threw her head back and screamed.

===

CESAR, MELISSA'S BROTHER, WAS PUTTING UP DRYWALL AT A construction site in Pearson, Texas, 130 miles north of Laredo, when Cristina called him on his cell phone.

"Mataron a mi hija," she said between sobs. *They killed my daughter.*

Cesar slumped to the dirt floor. After hanging up with his mother, he told his boss what had happened and was given permission to go attend to his family. One small wrinkle: he didn't have a car. Gracie had dropped him off earlier that morning. One of his coworkers, hearing what was transpiring, tossed Cesar the keys to his red Mazda.

"Go!" he told him.

Cesar got into the car and gunned it south on Interstate 35 toward Laredo, blasting past the speed limit. About an hour later, he pulled into the Webb County sheriff's substation on Highway 59. Cristina was in a room talking with Calderon and Salinas. They asked her about Melissa's friends: "Who was her best friend?" "Was anyone angry at her?" "When did you last see her?"

Cristina remembered the man with the black truck. She gave them David Garza's name and cell phone number, told them how strange and quiet he had been when he had come to her trailer with Melissa, how he just stared at her daughter. It was the last time she had seen her daughter alive. She also told them Melissa had been staying at the Pan-American Courts with Emily Varela.

Calderon had shown Cristina pictures of the murder scene to identify the victim. But Cristina wanted to see the body. She needed to see her daughter one last time. The body was less than a mile down

Highway 59, at the Webb County Medical Examiner's Office. Calderon cautioned against it.

"You don't want to see the body," he told Cristina. "It's not in good shape."

Cristina emerged from the interrogation room just as Cesar entered the building. They collapsed into each other's arms, sobbing.

Cesar took Cristina home to her trailer in Rio Bravo and comforted her as best he could. She couldn't stop crying. All those years of worrying over her daughter, hoping she'd stay safe, praying for her occasional return to her trailer—they all seemed like a blurred dream. She knew Melissa had problems. But she never lost hope that she would turn her life around, get help, and return to a normal, safe existence. In an instant, those hopes had vanished, replaced by an intolerable emptiness. Her daughter's smile, laugh, touch, smell . . . all forever gone.

"Mi Meli," she moaned, over and over.

That night, local TV station KGNS broadcast a one-minute, eighteen-second segment on Melissa, saying investigators were ruling her death a homicide but not offering any further details. Other than that, there was no publicity on the incident. Friends and neighbors dropped by as news of Melissa's murder spread, offering the family comfort.

Cesar was heartbroken. Memories of Melissa—hunting for grasshoppers in the yard in Rio Bravo, fighting off bullies, babysitting Carolynn—flickered endlessly in his mind. He knew she skated on the edge of danger but always expected her to pull through, always envisioned her around to see Carolynn start school, grow into a woman, marry. That deep pain mingled with a swelling anger at the thought that the person responsible for ripping his sister from their lives was still at large. Grief morphed into rage. He kissed his mother goodbye, told her to get some rest, then retreated to the small apartment he shared with Gracie and Carolynn.

Though the raid on the Arce household turned out to be an investigative dud, details of the sweep and Arce's truck, via La Gordiloca's reporting, nonetheless seeped into the homes and streets of Laredo, including the Ramirez household. Cristina Benavides followed La

Gordiloca fervently, as did Gracie and Cesar. It was no surprise that the details of the vehicle—a black Dodge Ram belonging to a law enforcement officer—easily reached Cesar Ramirez, minus the important context of Arce's subsequent interview and release.

Two days after Melissa's body was discovered, Cesar, still gripped by inconsolable pain, borrowed his wife's car and told her he was visiting a cousin. Instead, he drove to the house of one of his high school buddies—someone he knew well, someone he had helped in the past. The friend answered the door.

"I need a gun," Cesar told him.

The friend retreated into his home and returned with a .45-caliber stainless steel Colt 1911 Government Model handgun. He handed it to Cesar.

"I know what happened to your sister," he told Cesar. "I owe you and I'm not going to say no. Just be careful."

Cesar thanked him and returned to his car. He tucked the heavy pistol into the center console and drove north toward San Bernardo. Once there, he reduced his speed, slowly cruising up and down the four-lane avenue. Motorists drove to and from work, and people emerged from knickknack stores. Taco Mais was busy with diners. Cesar drove through the avenue's motel parking lots—the Relax Inn, Loma Alta, Pan-American Courts—as he always did when he searched for his sister.

This time, however, his eyes scanned the parking lots for a black Dodge Ram truck and his sister's killer, his right hand resting on the car's center console.

====

WORD OF MELISSA'S DEATH RIPPLED THROUGH SAN BERNARDO Avenue.

Through the usual channels sex workers use to communicate and keep one another safe—text messages, Facebook Messenger, motel parking lot gossip—details of the murder emerged, some true, others less accurate.

At the Relax Inn, the revelation that their good friend had been murdered staggered Claudine, Janelle, and Chelly. Pat Roth, the motel's manager, was saddened but not altogether surprised. Melissa, he knew, was prone to angering clients. She likely got into a fight with a customer or tried to rip someone off, he thought.

News of Melissa's death rattled Claudine the hardest. The oldest of the four women, she had stepped into the role of older sister and guardian for Melissa, helping her through some of her roughest patches. Now she was gone. A few days after Melissa's body was found, Claudine stumbled into the small lobby of the Siesta Motel, down the street from the Relax Inn. It was her custom to sit, sip some free coffee, and chat with the daytime manager, Rose Ortiz. They would talk about Claudine's kids or gossip about other sex workers. This time, Claudine was more serious, solemn, and noticeably high. Her fears poured out of her.

"That could've been me," she told Rose, her hands trembling.

Rose liked Claudine and tolerated her shooting up and turning tricks at her motel. She was older than the other girls, wiser somehow, with an inner glow missing in a lot of the others. "Please go with your family," Rose urged her. "Get off the streets. I don't want to open the paper and see you there someday."

"Don't worry," Claudine assured her. "Nothing's going to happen."

====

CHRISTOPHER CANALES, THIRTY-SEVEN, HAD BEEN ON THE SAN Bernardo scene for years, as a partier, occasional drug dealer, and trusted watcher over the girls. He had known some of them, like Chelly, for more than a decade, when he first started selling pot and pills from his north Laredo neighborhood. He got to know more of them as he spent more time on San Bernardo. He'd accompany girls to meet and size up prospective clients, waiting on the corner until they returned, or set them up with acquaintances or past clients he knew were safe and had money. Sex workers in Laredo generally didn't have pimps, but

Christopher, built thickly like a college running back with Mayan tribal tattoos splayed across his chest and stomach, was the closest they had to one. He didn't ask for a percentage of their earnings, only good-faith favors when he needed one: a pinch of chiva or an extra joint if they had one to spare. The women grew to trust him.

He first met Melissa in 2013. He would walk her to meet clients and watch over her on dates. Christopher said he was struck by how much fear pulsed through her, a paranoia that ran deeper than that of most of the other women on the avenue. Once, Christopher organized a date for Melissa with a customer who paid in advance. As they headed to the rendezvous, she began having doubts.

"Oh no, I can't do this," Melissa told him at the time.

Christopher explained that the guy had paid in full and had checked out. She needed to fulfill her end of the bargain.

"No, please, let's just go," she said. She began to cry and shake uncontrollably. "Please, I don't feel good about this. Let's just go."

He canceled the date. But he warned Melissa: "Don't be doing that. These guys pay and you put it in your pocket. You don't back out. That's how you get hurt."

Christopher was saddened but not entirely surprised when he heard of Melissa's death. He figured she tried to jack a client and it ended violently. "Her worst fear was to get attacked by one of the tricks, one of the johns," he said later. "It was her worst fear come to life."

As San Bernardo processed Melissa's death and detectives searched for leads, Cesar continued patrolling its side streets, looking for a black Dodge truck. Using the scraps of information leaked by La Gordiloca, Cesar peered into the driver's seat of any black truck he saw, hunting for a "police officer–looking" person inside. Once, he followed a Ram truck into a parking lot and pulled up behind it. He gripped the .45-caliber pistol at his hip, ready to exact revenge for his sister—until a woman stepped out of the truck. Cesar relaxed and drove on. Another time, he followed what looked like a good match for the truck until it came to a stop. But when children climbed out, he left.

He hunted Dodge trucks for three consecutive days following Melissa's murder, then, his rage ebbing and the search appearing increasingly futile, gave it up.

===

STILL BRUISED FROM THE FALSE START WITH RENE ARCE, SALINAS and Calderon pivoted to their next lead: David Garza, the older escort Melissa had brought home a few days before her murder. Cristina Benavides recounted to investigators the odd way he stared at her daughter and how strangely quiet he was in her living room. Calderon called Garza, and he agreed to be interviewed. On September 6, two days after Melissa's body was discovered, Salinas and Calderon drove to Garza's home in northwest Laredo and interviewed him.

He told them he was a divorced truck driver and, yes, he knew Melissa. He had picked her up on Saturday, September 1, and drove her in his black Chevy Silverado truck from her mother's home in Rio Bravo to the Pan-American Courts on San Bernardo, then drove her to his house. There, she got high and passed out. The next day, he had driven her back to San Bernardo and dropped her off at one of the hotels. That was the last time he saw her. When asked if he owned any weapons, he told investigators he owned a .40-caliber Springfield Armory pistol, which he hadn't fired in over two years. The weapon's caliber, matching the shell casings found at the scene, instantly piqued the investigators' interest.

Garza also told them that the day after dropping off Melissa, he had driven to Houston for work and had stayed there for several days. If true, that would place him more than three hundred miles from the scene when the murder happened. Garza was cordial and cooperative. Calderon confirmed his alibi through the GPS navigation system in Garza's truck—it all checked out.

Garza fell off the list of potential suspects. Investigators were back to square one.

More interviews followed, many of them taking place inside the sheriff's substation about seven miles east on Highway 59 from the sheriff's headquarters in downtown Laredo. The substation was a cream-colored, single-story, U-shaped concrete structure that housed the Criminal Investigation Division and Calderon's office. Just past the main entrance on the south side of the building was the muster room, a large space where deputies gathered each morning to discuss daily assignments. On one wall of the muster room were a flat-screen TV and a "Drug Identification Chart" displaying photos of seventy-seven different types of narcotics commonly found on the streets, along with their street names, next to rows of lockers. Down a hallway to the left was an eight-by-ten-foot windowless conference room used as an interview room. Inside were three chairs arranged around a small table. A tiny camera was hidden behind the thermostat control and another hung in the corner in plain sight. A light fixture on the ceiling hid a microphone.

It was here where Calderon and Salinas, in past cases, had interviewed drug runners and child molesters, most of whom ended up behind bars. Now, one by one, friends and acquaintances of Melissa's were picked up and brought into the interview room for questioning. One man had seen her Friday night before her murder but hadn't seen her since; another claimed not to know her at all and couldn't say why his name was associated with her. One acquaintance, Robert DeLeon, knew Melissa and said they would talk frequently on Facebook Messenger. He described how she routinely sported black eyes from fistfights with other sex workers or clients. He said he heard from a friend that Melissa may have been arguing with a client the night she vanished. Another friend said he saw her the night she was killed, walking along San Bernardo with another sex worker. He offered names and phone numbers of others who knew her, but had no direct knowledge of who may have done this to her.

Leads spawned more leads, more phone calls, more people brought into the substation's interview room. But nothing emerged worth pursuing, nothing pointing them to the killer. Investigators tracked down the owner of the phone number scrawled on Melissa's thigh; it came back to a Laredo woman who hadn't used the number in years.

While the two investigators questioned suspects and friends at the substation, plainclothes detectives fanned out across San Bernardo, knocking on doors at hourly-rate motels and talking with managers, sex workers, drug pushers, and others loitering there. All seven investigators from the CID canvassed the streets and alleyways around San Bernardo, hunting for clues. Calderon and Salinas also joined in, along with a handful of troopers Salinas recruited into the effort. Deputies who worked at Webb County Jail, who knew Melissa and the other women better, took part as well. Climbing into Salinas's agency-issued gray Dodge Ram 1500 truck, the two lead investigators perused San Bernardo Avenue, often until 2:00 or 3:00 a.m., stopping and talking with sex workers. Salinas paid a visit to the Relax Inn. He chatted with Pat, who pointed the ranger to Berto and Iris, a couple in room 111 who often hosted the girls and let them crash on their carpeted floor. The couple described Melissa as others had: tempestuous, with a knack for angering others. They said they wouldn't be surprised if she had tried to rip off a client and that's what got her killed. But they didn't know her whereabouts that day.

After speaking with more than a dozen people, investigators began noting a pattern in Melissa's life: she would hang out with some friends, drink or smoke crack, pass out for a few hours, then wake up and wander to the next friend's house and repeat. Her life was an endless cycle of nomadic partying and drifting, making any concrete leads of her whereabouts challenging. "We were being pulled in so many different directions," Calderon remembered later. "She had been at so many different places during the normal course of her day."

Sex workers were generally okay sharing what they knew with Calderon and Salinas, but others, such as known drug dealers who knew Melissa more intimately, were more hesitant to talk, especially when approached by Salinas in his starched white button-down shirt and Stetson hat. Detectives were also challenged by trying to glean information from people who were often noticeably high. When they were stoned, they were nonsensical. When they sobered up, they often refused to talk.

One person unleashed an angry barking German shepherd as investigators approached his house, forcing the detectives to sprint for cover. They later found the person hiding in the attic. He didn't have any information on the murders; he was more concerned about the disruption of his drug business.

Cristina Benavides offered investigators another tip: the name and phone number of Melissa's good friend Emily Varela, who she knew was staying at the Pan-American Courts on San Bernardo. Investigators descended on the motel. Guns drawn, they pounded on Emily's second-floor room, looked around, then escorted her back to the substation for questioning. For more than an hour in the substation's interview room, Emily recalled how Melissa was in her room the night before she died, how Emily had become upset with her and kicked her out. Hands trembling, Emily handed over her phone and allowed investigators to scroll through it. They found nothing significant and drove her back to San Bernardo.

Next, Calderon and Salinas zeroed in on the Canta Ranas neighborhood of west Laredo: rows of low-slung concrete homes with cement patios and corrugated roofs, crammed together and separated by rusty chain-link fences. Mexico, just across the churning Rio Grande, was visible down the street. San Bernardo Avenue was where sex workers made their money, but Canta Ranas ("Singing Frogs" in Spanish), just a few blocks away, was where many scored their black tar heroin and other drugs. At one trap house on Madison Street, a well-known drug dealer refused to let them in but spoke to Calderon and Salinas through a screen door. He hadn't seen Melissa for days but offered names and phone numbers of others who knew her better.

The detectives continued riding along San Bernardo, stopping sex workers on the street and asking if they knew Melissa. Most did. None offered a solid lead. After interviewing cleaning staff at the Siesta Motel, they searched a dumpster behind the motel, and Calderon fished out a pillowcase and bedsheets stained with dried blood and a pair of blood-splattered white shorts. The sheets, staffers told the detectives, came from room 141. Calderon and Salinas tracked down the man staying there, who said he had known Melissa but knew nothing about the murder. He and another person had been shooting up, and his friend caught a healthy vein with a needle and sent a spray of fresh blood all over the room. Large bloodstains were still visible on the carpet and mattress.

After more than a week of running down leads and interviewing people, Calderon and Salinas had little more than pages of hand-scrawled interview notes and a few false starts. Though no solid leads, the gumshoe investigating did yield further people to contact. Salinas compiled a list of persons of interest for whom they needed addresses, phone numbers, and prior arrests. He decided to call the South Texas Border Intelligence Center, known simply as the "BIC" to local law enforcement.

The BIC was housed in a two-story, seven-thousand-square-foot facility adjacent to the U.S. Border Patrol's Laredo Sector headquarters on West Del Mar Boulevard in north central Laredo, just off Interstate 35, enclosed by thirty-four-foot-tall precast concrete wall panels. On the facility's narrow second floor, rows of cubicles lined the walls, divided in the middle by a floor-to-ceiling glass partition with sliding glass doors that were generally maintained open. On the south side of the partition, a team of analysts from the National and Texas State Guards punched names and numbers through databases, trying to glean information on suspects or organized crime rings. Led by a DPS Texas Ranger, this half of the second floor was technically called the Joint Operations Intelligence Center. On the other side of the partition, U.S. Border Patrol and other federal agents analyzed data in what was the Border Intelligence Center. As a matter of practice, however, most law enforcement agents referred to the whole operation simply as the BIC. Each day, some twenty agents from the FBI, DEA, Homeland Security Investigations, DPS, Laredo Police Department, Webb County Sheriff's Office, and U.S. Border Patrol gathered on the second floor to browse state and federal databases, share information and tips on cases, and, collectively, try to untangle some of the region's most vexing criminal puzzles. Agents strolled freely through the open glass partition, often asking each other to run a name or a license plate through specialized databases.

Salinas worked at the BIC from 2011 to 2014, overseeing a team of state guardsmen, until his duties shifted back to the field office. But he still had contacts at the BIC willing to run names through databases. On September 11, seven days after Melissa's body was found, he called in his list of names that had emerged during the investigation, hoping to glean addresses and arrest histories on those people. One of the names on the list: Claudine Luera, a person suggested to investigators as being particularly close with Melissa. A Texas guardsman at the BIC answered Salinas's call.

Just beyond the open glass partition, Border Patrol analysts sat in their cubicles and busied themselves with the cases and tasks of the day. Less than twenty feet away from where the guardsman jotted down Salinas's leads, Juan David Ortiz, a U.S. Border Patrol supervisory agent and rising star at the agency, listened intently, straining to catch a few details.

PART 2

CHAPTER 5

Erik Aguilar was worried about how dramatically the phone calls and text messages from his navy pal Doc Ortiz had darkened from ebullience over his new job with the U.S. Border Patrol's Laredo Sector to disillusion and anxiety. There were also slurred voicemails and signs of substance abuse.

"This happened today," read one text sent to him in 2017 by Juan David Ortiz. Everyone who knew him from the military called him "Doc." The text was accompanied by an image of a migrant who had died crossing into South Texas. The corpse was fully clothed and shriveled by the South Texas sun. In a later phone call, Ortiz confessed to Aguilar the death and misery he witnessed each day on the border was gnawing at him. "Like going to war every day," he told him.

Aguilar, a former marine and longtime friend who had seen combat with Ortiz in Iraq, urged his friend to seek help. "He was struggling," he said later.

A few months later, Ortiz sent Aguilar a video of him doing the Ice Bucket Challenge—a popular social media trend at the time where people poured buckets of ice water over their heads, then called on friends to do the same, to promote awareness of ALS. In the video, Ortiz is slurring his words and noticeably drunk or under the influence of drugs. Aguilar barely recognized his clean-cut friend who married young and often talked about God while the two were stationed together in California. "He was stressed," Aguilar conceded later. "It was bad."

His friend was spiraling into a dark place, he thought. He had little idea at the time how far that fall would reach.

THE SOUTHMOST NEIGHBORHOOD OF BROWNSVILLE, TEXAS, IS, as the name suggests, the southernmost point of Texas's southernmost city. It's a collection of single-story brick homes and shops bunched together along winding streets, each hemmed in by rusty chain-link fences. Christmas lights dangle from roof eaves year-round, and plastic flowers and fake flamingos stand sentry in neatly trimmed front lawns. Sagging oak trees and sabal palms line the streets, their fronds baked brown by the borderland sun. There are neighborhood taco joints and beauty salons and tire shops. Storefront churches outnumber schools. The neighborhood derives its name from its proximity to the U.S.-Mexico border, which sits just a mile south, separating it from Matamoros, Mexico.

It's here where Guadalupe "Lupita" Rocha raised Juan David Ortiz, along with three younger half-sisters: Crystal, five years younger than Ortiz, and twins Stephanie and Samantha, fifteen years younger. Lupita would raise the children alone; Ortiz's father, a native of Matamoros, left them when Ortiz was just a newborn. Lupita later revealed to her son, then in middle school, that his father, Ramon Ortiz, committed suicide by shooting himself in the head with a .38 Special.

Like with most families in the neighborhood, Spanish was the predominant language spoken at home, and Lupita had familial ties to Matamoros across the river. Though Hispanics in the United States are predominantly Christian and tend to identify as Catholic, there were no shortages of Pentecostal and Evangelical churches in Brownsville's Southmost neighborhood, with names like Templo El Remanente, Templo Cristiano El Shaddai, and Templo Bethel Asambleas de Dios. Lupita took her family to Ministerio Restauración y Poder, an Evangelical/Pentecostal church on Zapata Avenue, where Ortiz and his family would sit through rousing songs about Jesus's healing powers or hear a minister recount scenes from the New Testament, all in Spanish. Around them, attendees jumped to their feet and raised their hands in ecstatic approval, at times speaking in tongues.

The Evangelical/Pentecostal teachings permeated the family's home life. Lupita, a paralegal, led Bible studies at her home with members of

Restauración y Poder. Ortiz spent Friday evenings at the church's youth ministry.

As he entered Gladys Porter Early College High School in Brownsville in 1998, fifteen-year-old Ortiz carried the church's influence with him. He joined Youth Alive Bible Study, a church-oriented, student-led group. The group met each Thursday during lunch in the school's computer lab and dissected passages from the Bible or talked about how to apply Jesus's teachings to everyday life. Ortiz, known to friends as David, became a leader of the group, able to quote Scripture by heart and give succinct meaning to ancient teachings. Outgoing, and with an inner confidence and easygoing smile, unafraid to spread the word of God to others, Ortiz was idolized by some in the group. "He was like a role model," said one freshman attendee. "I wanted to be just like him."

One passage Ortiz often repeated during the Bible study sessions was a quote from the apostle Paul in Romans 7:15: "I do not understand what I do. For what I want to do I do not do, but what I hate I do." It described the inner conflict that all humans, particularly high school students, struggled with: trying to do good under the constant specter of sin. To members of the group, there was no sign of inner conflict within Ortiz. He attended the study group regularly, always carried a Bible with him, and strode from class to class with a confidence that evaded other students.

He also had plans for his life. At around the same time, Ortiz enrolled in the school's Reserve Officers' Training Corps, or ROTC, and flashed photos of himself standing at attention in military garb, surrounded by other ROTC members. He told his fellow students matter-of-factly that he planned to join the navy after high school, go to college, and become a pastor. "He had a ten-year plan," one Bible study attendee said. "He knew exactly what he wanted to do."

=====

ORTIZ'S POPULAR, BIBLE-TOTING PERSONA AT PORTER HIGH, however, belied a troubled life at home. His mother, Lupita, brought home a string of different boyfriends, some of whom would physically abuse her. The encounters got so bad that at times Ortiz had to call police. To avoid the turbulence at home, he delved into school activities.

The Porter High School yearbooks from 1998 to 2001 are filled with photos of him in a variety of clubs and activities. In one black-and-white photo from 1998, Ortiz, still a freshman, is seen leaning on a piano with a music sheet in hand, singing along with three other students. The group was part of Estudiantina Juventud, the school's music ensemble club. In an accompanying photo on the same page, a smiling girl plays the guitar. The caption identifies her as Daniella Guajardo, who years later would become Ortiz's wife. Starting in 1998, Ortiz also joined the swim team. He began as an average swimmer but showed dedication, becoming competent, if not competitive, in the butterfly and relay races. Practice ran two hours each day after school at nearby Antonio Gonzalez Park, and Ortiz rarely missed one, putting in the time to learn the correct strokes and relay techniques, exchanges, and drills. The team traveled a few times a year to swim meets around the region, in McAllen, Weslaco, Corpus Christi. Before each meet, Ortiz would gather the other swimmers in a circle, bend a knee, and pray that the Lord strengthen their strokes and keep them safe.

Sal Cano, a swimmer on the team, took an immediate liking to Ortiz. A fellow Pentecostal Christian from the same area of Brownsville, he hung out with Ortiz at swim practices, sat next to him on bus rides to meets, and met him every Friday evening for youth services at Restauración y Poder. After the service, they would go for pizza or tacos and discuss the evening's teachings. Ortiz was jovial, joking, and Cano appreciated how seriously he took his faith. "He was a really likable fellow," Cano recalled.

In his freshman yearbook photo, Ortiz is wearing glasses with a striped shirt buttoned to the collar hanging on a skinny frame, his dark, shiny hair parted down the middle. By his senior year, Ortiz had added several pounds of muscle weight and carried a swimmer's physique. His senior year photo has his hair combed straight back and gleaming with product, his eyes no longer framed by glasses and staring intently into the camera. His fellow swimmers named him cocaptain that year, along with another student, Manny Galvan.

To Galvan, Ortiz seemed more mature than their peers. He carried a Bible from class to class and talked about church with a zeal other students used for spring break or weekend parties. While Galvan and others were discovering nightclubs and sneaking across the border to Matamoros, where they could drink at local bars without ID, Ortiz avoided the party scene.

One Thursday after practice late in their senior year, Galvan and his teammates organized an impromptu get-together at another swimmer's home to celebrate their season and the coming end of the year. They tried to get Ortiz to join them, but he declined. His mother was hosting a Bible study at their house and he had committed to be there. "He was a great guy. Everybody liked David," Galvan said later. "But he was also so uptight that it kind of pushed him away from everybody else."

===

ORTIZ GRADUATED FROM PORTER HIGH SCHOOL IN MAY 2001, and two months later, on July 5—a few weeks past his eighteenth birthday and two months before the terrorist attacks of 9/11—he did what he repeatedly said he'd do: he enlisted in the U.S. Navy. He signed up to become an emergency medical technician, doing his basic training first at Recruit Training Command, Great Lakes, just north of Chicago, and later at the Navy Medicine Training Support Center at Fort Sam Houston in San Antonio, Texas.

Later that year, he returned to Brownsville on a break from his military training and popped into the Sunrise Mall off Highway 83, where he ran into Manny Galvan, his former swim cocaptain. Galvan was working part-time at the Gap and was pleasantly surprised to see his high school buddy stroll into the clothing store. The two sat on a bench outside the store to catch up. His hair sheared nearly completely to the scalp and muscles filling out his T-shirt, Ortiz told Galvan how he had joined the navy and traveled around the United States. There was something different in his demeanor, Galvan noticed. That bright-eyed high school innocence was replaced by something sharper.

"We should grab some beers," Ortiz offered.

Galvan was surprised. He told Ortiz he didn't expect that from the Scripture-quoting student he remembered from Porter High School. "You don't even drink, man," Galvan told him.

"Nah, man, that's all BS from before," Ortiz said. "Don't worry about that shit. I know what's up."

Ortiz said he was ready to "party." The two swapped phone numbers and promised to get together before Ortiz had to return to the navy, but they never did.

It was the last time Galvan saw his high school buddy.

——

ORTIZ SLID INTO MILITARY LIFE WITH THE EASE AND ZEST OF someone chasing his calling. After basic training in Illinois and Texas, he was assigned, in April 2002, as a navy medical corpsman to the First Marine Division's Third Battalion, Eleventh Marine Regiment, at the Marine Corps Air Ground Combat Center in Twentynine Palms, California, a sprawling training base in the Mojave Desert just north of Joshua Tree National Park.

Ortiz roomed with other corpsmen and hung out with marines, watching movies in their dorm-like rooms or going into town for dinner and drinks. In their third-floor bunk room, Ortiz and his roommate, corpsman Charlie Javier, divided the room down the middle. Ortiz spent hours watching rented VHS movies like *Y tu mamá también*, the Mexican film starring Gael García Bernal, on his thirty-inch TV or chatting on the phone in Spanish with his mom and other Brownsville relatives. To beat the monotony of base life, Ortiz played *Madden NFL* on his PlayStation, dined on burritos at Santana's restaurant in downtown Twentynine Palms, or took road trips with friends to Palm Springs and other areas. Javier rarely, if ever, saw him drink alcohol.

Fermin Ayala, a marine with the Third Battalion, Twelfth Marines, who was assigned to the Eleventh Marines at Twentynine Palms in May 2002, hung out with Ortiz on base and grew to like the amicable corpsman. When another marine was getting married in El Paso, Ayala volunteered to drive the ten-hour trip. Ortiz and two other marines climbed into Ayala's Mitsubishi Galant, and they headed southeast toward the Texas border city. Along the way, Ortiz played his Tejano music on the Mitsubishi's radio and the other marines teased him. "That's not real music," one said. "That's just a tuba."

Ortiz talked about being a good Christian and reiterated his pride in his Hispanic heritage, pointing out that Texas was part of Mexico long before the Anglos came along. "The border crossed us," he told them.

The lives of navy corpsmen and marines at Twentynine Palms were constantly intertwined. Corpsmen accompanied marines on training trips into the desert, practicing first aid techniques as marines thundered 155mm howitzer artillery shells into the desert. By day, Ortiz would treat the marines for sprained ankles or heat exhaustion, and at night he'd squeeze into a sleeping bag under the night sky or stretch out in the cab of a truck for a few hours' sleep. His marine buddies got to calling him Doc Ortiz.

One marine who took a liking to Ortiz was Erik Aguilar, a sinewy former high school cross-country star from California. Born in the state of Morelos, Mexico, south of Mexico City, Aguilar immigrated to California with his mother when he was eleven years old and was encouraged to run cross-country by a high school coach. He racked up state accolades for races in high school and community college before joining the marines. Aguilar had already been at Twentynine Palms for more than a year when he met the younger Ortiz, a Hispanic corpsman eager to please and who seemed easy to get along with. Aguilar and Ortiz both came from Spanish-speaking backgrounds (Aguilar spoke a purer Mexican Spanish; Ortiz, a Spanglish version of Texan Spanish), both were churchgoing, and both believed in serving their country. They bonded immediately. Aguilar also had a less altruistic reason to befriend Ortiz. "He was a corpsman," he recalled. "If something ever happens to you, you want that guy by your side."

The two spent hours together on base, speculating on who would win the 2002 FIFA World Cup or listening to Tejano music in their rooms, their talks flowing freely between English and Spanish. "He was a pretty mellow guy," Aguilar said. "Very God-driven. Very patriotic."

====

IT WAS A HEADY TIME TO BE PATRIOTIC.

Ortiz arrived at Twentynine Palms seven months after the worst-ever terrorist attacks on U.S. soil. Images of the hijacked planes crashing into the World Trade Center buildings and the Pentagon on September 11 still burned fresh in the minds of service members around the country. In October 2001, President George W. Bush ordered U.S. special forces teams to Afghanistan to dislodge the Taliban and hunt down Osama bin Laden, and more army divisions and U.S. special forces were deployed in March 2002 to root out al-Qaeda, the terrorist group responsible for the attacks.

Military bases across America tensed in anticipation of more deployments, and Twentynine Palms was no exception. As early as August 2002, commanders of the First Marine Division, headquartered in Camp Pendleton, north of San Diego, huddled in conference rooms and discussed orders emerging from the Pentagon: to begin preparing for a U.S. invasion of Iraq, where questionable intel reports were linking the country's dictator, Saddam Hussein, to weapons of mass destruction. Iraq seemed destined to be the next target in the U.S.-led Global War on Terrorism.

And the vast desert environs of the combat center at Twentynine Palms provided the perfect backdrop for combat training for Iraq. Battalions were deployed into the sandy moonscape for a series of multiday exercises code-named Desert Scimitar, where artillery personnel fired howitzers into the desert while marines learned to live, sleep, and survive in the sunbaked environs, creating a battle rhythm for sustained twenty-four-hour combat operations. Marines, accompanied by their navy corpsmen, acted out covering long distances as quickly as possible, seizing key oil fields, isolating large cities, traversing impassable terrain, and conducting major river crossings—exercises that proved eerily similar to what they would later face in Iraq.

Intel officers estimated U.S. casualties in an Iraqi invasion wouldn't surpass 5 percent of the entire division—or about one thousand marines—but corpsmen nonetheless trained on how to treat the injured in the desert and to set up field hospitals. As UN weapons inspectors complained Hussein's regime was stymieing their efforts to search for weapons of mass destruction, military leaders feared Iraqis would unleash chemical weapons on encroaching U.S. troops. Starting in September 2002, division leaders at Twentynine Palms instituted "Gas Mask Wednesdays," ordering troops to carry gas masks on their uniforms all day and don them for thirty-minute intervals.

Though no details were revealed, staff sergeants urged marines to "keep training," hinting at bigger things to come. Many pulsed with adrenaline at the thought of traveling to foreign lands and testing their skills. Aguilar was based at Camp Butler in Okinawa, Japan, in 2001 when 9/11 occurred, and he and other marines bristled when their unit wasn't deployed to Afghanistan in the initial salvo in the Global War on Terrorism. But as the desert training intensified at Twentynine Palms, he and others itched to join the fight. "We were young and hungry for war," Aguilar said later. "It's like you practice for the Super Bowl but you never get to play. When you get a chance, you're excited. You're ready. It's what you've trained for."

By the fall of 2002, talk of deployment to Iraq was swirling through Twentynine Palms. The prospect sharpened into even tighter focus when, one day, Ortiz distributed anthrax and smallpox vaccines to the regiment. As marines and sailors headed home on their Christmas break, staff sergeants urged them to get some rest and enjoy their families—they'd be deploying soon after returning. Sure enough, after the holiday furlough, the marines were ordered to start packing: they were shipping out to Kuwait. The Eleventh Marine Regiment—activated during World War I and deployed in World War II and the Korean, Vietnam, and Persian Gulf Wars—was again heading to the battlefield.

And Ortiz would be wedged right in with them.

CHAPTER 6

In mid-January 2003, one battalion after another from the Eleventh Marine Regiment boarded charter planes at March Air Reserve Base near Riverside, California, and took the sixteen-hour flight to Kuwait.

The marines crossed into southern Iraq on March 20, 2003, and began their march to Baghdad. By all measures, it was a stunning success: a 350-mile military rout in just twelve days. But it was far from bloodless. In all, 138 U.S. troops were killed in the initial invasion. Navy corpsmen embedded with the marines were in the thick of the action. Corpsmen had legs blown off by mines as they tended to wounded marines, were killed by rocket-propelled grenades, or bore witness to friends maimed and slaughtered by war.

Ortiz was assigned to Lima Battery, Third Battalion, Twelfth Marines, who were reinforcing the Eleventh Marine Regiment out of Twentynine Palms. He was the most senior of three corpsmen attached to the unit of 134 marines. He rode in an armored Humvee in a convoy of six seven-ton trucks, each carrying a 155mm howitzer. Three times a day, Ortiz would tromp along the long lines of marines, checking on everyone's physical and mental health and reporting back to the commanding officer.

Just outside of Basra, they drove into a blinding sandstorm and took on friendly fire from the Fifth Marines, just one hundred meters away, who were firing at a truck that had crossed their path and refused to stop. Their bullets hit and flew past the civilian truck and pinged Ortiz's unit. When the gunfire ceased, Ortiz ran from marine to marine, making sure everyone was okay. Then he ran over to where the truck had finally stopped. Its Iraqi driver staggered out and collapsed, punctured full of bullets and clinging to life. Marines searched his truck but found only a few sacks of rice, no weapons or bombs.

Ortiz tried to save the man, but he died and they buried him in the desert.

Over the next two weeks, his unit trooped up through south central Iraq relatively unscathed, tallying no deaths and only a handful of minor injuries. On April 11, the Eleventh Marine Regiment rumbled into Baghdad.

Military resistance inside the capital had mostly vanished. Now, the Eleventh Marines were tasked with something not in the training manuals at Twentynine Palms: keeping a city of 5.6 million people—roughly twice the population of Chicago—with no governance or law enforcement from total collapse. They established a civil-military operations center for division leaders at the Palestine Hotel in downtown Baghdad and another for the regiment in eastern Baghdad. Units conducted patrols around the city, removing weapons caches and detaining looters. Others ferried fuel to water treatment plants, supervised the rebuilding of power plants, and secured hospitals.

Armed criminal gangs roamed the streets, robbing banks and hijacking vehicles. The Eleventh Marines tried to restore order during the day and hunted elements of the Fedayeen Saddam—specially trained paramilitary cadres—at night. Manning checkpoints, they were routinely raked with gunfire and rocket-propelled grenades.

One of the tasks assigned to Ortiz's unit was securing the Al-Rasheed Military Hospital in eastern Baghdad. As the marines entered the darkened lobby, they saw a macabre message scrawled on the wall in Arabic: 144 bodies had been buried in the hospital's lawn. As war arrived in Baghdad, the morgue had shut down and bodies had piled up at the hospital; workers had hastily put them in shallow graves throughout the hospital grounds. Marines, helped by former Iraqi soldiers, were tasked with digging up the bodies of men, women, and children and laying them in rows to await identification from family members and proper burial. Some had just recently died; others had been rotting for more than a month. Hospital staffers spent nights shooting at dogs trying to tear away a bone or other appendage from the rows of decomposing bodies.

Ayala, the marine who had driven Ortiz and others to El Paso, came up through southern Iraq with the Eleventh Marines and marveled at how the people there, mostly Shi'ite who had been brutally oppressed by Hussein, cheered their armored vehicles and offered them cigarettes. But their reception quickly darkened in Baghdad, populated more by Sunnis, Hussein's sect. Assigned to patrol the area around the Al-Rasheed Hospital, Ayala and his fellow marines were shot at repeatedly. Reprisal killings were rampant, and anyone seen cooperating with the Americans was kidnapped or killed. One young Iraqi woman working as a translator for the marines was murdered.

Ayala also helped secure the Al-Rasheed Hospital. More bodies were brought in, some bloodied and clinging to life, others days or weeks dead. Makeshift coffins were found in a nearby warehouse and commandeered to store the bodies. Family members arrived day and night to identify the dead. "We saw some gruesome stuff," Ayala said.

Ortiz spent most of his time in Baghdad driving in a Humvee with First Sergeant Gilbert Contreras, backing up other marine units when needed and treating the sick or wounded. But Iraqis were mostly on the receiving end of the violence. Once, Ortiz treated an Iraqi man who had stepped on a land mine and had both his legs blown off. Later, he and a marine attended to two men who were near a fuel tank when it exploded, their bodies burned scalp to feet.

One marine who was in Baghdad with Ortiz recalled the overwhelming stench of rotting bodies from the Al-Rasheed Hospital and the constant bloodshed. It took its toll, even on the war-hardened marines. "There was a lot of death going on," he said. "They could train you all day to shoot a gun, but they can't train you for what you're going to see."

=====

By the end of April 2003, with Baghdad slowly stabilizing, the Eleventh Marines handed over control of the city to a U.S. Army regiment and moved out. They headed to Al Diwaniyah, a dust-clogged city one hundred miles south of Baghdad, and set up camp at an abandoned Iraqi military base. Almost immediately, due to something in the air or the general lack of hygiene during combat, troops became violently ill. Marines complained of severe diarrhea and vomiting. Others were burning with fever or hallucinations. Most sought Ortiz for help. One marine needed five IV bags to stabilize. First Sergeant Contreras became incapacitated with the contagion for five days. Ortiz remained by his side the whole time, slowly nursing him back to health, as the commander writhed on a poncho in the dirt next to a Humvee.

The mysterious illness was so prevalent and made everyone so miserable that marines nicknamed the outpost Camp Diarrhea. Ortiz, as a corpsman, was in the middle of the outbreak. One night in Al Diwaniyah, just after dusk, Erik Aguilar was walking near the motor pool when he came upon his good friend Ortiz staggering drunk. Ortiz reeked of booze, and his words slurred when he spoke. Aguilar sat him on the dirt floor and reminded him that he could be in severe trouble—fines or the stockade or both—if an officer saw him inebriated. Ortiz told him he had gone outside the wire that day and scored some whiskey.

"What the fuck, man? We're at war," Aguilar told him. "You can't be drunk."

"My experience here has been bad," Ortiz slurred.

Aguilar found another corpsman and told him to move Ortiz out of sight until he sobered up. The next morning, Ortiz thanked Aguilar at breakfast for his help the previous night. Ortiz's face was morose, his stare darker. The easygoing smile was gone. They never spoke of the incident again.

As April turned to May, the marines trickled back to Kuwait to return to the United States. Their historic invasion of Iraq and toppling of Saddam Hussein's regime was officially over. Ortiz boarded USS *Dubuque,* a 570-foot navy transport ship, for the long ocean voyage to California. Aguilar took the same ship home. The *Dubuque* sailed for two months before docking in Southern California. The two friends never spoke.

=====

WITH COMBAT TOURS BEHIND THEM AND RELEASE FROM THE
military imminent, the marines and corpsmen now faced an equally
daunting task: reintegration into society, something for which the U.S.
military, at that point, had a less-than-stellar track record. Though the
majority of U.S. service members leaving the wars in Iraq and Afghanistan returned to their homes and families without issue, thousands
struggled with post-traumatic stress disorder and turned to alcohol,
drugs, or suicidal ideation to cope. By 2009, about 12 percent of the
nearly two million army, navy, and marine corps service members returning from at least one tour in Iraq or Afghanistan were diagnosed with
depression, anxiety, or acute stress. That percentage doubled with three
or four tours. One study showed that 43 percent of active-component
service members reported binge drinking within the preceding month.

Corpsmen were no exception. Anthony Ameen was a navy hospital
corpsman attached to the Second Battalion, Seventh Marines, in Hel-
mand Province, Afghanistan, in July 2008, when his company came
under attack. He was running to tend to another corpsman who had
stepped on a mine when Ameen himself triggered a mine, severing his
left leg. He came home to Phoenix to thirty-four surgeries and a battery
of excruciating physical therapy sessions. He received a prosthetic leg but
soon spiraled into depression and bouts of crippling anxiety, drinking
himself to sleep each night with a fifth of vodka or twelve-pack of beer.

Ameen was struck by how little guidance there was from the military to help veterans combat their anxiety and reenter society. There was
Veterans Affairs, which helped fix your body, and the Vet Center, which
focused on mental health counseling, but each entity seemed to rarely
communicate with the other, he noticed. Ameen was left mostly to figure things out on his own: "Nobody held my hand and said, 'Thank you
for your service, thank you for losing a limb for your country. Here's
what's available to you.'"

Ten years after leaving Afghanistan, after hunting down resources
himself, Ameen began visiting the local Vet Center, quit drinking, and

slowly improved his mental health. Today, he's married with four children and a sought-after motivational speaker. He founded Wings for Warriors, which helps connect veterans and first responders with resources and support. But he realizes his journey is an anomaly. Of the 1,200 marines who deployed with Ameen's company in 2008, twenty were killed in combat—and another thirteen died from suicide.

"In the military, you're spoon-fed," Ameen said. "When you sign that dotted line, you get three warm meals a day, clothing; you're told what to do. But when you get out of the service, it's all up to you."

The marines in Ortiz's unit, many felt, were also left to sort things out on their own. One marine who served with Ortiz was stunned by how little direction he received from the military after leaving combat. He was asked to fill out a questionnaire but never received a follow-up call. "The marine corps did a real shitty job of that," he said. "You just got chewed up and spit out."

═══

IF ORTIZ HARBORED ANY ILL FEELINGS OR DEMONS FROM HIS time in Iraq, he didn't initially show them. USS *Dubuque* delivered him back to California, and he returned to Twentynine Palms. Jerry Solis, a marine assigned to Twentynine Palms, met Ortiz shortly after, during training exercises in the desert. Solis was from Laredo. The two connected through their common border backgrounds and their mutual love for the Dallas Cowboys. They met for dinner or drinks in town or took weekend road trips together to Las Vegas or Palm Springs. Solis was struck by how much Ortiz talked about religion and readily recited Scripture. "He could quote you any quote from the Bible if you ask him," Solis remembered. "He knew the Bible."

In August 2003, Ortiz took a family leave to Brownsville. A jubilant cadre of family members and the local media greeted him at the Brownsville South Padre Island International Airport. His mother, Lupita, waved a tiny U.S. flag, while Ortiz's grandmother Tomasa Gonzalez gripped a flock of red, white, and blue balloons. The next day, a story appeared on the front page of the *Brownsville Herald* with a photo of a smiling Ortiz wearing a black Lima Battery T-shirt while being hugged by Gonzalez. The banner headline read: "A Hero's Welcome." The subhead mistakenly identified him as a soldier. Ortiz downplayed his time in Iraq, telling the reporter, "None of my Marines were seriously injured."

While in Brownsville, Ortiz ran into his friend from Porter High School, Daniella Guajardo. Pretty and cheerful, with an easygoing smile, Daniella captured Ortiz's attention. Sparks kindled, and the pair began dating. They were married a year later in Brownsville on August 11, 2004, and celebrated their reception surrounded by family in a hotel ballroom in Matamoros. Solis, now living in Laredo, drove to Brownsville to be the best man.

Now married and looking to return to Texas, Ortiz, after a short deployment to Okinawa, prepared to leave Twentynine Palms. Near the end of his term, in April 2005, Ortiz spotted Ayala walking near his barracks and called him over. He told his buddy he was leaving Twentynine Palms. "He was teary-eyed," Ayala remembered. "A grown man crying. It kind of threw me off. You go through something like Iraq, you get attached to people."

Ortiz reported to the U.S. Navy Element at the Defense Medical Readiness Training Institute at Fort Sam Houston on April 5, 2005, and later transferred to the Navy Medicine Training Support Center. Brandon Caro, another corpsman who served with Ortiz at Fort Sam Houston, was impressed at how Ortiz came to work each day in a crisp uniform, focused on his task, and carried on with the air of someone who knew where he was going. "He seemed like a real squared away guy," said Caro, who later moved to Austin and wrote *Old Silk Road*, a novel based on his time in Afghanistan. "He seemed really disciplined, someone who knew what was going on."

Ortiz and Daniella moved into a two-story redbrick home in the Adams Hill neighborhood of west San Antonio and settled into suburbia. Their neighbor Pearl Noriega relished seeing the happy couple's home fill with babies over the years: first a girl, then another girl, and finally a little boy. Pearl watched as Ortiz played in his backyard with his kids or chatted over beers after work with her husband, Arturo Noriega, in their garage. Grill outs with the two families were common.

Ortiz enrolled in American Military University, an online institution, earning a bachelor's degree in criminal justice forensics, and later a master's degree in international relations from St. Mary's University in San Antonio.

But the Rockwellesque image of family life the Ortizes exuded soon bore cracks. One day in the summer of 2008, with Daniella and the kids out of town, Ortiz met thirty-eight-year-old Amanda Callahan at Fast Eddie's billiards and bar in San Antonio. The two hit it off, and Callahan spent the night with him at his house. The next day, the pair went out drinking, and again she ended up spending the night with Ortiz. The next morning, Ortiz said there was something he wanted to show her and pulled out a small box from his closet. He opened the box to reveal what Ortiz claimed were C-4 plastic explosives he had retained from his military deployments. Ortiz later asked her if she had ever done drugs, and Callahan said she had not. He referred to people who used drugs as "disgusting and horrible people."

The two went their separate ways and never saw each other again.

═══

In May 2009, two weeks before his twenty-sixth birthday, Ortiz was honorably discharged from the navy. He departed the service with medical skills, two arms spackled with tattoos ("USN," "USMC," "Corpsman," and the American flag on one shoulder; tribal designs encircling a sun on the other; and small colorful birds flying atop each pectoral muscle), and a robust cigarette-smoking habit. In eight years of military service, he had also racked up a dozen accolades and honors, including a Navy & Marine Corps Achievement Medal, a Combat Action Ribbon, a Presidential Unit Citation, a Global War on Terrorism Expeditionary Medal, a Sharpshooter Marksmanship Ribbon, and a Pistol Marksmanship Ribbon.

Armed with a glowing military résumé, Ortiz had career choices. He was offered a position with the San Antonio Police Department and was slated to enter the police academy. Instead, his sights shifted to the better-paying U.S. Border Patrol, something he had considered for years. Ortiz told his San Antonio neighbors he wanted a career on the border because, as the son of immigrants, he could look out for the best interests of migrants arriving to the United States. To friends he said he looked forward to using his navy corpsman training to help those in medical need along the border. Pearl, also of Mexican descent, applauded his choice. "He understood immigrants wanting to come here for a better life," Pearl remembered. "I congratulated him."

When her husband, Arturo, was arrested in 2011 on felony murder charges for killing a man with his car while intoxicated, Pearl Noriega lapsed into depression. Ortiz visited her nearly every day, bringing her food and talking her through the malaise. He told her it wasn't fair, that everyone deserved a second chance. "He was very empathetic," she recalled.

Later, Ortiz attended Arturo's trial and spoke in front of the judge on his neighbor's behalf, describing him as an ideal neighbor and husband and urging leniency from the court. The judge was unimpressed. He sentenced Arturo Noriega to life in prison.

CHAPTER 7

Juan David Ortiz—Iraq War vet, navy corpsman, father of three—began his career at the U.S. Border Patrol with gusto. At the Border Patrol's academy in New Mexico, he was required to pass a drug test and trained to use an agency-issued .40-caliber Heckler & Koch P2000 semiautomatic pistol. Ortiz, now twenty-six, was assigned to the Border Patrol's Cotulla Station in South Texas, just over an hour's commute south from his home in San Antonio. There, he was tasked with chasing smugglers and drug mules and detaining undocumented migrants between ports of entry. Later, he was trained to stop cars and trucks suspected of drug or human smuggling.

Initially, he cherished the job. His annual salary was more than $80,000—greater than what he would have earned at a local police department—he was outdoors most of the time, and he could use the life-saving skills he acquired as a corpsman to help migrants. On more than one occasion, he came across migrants in the South Texas brush who were dehydrated and on the brink of death, and he furnished them with fluids and saved their lives.

Aguilar, his buddy from Twentynine Palms and Baghdad, hadn't seen or spoken to Ortiz in years. But in 2011 he signed in to Facebook and was delighted to stumble onto the profile of his old friend. Soon, Ortiz and Aguilar were swapping text messages and Facebook DMs. Ortiz boasted about his role at Border Patrol. "He was very grateful he was able to do his job and help migrants," Aguilar recalled.

To coworkers, Ortiz seemed smart, albeit aloof, often preferring to while away hours alone. He would hum songs and take smoke breaks by himself but was not considered a loner. While other agents tended to be loud, boisterous, and, often, off-color, Ortiz was quiet and stand-offish, sticking mostly to himself.

But just as Ortiz was adjusting to the pace and rhythm of the Cotulla Station, he was reassigned to the Border Patrol's South Laredo Station, a much larger—and busier—area sixty miles farther south on Interstate 35. For years, Ortiz had told friends he yearned to put his corpsman skills to good use. In 2016, he was about to test those skills in one of the busiest Border Patrol sectors along the southwest border.

═══

IF HE CRAVED ACTION, ORTIZ SOON FOUND IT. THE LAREDO Sector's 1,800 employees were responsible for patrolling 136 miles of U.S.-Mexico border and encountered more than three thousand undocumented migrants a month, along with drug runners, coyotes, and cartel operatives. In the area around Laredo, patrolling the border meant driving through miles of flat, arid private ranches, speckled with thornbushes and mesquite trees, north of town or tromping through marshland along the banks of the Rio Grande.

At times, large groups of migrants, mostly women and children or families, emerged from the bushes and surrendered to Border Patrol agents, opting to put their fate in the U.S. immigration system. They were often mud splattered, exhausted from long overland journeys from Nicaragua or Venezuela or other corners of Latin America, and very often had been victimized by the coyotes who brought them there. It was up to Border Patrol to coordinate transport and ferry the foreigners to holding cells, where they were processed and either released until their immigration court hearing or deported, depending on the believability of their story and the latest directive from Washington. Other times, the bushes would shiver and four, five, ten migrants would dart out in different directions, trying to evade the outstretched hands of agents and make it to stash houses or pickup points farther north.

Those were the lucky ones. The less fortunate migrants were dropped in remote ranches or vast deserts by unscrupulous smugglers and told to walk north until a second guide picked them up. Sometimes one did, often one didn't, leaving the ill-prepared migrants to wander for hours or days in triple-digit heat and searing sun in a sea of dust, chaparral, and prickly pear. Border Patrol agents encountered those unfortunate asylum seekers and, as often, their shriveled, sunbaked remains in jeans and sneakers.

High-speed chases of trucks weighed down with human cargo were also common, and temporary holding cells at times overflowed with masses of asylum seekers. The year Ortiz arrived in Laredo, agents encountered 35,888 undocumented immigrants in their sector. That was below the crush of the early 2000s, when more than one hundred thousand crossed each year, but it was still a steady current of crossings.

For his first year, Ortiz rode in Border Patrol airboats as they roared along the Rio Grande, rescuing stranded crossers or intercepting drug runners, then manned a Border Patrol checkpoint up on Interstate 35. The checkpoint was located right on the highway, and agents there inspected, one by one, each car or truck traveling north for signs of drug or human smuggling.

Initially, the gig exhilarated him. Once, Ortiz came upon a group of migrants in the desert badly dehydrated and near death. He kicked into action mode, hooking up the migrants with IVs and saving their lives. Later, he proudly relayed the story to Aguilar. "He was very grateful he was able to do his job," Aguilar said.

But the unending waves of migrants and the stress of saving lives while encountering drug runners, some of them armed, chipped away at the job's shiny veneer. Aguilar grew alarmed at the change in tone of the text messages he received from Ortiz. Messages praising his job or urging Aguilar to join him in Border Patrol devolved into texts denouncing the death and malice he saw on a near-daily basis. Ortiz, who once likened himself to a champion of migrants, now complained of how often they were sneaking into the United States. He told Aguilar he felt helpless as more and more groups of asylum seekers tramped across the border, many of them succumbing to the heat and harsh environments.

On three different occasions, he sent Aguilar pictures of the bodies of dead migrants he encountered near the border. Alarmed at the tone of the messages, Aguilar texted and called several times in response.

Several days passed before Ortiz replied. "Pretty stressful today," he texted. "Sorry I didn't respond. Very busy."

====

IN 2017, ORTIZ WAS ASSIGNED TO THE BORDER PATROL'S TAR-geted Enforcement Unit (TEU), a group of specially trained agents focused on raiding and breaking up smuggling rings. Backed by local and state law enforcement, Ortiz and others in the TEU would stake out stash houses where smugglers hid undocumented migrants, rush in and arrest the smugglers, and haul away the unwitting migrants. Once, they trailed a car to a gas station off Interstate 35 and found five hundred pounds of marijuana inside. More surveillance followed and more busts. Ortiz worked his way up to group supervisor, leading the team.

Many of the stash houses the group targeted were in the vicinity of Lafayette Street in central Laredo; Santa Rita, a working-class neighborhood overlooking the Rio Grande in south Laredo; and San Bernardo Avenue. With the freedom afforded to a supervisor, Ortiz drove around the neighborhoods in an unmarked vehicle, cruising up and down San Bernardo, looking for suspicious activity and delving into the city's criminal underbelly. He got to know the stash houses and drug dens—and the men and women who populated them. At times, he bragged to Border Patrol colleagues that he knew where all the sex workers in town were. Once, after lunch on San Bernardo with a few other agents, Ortiz offered to show them "where the whores worked." The agents, uncomfortable at the invitation, declined.

====

THAT YEAR, ORTIZ AND DANIELLA BOUGHT AN 1,800-SQUARE-foot home on Bur Oak Drive in a manicured subdivision in northwest Laredo for $238,000 and moved the family there. Daniella found work as a registered nurse at a local hospital, and the Ortiz family again settled into suburbia.

Shortly after arriving in Laredo, Ortiz reached out to Jerry Solis, his good friend from Twentynine Palms and a Laredo native. The two began hanging out. On weekends, they'd watch Dallas Cowboys football games together or hunt white-tailed deer on an expanse of wooded property in rural Webb County, which Solis rented from the landowner in an agreement known as a "hunting lease." On one such hunting trip, Ortiz and Solis were looking for deer while squatting in a cornfield when they spotted a javelina some sixty yards away. Ortiz sighted it with his AR-15 semiautomatic rifle and dropped the boar-like animal with a single round through its heart. "He was a pretty good shot," Solis remembered later.

The two hunted, shared beers, and reminisced about their time in the military. Ortiz loved the hunting trips so much that he split the cost of the lease with Solis, Solis's brother, and another friend. Meanwhile, his job duties were intensifying. The raids on stash houses and paperwork were piling up at an ominous rate, and he often worked deep into the night to catch up. After a few months, he informed Solis that, regrettably, he had to give up his share of the hunting lease. "Don't have time," he told him.

＝＝＝

In January 2018, Ortiz was promoted to supervisory agent and moved to the second floor of the Border Intelligence Center in north Laredo. He now oversaw a team of fourteen agents, who scoured reports and databases, looking for criminal trends and ways to break up cartel operations. Ortiz embraced his new position, tackling the workload and earning the growing respect of his superiors.

Slowly, however, the long hours and stress gnawed at him. He began getting crippling migraines. He'd wake up in the middle of the night covered in sweat and reeling from nightmares about his time in Iraq or scenes from the border. Panic attacks seized him at work. He began drinking more. At home, he was irritable and prone to bouts of anger. The slightest provocation would make Ortiz snap at his children.

Increasingly, Daniella took the kids out of town with her to visit relatives in Brownsville or San Antonio, leaving Ortiz alone in the house. Josue Lopez, who lived across Bur Oak Drive from Ortiz, often let his daughters play with Ortiz's daughters. The girls would draw with sidewalk chalk together or play tag in their yard. But by 2018, he stopped seeing the girls around the house for weeks at a time. Ortiz, strolling in and out of his house alone, would barely nod at his neighbor. "We were wondering, *What happened to the family?*" Lopez recalled later. "We didn't see the kids around. Only him by himself."

Aguilar also grew concerned at the misogynistic and mean undertones in Ortiz's messages. Once, Ortiz noticed a woman who had commented on Aguilar's Facebook page and texted him: "Who's the girl with the big tits?" It was a jarring comment from a friend who once preached Scripture and the importance of family.

By early 2018, then president Donald Trump's controversial border policies were in full throttle. As a cornerstone of his 2016 election campaign, Trump had promised stricter border policies and a heavy crackdown on undocumented crossings. His administration delivered, reducing the levels of legal immigration, ramping up raids on undocumented migrants living in the United States, and, most controversially, ordering the separation of families at the border. The new policies emboldened Border Patrol agents and leadership, allowing many to disregard migrants' civil liberties to carry out the directives.

Ortiz became an adherent. He told Aguilar he hoped Trump "closed the border" and said he supported the president's tactics. "I hope he deports everyone," he told Aguilar. Ortiz, who once said he wanted to join the Border Patrol to help protect migrants, texted Aguilar a picture of Trump emblazoned with the words "Deporter in Chief."

Paranoia crept into Ortiz's life. He felt as if people were constantly talking about him and plotting to harm him. He woke up four, sometimes five times a night, checking and rechecking the locks on the door. He would fill with a sudden, inescapable fear, imagining an enemy coming for him. At the office, dark thoughts overwhelmed him. While smoking a cigarette outside alone, he would suddenly blurt out, "Fuck my life!" or "Fuck this place!" unintentionally loud enough that coworkers could overhear. Other agents snickered at the outbursts, saying, "El pinche vato está hablando solo" (That fucking dude is talking to himself). Ortiz would do it at home, too, often without noticing, and Daniella would warn him to watch his language around the children.

Alarmed by his friend's deteriorating mental health, Aguilar suggested to Ortiz that he visit the local Veterans Affairs clinic to seek help. Spurred by his friend, Ortiz tried to get an appointment with a Laredo psychiatrist but couldn't find one taking on new patients. In February 2018, he turned to the VA clinic in Harlingen, three hours southeast of Laredo. From his first visit, Ortiz reported having trouble sleeping, mood swings, and bouts of anger and anxiety and shared the struggles he had at home growing up in Brownsville, including his mother's abusive boyfriends. "Veteran describes childhood as very unhappy and stated that is why he joined the military to get away from all that," an early assessment read. He was diagnosed with PTSD and depression and prescribed paroxetine (for anxiety and depression), divalproex (for irritability and anger), trazodone (for sleeping), gabapentin (to ease the migraines), and blood pressure medication, and Ortiz was also referred to a therapist who connected with him via teleconference every week for twelve weeks. Ortiz told the therapist about his mood swings and the nightmares, and he even confided that he had considered suicide. She warned Ortiz to be "very careful with what you're saying because you're in law enforcement." If he admitted to having suicidal thoughts, she would have to report it and he could potentially lose his job. She advised him not to say anything that could jeopardize his career.

After that, Ortiz kept his spiraling thoughts mostly to himself and focused on taking his medication. At first, the pills helped. Daniella commented on how refreshed and happy he appeared on mornings after taking his medication the night before. Coworkers also noticed he was more relaxed, less jittery. He told them he was taking hypertension meds. Despite the new meds, his erratic behavior continued. Juan Flores first met Ortiz when the two were at the Cotulla Station, then reunited with him in Laredo. Like Ortiz, Flores was a Border Patrol supervisory agent. Flores and Ortiz would occasionally get coffee together or meet for lunch. Flores found his colleague to be a reliable, albeit somewhat eccentric, worker. In the office, Ortiz whistled uncanny birdsongs, mimicking the high-pitched whistle of perhaps the red-crowned parrot or Audubon's oriole that was so prominent in South Texas, bemusing coworkers.

One day after lunch, Ortiz told Flores he wanted to check on a house where he had received intel there might be drug trafficking. He drove his colleague to San Bernardo Avenue. As he drove, Ortiz pointed out specific corners where prostitutes hung out, including one spot popular with a transgender sex worker. He drove past the house he allegedly wanted to check out, then pulled back onto the avenue and circled through the lots of some of San Bernardo's motels.

Flores, feeling increasingly uncomfortable, told Ortiz they should leave, since they had no business being there. Ortiz drove them back to the office.

Pedro "Pete" Gutierrez had been a Border Patrol agent since 2001 and a supervisory agent since 2009. He met Ortiz while working with him at the BIC. Like Flores, Gutierrez marveled at the birdsong whistles Ortiz produced in the office. Both smokers, Ortiz and Gutierrez took frequent cigarette breaks and lunched together. Driving to and from their lunches, Ortiz would point out suspected sex workers along San Bernardo. "I guess the city doesn't do anything about that," he commented to Gutierrez. The drives along San Bernardo with Gutierrez became a common occurrence.

Ortiz confided to Gutierrez that he suffered from anxiety and said he would buy beer sometimes after work, sometimes before, to deal with the condition. He told Gutierrez that, after their shifts, he would cruise around Laredo at night, drinking beer and picking up women on the streets. Once, he picked up a woman in a Denny's uniform; another time he gave a woman a ride from the bus station to her home.

He bragged to Gutierrez about sexual conquests he had had

around town, including one woman he had met at a bar near San Agustín Plaza downtown. He told his colleague that he often visited Mami Chulas, a drive-through liquor and convenience store in central Laredo that employed scantily dressed women, to buy booze and get in-car lap dances.* Ortiz asked Gutierrez for suggestions on discreet south Laredo restaurants. He said he had picked up a woman from Mami Chulas and planned to take her to lunch, then back to his house. When Gutierrez questioned Ortiz about taking women to his home, he replied that he always took an indirect route, so the woman wouldn't remember where he lived.

Another Border Patrol colleague, Joseph Peralta, described Ortiz's demeanor at work as "awkward" and "quiet." He noticed several tics favored by Ortiz, including whistling birdsongs and abruptly singing comments out loud, such as "*I wanna go home.*" Once during a shift, Ortiz confided to Peralta that he was drinking a lot and "wrestling with some demons." He said he was trying to clean himself up. By August 2018, Peralta noticed a sharp shift in Ortiz's demeanor: the birdsong whistles had ceased and his mood had darkened. When he asked him if he was okay, Ortiz replied that he had "fallen off the wagon." Peralta urged Ortiz to search for God and straighten out his path. "I don't know if I can get back on this wagon," Ortiz replied.

Ortiz was also what Peralta later described as a "Facebook stalker," endlessly scrolling through various women's profile pages. Another colleague would see Ortiz clicking through the Facebook photos of women and asking other agents, "¿Sí o no?"

One day in late August, just as agents inside the BIC were wrapping up to go home, Ortiz exclaimed to the group, for no evident reason, "Remember, snitches get stitches, and bitches wind up in ditches."

---

* Mami Chulas was forced to close in 2017 after state investigators alleged drugs were sold at the locale and a sixteen-year-old girl had been employed to dance provocatively in a bikini.

ORTIZ'S ANXIETY DEEPENED, AND HIS VA CLINIC ASSESSMENTS worsened. "Veteran reports he is struggling with sleep disturbances, anger and irritability, lack of trust, 'paranoid,'" another assessment read. "Veteran describes self as 'anti-social' and avoids going anywhere, hypervigilance and patrolling the perimeter of his home."

Anxiety lingered and Ortiz's alcohol consumption steadily increased; sometimes he'd have four or five tallboy beers in one sitting while popping his medication, creating a mental fog and mood swings that led to occasional blackouts. Once, he woke up in the parking lot of an event venue on Highway 59, still in his truck, foot on the brake; another time he woke up in his driveway. Between February and September 2018, Ortiz attended more than forty medical and mental health appointments, meeting with a battery of psychologists, psychiatrists, neurologists, and sleep specialists, at times shuttling between Laredo and Corpus Christi to make appointments. He also returned to the VA clinic repeatedly, where a clinician added Prozac to his list of daily meds. His regimen, as prescribed by the VA, included popping eight psychotropic pills a day— five in the morning, three at night—from Paxil first thing upon waking to ease his anxiety to trazodone before bed to help erase nightmares. As symptoms persisted, Ortiz returned again and again to the VA clinic. Each time, clinicians there upped his dosage.

━━━━

PHYSICIANS AND PSYCHIATRISTS HAVE BEEN PRESCRIBING MULtiple medications to treat multiple symptoms in patients for as long as drugs have been available. Psychopharmacology first emerged in the 1950s and '60s, and as medications grew in effectiveness through the 1970s, so did their popularity. The emergence of fluoxetine, better known by the brand name Prozac, in the 1980s led to an explosion of prescribed psychotropic drug use across the United States to treat depression, obsessive-compulsive disorder, panic attacks, and a myriad of other disorders. Psychopharmacology was on the rise. By the time the "decade of the brain" arrived (1990–2000), "new generations of antidepressants and antipsychotic agents placed psychopharmacology on a throne of power it had never had before." Prozac, Paxil, Xanax, Valium, Cipralex, Zoloft, Adderall, and others flooded U.S. homes with unforeseen intensity—all approved by the FDA and prescribed, often simultaneously, by licensed doctors and psychiatrists. The percentage of patients on three or more psychiatric medications being seen at the Biological Psychiatry Branch of the National Institute of Mental Health, for example, climbed from 5 percent in 1974 to 40 percent in 1995. Prescribing multiple drugs to treat mental health issues became so widespread that the industry coined a term for the practice: "polypharmacy," or the use of two or more psychoactive drugs for the management of behavioral symptoms.

But what effect all those swirling, mind-altering chemical compounds have on the human psyche remains an evasive mystery. Practitioners warn that there have been few clinical trials studying the effects of polypharmacy on patients—mainly because it's unethical to ask human subjects to ingest multiple psychotropic drugs for the sake of science. Polypharmacy remains a widely debated, murky branch of psychiatry. Though using the fewest number of drugs to treat a disorder is always the goal, applying multiple prescriptions has alleviated symptoms for millions of ailing Americans, according to Sheldon Preskorn, a professor of psychiatry at the Kansas University School of Medicine–Wichita. The drugs' interactions with other drugs are pre-studied by pharmaceutical companies, which could spend between $500,000 and $1 billion on research just to get FDA approval. Though more research would be helpful, "we know an awful lot about what the drugs do to the brain," Preskorn said. "We're getting better and better at that."

Still, polypharmacy has been repeatedly blamed for erratic behavior in patients. Attorneys for Lindsay Clancy, the Duxbury, Massachusetts, woman accused of strangling her three young children to death with exercise bands and leaping out of a second-story window in a suicide attempt, point to the cocktail of thirteen psychiatric drugs she was prescribed after experiencing postpartum depression in 2023 as a possible motive for her actions. The attorneys alleged the drugs, which included Klonopin, Valium, Prozac, Zoloft, and trazodone, turned her "into a zombie," and denounced the "horrific overmedication of drugs that caused homicidal ideation, suicidal ideation."

Though Clancy's case is a tragic outlier, researchers warn that over-prescribing psychotropic medications without sufficient studies reveal-ing their effects on the brain is a game of pharmaceutical roulette. Lisa Cosgrove, a clinical psychologist at the University of Massachusetts Boston, said the risk is not just the unknown effects of different medi-cations, but the unknown effects different *types* of medications, such as tricyclic antidepressants and selective serotonin reuptake inhibitors, or SSRIs, collectively have on the brain. Gabapentin, for example, was designed to treat seizures but has been prescribed to soothe nerve pain and migraines. What effect it may have on the central nervous system if taken together with an SSRI, like Paxil, is not definitively known. "In many ways, giving people multiple classes of psychotropic medications is making them guinea pigs," Cosgrove said. "We don't know what the outcome will be."

=====

WHATEVER THE REASONING, THE FIVE-MED PSYCHOTROPIC cocktail prescribed to Ortiz wasn't wildly beyond the norm of what many Americans take each day, especially veterans suffering from PTSD. But its effect on him was rapidly alarming friends. When not at work, Ortiz would meet his friend Solis at his family's truck yard, where they set up a wide-screen TV and a couch to watch Spurs or Cowboys games over beers. Increasingly, Ortiz complained of his job. One night at the yard, in the spring of 2018, Solis witnessed Ortiz pop a pill with his beer. He asked him about it. "Dealing with depression," Ortiz replied. He told him about going to the local VA and being prescribed antidepressants. He didn't delve into why. Two months later, in late summer 2018, they were back at Solis's yard. This time, he watched as Ortiz swallowed three or four pills at a time and washed them down with a beer. Solis warned his friend not to overdo it, unless he wanted a DUI.

"Nah, it's okay, I can handle it," Ortiz answered.

"You're going to whack out," Solis told him. "You're going to do something stupid."

"I could handle it," Ortiz repeated.

But Solis noticed his friend's mood shift. Each time they would meet—at the truck yard or at a Buffalo Wild Wings for dinner—Ortiz would drink too much and pop what seemed like an increasing number of pills. He grew confrontational. At a party at the house of a friend of Solis's, Ortiz, buzzing after a few beers, challenged the host to a wrestling match. Solis pulled him aside.

"Bro, chill out," he told him.

"I could take him," Ortiz slurred.

One evening, when they were alone together, Ortiz scrolled through the photos on his phone and showed Solis a picture of a smiling girl he said he had met at the gym: she was young, fair-skinned, almond-eyed, dark-haired, pretty. Ortiz said he was hooking up with her and she knew he was married. Daniella had increasingly been taking the kids to stay with her sister in Brownsville, and he was taking advantage of the empty house, he told Solis. "Be smart about it, dude," Solis counseled his friend. "I hope you know what you're doing."

At six feet one inch and 215 pounds, with a dense, muscular build sculpted from hours at Gold's Gym, Ortiz could usually hold his liquor. But the quantity had become copious. One or two Michelob tallboys led to four or five, then a six-pack in one sitting, accompanied by more antidepressant pills. By mid-2018, he was drinking eighteen beers a day. In late August, Ortiz went to Solis's truck yard to watch a preseason Cowboys game with friends. They grilled steaks and had a cooler full of cold beer. Everyone was drinking and joking and barking commands to the players on the screen. Ortiz sat quietly, sullenly, on a corner of the couch, nursing a Michelob tallboy and smoking Marlboro Lights. Something was noticeably wrong. Solis thought of asking his friend if he wanted to talk, but there were too many people around. He asked Ortiz to accompany him to the store to get more beer.

"Nah, I need to get home," he said. He got up and left the party.

If anyone at Border Patrol noticed Ortiz's spiraling condition, no one officially reported it. Ortiz himself was inclined not to mention anything, fearing a reprimand, demotion, or worse.

Instead, on August 27, 2018, Ortiz, in line for another promotion, was given a T5 security clearance interview. The Tier 5 clearance would give him access to some of the sector's most sensitive information. Along with the thirty-five-minute interview at CBP's Laredo Sector headquarters, he had to fill out a questionnaire. An agency investigator checked his references and background, noting a "letter of caution" Ortiz was given in 2016 while in Cotulla after a migrant accused him of taking a cigarette from him, but he was cleared of wrongdoing by a supervisor. Nothing else came up. He passed the exam. "The record checks and interviews, as appropriate, were favorable unless otherwise indicated," the investigator wrote.

The fact that no Border Patrol overseer picked up on what appeared to friends and coworkers as increasingly unhinged personality traits from one of its supervisory agents may seem improbable. But, in fact, Ortiz was employed at a federal agency that, by design and nature, was prone to overlook such things.

CHAPTER 8

Decades before the birth of the U.S. Border Patrol in 1924, gunmen and vigilantes prowled the United States' border with Mexico, chasing outlaws, turning back foreigners, and clashing with Indians for dominance of the region.

The Texas Rangers formed in the 1820s to protect early Texas colonists from warring bands of Comanches and Karankawas, smugglers and outlaws. They allowed Anglo-American settlers to elbow into the region by imposing their will, often by force, on surrounding Texas Mexicans.

Following the end of the Mexican-American War in 1848, the Treaty of Guadalupe Hidalgo created the modern-day U.S.-Mexico border. The agreement shrank Mexico's border by more than one thousand miles, pulling its northwest border down from southern Oregon to the current San Diego–Tijuana demarcation and gifting five hundred thousand square miles, including Arizona and New Mexico, and more than eighty thousand people to the United States.

The Chinese Exclusion Act of 1882, passed during a violent wave of anti-Chinese sentiment in America, prohibited Chinese workers from entering the United States and led to mounted Chinese inspectors, who rebuffed unsanctioned Chinese border crossers on America's southern and northern borders.[*]

By 1924, when Congress created the Border Patrol, the Immigration Bureau had a pool of willing cadets to choose from, including veteran mounted Chinese inspectors, former Texas Rangers, and members of the Ku Klux Klan. Many were longtime borderland residents who knew

---

[*] The Chinese Exclusion Act was repealed in 1943, after China allied with the United States against Japan during World War II.

the territory well. Others were hardened settlers of the western frontier who had survived hostile Comanche attacks, chased bandidos deep into Mexico, and used raw physical violence to impose their will. A year after forming the Border Patrol, Congress awarded its agents broad authority to interrogate, detain, and arrest without warrant anyone suspected of breaking U.S. immigration law. The Border Patrol would go through countless transformations in its century of existence. But its Congress-appointed powers, paired with the backgrounds and mindset of its early agents, created an aura of aggressive, often unchecked policing at the border that, one hundred years later, still radiated.

=====

BY THE 1970S, THE BORDER PATROL HAD GROWN FROM A FEW hundred agents at its inception to more than two thousand, most of them patrolling the 1,954-mile southwest border. More agents meant more opportunities for abuse. In his 1983 book, *The Tarnished Door: The New Immigrants and the Transformation of America,* Pulitzer Prize–winning *New York Times* journalist John Crewdson spoke with Border Patrol agents who described abusive tactics, such as handcuffing migrants to cars and making them run alongside them to the border or "pushing illegals off cliffs . . . so it would look like an accident."

Beginning in 1971, investigators at the U.S. Department of Justice began looking into allegations of widespread corruption and abuse within the Immigration and Naturalization Service, which, at the time, oversaw the Border Patrol. In the effort, tagged Operation Clean Sweep, they unearthed not just cases of abuses but, equally disturbing, leaders within the agency willing to overlook the crimes. One case involved a Texas Border Patrol agent who had been charged three times with sexually abusing his fifteen-year-old Mexican maid but had never received more than a five-day suspension from duty. Another involved an inspector in San Francisco who remained on the job, even after being caught stealing jewelry and other valuables from arriving passengers, smuggling pornographic films, and selling immigration documents. Despite compiling a formidable case file and winning grand jury indictments, Operation Clean Sweep sputtered between the Nixon and Ford administrations, then faded. Out of the more than three hundred potential criminal cases against past and current INS personnel, only seven officers were indicted and five convicted. Today, not even Wikipedia carries mention of the effort.

=====

THE TERRORIST ATTACKS OF 9/11 PROFOUNDLY CHANGED HOW America policed its borders. In the wake of the attacks, lawmakers folded the Immigration and Naturalization Service and created in its stead U.S. Customs and Border Protection, under which Border Patrol was placed. Both CBP and the newly minted Immigration and Customs Enforcement fell under the new Department of Homeland Security as a strategy to prevent future foreign attacks on American soil. Border security became a top national priority, and this renewed focus, coupled with an upsurge in border encounters (Border Patrol agents apprehended 1.6 million migrants nationwide in 2000, a fourteen-year high), spawned an unprecedented hiring spree at the agency. New recruits flooded Border Patrol stations in the Southwest so fast that some stations held their daily musters in the parking lot to accommodate everyone.

By 2011, the Border Patrol had more than doubled its workforce to about twenty thousand agents, becoming the biggest federal law enforcement agency in the country—and Congress poured in money to equip and pay these new employees. By 2014, the United States was spending more each year on border and immigration enforcement than the combined budgets of the FBI, ATF, DEA, Secret Service, and U.S. Marshals, plus the entire NYPD annual budget. All told, the United States government has invested more than $300 billion in border and immigration control since 9/11. In the rush to swell the ranks, among the candidates that slipped into Border Patrol service were cartel operatives, ex-criminals, and the mentally unsound. CBP, which oversees the Border Patrol, was unable to fully screen its thousands of new recruits.

Unlike the FBI, which requires all applicants to take polygraph tests, CBP administered preemployment polygraph examinations to only 10 to 15 percent of applicants between 2006 and 2009. Of the around one thousand CBP applicants who took the polygraph test in that period, nearly 60 percent were determined unsuitable for service, largely because they admitted during the examination to "prior criminal activity, including violent crimes and involvement with drug cartels and smugglers." CBP did not begin requiring polygraph tests for all law enforcement applicants until mid-2012, and only after being mandated by Congress.

As more agents flooded stations, incidents of misconduct climbed. Between 2004 and 2014, "roughly 170 CBP employees, including Border Patrol agents, [were] arrested or convicted on corruption-related charges," such as smuggling, money laundering, and conspiracy, according to CBP's former head of internal affairs. Arrests for general misconduct were far greater: from 2005 to 2012, approximately 2,170 CBP officers or agents were arrested for offenses ranging from domestic violence to drunk driving. As misdeeds piled up, watchdog groups criticized the Border Patrol for not doing enough to discipline its agents. An audit report by Homeland Security's Office of Inspector General in June 2019 concluded that the department, including CBP, "does not have sufficient policies and procedures to address employee misconduct." Reports of abuse rarely resulted in discipline. Out of 809 complaints of alleged physical, sexual, and verbal abuse lodged against Border Patrol agents from January 2009 to January 2012, 97 percent of the cases that reached a formal decision resulted in "No Action Taken," according to CBP records obtained by the American Immigration Council.

The report underscored an unspoken truism at Border Patrol: agents who violated the agency's use-of-force policy rarely faced consequences. From 2006 to 2014, the height of the hiring surge, only a single agent faced a criminal trial for a shooting incident—in an agency that employed more than twenty thousand agents. That case, in 2008, was dismissed after a mistrial. The agent went back to work for Border Patrol.

AN AFFABLE, STRAIGHT-SHOOTING FORMER POLICE CHIEF IN Buffalo and Seattle, Gil Kerlikowske was tapped by President Barack Obama in 2014 to head the embattled CBP. Kerlikowske learned first-hand of CBP's opaque handling of agent misconduct his first week on the job. Shortly after arriving at his new position in March 2014, he received a phone call at his office at CBP headquarters in Washington. Kerlikowske was a police veteran and national drug czar who had witnessed more than his share of vile criminality. But the story relayed to him by the official on the other line left him breathless.

Esteban Manzanares, a Border Patrol agent based in McAllen, Texas, had picked up three Honduran women in the South Texas brush near the Rio Grande. The women—two teenage girls and the mother of one of the teens—had just floated across on a raft and were wet, muddied, and exhausted. They had no intention of sneaking past agents; they wanted to turn themselves in to the first Border Patrol agent they saw and ask for asylum, which they did as soon as they came upon Manzanares.

Manzanares, however, had other plans. He loaded them in his Border Patrol SUV, drove them down a gravel road, and stopped at the edge of the woods. Manzanares pulled the mother from the back of the SUV, dragged her into the woods, duct-taped her mouth, strangled her, slashed her arms and wrists with a knife, and left her to die. Next, he dragged the woman's fourteen-year-old daughter from the vehicle, sexually assaulted her, took pictures of her half-naked body, slashed her wrists, and left her to die as well, covering her limp body with dirt and branches as the teen feigned death.

Manzanares then drove the last victim, a fifteen-year-old girl, to a stand of trees on the edge of a field and handcuffed her to a tree. He then returned to work. At the end of his shift, he changed out of his Border Patrol uniform, retrieved the chained victim, duct-taped her mouth, and drove her to his apartment in nearby Mission, Texas. There, Manzanares tied his young victim to a bed. He took pictures of her naked body with his smartphone and sexually assaulted her. Unbeknownst to him, his other two victims had survived and alerted the police. A team of FBI agents and Mission police officers circled in on his apartment. At around 1:00 a.m. the next morning, as police and federal agents banged on his apartment door, Manzanares shot himself with his agency-issued .40-caliber handgun while sitting at his dining room table, killing himself instantly. A two-page suicide note lay on the table, in which Manzanares apologized for his actions. "I am a monster," he wrote.

As he absorbed the details of the case, Kerlikowske's heart sank. The women were vulnerable and had arrived in this country under tough circumstances to seek help and better their lives. They deserved more than a boilerplate statement from his agency. He wanted to portray genuine empathy for the victims, work in details of the crime, and promise to take action to prevent such a horrific event from ever reoccurring. He wrote up a draft.

But top officials at Homeland Security, which oversees CBP, balked. They wanted the new commissioner to remove any empathy for the victims, avoid personal thoughts, and just say the agency "takes any such complaints seriously." Kerlikowske was stunned.

"This was such a horrific incident," he remembered later. "You would never be able to get away with that at a police department."

Kerlikowske put in a call to Jeh Johnson, then Homeland Security secretary, who urged him to do whatever he felt was right. Backed by the department's highest official, Kerlikowske released a statement saying he was "deeply sorry" over the incident, promised the victims would receive proper care, and vowed to do everything in his power to prevent anything like that from reoccurring at the agency.

Kerlikowske was proud of the statement—sincere, empathetic, hitting the right tones—but the experience taught him a valuable lesson. "I realized that federal law enforcement doesn't have to abide by any of the transparency standards or be answerable to the public the way that a local police chief has to," said Kerlikowske, who, after retiring from CBP in 2017, became an outspoken critic of Border Patrol's lack of transparency. "That was a big part of our problem."

=====

LACK OF TRANSPARENCY AND ACCOUNTABILITY WERE JUST SOME of the challenges facing officials at CBP and Border Patrol. As U.S. wars in Afghanistan and Iraq dragged on, many discharged veterans turned to Border Patrol for employment. Military veterans had been joining Border Patrol for generations. It was an ideal fit: at Border Patrol, you were often outside, carried a weapon, fraternized with other, mostly male agents, and were left mostly to your own devices, spending long hours patrolling desolate stretches of the Southwest. One former Border Patrol supervisory agent from the Laredo Sector recalled Vietnam vets flooding the ranks of his sector in the 1980s. Then, the mood was laid-back and supervisors urged agents to avoid drawing weapons in the field.

That attitude changed after 9/11, he said. Young vets streamed in, fresh from deployments in Iraq and Afghanistan. The discharged marines and soldiers were disciplined and skilled at taking orders and carrying out tasks. But the directive from CBP headquarters felt harsher: vigilance at all cost. Military hardware poured in. The Laredo Sector agent noticed with alarm how M4 semiautomatic carbine rifles piled up in the sector's armory and the overall mindset grew more militarized. Even the uniforms looked more military. "After 9/11, it changed," he said. "It got more intense."

In the years since 9/11, Border Patrol agents have earned a reputation of heroism in often harsh and perilous circumstances. They've rescued countless migrants from sweltering border deserts or saved them from drowning in the Rio Grande. Many have repelled or captured dangerous smugglers along the border or processed large groups of foreign nationals without incident. Agents, particularly in the vast desert stretches of southern Arizona or Texas, risk personal safety while chasing smugglers or corralling migrants under a punishing sun and are always at risk of running into an armed cartel member. From 2003 to 2017, thirty-three border agents died in the line of duty, including sixteen from driving accidents and six shot or run over by smugglers.

But stories of abuse—and subsequent lack of discipline—at the hands of Border Patrol agents have equally flourished. Immigrant advocates complain that the agency's military mentality has led to more use-of-force incidents by agents and deem the strategy inappropriate for dealing with unarmed civilians, many of them hungry and exhausted from long journeys north. "There is a certain way that people are trained to fight wars," said Vicki Gaubeca, a Tucson-based associate director for the U.S. Program of Human Rights Watch and longtime Border Patrol observer. "And that should be completely removed and different from how we deal with immigrants."

===

THE BORDER PATROL HAS ALSO BEEN DEALING WITH A GENDER challenge: its ranks are overwhelmingly male, leading to issues of misogyny and, in some cases, sexual assault.

After graduating with honors from Auburn University, Jenn Budd considered going to law school. But she yearned for adventure and, as a gay woman from Alabama, ached to leave the South. Acting on a tip from a friend, Budd, then twenty-four, signed up with the Border Patrol in June 1995 as a way out of her comfort zone and a chance to see the country. Shortly after arriving at the Border Patrol training academy in Glynco, Georgia, Budd was warned by other female agents to watch her drinks at the campus bar around the male recruits and was told about the "Game of Smiles," a sexual predatory game where a drunk or drugged female trainee is forced to perform oral sex on her male peers.

One night, Budd was heading to her dormitory when a male recruit asked if he could walk her home. As they reached her dorm building, the recruit threw her against a wall and told her to "play ball" as he proceeded to sexually assault her. Budd managed to knee him in the groin, and the two exchanged blows before she ran upstairs and locked herself in her room. The next day, nursing a bruise under her eye and a busted lip, she returned to class but never reported the incident. Despite urging from friends, Budd said she feared being kicked out of the academy for starting trouble and needed the job. She set her sights on getting to California, her first choice for placement. "That's how bad I didn't want to go back home," she said.

Upon graduating from the academy, she was stationed in San Diego County when she saw her attacker again. Afterward, she was plagued by rumors that she had slept with a supervisor to secure a promotion, and Budd filed a formal grievance with the Equal Employment Opportunity Commission, complaining of the agency's general misogynistic environment. The complaint went nowhere. She retired from the Border Patrol in 2001, after six years at the agency. Today, Budd lives in San Diego and has become an immigrant rights advocate.

Budd said she was taken by surprise by her sexual assaulter—but further stunned at just how rampant that attitude was at Border Patrol and how little weight women's complaints carried. "This is the system," she said. "This is what they tell the agents: Women's voices don't matter for shit."

═══

THE EMERGENCE OF DONALD TRUMP AS A PRESIDENTIAL CANDI-date in 2016—and his brash, tell-it-as-it-is style—ignited a fervor with Border Patrol unionists. Trump's mix of tough speak and promises of strict border policies as a cornerstone of his campaign made him a heady pick for many in the agency. For the first time in its forty-nine-year history, the National Border Patrol Council, a union which boasted 16,500 members at the time, endorsed a presidential candidate, throwing its support behind Trump.

Later that year, the "I'm 10–15"* page emerged on Facebook in 2016 as a sounding board for thousands of Border Patrol agents across the country. Agents posted jokes and memes on the invite-only group's page and vented about life on the border; the page's "about" section

—————————————

* "10–15" is Border Patrol code for "aliens in custody."

urged agents to share posts that were "funny, serious and just work related. We are family, first and foremost. This is where the Green Line starts, with us." But the group soon became a dumping ground for racist and anti-immigrant vitriol, illustrations showing members of Congress being sexually assaulted, and wisecracks about the deaths of migrants. Some of the more graphic posts targeted U.S. representative Alexandria Ocasio-Cortez, the outspoken Democrat from the Bronx, including a photo illustration of her engaged in oral sex at an immigration detention center. When a sixteen-year-old Guatemalan migrant died in 2019 while in custody at a Border Patrol station in Weslaco, Texas, one "I'm 10–15" user posted a GIF of Elmo with the quote "Oh well." Another responded with an image and the words "If he dies, he dies." At its peak, the group boasted 9,500 members.

The private Facebook page came to light in July 2019 after ProPublica and *The Intercept* acquired screen grabs or access to the page and revealed its contents. CBP officials denounced the page and said they would launch an internal investigation, but the agency had known about it for years and let the posts continue, according to media reports. In October 2021, the U.S. House Committee on Oversight and Reform, chaired by Representative Carolyn Maloney, launched its own investigation into the matter. CBP documents obtained by the committee showed that the agency had conducted 135 investigations into employees connected with "I'm 10–15" and other, similar Facebook groups. But discipline recommendations by CBP's Discipline Review Board were drastically reduced by CBP officials. Of the sixty Border Patrol agents determined to have committed misconduct, only two were removed from their jobs. One agent who posted a sexually explicit doctored image of a member of Congress had his discipline reduced from removal to a sixty-day suspension. He was awarded back pay. Most of the other agents returned to working with migrants.

=

IN RECENT YEARS, CBP HAS LAUNCHED INITIATIVES LAUDED BY immigrant advocates as positive steps toward better accountability and transparency. It made public the agency's use-of-force handbook, which details when and how agents should draw guns on suspects; began publishing annual *Discipline Overview* reports, which list disciplinary actions taken on agents (albeit sans any identifying details); and started testing and deploying bodycams on agents.

Immigrant advocates, however, say that a culture of patrolling with impunity remains stubbornly intact—and is changing at a glacial pace. "History seems to loom much larger there than it does for other agencies," said Chris Rickerd of the Project on Government Oversight, who monitors Border Patrol. "All the imagery and symbolism of Border Patrol history—they're very much aware of their past."

═══

JUAN DAVID ORTIZ REPORTED TO THE BORDER PATROL training academy in New Mexico on August 27, 2009, at the tail end of the agency's massive post-9/11 hiring spree. He entered a world where misogyny was rampant, agents often went unpunished for misdeeds, and secrets, no matter how dark and damning, tended to remain concealed. Any struggles he may have been having with post-traumatic stress disorder from his time in Iraq, any nightmares or panic attacks or creeping paranoia, went wholly undetected by the agency. He was never given a polygraph test.

And in 2018, as one of the Laredo Sector's rising supervisory agents spiraled into deepening paranoia, alcoholism, blackouts, aggressive behavior, and suicidal ideation—observed by coworkers, therapists, family, and friends—Ortiz's work record remained unblemished. He was free to enter and leave the sector's Border Intelligence Center at will, privy to some of the region's most sensitive criminal cases—including his own.

CHAPTER 9

By the time he started hanging out on San Bernardo Avenue, Edgar "Güero" Rios had been in and out of Webb County Jail four or five times, on charges ranging from drug possession to sexual assault of a child. At forty-one, he was older than the other drug pushers, users, sex workers, and outcasts who congregated on the avenue and considered himself more street-smart. Color-splashed tattoos branched across his chest, back, arms, and neck. Some depicted elaborate Mayan gods, others dripping rosaries. One across his chest read: "Mexicano Verdadero." *True Mexican.*

Edgar knew where to score the good chiva and crack rocks and shared them generously with female acquaintances. His connections to Mexican prison gangs and gigs with crime rings once brought him enough money to own real estate and host nonstop parties. All that wealth, however, had vanished into a heroin and crack cocaine addiction. Girls around San Bernardo naturally gravitated to him, including Melissa and Claudine. He lived at his mom's house on Main Avenue near the Canta Ranas neighborhood and routinely invited girls back there to party. But his freewheeling ways with women slowed in early 2018, when he met Erika Peña.

One of five siblings, Erika, twenty-eight, was from Laredo. As a young girl, she had shown flashes of being a good student, but starting in her early twenties, like others along the avenue, a growing drug habit pulled her to San Bernardo. Before long, she joined the ranks of sex workers there, sharing motel rooms, drugs, and clients with Melissa, Janelle, and the others.

Pretty and feisty, with a full figure, Erika caught Edgar's eye immediately. Thirteen years his junior, she partied like the other girls and had a drug habit that outpaced his. But there was a sweetness to Erika that made her unique. Her smile was radiant and sincere. Her loyalty to friends was admirable. Edgar and Erika started hanging out and were soon dating. Edgar knew how Erika earned her money, and he accepted it. He spent day after day with her, driving her to jobs or hanging out and shooting up black tar heroin together at his mother's house. Edgar admired how Erika was a "coaster," how heroin sent her sailing on a gust of bliss, eyes closed, slight smile, mind swimming. The drug, in contrast, perked him up and made him anxious. He still did it plentifully; anything was better than withdrawal sickness. Erika grew to trust Edgar. After a job, she'd hand him her earnings, letting him divide the cash needed between drugs, cigarettes, and food. "I fell in love with her," Edgar remembered later. "She was so fucking awesome."

At around the same time, Erika's awesomeness was catching someone else's eye.

⸻

By the spring of 2018, Juan David Ortiz was reeling from the effects of mixing prescription pills and booze. Daniella increasingly took the kids to visit family in Brownsville and San Antonio, no doubt happy to steer clear of her husband's mercurial mood swings and angry outbursts. And, more and more, Ortiz was exploring the dark crevices of San Bernardo and San Agustin Avenues he had discovered during his time with the Border Patrol's Targeted Enforcement Unit. Ortiz was no longer a detached observer; he was stopping and chatting up some of the women on the avenue.

One night in April 2018, Ortiz saw Erika Peña strolling near San Bernardo, near the Evelyn Motor Inn. He pulled over and asked if she needed a ride. "Sure," she said, and hopped into his white Dodge Ram pickup. The two hit it off. He was clean and charming with plenty of cash. They retreated to one of the avenue's hotels, had sex, and agreed to meet again. Ortiz became not just another customer for Erika but that coveted score in turbulent San Bernardo street life: a steady, repeat client. After securing her phone number, Ortiz called her repeatedly after that, picking her up from different points around Laredo or randomly rolling up to her on San Bernardo. He revealed to her he was a Border Patrol agent.

Erika bragged to Edgar about her latest conquest. "Man, that Border Patrol, he gives me money. Sometimes I don't even have to have sex with him," she told him after a date. Ortiz picked her up, sometimes from her mom's house, where she was staying, or from wherever she might be along San Bernardo. Other times he would pull up to Edgar's mom's house to drop off cash owed to Erika. He'd pay her $50, $150, $200, sometimes $300 a visit—exponentially higher than the going rate for sex at the time. When Erika was low on heroin and the tentacles of withdrawal were creeping in, she'd text Ortiz, who would drop off cash with Edgar to get her a fix.

On at least two occasions, Edgar drove Erika to Ortiz's home. Initially, he waited outside in the car while Erika was inside with Ortiz. But after a while, Ortiz came out to the car, sipping a beer and smoking a cigarette, and invited him in. Pictures of Ortiz and Daniella dotted the living room. Edgar asked Ortiz if he minded if he and Erika shot up.

"Nah, just go to the bathroom," he said, "and make sure you don't leave any blood."

Edgar never saw Ortiz shoot up or take drugs. But there was something familiar about his wild-eyed look, pupils dilated. He had seen it plenty over the years. Ortiz was on something, he just didn't know what.

Occasionally Ortiz would set up Erika at the Motel 9 off Interstate 35, about two miles north from the BIC, or the New Cactus Courts Motel on Santa Maria in west Laredo. He would let her stay there during the day and meet up with her at night. Parties ensued. Other times, they would drive to the parking lot of the Walmart on upper San Bernardo or of a darkened park at night and have sex in the cab of his truck.

Once, Edgar was home when he received a call on his cell phone from Ortiz. Erika was at his house and had run out of dope. She was curled up naked on his bed, unable to move, the excruciating pains of withdrawal clawing at her.

THE DEVIL BEHIND THE BADGE — 109

"Hey, man, your girl needs a fix," Ortiz told him.

"What the fuck you want me to do?" Edgar spat back.

He handed the phone to Erika. "Yo, call a connect, motherfucker, and bring me something. He'll pay for it," she said.

Edgar scored some chiva and rescued Erika from her withdrawal. Ortiz paid for everything, including Edgar's roundtrip Uber fare.

When Ortiz called, Erika would drop what she was doing and meet him. Once, he picked her up in his green Border Patrol uniform with the shirt worn inside out, the "U.S. Border Patrol" patch on the left shoulder hidden from view. He lavished Erika with cash, clothes, a mobile phone, gift cards. Erika bragged to workers at the Relax Inn that a "Border Patrol agent" would pay her $300 just to be with him. Ortiz told her she was his "favorite" and confessed struggles he was having with Daniella, who didn't much care for Laredo. In intimate moments, Ortiz would ask Erika to say she loved him, but she always refused, not wanting to complicate their relationship. Deeper feelings, however, were germinating. She once confided to Edgar that she may be falling for her prized client. "I'm scared to fall in love with him because he's married," she told him. "But he gives me everything."

=====

IT WAS NOT SURPRISING—OR UNCOMMON—FOR LAREDO SEX workers to land law enforcement clients. Laredo teemed with agents from CBP, Border Patrol, Homeland Security Investigations, DEA, FBI, and state and local agencies; the odds were good that a stray agent or two would occasionally dabble in one of the city's oldest professions. Meli Rodriguez had slept with three U.S. Border Patrol agents and one Texas Department of Public Safety state trooper, some of them while still in uniform, during her time on the streets. In her late thirties, Rodriguez was on the older side of sex workers and knew Melissa and Chelly well from serving stints together at Webb County Jail. She preferred the truck stop off Santa Maria Avenue on the city's west side to San Bernardo Avenue for luring clients. On San Bernardo, you got in the client's car and drove off, instantly at the mercy of the stranger behind the wheel. At the truck stop—a darkened, two-pump lot popular with long-haul drivers—the transaction usually occurred within the cab of a parked truck and often with repeat customers. Sex, cash, then hop out of that truck and into the next one. The money wasn't bad, either. Meli could score $40 for oral sex or $100 if the client wanted her to spend a few hours in his cab. The goal was to get to $500 each night, enough for a San Bernardo motel room and a night's worth of black tar heroin.

One evening, a Border Patrol agent approached her. Instead of staying at the truck stop, he suggested driving to his house. Meli was skeptical but also in need of cash, so she accepted. The agent, a young Anglo man, drove her south on Highway 83, past Rio Bravo, more than fifteen miles outside of town. Just as she was growing anxious, he pulled up to a mobile home where he was staying. He paid up front, and overall the experience was fine; he later drove her back into town. But being so far from the safety of her friends and the city unnerved her. "You don't know what they have in their house," she remembered later. "It's scary."

═══

ORTIZ AND ERIKA'S RELATIONSHIP MAY HAVE BEEN EVOLVING beyond transactional, but she wasn't the only woman on San Bernardo drawing his interest. Ortiz was also a repeat customer of twenty-one-year-old sex worker Anna Karen Herrera, nicknamed "Barbie" for her blond hair and youngish good looks. Ortiz and Anna would sit in his truck and drink beers or she would smoke crack. Anna told him how she wished to get off drugs to reconnect with her children, and Ortiz offered to help her with Child Protective Services. His questioning often turned to Erika: Did she use needles? Did she take showers? Did she have any diseases? During one drive, Anna reached under the truck's seat for her dropped phone, and Ortiz warned her he had a weapon down there.

"Don't take it out," Anna pleaded.

"Don't worry about it," he said. "I'll just leave it there."

Earlier that day, just before Ortiz picked her up, Anna pulled aside her good friend Robert DeLeon and told him she had methadone pills on her. She had already purchased them, but to make a few extra bucks, she wanted Robert to pretend like she owed him for the pills. Her client would then give her cash, she said.

From his house on the corner of Ugarte Street and San Agustin Avenue, Robert had a front-row seat to all the daily dealings, drama, and transactions that occurred around San Bernardo. He got to know the women on the avenue and empathized with their struggles. When thunderstorms rolled through or one of them felt threatened, Robert would let them crash on his couch. As Anna explained her ploy to make some money, he agreed to play along.

Later that day, he watched from his front porch as Ortiz picked up Anna in his white truck. Sometime later, Anna called with Ortiz on the line and pretended to want to pay for the pills.

"Can you do forty or fifty for all the pills?" Ortiz asked.

"Let's do fifty, that's what they're worth," Robert answered.

Ortiz's voice was calm, agreeable. He gave Anna the money.

Later, after dropping her off, he texted her: "I hope you change later on. You make me proud. You'll change."

===

AROUND THE TIME ORTIZ WAS COURTING ERIKA AND ANNA, twenty-year-old Cassandra "Cassy" Rubio was also trying to score clients along San Bernardo. On the streets for about two years, Rubio was tall, long-legged, and olive-skinned with short brown hair and long, natural eyelashes that batted over almond-shaped, coffee-hued eyes. In other circles, she might have earned a decent living as a magazine model. But long abscess scars running up and down her legs betrayed her heroin use and addiction. She ran with the usual crowd on San Bernardo. She got along great with Janelle, whom she found to be jovial, protective, and hilarious, and clashed with Melissa. The two once had an argument over $10, which escalated into a fistfight. Two days later, the topic reemerged and again Cassy and Melissa came to blows. The two women patched things up later but mostly stayed out of each other's way.

One day in March 2018, Cassy was loitering in the empty lot on the corner of San Agustin and Ugarte, a block off San Bernardo, wondering how to scrape enough cash together for her next fix, when Ortiz pulled up and motioned her over. She got in, and they drove off. As the truck ramped onto Interstate 35, something about Ortiz's vibe—his intensity, that stare—triggered alarm bells in Cassy.

Instinctively, she asked, "You're not a cop or anything?"

"No," he answered. "But I do have something to do with law enforcement."

The answer didn't help put Cassy at ease.

"I'm Border Patrol," he said.

They drove north on Interstate 35, and Ortiz asked Cassy to perform oral sex on him while he drove. She did and was surprised at how quickly he climaxed. He paid her $100—more than double the market rate—and returned her to a house near San Bernardo, where she was staying with a friend. The entire visit lasted thirty minutes. He asked if he could see her again. "I really like you," he told her.

Cassy marveled at the quality of this latest client. He was clean, quick, and paid well. She readily agreed to see him again. She didn't have a phone at the time, but they agreed that he'd come looking for her again around San Bernardo. Two weeks later, at around 10:00 p.m., she was near the same spot on San Agustin when Ortiz pulled up. Cassy got in. This time his demeanor was markedly different. Bluish bags hung under his eyes, and there was a jittery energy to him that wasn't there before. Ortiz kept asking about Erika Peña: Had she seen her? Did she know where she was? He drove the truck aimlessly around residential streets. Cassy started to feel edgy. It had been a while since her last fix, and she needed to score some chiva soon.

"So, what's up?" she said finally. "What do you want to do?"

Cassy could tell Ortiz had been drinking. Empty beer cans littered the floor of the truck, and his breath had a boozy tinge. He pulled the truck over and removed a crumpled fifty-dollar bill from a pocket with what appeared to be cocaine inside. He dug out a tiny pile of the powder with a corner of a credit card and inhaled it up a nostril. "Want some?" he asked Cassy. She declined, and he continued driving.

Twenty minutes passed, then thirty, as Ortiz wound through more streets. Cassy was losing patience.

"Come on, dude," she told him. "I need to go. How much do you have?"

"I have sixty dollars," Ortiz said, handing her the cash.

He drove west on Jefferson Street, past warehouses and railroad tracks, nearly to the banks of the Rio Grande—the edge of America—and pulled into a darkened parking lot. They tried to have sex, but, the effects of the powder and the beer apparently clouding his libido, Ortiz struggled to perform. Cassy, her patience at an end, gathered her things and jumped out of the truck.

"Man, fuck you," she said, and walked off down the dark street.

Ortiz called after her, urging her back. But Cassy kept walking.

IN THE UNSPOKEN CODE AMONG SEX WORKERS OF SAN BERNARDO Avenue, certain things were taboo, such as lowering the price for sex acts (a woman got jumped once by a cabal of sex workers for offering $10 blow jobs at a truck stop—well below the going rate) or snitching to the police. Sharing clients was not one of those taboos. Workers may be territorial about boyfriends, motel rooms, or drugs but readily share customers, passing them around from one woman to the next, depending on who was available or who may be in more desperate need of cash.

So, no one found it strange that the Border Patrol agent who was connecting with Erika, Anna, and Cassy also wound up with Melissa. He met her the same way he met the rest: cruising down side streets along San Bernardo and stopping for a chat. Erika couldn't have been overjoyed seeing him go with Melissa—Ortiz provided a steady stream of income, and wasn't there something a little more between them?—but she considered Melissa a friend. They had been through a lot together, including stints in the county lockup and tough scraps on the street. Plus, she knew the rules: clients were fair game. Like the others, Ortiz had picked up Melissa on several occasions, at times taking her to buy cigarettes or dope. For him, she was one of his "regulars."

Through the summer of 2018, Ortiz oscillated between different women on San Bernardo. As late summer approached, his obsession over Erika intensified. On September 1, he used the browser on his iPhone to google "Erika izamar pena webb county jail," then pulled up the Webb County Criminal Records site to search her arrest record. Later, he deleted the searches from his browser history.

=====

IN THE PREDAWN HOURS OF MONDAY, SEPTEMBER 3, 2018 (Labor Day), Melissa staggered around San Bernardo, feeling the familiar pangs of hunger and cocaine withdrawal and deciding where she was going to spend the night. Ortiz pulled up alongside her in his white Dodge Ram truck. She was more bedraggled than usual: hungry, thirsty, in growing need of a hit and with nowhere to go. His was a familiar face.

"I'm really bad right now," she told Ortiz.

Ortiz pushed open his passenger-side door and she climbed in. He offered to take her to McDonald's. Instead, they made a stop at a convenience store for a bag of spicy Mexican Takis chips.

"Ay pa'," she told Ortiz, "dame dinero para ir agarrar algo." Ortiz knew what that "algo" meant. He handed her a twenty-dollar bill and drove her to a trap house near Sanders Avenue in central Laredo so Melissa could score.

Along the way, the two slipped into Spanglish small talk.

"Hey, ¿andas bien or todavía andas junto con la Erika?" Melissa asked.

"No'mbre, buey," Ortiz said. "I haven't seen Erika in a while."

They arrived at the corner house with the green fence near Sanders Avenue, a favorite source for crack rocks and heroin to many of the inhabitants of San Bernardo. Melissa slipped inside while Ortiz waited outside in the truck. She returned a few minutes later, clutching a bag of peanut M&M's, eyes swirling from a drug high, and climbed into the truck—and passed out immediately, slumping onto the dashboard.

Ortiz shook her, tried to wake her, but Melissa remained in a stupor. He sat in his truck, puzzling out what to do next. His initial thought was to drop her on the curb outside the emergency room at the Laredo Medical Center, about two miles northeast from where they were. But the hospital, he figured, was probably covered in outdoor cameras. Someone could easily pick up the license plate of the truck dropping off an unconscious woman.

As his mind raced with what to do, Erika Peña arrived and was walking into the drug house. The two locked eyes before Ortiz drove off with his unconscious human cargo.

He drove west away from the neighborhood and got on the north ramp for Interstate 35, Melissa still breathing but in a heavy drug stupor next to him. He drove north on the highway through the dark night, his mind swirling. What to do with Melissa? What would Erika think later? Did he just sabotage that connection? At the Mile Marker 18 exit, near the Laredo Travel Information Center, Ortiz exited Interstate 35 and drove north along Highway 83, a dark two-lane hardtop, then west on State Highway 255.

Just as he approached Jefferies Road, Melissa awoke. She sat up in her seat, nervously looking around.

"¿Dónde chingao ando?"

Ortiz told her where they were, in a rural stretch of northwest Webb County.

"¡Párate a la verga!" Melissa told him.

Ortiz pulled off on Jefferies Road. Melissa got out of the truck, unleashing a stream of obscenities at Ortiz as she struggled to gain her bearings. She staggered to the side of the gravel road to urinate but lost her balance and keeled over.

Whatever darkness had been slowly mounting in Ortiz—hatred, fear, disgust—swelled into a ferocious wave. He pulled his agency-issued .40-caliber H&K P2000 semiautomatic pistol from its holster by his seat with his left hand and stalked up to Melissa, approaching her from behind and slightly to her right. He got within a few feet and raised the handgun, aiming its barrel just behind her head. He pulled the trigger. Then again. And again. *Boom. Boom. Boom.* Slugs tore through Melissa's jaw, neck, her right wrist. She slumped facedown into the thornbush, still clutching the bag of peanut M&M's. A pool of dark crimson spilled from her skull and seeped into the orange dirt around her.

Ortiz drove off, anxiety strangling him as his actions dawned on him. He reached his home, paranoia spiking through him like disease. Did anyone see him do it? Were there cameras out there? Could they have recorded the entire scene? Was his life about to come crashing down? Ortiz used the web browser on his iPhone to google "homicide laredo tx." Nothing came up. Again, he deleted the search from his browser history, trying to carefully cover his tracks. He went to sleep.

A few hours later, he woke up, showered, shaved, and drove to work. The BIC was buzzing with news of the dead body on Jefferies Road. Ortiz strained to keep his face from betraying him.

After fielding a phone call from agents on the ground, an investigator at the BIC walked over to Ortiz and filled him in on the case. He told him a witness at the scene had seen a car drive off that day and had the license plate. Investigators wanted the plate run through the Border Patrol's Perceptics system, a camera-based software that captures license plate images around the county. Relief washed over Ortiz. They already had someone else's license plate—Rene Arce's, the police officer wrongly pegged as a suspect—and just needed it run through the system. At the time, he was the only one in the BIC with access to the Perceptics system.

At first, Ortiz tried avoiding getting involved. "No'mbre, ¿pa' qué, bro?" he told a colleague.

Later, when asked again to run the plate, Ortiz balked. "¿Pero pa' qué, buey?" he said. "Who gives a fuck, man?"

When they insisted a third time, he finally relented. He logged in to the system and typed in the numbers to Arce's license plate. The truck had been spotted once, over a month ago, at the Border Patrol checkpoint on Interstate 35. He passed the information on to investigators.

As he contemplated his actions of the previous twenty-four hours, Ortiz wrestled with what effects his multiple medications may have been having on him. Later that day, he used his iPhone browser to visit Drugs.com and search "side effects and uses" for divalproex, the med he took to ease his anger, and later did a similar search for paroxetine, prescribed for anxiety and depression. Whatever results emerged, they didn't stop him from continuing to take the pills.

That evening, a one-minute KGNS newscast segment described investigators finding the body. The reporter named Melissa as the victim, flashed a picture of her from her Facebook page, strands of straight black hair framing her smiling face, and said authorities weren't releasing cause of death or saying if any arrests had been made in the case.

Ortiz's initial burst of paranoia simmered, and he resumed the daily routines of his life, meeting with friends after work and expressing joy when Daniella let him know one of his daughters got As and Bs on her report card. "Good!" he texted his wife.

But stress from the mounting workload of a Border Patrol supervisory agent, coupled with fresh anxiety acquired outside the job, was starting to show. Jerry Solis noticed how his easygoing good friend had been supplanted by someone morose and easily irritable. Ortiz rarely, if ever, met up with Solis and his brothers to watch sports or eat wings anymore. When they did get together, Ortiz's alcohol consumption was out of control. Whereas before he would sip one or two Michelob Ultra tallboys at a sitting, lately he would down four or five, absorbing 125 ounces of alcohol at a time—consuming nearly a gallon of beer. A few pills would usually follow.

On September 4, the day after Melissa's body was discovered, Jerry called Ortiz and his friend answered. Radios crackled in the background, and Ortiz said he was at work. Jerry said he and a few friends were headed to a ranch to cook out and kick back. He invited Ortiz along. "I can't," Ortiz said. "Too much work." They promised to stay in touch. After returning from the ranch a few days later, Jerry texted Ortiz again, checking up on him. He never answered.

Ortiz was preoccupied with staying abreast of the investigation into the dead body found on Jefferies Road. The subject of Melissa's slaying had become a popular topic in the BIC's second-floor offices. Pedro Gutierrez, Ortiz's lunch buddy, speculated that the gunman could very well be in law enforcement, given the desolate area where the body was found. Ortiz didn't offer any noticeable reaction.

He repeatedly asked Gutierrez and others in the BIC for information on the initial suspect, Arce, and whether he was still in custody. When Arce was released, Ortiz became noticeably upset.

Juan Flores, another Ortiz colleague, wondered aloud about the possibility of the shooter targeting more women. "Man, what if this guy turns out to be a serial killer?" he asked agents in the BIC. Ortiz grinned and jutted a thumb at Gutierrez.

"That's what I was telling this guy," he said.

Comforted in the knowledge that investigators were busy chasing other leads, Ortiz refocused his attention on San Bernardo. That familiar tug had reawakened.

CHAPTER 10

Wayne Garcia was a soft-spoken sixty-two-year-old retired accountant and comptroller from Laredo. His talents as a financial and political consultant, he claimed, helped several local officials get elected. He had salt-and-pepper face stubble, dark pouches under gray-green eyes, and a short, thin frame with a generous belly. His easygoing smile was warm and inviting, despite missing one of his two front teeth—the result, he said, of a late-night brawl with two gangbangers outside of a San Bernardo Avenue watering hole.

In 2014 he retired and turned his attention, and bank account, to Laredo's party scene. Sweet, monied, and unintimidating, Wayne became a favorite in San Bernardo's sex worker scene. "Right now I play rock and roll, do drugs, and chase women," he said. "Not necessarily in that order."

At around 9:30 p.m. on Wednesday, September 12, 2018, Wayne was driving north on San Bernardo, on his way to karaoke at Applebee's, when he heard a familiar whistle. Claudine Luera, dressed in blue jeans under peach-colored shorts and a pink top, waved him over. Wayne picked her up, and the two cruised along San Bernardo. It had been a few days since he had seen Claudine and he smiled, happy to have her near again. They stopped at a Stripes gas station to buy Hawaiian Punch and cigarettes for Claudine, then went to a nearby McDonald's for dinner. They dined on cheeseburgers and chatted about the usual topics: Claudine's kids, Wayne's karaoke prowess. As he had countless times before, Wayne urged her off the streets. "You don't belong here," he told her. "It's a weakness." Claudine just smiled.

They drove around some more, stopped for a drink, then went to pick up a friend, Anna Karen Herrera, who was staying at the Hotel Plaza down the road. Anna climbed into the back seat of Wayne's

Nissan Versa, and the three cruised up San Bernardo. He made a left on Ugarte Street and pulled into a dark, empty lot behind an apartment complex on San Agustin Avenue. Anna pulled out some crack rocks, and the three passed around a pipe, breathing in the acetone-scented smoke. They puffed, giggled, and gossiped about recent happenings on the avenue. At around 11:00 p.m., Claudine glanced at her watch and popped up in her seat.

"Oh my God, I gotta go," she said, gathering her things.

Even for Claudine, it was an abrupt departure. Wayne asked where she was going and urged her to stay. He offered to rent her a hotel room for the night or take her back to his apartment. They could chat, smoke some more, and she could get a good night's sleep. No need to work tonight, he told her. "Just stay with us," he said.

Claudine was adamant. "I gotta go," she kept repeating. She shouldered her bag, thanked Wayne for the evening, and walked off into the night.

Wayne worried, as he always did. But he reminded himself that Claudine was from Laredo and knew its streets, and drew some comfort from that thought.

═══

CLAUDINE ANNE LUERA WAS BORN ON DECEMBER 3, 1975, IN Laredo, the third of four daughters to Ramon and Ann Catherine Luera. Ann, a native of Glasgow, Scotland, met Ramon at a London nightclub while he was stationed in the UK with the U.S. Air Force. They married a few years later, and he coaxed her into relocating to his hometown of Laredo to raise a family.

Claudine grew up surrounded by siblings, cousins, and family gatherings. Summers were spent climbing trees and splashing around in Mc-Guire Lake near College Station, Texas, where relatives lived. She was a pretty, shy girl with sparkling blue eyes and sandy hair who preferred stomping around with male cousins to playing with dolls.

At Bruni Elementary School in Laredo, Claudine got good grades and received the presidential award for high marks and exemplary behavior. More good grades followed in junior high. Like her sisters, Claudine seemed on track to finish school and pursue a career.

But two things occurred in Claudine's childhood that irrevocably altered the course of her life. When she was around six years old, an older relative sexually assaulted her. Shortly after the incident, when she brought it up to family members, no one believed her—not her mother or paternal grandmother—a lack of support that confused her and clung to her the rest of her life. Years later, as she recounted the incident to friends and family members, it was that lack of belief from family elders that most stung. She never shook the incident; it left her with a deep mistrust of men and a lifelong aversion to sexual intimacy. Throughout her life, she often recoiled at a man's touch.

The second was meeting Hector Zambrano Jr. Claudine first met Zambrano, known as "Junior," briefly in elementary school, but the two reconnected in junior high. Born in Laredo, Junior was tall and thin, with arms and neck already filling with bright tattoos. He was known as a tough street brawler with connections to the local Mexican drug cartel in Nuevo Laredo. He and Claudine had immediate chemistry. Claudine would accompany him to Nuevo Laredo to deliver payments from drug deals or connect with cartel members. She started skipping school. School officials would call her house, looking for her on days she didn't show. Her grades spiraled.

She kept seeing Junior as she started Martin High School. Drugs entered her life. She would smoke weed and help Junior inject heroin. Her sisters would come see them and notice him nodding off, with Claudine nearby to prop him up or shake him awake. Her family warned her away from him.

"Get the fuck away from that guy," her sister Colette Mireles told her repeatedly.

"I can't," Claudine replied.

She loved him—but was also afraid of him. Junior had a violent side, which he wielded to enforce cartel directives but also occasionally aimed at Claudine. In her freshman year at Martin High, as her grades plummeted and absences piled up, Claudine dropped out of school, turning her attention to life with Junior. The two moved into a small apartment in Nuevo Laredo. She did her first hit of heroin, relishing how the molecules buzzed through her and erased all traces of pain. She lost weight, and her face, once rosy and flush with vitality, grew sallow. Now rail-thin, Claudine would periodically visit her mom or sisters with Junior, but his dominance over her became clear. Once, when Junior said it was time to go and Claudine begged for a few more minutes with her family, he grabbed her by one of her exposed ribs and yanked her toward the car, screaming. The relationship tormented Claudine's parents.

One time, while Claudine and Junior visited her sister Angie Perez's home in Laredo, a Webb County sheriff's SWAT team, dressed in Kevlar helmets and wielding assault rifles, stormed the home and arrested Junior on kidnapping charges. Claudine's mom later confessed to calling the police, fearing he was holding Claudine against her will.

With Junior in jail, Claudine's life improved. She went to rehab, cleaned up, got a high school equivalency diploma, and landed a clerical job at the Webb County Courthouse. She began seeing other guys. At twenty-one, just three years after shooting heroin in Nuevo Laredo apartments, she got pregnant and had her first child, Ciara. The dad vanished from their lives, but Ciara brought a renewed peace and purpose to Claudine's life. She found an apartment downtown and lined the window ledge with pots filled with wildflowers, aloe vera, and serrano peppers. She doted on Ciara and taught herself to cook, whipping up elaborate plates of enchiladas, chiles relleno, tamales, and seafood stews with shrimp and octopus.

More men followed, and more kids. In 2000, Claudine gave birth to twins, Ramon and Rudy. A year later, another set of twins arrived, Malena and Elian—all with different men. Suddenly, Claudine was on her own, caring for five kids—three of them autistic, two of them severely so. Her small apartment rang with the cries and fits of special-needs kids. Claudine would prop headphones on Ciara and have her watch Hooked on Phonics on a computer, as Elian and Rudy erupted into prolonged screaming fits. As they got older, the kids evolved from screams to violent tantrums, throwing pans at their mom or attacking one another, as they struggled to verbalize feelings. When she was old enough, Ciara would help her mom hold down Rudy and Elian to give them their daily dose of Risperdal as they kicked and yelled and pushed the medicine away. Claudine qualified for and collected federal Supplemental Security Income, or SSI, for her special-needs kids—totaling around $2,500 a month—but the stress of raising her children was slowly eroding her sanity.

One beacon through all the turmoil was Claudine's mom, Ann. Claudine had always been close to her mom, sharing secrets with her and relying on her for advice. Now, Ann helped with her grandchildren, visiting them often. Ann and Claudine would go downtown together, shopping for knickknacks, or cross over into Nuevo Laredo for hot chocolate or cocktails. By 2008, Claudine's life began to improve. She moved herself and her family to a four-bedroom home in south Laredo. Besides the SSI checks, she received child support checks from the children's fathers, earning enough to feed and support her family. Ciara was thriving, getting good grades at Harmony Science Academy, a high-performing charter school.

Even as she helped her daughter and cared for her grandkids, however, Ann was growing sick. A longtime smoker, she had congestive heart failure and her kidneys were failing. In August 2008, after years of declining health, she died, plunging Claudine into depression. She spent days without getting out of bed. Neighbors came over to rustle her awake or bring food for the kids. Claudine began drinking, mostly cheap beer. Barely able to function, she finally visited a doctor friend who prescribed Xanax and Vicodin. The benzodiazepine and narcotic helped soothe her anxiety and numbed her pain. They also deployed molecules that attached to her opioid receptors, reawakening addictive urges.

Around that time, Junior was paroled from prison and jumped house arrest. He moved in with Claudine and the children. Her sisters were alarmed when they saw his face flash on their TVs as "One of Texas's Most Wanted." Angie called Claudine.

"No, they made a mistake," Claudine told her sister. "That's his brother." She added: "He's not that bad."

Ciara, now eleven, initially welcomed Junior's presence. Over the course of a few weeks, he helped wean Claudine off the pills and got her to quit drinking. He instilled discipline in the other kids that seemed to tamp down the screaming and outbursts. Claudine seemed happy, reinvigorated. She began cooking again. For the first time in Ciara's life, the family had a car. They would take trips to the mall or Walmart. There was a new bounce in Claudine's step. She talked about starting her own business: a catering company.

But dark habits crept back into their lives. Junior, technically on the lam and with no job skills, began dealing drugs to make money. Claudine helped. Strangers cycled in and out of the home. Parties raged deep into the night, with the children sleeping in their rooms. The happy family life Ciara treasured deteriorated into lies and cover-ups. Claudine began wearing long-sleeved blouses, even in the high heat of summer, concealing tracks on her arms. "Spider bites," she lied to Ciara when asked about the marks dotting her forearms. Junior would stagger out of his room, begin talking to Ciara, then slump into a stupor, saliva dribbling down his chin. One day, Claudine and Junior showed up at Ciara's school, pulled her out of class, and made her pee into a cup to help Junior pass a drug test. Ciara loved and feared for her siblings and dreaded leaving them alone in the deteriorating scene at home. But she couldn't take it anymore. At twelve years old, she asked Angie if her aunt would take her in.

Word reached Angie that Junior was now working as a hit man for a Mexican crime syndicate. The family was terrified of calling the police on him for what he might do to Claudine and the kids. Ciara feared for her siblings. In the spring of 2014, Ciara was visiting her mother and siblings when a SWAT team again stormed the home, wielding batons and shields. Ciara and the other children were kept in one bedroom as the police swarmed through the house. Junior wasn't home at the time, but they found syringes, bags of heroin, and guns wrapped in blankets and hidden in closets. A warrant went out for his arrest. A few weeks later, Ciara flicked on the TV news and saw Junior being arrested for smuggling undocumented immigrants in her former home. She watched with dread and dismay as the agents muscled through her mother's house. She recognized the Spider-Man curtains from her brothers' room in the images.

With Junior back in prison, Claudine, saddled with a heroin habit, began to spiral. In the summer of 2014, behind in mortgage payments and unable to hold down a job, she lost the house. She gathered her things and her four kids and moved everyone into the Pan-American Courts on San Bernardo Avenue. Rent was cheaper, and she could be nearer to the trap houses that could remedy her withdrawals. She lived on federal assistance and child support that trickled in. Still, money passed through her like water through a sieve.

At the time, Junior Casas, a transplant from Wisconsin, was staying a few doors down in another room at the Pan-American Courts. He sat outside his room, observing the happenings. One day, Claudine walked over and introduced herself. Casas was struck by her beauty: sparkling blue eyes; high, round cheekbones; fair skin; chestnut-colored shoulder-length hair. The two hit it off. Claudine was soon coming over regularly, confiding in Casas about how hard her boys were to handle, how scared she was that they might try to hurt her someday. Casas would cook her burgers on a small grill or she would whip up Mexican dishes on the small hot plate in his room.

Her sons continued wreaking havoc, erupting into tantrums in the parking lot or fighting each other. Claudine slipped deeper into her addiction, asking her dad for money or selling food stamps for cash. One day, a few months after moving into the Pan-American Courts, Texas Child Protective Services knocked on her door. Her lifestyle wasn't conducive to raising kids, they told her. The children were taken into temporary protective custody. Her sister Colette took guardianship of two of the children, Rudy and Elian, while Ramon and Malena went to an aunt.

Losing custody of her children devastated Claudine. She spiraled further into substance abuse disorder. The SSI and child support checks stopped arriving. Claudine was in a personal and financial abyss. Faced with an opioid addiction and no income, she did what scores of others have done over the years on San Bernardo: she hit the streets.

Claudine began nightly strolls along San Bernardo, lingering at the Relax Inn or down the street at the Siesta Motel. She became friendly with Melissa, Chelly, and Janelle. Claudine was thirty-eight, older than them, and came across as more educated and had an older-sister vibe the others were drawn to. They became close friends.

At night, Claudine would pull on a tight dress and pumps and flag down passing clients. She would rarely let customers engage her for full sex, offering instead oral sex for $20 or $30 per transaction. Her twinkling blue eyes and mature air set her apart from the other, younger women on the strip and earned her a string of steady, repeat customers. She scraped together the money she made each day to pay for the $39-a-night room at the Pan-American Courts and the small bags of black tar heroin she consumed to the tune of hundreds of dollars a day. Her arms, legs, and neck soon filled with scars from repeated needle stabs. When her veins collapsed and vanished, she asked friends to stab her between her toes. When that stopped working, she injected straight into the skin, a practice known as "skin-popping" that led to lesions and the occasional abscess. She went back to long-sleeved shirts and dresses to hide the scars.

Her chats with Casas grew morose. They would eat heated-up Hamburger Helper or watch Discovery Channel documentaries on Casas's TV. Claudine confessed that she wanted to go to rehab, get cleaned up, and return to her kids, but she didn't see a path there. Even if she did go, she told Casas, she would have to return to Laredo and would slide right back into her disorder. Casas saw her physique disintegrating; the beautiful girl who had introduced herself in the parking lot had lost weight, collected dark bags under eyes, and become jittery. Casas let her shoot up in his bathroom. He would worry when she was in there for twenty, twenty-five minutes, as she struggled to find a vein, thinking she was overdosing.

Claudine abhorred her substance abuse disorder, how it had

wrenched her life apart and kept her in shackles. She tried quitting various times; the best opportunities were always when she was arrested and had to sober up in jail. Between 2011 and 2018, she was arrested five times on various drug and prostitution charges. The moment she got out, however, she returned to the needle. The alternative was too terrifying to face. If heroin was out of her system too long, she would break out in sweats. Her joints would ache like she had contracted a crippling flu. It would pain her to walk from one side of the room to the other. Most disconcertingly, her pants would soil with waves of uncontrollable diarrhea. Withdrawal felt like her body was slowly wrenching itself to death an inch at a time. She once told a relative she would prefer actual death to heroin withdrawal. One small hit of chiva, however, and everything clicked back into place. Unlike other drugs that slurred voices or blurred perceptions, heroin made Claudine feel normal again. She could hold a conversation on the intricacies of making homemade tamales while sky-high on heroin without anyone noticing.

Claudine grew to love the other girls on the strip. Melissa was more than a decade younger and brash. Still, the two were often together. If Melissa had a few extra crack rocks, she'd share them with Claudine, and if Claudine had a room, she would let Melissa drop by to shower or rest or use it for a multiday party.

Pat at the Relax Inn liked Claudine. She would come over to use the pool or rent a room for a few days, usually paying the $55 per night on time and keeping the rooms clean. Nora found Claudine more educated and easier to talk to than the other girls. One day, as Pat grilled meat nearby, Claudine sat and opened up to Nora, telling her, in Spanish, how she once wanted to be a teacher, how she once had a house but lost it, how her kids were taken away but she was going to win them back someday. She pulled out her phone and showed Nora photos of her kids, the house, her sisters. "I know there are people who disrespect your hotel," Claudine told Nora. She promised never to be one of them.

At the Siesta Motel, front desk manager Rose Ortiz often saw Claudine and Melissa together and marveled at how different the two were.

She preferred Claudine and their talks on current events. Claudine also talked incessantly about her kids, how proud she was of them, especially the oldest, Ciara, who was readying to graduate high school, and about how her autistic sons were making good progress at school. She missed them all, especially Ciara, whom she hadn't spoken to in months.

There had been an ugly incident in 2016 where Claudine had arrived stoned and slurring her speech to a meeting with CPS officials. Ciara was so embarrassed she vowed never to speak with her mother again. Years passed. The drugs, her mom's obsession with Junior, the drama, the lies—it was all too much for a teenager trying to get through high school. Still living with her aunt, Ciara graduated high school and found a job at a plasma center downtown but severed all ties with Claudine. Her mom had called her the day she graduated in May 2016, but since then months had passed and the two hadn't talked.

===

IN EARLY DECEMBER 2017, CLAUDINE WAS TALKED INTO A BLIND date by her cousin. Wayne Garcia was older than the men she usually dated, but he was sweet and funny and had an aura about him that allowed her to let her guard down, a rarity given her line of work. They became inseparable. Wayne took her shopping for new pantsuits at Dillard's at the Mall del Norte or dinner at Red Lobster. He bought her a new Galaxy smartphone with prepaid service and asked her to call or text him each night when she got home, just to know she was okay. He rented her rooms at the Pan-American Courts, Siesta Motel, or Relax Inn so she could get a few hours' rest in between jobs.

Wayne freebased with her but urged her to quit heroin. He allowed her to shoot up in the bathrooms of their hotel rooms, knew that without the chiva a violent illness soon followed, but he constantly counseled her to quit.

"I worry about you and I worry about your health," he told her.

Claudine's legs became dotted with scars from heroin use. One large abscess yawned on her calf, creating purpled skin that looked like pus-filled, shriveled meat yet was hard to the touch. Wayne convinced her to go to the hospital and have it removed. After being released, Claudine returned to San Bernardo and turning tricks for cash. She promised Wayne to continue texting him to let him know she was okay. When Wayne's phone buzzed with a new text from Claudine, saying she had made it back to her room, often it was already light outside.

THE EMOTIONAL DISTANCE BETWEEN HERSELF AND HER MOTHER clawed at Ciara. She missed having her mom to talk to, the long, confiding chats they once shared.

In January 2018, urged on by her grandfather, Ciara, now twenty, set out to find Claudine. Years had passed since their last contact. She didn't know what to expect and braced herself for a fresh wave of disappointment.

Ciara found her mom on San Bernardo Avenue and invited her to lunch. They went to Tacos Kissi, a popular spot on the strip known for its "Mexican sushi": deep-fried sushi rolls. Over steaming plates of beef fajita tacos and Mexican sushi, mother and daughter began talking, hesitantly at first, then building into a torrent of emotional mea culpas and confessions. Claudine apologized for messing up their lives so badly. Through tears, she told Ciara how much she missed her and the other children. She told her about the sex work and her grade school rape all those years ago and her dependence on heroin. She said she was weak, not built like everyone else. But she did truly love all her children and wanted to be back in their lives. Ciara told her mom about the fits of depression she struggled with and a recent fallout she'd had with one of her aunts.

"I really want my mom back," she told Claudine through tears. "It's really all I want."

Claudine vowed to do all she could to return to them. "I want to clean up," she said. "I want to do better."

Ciara promised to help her. The lunch was designed to be an initial connection, an opening salvo in a long trek toward regaining trust between mother and daughter, but it flourished into much more. They swore to make their relationship work this time. Ciara began researching apartments she and her mom could move into.

After the lunch, Ciara called her aunts and told them about the meeting.

"Be prepared for disappointment," Colette warned her. They had been down this road before and Claudine had always managed to upend things, she told her niece.

This time felt different, Ciara insisted. Colette said she and the other sisters would help any way they could. First things first: they needed to get Claudine off drugs. She had been in and out of different rehab programs over the years, none of which stuck for long. Part of the problem was that, at the time, Laredo didn't have a long-term overnight detox center, only outpatient rehab. A twelve-bed recovery center in nearby Rio Bravo required that the patient be clean before entering; thus, it wasn't a true detox center. For many users, the only inpatient detox center was Webb County Jail. The closest actual detox center was Charlie's Place Recovery Center (now Cenikor) in Corpus Christi, a two-and-a-half-hour drive to Texas's coast. Colette made some calls.

After multiple conversations with an array of officials, Colette got Claudine a prepaid spot for three months at the rehabilitation center. If she stuck with it, her stay at Charlie's Place would truly flush the drugs from her system and deliver her back to their lives. After rehab, if she was clean, she could move in with Ciara in a two-bedroom apartment she had found in north Laredo.

Claudine was giddy; she readily agreed. Rooming with her daughter and reconnecting with her family: her dream of straightening out her life was actually materializing.

"I really want to do this," she told Ciara.

As the first day of rehab approached, Angie bought Claudine two pink spiral notebooks to use as journals and printed out photos of all her children. Inside one of the notebooks, next to the photos, Angie scribbled a message to her sister: "This is why you're here, so open this book whenever you feel in doubt." A new stage in her life was emerging.

At 7:00 a.m. on February 10, 2018, Ciara and Colette packed the journals, family pictures, and sets of new underwear and drove to San Bernardo Avenue to find Claudine and drive her to Corpus Christi. They arrived at a friend's house where she was staying, but Claudine wasn't there. "Never came home last night," the friend said. Familiar feelings of dread and regret crept into Colette.

Colette and Ciara drove to another friend's house and found Claudine there, loopy and drowsy from an all-night drug binge. They corralled her into the car. As they pulled onto Interstate 35, Claudine panicked.

"Stop the car," she told them. "I can't do it."

"Oh, you're doing it," Colette answered.

The car was mostly quiet for the rest of the long drive, as the sun emerged over the ranches and cactus fields along Highway 59. In Corpus Christi, Colette and Ciara had breakfast with Claudine at a small diner, then dropped her off at Charlie's Place. They reassured her she could do it. Claudine smiled shakily and disappeared inside.

Ciara and Colette cheerily drove back to Laredo, basking in their accomplishment. Could this be the moment Claudine conquered her disorder and regained her life? Did they pull it off? Ciara went back to her apartment to plan her mom's return. Claudine would need close supervision and support to weather the coming months if she was truly turning a page on her drug use. Keeping an addict away from heroin is no easy task, but Ciara felt up to the challenge.

"Nobody fueled me like my mom," she remembered later. "She wanted to do better. She wanted a relationship with us. And I was going to help her do it."

Just four days later, however, on February 14, Colette called her father to wish him a happy Valentine's Day. Claudine was there at his house, he said. She had walked out of Charlie's Place, and a friend had wired her money for bus fare back to Laredo. Her three-month rehab stay—a coveted slot that took time and pleading and money to secure—

had lasted just ninety-six hours. All the dreams of Claudine getting a job, moving in with Ciara, and reconnecting with her children vanished. A few hours later, she was back on San Bernardo Avenue.

Ciara, feeling betrayed, was livid and didn't speak to her mom for more than a month.

Slowly, however, Ciara and Claudine reconciled. Ciara recognized the stranglehold heroin had on her mom. She realized it was going to be a long, tough slough. And she wasn't giving up. They talked nearly every day. Claudine's texts to her daughter were peppered with emoji faces or selfies of herself with freshly shampooed straight hair and new lashes, requests for more photos of her or snippets of advice. They chimed into Ciara's phone randomly all hours of the day and night:

"Hey mamas, what you up 2? Send me more pics."

"You need to be careful, it's a crazy world out there."

"Life is like a box of chocolates, you never know what you're going to get."

Although Claudine abandoned her rehab stay, she held on to her journals and wrote in them regularly. The pink spiral-bound notebooks soon filled with scribbles, doodling, and "Junior" and "Hector" scrawled in a variety of fonts. Claudine also dedicated page after page to writing personal letters to her eldest daughter. "To my Dearest Ciara," they often started, and expressed an aching love for her and the other children. She wrote in looping cursive handwriting, the pages often marred with inkblots or food stains, and at all hours of the day and night. In one entry, dated March 29, 2018, 2:07 a.m., she stressed how much she loved her daughter and missed her "every hour, minute, second, day, week, month, year." She lamented the time lost between them and dreamed of a world where life had turned out differently, placing blame heavily on herself.

"How I wish I could turn back time," Claudine scribbled. "How I beg God and you all for forgiveness."

CHAPTER 11

In early September 2018, a slow-moving upper-level trough collided with remnants of Tropical Storm Gordon from the Gulf of Mexico and dumped heavy rain on South Texas. The downpours started on September 2 and continued on and off for more than two weeks, turning the arid landscape from drought to deluge, flooding parts of Webb County with up to four inches of rain. Submerged cars were abandoned in flooded parking lots, and streets moved like shallow rivers.

Rain lashed at Laredo as San Bernardo hummed with reports of Melissa's death. Claudine was particularly distraught. Her good friend, whom she had hung out with and shared a cigarette with just days before, was lying dead in a morgue. Pat Roth saw Claudine emerge from a room at the Relax Inn, pale as a bedsheet.

"I can't believe this shit," she told friends over and over again.

On September 4, Ciara received several urgent text messages from her mother. Heavy rains pounded Laredo as Claudine told her daughter she needed to see her immediately. Ciara didn't want to drive in the rain, so she told her mom to take a cab to her apartment and she would pay for it. Claudine arrived past midnight that night, soaked from the rain and trembling with fear. She towel dried, and she and Ciara ate bowls of Special K cereal with milk, then climbed into the only bed together. They talked about Melissa. Claudine said the women on the strip were unnerved by it and some were too scared to work.

Claudine hinted to her daughter that she may know who killed her friend.

Her words terrified Ciara. She urged her mom to stay with her for a few days. She'd be safer in her apartment than roaming San Bernardo Avenue. Claudine agreed.

The next morning, Ciara got up early and left for her job at the

plasma center downtown, where she worked as a donor center technician. As she left, Claudine slept in her bed. The conversation she had had
with her mom the night before unnerved her. What did Claudine know
about Melissa's murder? She made a mental note to talk further about it
with her mom later that day when she got home from work. For now, at
least, she'd be safe in her apartment, Ciara thought.

But when she returned home later that day, Claudine was gone.

=====

WHEN SHE WAS SHORT ON CASH TO PAY FOR A ROOM AT THE PAN-
American Courts or the Relax Inn, and she didn't feel like pestering
Wayne, Claudine routinely stayed at the home of Evangelina Torres,
known as "Doña Eva" in the neighborhood. Eva, seventy-three, lived
on Ugarte Street one block from San Bernardo with her two grown
sons, Carlos and Rafa. She had silver hair pulled back into a tight bun
and crystalline blue eyes. She had the handsome, elegant air of an aging
movie star but was actually a former regional lawmaker from the state
of Tamaulipas, just across the river in Mexico, who once prosecuted
corrupt Mexican police. When the violence and death threats became
intolerable, she retreated across the border and made her home in Laredo where she had lived for nearly twenty years. Both her sons spiraled
into cocaine and heroin addictions, but she routinely welcomed their
drug-addled friends into their two-bedroom cottage, including many
of the neighborhood's sex workers. Realizing Laredo's lack of a detox
center, Doña Eva often ventured across the bridge into Nuevo Laredo
to retrieve vials of methadone, which she distributed to any woman trying to quit heroin, charging them only what she had paid for the pills,
about $7 each—far less expensive than methadone treatments in the
United States. Her cramped home often overflowed with sex workers,
vagabonds, and junkies, shivering through withdrawals or napping on
the couch.

Like others, Eva enjoyed chatting with Claudine and always allowed
her to stay in the extra bedroom in the back. Claudine admired Eva's

cooking, especially her yellow rice with carne guisada. Claudine would hang around the house, then leave for her escort dates at around 2:00 or 3:00 a.m. When not working, Claudine and Eva would chat into the night. Eva always offered to get her methadone to help her kick her addiction. Claudine would burst into tears. "I want to clean up," she said. "I want to be with my kids." Always, however, she returned to the streets and her drug use.

On September 11, 2018, Claudine called her sister Colette to check in on her kids. Colette had good news: Claudine's son Elian had progressed enough with his autism at school that he was being placed in a mainstream class. Elian got on the phone with his mom and cheerfully told her he would soon be taking chemistry, math, and other "regular" classes. Claudine was elated. "Oh my God!" she told her son. "I can't believe it!"

Shortly after that call, Claudine visited Eva at her home. Buoyed by the news from her kids, she told Eva she was ready to start the methadone treatments. She knew a friend who would lend her the money to pay for the pills. She was ready to get clean.

The next day, at around 6:00 p.m., Claudine sent her daughter a flurry of text messages: "Urgent—Plz A.S.A.P. . . . JUST WANT, NEED 2 TALK 4 ONE MINUTE." Ciara texted her back, along with some pictures of herself. Claudine urged her to call. "Call me whenever u can, no matter what time . . ."

That night, Claudine was roaming through Eva's house, peeking in on what she was cooking in the kitchen and scolding Carlos and Rafa for not appreciating their mother more. "You don't realize how much you need her until she's gone," she told them, sparking an argument between the three of them.

Later that evening, she got dressed earlier than usual. Claudine told Eva about her desire to, once and for all, shake her addiction. This time for real. She told her she had lined up a date with someone who would give her enough money for the methadone pills. She really wanted to give it another shot and start weaning herself off the chemical substance that had wreaked so much havoc on her life. Eva beamed; she told Claudine she was proud of her for making such a life-altering decision. She told her to be careful—and God bless.

Claudine left at around 9:00 p.m., earlier than normal for her. She walked over to San Bernardo and met with Wayne and, later, Anna Karen Herrera. After freebasing in his car for a few hours, she readied to leave. Wayne urged her a final time to stay.

Sorry, Claudine said, she had to go.

"Call me in the morning," Wayne told her.

Claudine agreed and hurried off.

═══

ORTIZ HAD EXTRACTED HIS SHARE OF COMPANIONSHIP AND SEX from the women he picked up along San Bernardo Avenue. But part of him had other motives: he aspired to rid Laredo of this population of individuals he considered "mierdas" (turds) and "descarados" (shameless people). He saw himself as a spy on the inside, someone with a growing body of intel on a segment of society he felt was better off eradicated. After escorting Erika and Melissa multiple times to the drug dealer's house near Sanders Avenue, he put in a call to a contact he had at the Webb County Sheriff's Office and tipped him to the illicit activity at the house, giving him an address and description. Another route was taking matters into his own hands.

Eight days had passed since Melissa's body had been found, and, as far as he knew, nothing in the case pointed in his direction. From his desk at the BIC, Ortiz had tried to casually glean details about the murder investigation from colleagues, asking one Border Patrol intel agent what he knew about the case. The agent was puzzled by the question. "What do you care?" he asked Ortiz. "That's not your case." Ortiz shrugged it off. He was confident detectives didn't suspect him. Emboldened, his interaction with the women of San Bernardo, along with his drinking and erratic consumption of meds, continued unabated.

As midnight neared on Wednesday, September 12, Ortiz climbed into his Dodge Ram and headed to San Bernardo. Unlike past drives, fueled mainly by the thrill of forbidden sex, now more sinister motivations bubbled within him. "Fuck these people," he muttered to himself. "They are all fucking mierdas."

Ortiz reached San Bernardo Avenue just as Claudine emerged from one of the strip's motels. He pulled over, she got in, and they sped off. Buzzing from a night of heavy drug consumption, Claudine was chatty. She talked about her life on the streets, how she'd been living in and out of motels. As others had before her, she asked if Ortiz could drive her to the house near Sanders Avenue to score some chiva and shoot up. He obliged.

After she scored the heroin, Ortiz drove Claudine through Laredo's dark streets and ramped onto Interstate 35, heading north. As they drove along the highway, Claudine brought up Melissa's murder.

"Yeah, I heard about that shit," Ortiz said.

"Dude, do you know where it happened?" Claudine asked.

Ortiz said yeah, he knew.

"Would it be really fucked up if we go see it?" she asked.

He couldn't believe what he was hearing.

"Okay," Ortiz told her. "I don't have anything better to do."

He piloted the Dodge Ram north on Interstate 35. They were headed to the scene of the crime. The night's earlier sheets of rain had eased into a steady drizzle, painting a slick sheen on the highway. Ortiz pulled off on the Exit 18 ramp and headed north again on Highway 83, retracing the route he had taken with Melissa. Suddenly, something clicked inside Claudine—or enough of the drugs wore off to spark a glint of insight. An odd curiosity about seeing the spot where her friend spent her final moments shifted into the horrific realization that Melissa's killer may be driving her there. Terror seized Claudine.

"Fucker!" she said, panic tugging at her voice. "You were probably the killer!"

She stared at him.

"You were probably the killer! You're the . . ."

"Shut the fuck up," Ortiz commanded. He turned east on State Highway 255, then pulled over on the shoulder of the highway. "Get out of my truck."

Claudine could only repeat, over and over, "You were probably the killer! You were probably the killer!"

She gathered her things in a ball to her chest, stumbled out of the truck, and began walking through the scrub next to the highway, away from the truck. Ortiz got out, too, grabbing his .40-caliber handgun, and followed. Claudine tromped through dark scrub brush. From where she was, she could see the zipping headlights of cars and trucks speeding along Interstate 35, less than three miles away. All around her, darkness. Ortiz silently walked up behind her, raised the gun to the back of her head, and squeezed the trigger twice. *Boom. Boom.* The sound of the blasts carried through the dark, wet night, dissolving across open fields. Even though he stood just a few feet away, the first shot missed its target completely. The second found the back of Claudine's head. As designed, the jacketed hollow-point bullet mushroomed on impact and tore a dime-sized hole through the bone and tissue in the back of Claudine's head, ripping through the occipital lobe and lodging in her left temporal lobe, one of two plum-sized sections of brain vital for memory and language. She crumpled to the ground.

Ortiz drove off. As he headed toward Interstate 35, unlike after Melissa's murder, he was surprised to find that there were no shakes, no panic rushing in him, no stifling paranoia about being caught. The task had been, in his eyes, clean and efficient. He drove the twenty-five miles south back to his home on Bur Oak Drive, showered, and slipped into bed with his sleeping wife.

═══

AT DAYBREAK ON SEPTEMBER 13, A TRUCK DRIVER CRUISING along State Highway 255, just east of Highway 83 north of Laredo, noticed what appeared to be a person lying on the side of the road. The driver turned around, parked, and approached the female body. The woman was splayed on the ground, surrounded by streaks of blood, but still breathing. The driver called 911, then knelt next to her to wait for help to arrive. He offered her a towel and a bottled water, but she pushed him away. "I'm thirsty, leave me alone," she muttered in her haze.

The emergency call went through the Webb County 911 dispatch center and pinged to Rey Veliz, a paramedic with Angel Care, the ambulance company that contracted with the county to retrieve patients in unincorporated Webb County. He had answered that type of call in that corner of the county at that hour of the day many times before. It usually meant an oil field worker or migrant laborer had wandered onto a highway and was hit by a passing truck. The ambulance with Veliz sped toward its destination just as dawn leaked into the Laredo sky.

Texas Department of Public Safety state troopers were already at the scene, looking at tire marks, and asked Veliz and his partner not to bring a stretcher to the victim, so as not to disturb any evidence. Two cell phones, pages from a notebook, and sneakers were strewn near the victim, a woman in her mid-forties, who was crumpled in the grass, groaning. He knelt next to her.

Veliz reached behind her head and felt a sticky mass of blood there. He didn't notice any other injuries and assumed she had been hit by a truck in the twilight. Suddenly, the woman began flailing her arms, fighting off the paramedics. Veliz held her down as his partner strapped her onto a backboard and slid on a cervical collar, and together they carried her to the ambulance. Fighting off paramedics was not unheard-of with trauma victims. Veliz had seen it many times before, where accident victims suddenly, subconsciously, started fighting off the people there to assist them. This female victim, however, was being particularly combative, struggling to free her arms from the straps and mumbling incoherently.

"Just calm down," Veliz told her as the ambulance sped toward Doctors Hospital of Laredo, nineteen miles away. "You're in good hands. We're getting you some help."

The ambulance sped into the hospital's emergency bay, sirens blaring, and Veliz handed the patient over to a team of waiting doctors, who wheeled her inside, strapping IVs and pulling an oxygen mask over her face. As they worked to find and patch her wounds, they wheeled her straight to radiology for X-rays. Outside, Veliz filled out paperwork and cleaned up the rear of the ambulance, wiping the victim's brain matter off his backboard. Sheriff's deputies arrived and asked him a series of standard questions about the patient. Did she say anything during the ride? Did she talk about anything specific? No, Veliz said. She was mumbling but incoherent.

As Veliz and the detectives chatted, a doctor emerged from the X-ray room. The victim had died, he said. X-rays had shown a scorched, dime-sized wound in the back of her head. A metal projectile was still lodged in her brain. It wasn't a traffic accident, the doctor told them. It was a gunshot wound.

———

CAPTAIN CALDERON DROVE INTO THE SHERIFF'S SUBSTATION ON Highway 59 early on the morning of September 13 and parked around the back. Another long day lay ahead. The case of Melissa Ramirez's murder had gone frustratingly cold. Dozens of leads and interviews he and Ranger E. J. Salinas had pursued over the past nine days had yielded not much of anything. No clear suspect. No motive. No witnesses. Nothing other than a dead sex worker on the side of a rural gravel road and .40-caliber casings sprinkled nearby.

Calderon's cell phone buzzed. A sheriff's deputy, Sergeant Felix Nuñez, who had arrived at the scene on State Highway 255, was calling to advise him that a woman had been found just east of Highway 83 in northwest Webb County. Investigators and paramedics believed it to be an "auto-ped"—sheriff's office lingo for "auto-pedestrian," or someone struck by one of the thousands of trucks rumbling through that area each day. Calderon thanked him and said to keep him posted.

The details tumbled in Calderon's mind for a few moments. He mentally calculated spots on a map and distances. The area where the auto-ped occurred was just a few miles from where Melissa's body was found nine days prior. But auto-peds happened there all the time, especially with asylum seekers who wandered out of the brush disoriented and into the path of a speeding semitruck. The Patrol Division—not CID—handles auto-peds. They'd deal with it.

He had just closed the driver's-side door to his truck and was headed around the vehicle when a second call came in. Again, it was Nuñez.

"Correction: not an auto-ped," the deputy told Calderon. "Gunshot victim. Female."

Calderon climbed back into his truck and sped off to the crime scene.

══

By the time Calderon reached the scene on State Highway 255, CID detectives had cordoned off the area and were combing the grass for clues. He surveyed the scene. The tall grass was littered with plastic bags, a black purse, a Bic lighter, a pair of low-cut black Nike sneakers, pens, hairspray, two pink spiral notebooks filled with cursive writing and doodling, and two cell phones. The purse contained condoms, makeup, and a cigarette box filled with syringes. The items were spread about haphazardly, as if flung abruptly. Clumps of flattened grass and dirt were stained with Claudine's blood. Streaks of dark blood ran from deep in the brush to the shoulder of the highway. Shot in the head but still alive, Claudine had dragged herself about ten feet to the road, where she would more likely be rescued.

Calderon jotted down details in his notebook, as deputies around him tagged the items—each a potential clue—with yellow numbered markers and took pictures. Salinas arrived and snapped his own pictures of the site, adding to his burgeoning case file.

As they scoured the field, one of the deputies picked up a Texas ID nestled in the overgrown grass near the purse. He read it: Claudine Luera, forty-two years old. The detective recognized the name as one of the people they had been trying to locate, a friend of Melissa's and a fellow sex worker. Another deputy recovered two casings from the scene: federal-brand .40-caliber shells.

The realization hit Calderon like a spray of ice water to the face. The bullet casings, the wounds, the victims' professions, and the proximity of the murder scenes were all too similar to be coincidental. This was no longer a routine homicide, he thought.

Laredo had a serial killer on the loose.

PART 3

CHAPTER 12

September 14 began as most Fridays do in Laredo. Highways filled with commuters headed to work downtown. The port of entry busied with steady streams of Mexican nationals crossing into Laredo. Downtown shops rolled up their shutters and put out bins of suitcases and soccer balls, readying for customers.

Word of a second victim found in Laredo's outskirts, however, had started to seep into the community. As usual, La Gordiloca was one of the first to report on the unidentified woman found clinging to life on State Highway 255. On the afternoon of Thursday, September 13, just hours after Claudine was found, La Gordiloca addressed her audience in a live selfie video on her Facebook page. Wearing a bejeweled trucker's cap and low-cut blouse revealing shoulder and neck tattoos, La Gordiloca recounted the incident. This time, her report was remarkably accurate. Speaking first in Spanish and then retelling it in English, she described how sheriff's deputies—or "sherifes" in Tex-Mex Spanglish—received a call at around 7:30 a.m. for an injured woman believed to have been badly beaten, off a highway not far from where Melissa's body had been recovered nine days earlier. The victim had been taken to a hospital, where she died of her injuries, La Gordiloca told her followers.

A few hours later, she went live on Facebook again with an update: deputies had thought the woman had been beaten, but, in fact, she died of gunshot wounds, La Gordiloca reported, again relaying the news first in Spanish, then repeating it in English. Her words and demeanor took a somber tone. "We hope they solve both these cases soon," she said. "It's very serious. Now it's two."

The next morning, at 8:21 a.m., *Laredo Morning Times* posted a story to its website with the headline "DPS: Woman Found Critically Wounded off Roadway in Webb County Dies." The 206-word story said the victim had suffered "head trauma" and died after being transported to the hospital, but didn't mention gunshot wounds. It described how the victim had been discovered "around the area" where Melissa was found slain ten days earlier. Authorities were not releasing her identity, "pending the notification of next of kin." TV broadcasts also ran short reports on the incident, with similar information.

Angie Perez, Claudine's older sister, was at home getting ready for work when an anchor on the morning TV newscast announced the discovery of a "second body." Strange, she thought. Perez had been out of town on vacation and hadn't yet learned of Melissa's murder. *What second body? Who was the first one?*

Later, at work, her phone rang. It was Junior's mom—and she was crying. She told Angie that the body authorities had found was Claudine's. Someone in law enforcement had leaked the news to her son. "It's Claudine," she cried into the phone. Angie's heart sank. She started to tremble. Her first thought was: Junior killed her. She hung up with Junior's mom and, hands shaking, called Colette.

Colette had heard of Melissa's murder but refused to believe the second victim could be her sister. Hadn't she talked to her just three days earlier? She sounded fine, better than usual, actually. "How does she know that for sure?" Colette asked Angie, questioning Junior's mom's news. They needed confirmation. She called the Webb County Sheriff's Office and asked to speak to the person in charge of the murder investigation but was told the investigator was out of the office. Someone would get back to her. She left her name and phone number. And waited.

Meanwhile, Colette's phone chimed with text messages from friends of Claudine's from San Bernardo. "Have you seen Claudine?" one person texted. Another one read: "We're worried about her." Colette's heart sank. Something wasn't right. Claudine was in trouble. Those painful thoughts that had tormented her ever since her older sister slipped into a life on the streets roared to life. Overdose? Hospital? Murder? She started a text thread with Angie and her niece Karina. "We need confirmation," Colette typed out in a text. Also: "No one says anything to Ciara."

Hour after excruciating hour passed. No callback from the sheriff's office. The sisters dialed in to the Webb County Medical Examiner's Office and explained to the person on the line that they were potentially the family of the victim found by the highway. The employee who answered the phone asked if they could name any identifying marks on the victim, such as tattoos or scars. Colette described the tattoo of a cartoonish devil on Claudette's left shoulder blade, the rosary beads circling her mom's name on her right hip, and the various men's names inked throughout her body. Silence on the line while the employee confirmed the details. After what felt like millennia, the person returned to the line.

"With the information you've given us," the employee said, "and we just ran her fingerprints, we can confirm that it is her."

Color drained from Colette's face. She hung up the phone. Her heart felt shredded. Years of worrying and stressing about her sister, fighting and pleading with her, praying and hoping for her—all evaporated with a single sentence from a stranger. The pain was excruciating but intensified when she thought of Claudine's children. How would they break the news to the twins? How about *Ciara*?

Karina suggested calling Ciara. "No," Colette said. "We're going to her."

═══

THE BIOMAT USA PLASMA CENTER ON HIDALGO STREET DOWN-town swarmed with activity. Potential donors filled out consent forms or waited on gurneys to have a needle inserted into their arm and plasma extracted. Plasmapheresis machines whirled, separating plasma from red and white blood cells, platelets, and other cellular components of the blood. The center had been nonstop with donors since opening at 7:00 a.m., and Ciara, managing much of the steady flow, had been in the middle of it. She had been so preoccupied with the demands of the workday that she didn't notice the text messages and missed calls piling up on her cell phone.

At around 3:00 p.m., Colette, Angie, and Karina walked into the center and asked to speak to Ciara. "It's a family emergency," Colette told the receptionist. Ciara emerged from the back offices and was surprised to see her aunts and cousin standing there. Confusion and panic stirred in her. Why are they here? she thought. They know I work Fridays. The stern looks on their faces weren't good.

"What are you doing here?" Ciara asked, pushing down the panic.

"We have to go," Colette told her.

Realization dawned on her.

"No," Ciara said.

She knew why they were there. It was the moment she'd expected and dreaded for years, the moment someone came to tell her her mom was dead. Living with a mother sickened by heroin addiction and forced into street life by her disorder carried with it an innate knowledge that it could all end at any moment. She could overdose or die at the hands of an unkind client. Ciara accepted and lived with the knowledge that that dark day could arrive at any moment. Still, when it finally did, it failed to compute.

"No," she repeated. "No, no, no, *no.*"

She pushed past her relatives, ran out a back door, and vomited repeatedly in the alley.

===

CALDERON GATHERED HIS GROUP OF DETECTIVES IN THE WEBB County sheriff's substation on Highway 59. He stressed the significance of having one shooter targeting women on San Bernardo. Claudine's death, he told them, was the single most important clue they now had to collaring the gunman. They needed to work backward and find out everything they could about that stretch of time from when she was discovered on State Highway 255 to the last time anyone saw her alive. They needed to find friends, relatives, customers—anyone and everyone who could help them with a lead.

Time was crucial. The last thing Calderon wanted was for days to tick by again without a significant break in the case, as with Melissa's murder. "This one is very, very recent," he told them. "We need to find out where she was the last twelve, eighteen hours." Detectives fanned out across the city and got to work, checking with sources and following up on leads.

One of the first names they unearthed was Encarnacion "Chon" Treviño III, a known San Bernardo character who had been in and out of jail and was Claudine's on-again, off-again boyfriend. If anyone knew what happened to Claudine, sources told detectives, it'd be Chon.

On the afternoon of September 14, a half dozen detectives descended on Chon's house on Gustavus Street in central Laredo, just a few blocks from the popular drug den off Sanders Avenue. No one answered the door, so detectives decided to wait for him on his concrete front patio. Just then, Chon pulled up in his four-door black Cadillac, saw the lawmen loitering outside his home, and sped off. Deputies scrambled to their cars, flicked on lights and sirens, and gave chase, but Chon had too big of a lead. He vanished among Laredo's tightly winding streets.

Detectives stopped short of issuing an official BOLO—"Be on the lookout"—alert for his arrest, which would ping into the radios of all deputies across Webb County. But the dozen or so deputies involved with investigating the recent murders spread across the city hunting for Chon, now the top suspect in Claudine's—and possibly Melissa's— murder.

A few hours later, Chon, still lying low and out of sight, called a contact he knew at the Laredo Police Department and described the earlier scene: a bunch of uniformed armed guys outside his home. Seeing so much law enforcement in one place, he instinctively fled, but he still didn't know why they were there. The Laredo police official assured him it wasn't their guys and promised to look into it. After a few calls, he called Chon back and informed him those were Webb County sheriff's deputies, who wanted to talk to him about Claudine's recent murder. Through his police intermediary, Chon agreed to meet with detectives.

At 5:50 p.m. that day, Chon walked into the substation on Highway 59 and sat in the interview room with Calderon and Salinas. They went over his relationship with Claudine, the people he hung out with, when he last saw Claudine or Melissa. Chon told them he saw Melissa with another sex worker named Jessica on San Agustin Avenue the night she was killed. He disparaged Melissa, calling her a "snitch" and a "bitch" and a "güera." Claudine had stayed with him at the Relax Inn, on and off, but he hadn't seen her in days. He had no idea how she ended up on the shoulder of State Highway 255, a gunshot wound to the head.

Calderon and Salinas didn't completely strike Chon off their list of suspects, but he was free to go. Detectives didn't have enough there to detain him. Once again, they had no suspects.

＝＝＝

NEWS OF CLAUDINE'S DEATH DROPPED ON SAN BERNARDO Avenue like an anvil. Even before law enforcement had publicly identified her as the "second body" found on State Highway 255, Claudine's name had rippled through the cell phones and Facebook messages of her fellow sex workers and friends along the avenue. The theory of Melissa's temper somehow leading to her death no longer held. It was now evident that someone out there was targeting the sex workers of San Bernardo. Some of the women retreated home to their families for a while to lie low. Others huddled in motel rooms and abandoned lots, sharing intel on clients and pocketknives. San Bernardo Avenue, once humming with illicit activity, grew quiet as church on Sunday.

On the evening of Friday, September 14, a group of sex workers gathered in room 138 at the Siesta Motel. Some cried; others asked about the whereabouts of other women they hadn't seen for a few days, wondering if they, too, had been targeted. The group didn't emerge for more than two days. "They were really scared," motel manager Rose Ortiz remembered later.

Still others returned to work. The threat of a killer loomed over the avenue, but even stronger in some women was the menace of a painful heroin withdrawal. Berto and Iris, the couple from the Relax Inn who often let sex workers sleep on their hotel room floor, counseled some of them to travel in groups and check out any cars before getting into them.

Less than twenty-four hours after Claudine's murder, some of the women on the avenue, including Janelle, Chelly, and Erika Peña, were back out on the street, looking for a quick score.

<hr>

It was billed as the "Final Judgment."

The middleweight championship boxing match between Canelo Álvarez and Gennady Golovkin II was a rematch between the world's two top boxing goliaths and expected to draw millions of viewers around the globe. It was scheduled for September 15, 2018, at T-Mobile Arena just outside Las Vegas. Their first match the previous year had ended in a controversial split draw decision after twelve rounds, and boxing enthusiasts everywhere were eager to pay the $85 to bring the HBO pay-per-view event into their living rooms. Álvarez, originally from Guadalajara, was a source of pride for Mexico and legions of boxing-loving Mexican Americans in the United States.

Ortiz planned to watch the bout at a coworker's watch party that he was having at his house in San Antonio. He planned to bring his wife, Daniella, along. The family would spend the night at Daniella's sister's house, making it a San Antonio family weekend. The day before they were scheduled to leave, however, a leak sprung in their home. Ortiz told his wife to go ahead with the kids. He'd wait for the plumber to fix the leak, then meet them there the following day. Daniella left and waited to hear from her husband.

With an empty house to himself, his wife and children more than 150 miles away in San Antonio, dark, familiar feelings began percolating inside Ortiz. He hopped in his truck and headed to San Bernardo Avenue.

Ortiz hadn't seen Erika in more than two weeks. The last time they had met, they had gotten into an argument, and he had broken her phone, rendering it inoperable. The phone was her lifeline, her main connection to clients and cash, and she got pissed at him. Whatever animosity toward Ortiz that had been brewing in Erika, however, seemed to evaporate on the evening of September 14, when she spotted his familiar white truck rolling along San Bernardo.

=====

RAIN AGAIN PELTED LAREDO IN THE EARLY EVENING OF FRIDAY, September 14. The avenue was mostly quiet except for a few girls huddled under awnings or at bus shelters, hoping to score a client. The deaths of Melissa and Claudine had spooked many of the women off the block. But Erika was saddling a $400-a-day heroin and crack habit. She needed a score.

At around 6:00 p.m., Ortiz spotted Erika sitting on a bus bench on San Bernardo. He pulled over.

"I've been looking for you," he told her.

Erika was dressed in ripped white jeans, a floral blouse, and white sneakers and clutched a small flower-print bag containing some foundation makeup, condoms, ChapStick, three dollar bills, and a ceramic pipe for smoking crack rocks. She climbed into the truck.

They drove first to a drug house near Clark Boulevard and North Arkansas Avenue, where Erika bought a foil of chiva, then a few blocks north to another house to buy a clean "rig," or syringe. Back in the truck, Erika brought up the topic everyone on San Bernardo seemed to be talking about. "Did you hear what happened to Melissa and Claudine?" she asked.

Ortiz said he saw something about it in the news. "What's the word on the street?" he asked.

Erika described how investigators had been around San Bernardo, knocking on motel room doors and people's homes, asking about the two slain women. She said some people in the neighborhood had been picked up by detectives and questioned. She hadn't been questioned, she said. Ortiz kept driving.

He drove them to a convenience store and handed Erika a hundred-dollar bill. She went inside and returned a few minutes later with a twenty-five-ounce Bud Light tallboy—or "tally," as they're commonly referred to in Laredo—a blue Powerade, and a pack of Marlboro Lights and handed him the $89 in change. He drove them to his house in north Laredo.

=====

THE SAN ISIDRO NEIGHBORHOOD WAS A DEVELOPED COMMUNITY of newish, roomy homes and manicured lawns on the northern edge of the city. It was home to a variety of law enforcement agents, including Border Patrol, whose stouter salaries afforded them the city's more comfortable homes. Beyond the houses to the north was an expanse of scrub desert stretching all the way to Cotulla and, beyond that, San Antonio.

Ortiz drove into the neighborhood down a street lined with Madagascar palms and prickly pear cacti, past the concrete sign for San Isidro Ranch, and pulled into the driveway of his home on Bur Oak Drive. Inside, Erika retreated to a seat at the dining room table to prepare her chiva for consumption. She bent the handle of a spoon to keep it from rocking, added a pinch of the gooey black substance and a few drops of water and mixed them in the spoon's bowl, then drew the mixture into the syringe. She busied herself with the ritual, found a workable vein, and slowly injected the drug into herself as she and Ortiz chatted.

From the moment Ortiz had stepped into the home, Erika had sensed something different about him. He seemed nervous, jittery, out of sorts. Her usually charming, funny client who had become more of a friend was unnerved about something. As the morphine molecules flooded her system, Erika sensed a dark change in Ortiz. The small talk took a morose turn. Ortiz told Erika he was worried police would check his DNA, since he was the "next to last one" to be with Melissa. He told her Melissa had given him oral sex the last time they were together. The comment was odd, unprompted, and sent small, cold daggers through Erika. She strained to keep her composure.

"If you didn't have anything to do with it, you shouldn't be scared," she offered. But inside her, alarm sirens blared. For the first time since Melissa's death, a sickening kernel of logic formed in her mind: What if *he* was the killer? That theory—however wild and incredulous just moments before—suddenly had a veneer of truth around it. Erika asked to borrow Ortiz's phone to call her mother. He said maybe later.

"I feel strange," Ortiz said. His face seemed to contort as he pressed his palms against his temples. "I feel stressed."

Erika reached for a pack of cigarettes and noticed her hands badly trembling. Ortiz watched as her body trembled uncontrollably.

"Why are you scared of me?" he asked, his voice flat, emotionless.

Ortiz said they should go to his bedroom, but Erika suggested going to the backyard instead to have a smoke together. This was something they often did with her sitting on his lap, an affectionate ritual laced with gentle teasing and laughing. This time, however, Erika made sure to secure her own patio chair, afraid to give Ortiz her back.

As they settled into the patio chairs, a primordial terror gripped her insides. Something felt horribly wrong. Erika suddenly felt the tendrils of death around her: in the memory and talk of her freshly murdered friends, in the eyes of Ortiz as he stared emptily back at her. Suddenly, a disembodied male voice, the voice of an ex-boyfriend who had died years earlier, swelled inside of her and bubbled into her head. *Sal de la casa,* it told her. *¡Vete ya!*

Erika's mind raced and flickered as a wave of nausea swooned through her. She told Ortiz she'd left something in his truck. She abruptly stood up, staggered through the house, rushed outside, and threw up on the sidewalk.

===

ORTIZ STARED ANXIOUSLY AS ERIKA FINISHED EMPTYING THE contents of her stomach on the sidewalk in front of his home.

"Maybe it's because I haven't eaten all day," Erika said, her mind fumbling for an excuse. Ortiz suggested going for a hamburger, and she agreed, anxious to get somewhere—anywhere—with more people and lights. She asked to be driven back to San Bernardo, but Ortiz said there were nearer places they could try. She gathered her stuff, got into the truck, and watched as Ortiz locked the front door of his home and climbed into the driver's seat.

On the drive, Erika again became consumed by a powerful dread. "David," she said, "la muerte anda cerca."

Ortiz told her to chill. "¿Qué chingao traes?" he said.

Erika asked if he could just take her through a fast-food drive-through, then return her to San Bernardo. But Ortiz said the Circle K at the Valero gas station near his house off Highway 69 had good burgers, very popular with truckers.

He pulled into the gas station and drove around the Circle K to the less populated trucker parking lot in the back, gliding in between two semitrailer trucks. Erika again asked to go back to San Bernardo. Ortiz ignored the request. Instead, he bent over, reaching for something near his door.

"What are you doing?" she asked.

"Just fixing my pants," he said.

When he sat up, he was holding the .40-caliber H&K P2000 semi-automatic with his left hand. Wordlessly, he pointed the black pistol at Erika's chest.

Erika's eyes widened and her heart hammered wildly. All her instincts, all the hushed rumors, all the pain and terror sparked by her friends' deaths—all of it crystallized into the reality of the four-inch steel barrel now pointed at her. Ortiz held the gun and stared silently, his eyes glassy and intent. A single thought formed in Erika's mind: I'm going to die.

"Please don't shoot me," she told Ortiz.

Then something inside her snapped. A decade of living and surviving on the streets of Laredo had forged an instinct to, if threatened, lash out first, explore other options later. She lunged at the steering wheel, attempting to honk the truck's horn, and pushed open the passenger-side door. "Help me!" she screamed out the open door. Ortiz reached over and grabbed a handful of Erika's blouse with his right hand, his left hand still aiming the pistol at her chest. They struggled; his grip was strong, but it had more purchase on the blouse than her shoulder. She squirmed and fought and twisted her way out of the blouse and jumped out of the truck's passenger-side door. Suddenly, she was on the street, shirtless, the night breeze touching her bare shoulders. "Help me!" she screamed again, and she ran, as hard and fast as she could, toward the lights, toward the Circle K, and away from the man with the gun.

Just before 9:00 p.m., she emerged from behind the store. Her arms were crossed over her chest and her head pivoted from side to side, looking for Ortiz and his white truck. She asked a person loitering in front of the Circle K, the first person she saw, for help. He pointed her to the black Texas DPS SUV parked at pump number four and the trooper standing beside it. Erika walked up to him, arms still covering her chest, struggling to form words and keep her breath from galloping away from her. Trooper Francisco Hernandez, a thirteen-year veteran of the force, calmly listened.

As she unspooled her story, most of it coming out in Spanish, Erika nudged herself toward the open driver's door of the trooper's SUV, as if wanting to disappear into the dark safety inside. Hernandez asked her to move aside so he could reach his radio. He called in the incident: assault on a woman. "Tranquila," he told her. *Relax.*

Trooper and victim spoke for forty minutes at pump number four, sliding effortlessly between Spanish and English and, at times, a hybrid of both. Erika's head swiveled left and right endlessly, looking for Ortiz's truck. Her breath noisily gusted in and out, in and out.

"Tengo miedo, sir," Erika said as she leaned against the pump's concrete pillar. "He has a gun."

"Don't worry about it," Hernandez said. "You're safe right now. Estás bien."

Perhaps it was the trauma of having a gun drawn on her, the heroin clouding her thoughts, or the innate instinct to not totally trust law enforcement—or a mix of all three—but Erika changed her story in small but substantive ways as she told it to Hernandez. She said the person she knew only as "David" had picked her up downtown earlier that evening and bought cigarettes and beer with her before offering to take her on a drive, omitting the dramatic scene at his house. She did say, however, she knew where Ortiz lived and could take authorities there. Perplexingly, she also repeatedly called Ortiz an "oil field worker," even though she knew him to be a Border Patrol agent.

Her words rambled from one turn in the story to the next, at times colliding into one another. She talked about how David liked to cruise Sanber and had picked her up there, how he offered to buy her a hamburger, how she had jumped out of her own blouse to save her life. Hernandez strained to follow the story. "Just take deep breaths," he instructed her.

Erika asked for a cigarette; he said he didn't smoke. "Cigarettes are bad for you right now," Hernandez told her.

Then Erika, still struggling to catch her breath and organize her thoughts, told Hernandez what she and Ortiz had talked about that night.

"We started talking about the muchachas que acaban de fallecer," she said.

A light flickered in Hernandez's mind.

"¿Las que dumpiaron allá?" he said.

"Sí."

Earlier in the week, Hernandez, along with a handful of other DPS troopers, had been recruited to help Calderon and Salinas on the "knock-and-talks" around San Bernardo. He had interviewed a resident of a home who allegedly knew Melissa well. Not much came out of it, but the exercise had awarded him valuable insight into Laredo's top murder investigation. He knew all too well what Erika was referring to.

He asked her to stay by his vehicle and relax.

"Let me just check something."

Hernandez knew what to do with the information, but since they were within Laredo city limits, protocol was to call Laredo police first, which he did. He called in an assault on a woman at the Valero gas station. The Laredo police dispatcher told him a unit was on the way.

Five minutes passed. Then ten, fifteen. After waiting eighteen minutes with no sign of Laredo PD, and Erika growing increasingly fidgety, he pulled out his cell phone and texted Salinas.

CHAPTER 13

Ortiz watched as Erika ran through the dark parking lot and disappeared around the Circle K. He was faced with two options: go after her or flee. He chose the latter.

He pulled the passenger-side door closed, revved the Dodge truck out of the gas station, and made the quick five-minute drive back to his house. Ortiz entered his empty home and cracked open another Bud Light tallboy, chugging it, hoping the beer could dilute the anger and panic. Why had Erika brought up Melissa? Why had he pulled a gun on her? She was different from the others; they had a connection. His mind raced back to his last night with Melissa, how Erika saw them together at the drug house.

She knew. *She knew.*

Sharp pain radiated from his neck. Erika would surely go to the police, and those officers would be knocking on his door at any moment. Ortiz had killed two women and pulled a gun on a third. When police come, he thought, they won't be doing so with polite smiles and handshakes. They'll be wielding their own hardware. He was now the hunted.

"Fuck this shit," he muttered to himself. "Fuck. This."

He stomped through the home, gathering and loading his weapons.

9:20 P.M., FRIDAY, SEPTEMBER 14

Calderon and Salinas were at the substation on Highway 59, resigned to another long night of poring over interview transcripts and prioritizing leads. Calderon hadn't had a full night's sleep in a week. His days consisted of arriving early to the substation, planning out which people to try to reach or section of Laredo to canvass, interviewing a variety of different leads, returning to the substation and working through paperwork and databases until past midnight. Then starting again the next morning. The case had consumed him. So far, the effort had yielded frustratingly little. They had approached or interviewed about sixty people, but none had led to a workable lead. They were encouraged by the initial reaction Chon Treviño had when police visited his home, but that proved to be a dead end as well. Calderon couldn't remember the last time he had worked so hard on a case and gained so little. Now, with the discovery of a second body, there was pressure to find whoever was doing it before they struck again.

Just then, a text message pinged in Salinas's phone. It was Trooper Hernandez. He called him back. Hernandez told the ranger he was standing at a Valero gas station in north Laredo with a woman dressed in a bra and jeans who allegedly had just been assaulted by a gunman. The woman knew Melissa and Claudine.

"She mentioned something about the other two girls, and that's when the guy got nervous," Hernandez told Salinas. "She knows who they are, esas muchachas."

"Bring her in," Salinas instructed.

9:30 P.M.

Ortiz surveyed the weaponry spread across his kitchen island: a Beretta Px4 Storm 9mm pistol, his agency-issued H&K .40 handgun, and a Bushmaster AR-15 semiautomatic rifle. He yanked back sliders and checked magazines, making sure they were fully loaded, safety buttons off. He glanced around briefly for his twelve-gauge single-shot Remington shotgun but couldn't remember where he had left it. (It was propped, undisturbed, in a corner of his garage.) From a stash of more than fifty boxes of bullets in his garage, acquired over a decade in law enforcement, he also pulled out a box of Federal-brand .40-caliber jacketed hollow-point rounds, a box of extra ammo for the AR-15 rifle, and a box of 9mm bullets. All told, between chambers, clips, and boxes, Ortiz had amassed more than one hundred rounds of ammunition on his kitchen island.

If they wanted him, they would need to penetrate a fusillade of flying lead to reach him. He sat, sipped his beer, and waited for the first knock.

9:55 P.M.

Erika Peña emerged from Trooper Hernandez's SUV in the back parking bay of the Webb County Sheriff's Office substation, shivering and shirtless. Though she was at the sheriff's substation, surrounded by deputies and troopers, she still feared for her life, scared that her tormentor would somehow find her and finish the job he had started. It was hard to shake the image of the gun pointed inches away from her—the same gun, she was now sure, used to kill her two friends.

Someone found her an oversized white T-shirt from within the substation, and Erika pulled it on. Just outside the substation, under an aluminum awning, she recounted the events of the night with as much detail as her rattled, drug-clouded mind could muster. She spoke clearly and animatedly, raising her voice enough to be heard over the steady drumming of rain on the tin roof overhead. Calderon and Salinas listened intently to her story, which this time included the trip to Ortiz's house. She told them about meeting Ortiz on San Bernardo that night, stopping for beer and cigarettes, then driving to his house, and the way his mood shifted when she mentioned Melissa and Claudine. Her story flowed so freely, and credibly, that investigators decided to keep her outside and talking. Erika again asked for a cigarette—*pleaded* this time—and Calderon produced a pack of Marlboros for her. Erika nervously shifted her weight from one foot to the other, chain-smoked cigarettes, and retold her story for detectives, reliving how crazed Ortiz had appeared at the mention of her two friends. She would pause occasionally to take a long, shuddering breath or pull on her lit cigarette. Every few minutes, she'd cover her face with her hands and sob.

Calderon and Salinas stole glances at each other. After ten days and more than sixty interviews, this was the best lead they had. Gliding between English and Spanish, they asked her to repeat parts of the story, making sure they understood the details. Erika still only knew him as "David," but she was fairly sure she could lead them to his house. She remembered one cross street in his neighborhood: "Chisom," or possibly "Chisos." Calderon pulled up the map app on his iPhone and zoomed in on the area just east of the Valero station. He showed it to Erika. Together they spotted Chisos Oak Drive in the San Isidro neighborhood. The house was right around there, she told investigators.

"We'll get there," Calderon assured her. "I think I know where that is."

They spoke with Erika for more than an hour under the awning outside of the substation. When she was done, detectives hatched a plan: Erika would ride with investigators in one vehicle around Ortiz's general neighborhood and try to point them to the house. Calderon and Salinas would follow in Salinas's truck, while two more deputies would trail in a third vehicle. They were not yet prepared to knock on his front door; confronting an armed murder suspect would require significantly more manpower and weaponry. For now, they just wanted the house—and a potential ID.

The three-car convoy pulled away from the substation and drove south on Highway 59, heading toward the San Isidro neighborhood.

10:30 P.M.

Ortiz waited. And waited and waited and waited. After more than an hour, when the knock bringing the posse of lawmen to his doorstep never materialized, he reconsidered his options. The buzz of confronting a team of police officers in a final, violent firefight faded, replaced by a new realization: Maybe he *had* gotten away with everything after all. Maybe Erika didn't go to the police. There was some logic to that theory.

Erika wasn't like the other women. She was special; they had definitely shared moments that transcended the typical sex-for-cash transaction. She wouldn't rat him out. She'd keep her mouth shut and return to life on San Bernardo.

Maybe this was a sign. Maybe he had a higher calling that had less to do with sexual gratification and more with stepping in where Laredo police, vice squads, and the courts had all failed. Ortiz locked up his house again and got back into his white Dodge Ram pickup, his mind swimming with the buzz of multiple tallies and the growing courage from having dodged his own demise. He hatched a new plan. But first things first. He drove along Crepusculo Drive and out of the San Isidro neighborhood, crossed busy Bob Bullock Loop, and pulled into the Murphy Express gas station across from the Walmart. He parked at a pump and marched across the lot and into the convenience store. Dressed in jeans, a long-sleeved khaki button-down shirt, and a camouflage cap, Ortiz walked to the ice cooler, pulled out three more Budweiser tallboys, paid for the beer and a pack of Marlboro Special Blend cigarettes with a credit card, and left.

He pointed the Dodge Ram toward Interstate 35, then south toward San Bernardo. It was nearing midnight and the workers would be out. This time, he wasn't going for sex.

11:15 P.M.

The caravan of Calderon, Salinas, Erika Peña, and a bevy of other law enforcement agents wound itself through the San Isidro neighborhood, along Crepusculo Drive and Spanish Oak Drive, passing stucco homes with closely cropped lawns that would appear nearly identical to anyone else. Erika sat in the back seat of an unmarked white Chevy Tahoe, used by sheriff's deputies for undercover operations. Two sheriff's deputies sat up front; Erika was wedged in the middle of the back seat between Trooper Hernandez, the DPS trooper who had driven her away from her encounter with Ortiz, and a crime victim coordinator. Their instructions were to find the house and, if any threat emerged, to protect Erika at all costs and speed her away at the first sign of trouble. She directed the Tahoe to turn left here, right there, winding through the quiet neighborhood. As they neared Ortiz's street, Hernandez rolled down his rear window so Erika could get a better look. She leaned toward the open window, peering at the homes. The Tahoe pulled onto Bur Oak Drive. "¡Ahí está!" She pointed to a house.

The Tahoe slowly rolled past the cream-and-brown single-story Texas-style ranch home. Erika looked out the back seat window. The puddle of her vomitus was still visible on the sidewalk, congealing in the warm night. "Sí, esa casa," she told the team in the Tahoe. She was sure of it. Sergeant Joe Peña, driving the vehicle, radioed Calderon and Salinas, who were trailing them in Salinas's pickup truck. They now had an address: 204 Bur Oak Drive.

There was no white Dodge truck in the driveway, and the three law enforcement vehicles rolled past the home and came to a stop down the street. Using a browser on his iPhone, Calderon punched the address into the Webb County Appraisal District Property Search site. The name of the homeowner populated in the results field: Juan David Ortiz, along with his date of birth. Sergeant Peña, who was head of the CID's cybercrimes team, ran the name through a law enforcement database on a laptop from inside the Tahoe and found a driver's license number for Ortiz, while Hernandez obtained his driver's license photo through another database. The photo showed Ortiz with short dark hair, a round face, and intent dark eyes staring blankly back at the camera. Detectives caught a troubling detail on the driver's license. In all caps, just under the license's expiration date, was written: "VETERAN." They were dealing with someone who knew how to handle a weapon and may have had combat experience. Peña showed the driver's license photo to Erika. "That's him," she said, without the slightest hesitation. They had their suspect.

Peña radioed the lead investigators about the positive identification, then drove Erika back to the substation. Calderon and Salinas parked down the street and settled into the truck's cab, waiting to see if anyone entered or emerged from Ortiz's home.

Perched in the front seat of the ranger's Dodge truck, Salinas and Calderon marveled at the recent turn of events. Less than an hour ago, they were nearing the eleventh day of a double murder investigation with dozens of leads and names but no suspect or theory, other than a killer was preying on the sex workers of San Bernardo. Now, suddenly, they had a name, an address, a driver's license, and a photo of perhaps their strongest suspect yet. At 12:07 a.m., they issued another BOLO—the third of the investigation. This time it was for Juan David Ortiz. The bulletin included a description of the truck, the license plate number, and Ortiz's Texas driver's license photo. It also warned agents that Ortiz was "armed and dangerous." The Webb County sheriff's radio dispatch put out the BOLO, pinging it into the radios of the two hundred or so deputies in the county, then notified DPS dispatch, which sent out its own BOLO, alerting several hundred troopers in the Webb–Starr–Jim Hogg County area. More than four hundred local and state law enforcement agents were now on the hunt for Ortiz's white 2015 Dodge Ram 2500 truck, license plate number 324885DV.

Salinas ordered several DPS troopers to patrol the area around San Bernardo and look for the suspect, as well as the I-35 corridor around the Webb County Exchange, where he took past victims. Webb County sheriff's deputies were also dispatched to the area. Salinas also called the BIC requesting U.S. customs officials detain Ortiz at any U.S.-Mexico crossing or at the CBP checkpoint on I-35 north of town.

Sitting in Salinas's truck, still working on the faulty info given by Erika that Ortiz was an oil field worker, Calderon and Salinas pondered their latest suspect. Did he work seven days on, seven days off, as most oil field workers in the region did? And if so, was he currently on one of his leaves? They tried puzzling out how he targeted the women and when he might vanish into an oil field again. Or had he already left to his oil field job, and, if so, how long before he reemerged in Laredo? If he lived in Laredo, he most likely worked in the Eagle Ford Shale, a Cretaceous-age underground rock formation spreading four hundred miles from the U.S.-Mexico border near Laredo to just east of Waco, where oil and natural gas were extracted. But for which company? The whole time, the investigators kept their eyes glued to 204 Bur Oak Drive, waiting for a white Dodge truck to pull up.

If their intent was to stealthily monitor Ortiz's house, they weren't entirely successful. The unmarked truck with two men huddled inside, the glow of cell phone screens and vehicle instruments lighting their faces, drew the attention of neighbors, one of whom called the police. A Laredo police officer drove up alongside Calderon and Salinas and asked what the men were up to. The investigators rolled down their window, flashed ID badges, and explained they were on a stakeout. The officer nodded and drove off.

After over an hour on stakeout, with the house as dark and still as when they first arrived, the two detectives left as well.

CHAPTER 14

Sara Sotelo was losing patience.

Her mom, Guiselda Alicia "Chelly" Cantu, thirty-five, had just broken up with her latest boyfriend, known to most as "Bebo," and she cried as she recounted the split to Sara. She told Sara, twenty-one, how much the man meant to her and how this time he had really gone, leaving her alone with a strangling heroin addiction and the daily risks of turning tricks along San Bernardo. Chelly had been eking out a living as a sex worker on the avenue for more than two decades and had grown a tough emotional veneer, but this latest breakup seemed to shatter her.

Sara wanted to comfort her, but she also despised when her mother weakened over men. Especially *this* one. To nearly all Chelly's friends, Bebo was a deadbeat: perpetually unemployed, unable to raise even a few illicit dollars and mooching on Chelly's meek income from sexual trysts to feed his own heroin habit. But there was a connection between Chelly and Bebo few understood, born of enduring together daily threats of violence, homelessness, sickness, and heroin withdrawal. They had fought in the past—Chelly once slapped him across the face, urging him to earn his keep—but this latest one had raged out of control, and he had walked. Now, Chelly felt truly alone.

"Mom, fuck him," Sara told Chelly in the room the two shared. "You don't fucking need him."

Sara, fifteen years younger than her mom, had grown up with foster parents after Chelly hit the streets. Recently, unable to hold down a job and stifled by her own crack cocaine addiction, Sara had joined her mom turning tricks around San Bernardo Avenue. The two shared friends, drug connections, and, lately, a small $400-a-month detached room with a single bed in a home in central Laredo. They had become closer while on the streets, sharing dreams of cleaning up and reconnecting with their children: Chelly with her three other children, all of whom lived with relatives or foster parents; Sara with her one-year-old son, Angel, also in foster care. Chelly even offered to pay for Sara's latest tattoo: "Hope," written in cursive on her left wrist, framed by vines and flowers. But they also fought, sometimes viciously, as Sara had little patience for her mom's dependence on men. That day, as her mom mourned the loss of Bebo, she felt that familiar anger rising.

Chelly asked her daughter for a hug, but Sara was annoyed. She ordered her mom to "get your shit together."

"But I love him," Chelly said.

"Okay, I understand. But he's a fucking asshole."

Sara didn't understand why Chelly couldn't just drop her need for him and other guys. The streets were tough, but they could navigate them on their own, together, as mother and daughter.

"I don't like you crying all the time," Sara told her mom.

She got dressed and left the apartment. It was getting dark and time to hit the avenue. Chelly was depleted. She wanted to stop this endless cycle of drugs and sex, but heroin had its claws in her. She missed her kids, and the lesions along her legs and arms had turned into painful, pus-weeping wounds. But nothing—*nothing*—was worse than the agony of withdrawal.

A little later, Chelly dressed and left as well, hoping to score a few more clients.

══

CHELLY WAS BORN INTO WHAT, BY MOST MEASURES, WAS A CARing, albeit unorthodox, family. Her mother, Sara Alicia Cantu, was still in her twenties when she had Chelly and her older brother, José "Joey" Cantu, by two different men. Chelly's dad, Gustavo Montemayor, originally from Mexico, cycled between the two countries and wasn't around in the early years of her life. Sara doted on her children and was supported by a platoon of cousins and relatives in South Texas. But the young family shattered in 1985.

Early on the morning of September 7, 1985, with Chelly just two years old, Sara Alicia Cantu was shot once in the head with a .22 revolver. Still breathing, she was rushed to Mercy Regional Medical Center but died from her wound about an hour later. *Laredo Morning Times* ran a story on its front page the next morning on the incident, revealing that police had arrested a thirty-seven-year-old oil field worker in the shooting. It said police suspected Cantu's murder "was possibly the result of a domestic problem." The following day, the paper ran an even smaller story on page six listing survivors and funeral details. There was no further mention of the suspect or whether he was ever indicted for the shooting.

Abruptly parentless, Chelly and Joey moved in with their maternal grandmother, Ramona Cantu, in her six-hundred-square-foot trailer home in El Trompe, a working-class neighborhood that housed many of Laredo's recent arrivals from Mexico, as well as an array of drug dens and stash houses. Youth gangs and drug runners ran the streets. Lacking parental supervision, Joey and Chelly grew up by the rules of their hardscrabble neighborhood. They played tag in the street and walked along the dry bed of Zacate Creek three and a half miles north to the newly renovated Mall del Norte. On Easter and Christmas, Ramona would drive them to an uncle's ranch outside San Antonio, where they would scramble up trees, play hide-and-seek until dark, and have epic water balloon fights with their cousins. Chelly smiled often. Joey adored his sister's laugh, a high-pitched guttural guffaw that reminded him of cartoon hyenas.

After serving time in a Mexican prison, Gustavo Montemayor resettled in Laredo and tried to rekindle a relationship with his daughter. He showed up to birthday parties and bought her dresses. Chelly as a young girl was obsessed with ballet. Her father would watch her at dance recitals and listened to her dreams of one day becoming a ballerina. But he was married to another woman by then, and most of his focus remained with that family.

In El Trompe, Chelly and Joey learned to stick together. When kids tried to bully Joey, Chelly stepped in and chased them off, flashing a ferocity few wanted any part of. Once, when Joey was in fifth grade, a classmate took his trompo—a spinning top-like toy—sending Joey into tears. Chelly stalked over, snatched the toy back for Joey, and beat the kid until *he* cried. But under the toughness hid a softer Chelly that few people got to witness. Seeing someone sad or watching an emotional movie would often send her into crying fits, a habit that trailed her into adulthood.

As he got older (and bigger), Joey learned to take care of himself. He started hanging out with a neighborhood gang and getting into fist-fights. The carefree days of water balloon fights at his uncle's ranch near San Antonio faded into memory. Now, an inexplicable anger and hate filled him most days, surfacing in frequent fights with other kids on the block. By the time he was fifteen, Joey was a stocky five feet five inches and 193 pounds of mostly muscle and could put a hurting on anyone who crossed him. He gained a reputation in El Trompe as someone who had your back if he was your friend and someone you didn't want to cross if he wasn't.

In July 1996, a friend told Joey that the friend's mother was being physically abused by a man she was dating. The two teens, plus a third friend, lured the thirty-eight-year-old man to a backyard cookout, then jumped him, beating him with bricks, cement blocks, and dumbbell bars. The man died from his injuries, and Joey was arrested and charged with homicide.

At fifteen, he was tried as an adult and sentenced to forty years in prison for murder. He spent a few years in the Webb County Jail before being sent away to the William G. McConnell Unit state prison in Bee-ville, Texas, sixty miles north of Corpus Christi. Joey's childhood was over and Chelly's best friend wrenched away from her.

=====

CHELLY'S LIFE BEGAN TO UNRAVEL. AROUND THE TIME OF JOEY'S conviction, she was at the house of a family friend when the man slipped her a pill. She passed out and woke up with blood on her undergarments. She had clearly been raped. She went home and told her grand-mother. What happened next is unclear and the subject of conjecture, as Chelly later told different versions of the same story to different people. To some, including Joey, she said that no one believed her story of being sexually assaulted, a lack of trust that weighed on her for years to come. To others, she said that after she told her grandmother, her grandfather had marched her back to the family friend's house, had her identify her assailant, then shot and killed the man in front of her. Whichever ending is accurate, there's no debating the incident left her emotionally marred.

In middle school, she began experimenting with drugs, starting with marijuana and Xanax and escalating to the heroin proliferating through Laredo at the time. She was partying and hanging with rowdy crowds, returning late to her abuela's trailer, if at all. At fifteen, she gave birth to Sara, followed by Juan a year later, and, a few years after that, Brianna and then Jacob. At each birth, Texas Child Protective Services placed the baby in foster care or had them adopted by family members; Chelly's lifestyle was deemed unconducive to parenting. She dropped out of high school and plunged deeper into drug use. She bounced in and out of rehab. Nothing seemed to work.

In 1998, while Joey was still being held at the Webb County Jail in Laredo on homicide charges, Chelly paid her brother a visit, carry-ing tiny, chubby Sara, then just a few months old. Joey cooed over his new niece, and Chelly played with her as well. The two siblings didn't say much to each other, the enormity of Joey's fate pressing on them. At the end of the visit, Joey told Chelly he loved her and was led away in manacles. He didn't know it at the time, but it was the last time he'd ever see her in person.

——

As Joey was transferred to state prison, Chelly hit the streets, the start of what would become a two-decade odyssey through the motel rooms and drug dens along San Bernardo Avenue. Berto

Ramirez first met Chelly while he was still in school. She was older and already well entrenched in the trap houses of El Trompe and San Bernardo. At the time, Berto was dealing with a heavy heroin habit. One day, he ran out of money and chiva and was shivering through withdrawal. Chelly, who had just met Berto, saw him suffering on the couch of a friend's house. "I'll be right back," she told him. She left and returned shortly with a foil filled with heroin. She cooked up the substance, drew it into a clean syringe, and injected it into Berto, easing his pain. "She was just like that," he remembered. "She helped us a lot."

Even as the streets hardened her, Chelly retained a vulnerable interior. Meli Rodriguez, a close friend and fellow sex worker, said she was impressed by how Chelly would tell off a rude client, yelling and shaming him until he slinked away. And if someone crossed her—friend or foe—she was ready to beat her point across with flying fists. But when they would get high, a state of euphoric pleasure for most, Chelly would often dissolve into sobs. They'd mix heroin with cocaine and smoke freebase cocaine. Where others "glided" away into their euphoric state, Chelly would cry and say how much she missed her children, how much she wanted to stop using drugs and get her life in order. "She was very deep inside," Meli said.

In February 2013, Chelly was picked up by Laredo police on eleven counts of forging checks. She was ordered to serve two years behind bars and transferred to the Lucile Plane State Jail for women, just outside Houston. For most people on the streets, it would've been a debilitating blow, a prolonged roadblock to income and daily activities. But Chelly cherished the lockup. She saw it as a chance to detox, albeit through painful withdrawals, and think clearly again. She wrote to her brother, Joey, at his state prison in Beeville. The incarcerated siblings struck up a correspondence, each receiving two to three letters a week from the other. They lamented about the paths their lives had taken, the family members they'd let down, and pondered what forces had led them down such dark paths. "I don't know what happened," Chelly wrote to her brother. "I just started feeling angry all the time, and hateful."

Joey could relate. For as long as he could remember, he harbored a similar swelling of hate and loathing that seemed to arise out of no-where. It began on the streets of El Trompe in Laredo and carried over to his early years in prison, where he joined a gang and used violence to resolve any perceived transgressions against him. Midway through his sentence, however, his life took a sharp turn. One day, for no particular reason, he wandered into a session of God Behind Bars, a faith-based group that ministers to incarcerated individuals. The music emanating from the ministry brought him to tears. He felt something unlock in him, and the pain and anger, which had ruled his life for so long, be-gan to recede. The next day, he quit the prison gang he was affiliated with and turned to the Bible. He began dwelling in forgiveness and love rather than revenge and hate.

Joey counseled Chelly as best he could through their letters, describ-ing his change of heart and urging her to exercise patience and stay off drugs. But he knew she needed help. He felt reborn with a new mission in life: stay out of trouble and get released from prison so he could help his sister get off the streets. Chelly wrote to her brother how much she wanted to quit heroin. She vowed to do her best to stay off it for good this time, reconnect with her children, and live a better life.

After she was released in 2017, however, the opiate's pull again took over. Within weeks, she was back on San Bernardo Avenue.

—————

GUSTAVO MONTEMAYOR HAD GROWN ALARMED AT HIS DAUGH-ter's condition. He would cruise around the city and find her sleeping under a bridge on a flattened cardboard box or sitting on a bus bench on San Bernardo, waiting for clients. She'd show up at his house in east Laredo when she needed cash for food or rent, and Gustavo would give her money or buy her dinner. He urged her to try rehab again. Nothing worked. Desperate, Gustavo turned to his older brother, Javier "Javi" Montemayor, for help. The two had met only as adults, having the same dad but different mothers. Javi, then sixty-two, had struggled with his own addiction to heroin and cocaine but had been drug-free for two years and was taking methadone to help with the opioid cravings. He knew the area and characters around San Bernardo well. He lived in a lean-to on Flores Avenue, just two blocks west of San Bernardo, with his elderly mother, Angela. Javi had never met Chelly but assured his brother he would look for her and try to help.

Javi and Chelly met one day near Javi's house. Javi considered himself a veteran of the run-down characters of San Bernardo, but Chelly's appearance stunned even him. Her cheeks were sallow and sunken, her hair stringy, and the stench emanating from her legs made him wince. Still, he saw a glint in Chelly's brown eyes, and she gave off an inner warmth that was rare among the avenue's sex workers. Javi also sympathized with San Bernardo's most downtrodden characters, having been through its darkest valleys himself. Chelly immediately called him "tío," and the two kicked off a friendship. Soon after, she moved into the small apartment with Javi and his mother.

Javi gently urged her to get off heroin. But having gone through the process himself, he knew nagging her wouldn't work; he had to gain her trust. He counseled her on the ways of the addict and offered small tips, such as always saving a pinch of chiva for the morning, when withdrawal symptoms hit the hardest. He offered to pay for an occasional fix—but only if she showered and cleaned her legs first. "I taught her how to manage her time, manage her life," he said. Javi was careful never to criticize her lifestyle or put down her appearance.

He allowed Chelly to bring friends over to their tiny abode and shoot up inside, preferring to have his niece there than in some dark lot somewhere. He was alarmed at how much Chelly was shooting up; she would cook enough junk to knock out someone twice her size—then double the amount and inject it. He cautioned her to reduce the amount of each fix, even if it meant increasing the frequency. She slowly heeded her uncle's advice.

Javi got to know Melissa and Claudine, too. As others did, he found Melissa to be erratic and Claudine to be sweet and wise beyond her years. When not partying, Javi and Chelly spent hours watching Martha Stewart's *Martha Bakes* and other shows on TV. She talked to him about missing her children, about her desires to get off drugs and return to a normal life. She told him about her adolescent rape. She also revealed, in detail, some of her recurring nightmares. In one, an angry leprechaun, his face scarred by burn marks, tugged at her blanket until she woke up, then vanished into a hole in the wall.

═══

In July 2017, Javi began struggling with a withering cough and had trouble breathing. A stroll across a room would send him into coughing spasms. He initially refused to visit a doctor, but Chelly pleaded with him to seek medical attention. He finally relented, and Chelly accompanied him to the emergency room of a nearby hospital. There, doctors found stage 4 cancer in his kidney, liver, lungs, and pancreas. They told him he had roughly four months to live. As Javi wallowed on his hospital bed, pondering the short life left in him and whether he would die alone, Chelly visited him each day. She brought him his favorite lunch from Wendy's: a single cheeseburger with jalapeños and fries. She stayed with him as he was wheeled in and out of intensive care and was by his side for all twelve days he was in the hospital. Finally, doctors told Javi they were transferring him to a hospital in Dallas to continue treatment. He said goodbye to his niece, and they promised to stay in touch.

Chelly resumed her life on San Bernardo. She met and started dating Bebo. The two moved into the Relax Inn together. Berto Ramirez and his girlfriend, Iris, were also staying at the Relax Inn, and he was initially happy to see her again. He never forgot how generous she had been to him when they first met years ago. Pat, the Relax Inn's manager, also liked having Chelly there. She paid on time and respected the property. The legs, however, were a growing problem.

CHAPTER 15

Years of heroin use had caused Chelly's veins to severely retreat, and she increasingly turned to skin-popping to deliver the drug into her system. Many users along San Bernardo bore scars from longtime heroin use; none had it worse than Chelly. Both her legs, from ankles to upper thighs, were covered in painful, blistery scars, as bacteria infected and consumed nearly every inch of her lower extremities. Though never diagnosed, Chelly likely had necrotizing fasciitis, also known as "flesh-eating disease." Her legs reeked of rotting meat, and a gaping wound yawned just under her left knee, revealing pink flesh to the bone, like the open mouth of a shark. The pain in her legs was so severe that Chelly tiptoed rather than walked everywhere to lessen the impact of her feet hitting the ground.

Pat Roth, the manager at the Relax Inn, liked how Chelly respected the property and protected him and Nora from the more unscrupulous characters around town. She was also one of the few sex workers in his orbit who would pay back the money he lent them. But secretions from her legs were ruining the linens in her room. Finally, Nora gave Chelly a set of personal towels. Cleaning staff were directed to wash those towels periodically for her and return them only to Chelly's room. They were taken out of general circulation.

Berto and Iris were happy to connect with Chelly again at the Relax Inn. They had been clean from heroin for months and knew it was risky being in such close contact with active users, but they took a chance with them. Despite the smell from her legs, they socialized with Chelly, sharing beers and gossip. Chelly would leave each night from 7:00 p.m. to 6:00 a.m. and tiptoe the streets around San Bernardo and San Agustin, hunting for clients. Before she left each evening, Iris would wrap her legs in blue plastic and tape them down, so their smell wouldn't offend potential clients.

Despite her tenacity, however, money dried up. A growing percentage of it was going to chiva, less to rent or food. Pat lost his patience with Chelly and her unemployable boyfriend. After one too many missed payments, he kicked them out of their $50-a-night room at the Relax Inn. Facing homelessness, Chelly and her boyfriend turned to Berto and Iris. The couple, again, opened their room to them, allowing them to move into room 111. Chelly and Bebo would sleep on blankets on the floor, while Iris got them extra pillows from the hotel's laundry room. But the arrangement was short-lived. Constant drug use and the stench from Chelly's legs became too overbearing. Berto wanted to help his friend when she was in need, but he felt he had no choice. He asked Chelly to leave.

Just before leaving, Chelly and Bebo had a drawn-out fight, and he left her. She was now homeless and alone.

=====

As Chelly struggled to keep a roof over her head, Joey Cantu prepared to leave prison. Years of good behavior and his newfound focus on religion had earned him an early release. On June 18, 2018, Joey walked out of the McConnell Unit unshackled, eighteen years earlier than his full sentence. He was far from a free man, however. He was still on parole, needed to wear an ankle monitor, and couldn't stray far from home without prior approval from his probation officer, unless he was going to court-mandated Alcoholics Anonymous meetings at a nearby church. But he was outside the walls and system that had raised him since boyhood. He had walked in an angry, scared teenager and walked out a thirty-seven-year-old man, hardened by more than two decades of prison but sober, brimming with God's love, and motivated to get his little sister off the streets.

After moving into his aunt's house in north Laredo, Joey called

Chelly via FaceTime on his aunt's phone. He barely recognized the woman who answered the video call. Chelly's face was sallow and hardened from years of drug use; her eyes, once dancing with light and laughter, were droopy and dark. He could see scars and ulcers on nearly every inch of exposed flesh. Her smile, though, hadn't changed. Chelly told her big brother she was happy he was out of prison and couldn't wait to see him again.

Joey became rejuvenated with the prospect of reconnecting with his sister, though his freedom of movement was limited. His family was also keen on limiting Joey's contact with Chelly, fearing her lifestyle would complicate his parole and land him back in prison. Even without all the limitations, connecting with Chelly would be a continual challenge. She had long ago lost (or sold) her cell phone and relied on the phones of friends or clients for contact with her family. Joey managed to chat with Chelly through occasional FaceTime or Facebook Messenger sessions via phones of friends. They would chat about their days, and Joey would urge her to meet him somewhere. He knew seeing her in person would be a major step to getting her off the streets. Chelly deflected his invitations, saying she was embarrassed to have him see her in her present condition, embarrassed mostly of her legs.

"Dude, I don't care," Joey told her. "You're my little sister."

One day, as they talked on the phone, he asked her to meet him at one of his AA meetings at the Laredo First Assembly of God Church on McPherson Road. To his surprise, she agreed. It would be the first time the siblings would see each other in person in twenty-two years. Joey arrived at the church early and waited outside by the parking lot. One minute stretched into the next, which stretched into an hour. Chelly never showed.

Joey was resigned to seeing his sister through occasional FaceTime chats and worrying constantly about her. He needed her to hold on for a few more months, until his house arrest lifted and he was able to travel more freely. Then he'd seek her out and, slowly, surely, extract her from the streets. It became his life's top focus.

After being kicked out of the Relax Inn, Chelly turned to Sara. The two reconnected, and Chelly moved into the room in the house Sara had been renting. She told Sara about breaking up with Bebo, how it stung but how she realized he was just draining her of emotion and money. The room she shared with Sara was smaller even than the room at the Relax Inn but cheaper, and there was less pressure to come up with room rent every single night. If she caught a good streak, she could make her half of rent over the course of just a few days. Chelly mostly offered clients oral sex, as the condition of her legs wouldn't allow much more. Her legs were often a deterrent, but her wit, charm, and face won her a stock of repeat clients.

Sara enjoyed the long chats she had with her mother, how they both recognized street life was ruining their lives and strategized how to leave it all behind someday. They argued, but Sara realized she had gained a best friend with Chelly, one of the few people along the avenue she could fully trust.

Strangely, Chelly didn't say much to Sara about the murders of first Melissa and later Claudine. Sara knew them both as well and was saddened by the news of their deaths. After news of Claudine, Chelly urged Sara not to go out. But Chelly knew her own heroin habit wouldn't wait for the police to catch up with a killer. She needed money and needed it soon.

In May 2018, Gustavo Montemayor had a vivid dream that involved Chelly's mom, Sara. He hadn't seen the mother of his daughter in more than thirty years, yet here she was in his dream, resplendent in a white gown, floating toward him, embracing him. She never spoke, but somehow he knew she was there to take Chelly. He woke up not alarmed but comforted. Chelly's suffering would soon end, he thought, and she'd be with her mother. It wasn't the worst thought in the world. He never told Chelly about the dream.

Four months later, on Thursday, September 13, Chelly walked the two miles from San Bernardo to her grandmother's trailer in El Trompe, where Montemayor was visiting. Chelly looked in worse shape than usual. She was unbathed, and her face was hard and weathered. Her eyes sagged and were ringed by bluish bags. She asked her dad for $20. Montemayor couldn't do it anymore; he was done feeding the habit that had brought so much ruin to his daughter's life. He refused to give it to her.

Chelly turned and walked off. Montemayor sensed it may be the last time he'd see his daughter alive.

The following evening, on Friday, September 14, still stinging from the breakup with Bebo, Chelly was back on her usual corner of San Agustin Avenue and Ugarte Street, cajoling potential clients and hoping for a score. Just before midnight, as Calderon and Salinas were typing up the BOLO on Ortiz, a white Dodge pickup rolled up to the corner.

Chelly climbed inside, and the truck drove off.

═══

THE SMELL HIT HIM INSTANTLY.

Ortiz didn't know Chelly and was unprepared for the stench emanating up from his passenger's legs and filling the cab of his truck. He lowered his window.

Blood trickled from a corner of Chelly's mouth, and she complained that she had just been picked up by a man in a black truck who had struck her. It wasn't the first time it had happened; some clients felt deceived after picking up Chelly and noticing the condition of her legs, while others didn't care as much. "Me dió un chingazo," she said to Ortiz, pointing to her lip. "Mira."

Ortiz listened to Chelly's chatter, but the words barely registered. He was focused on the task at hand. Still buzzing from the events of the night—pulling a gun on Erika Peña and having her run off at the Valero gas station—and the alcohol from three Budweiser tallboys, Ortiz's resolve hardened to rid the city of what he deemed "undesirables," starting with the reeking sex worker next to him. Rain thumped the windshield as he drove north on Interstate 35 and pulled off at the Mile Marker 18 exit near the Laredo Travel Information Center, then headed north on Highway 83. It was a familiar route, the same path he had taken during the final minutes of Melissa's and Claudine's lives. As he headed north on Highway 83, however, an unexpected sight made Ortiz's heart leap: a law enforcement vehicle—either DPS or Webb County Sheriff's Office, the details didn't register or matter—parked on the shoulder of the highway.

Ortiz turned right on State Highway 255, near where he had shot and killed Melissa; drove east on the roadway, passing the field where he had left Claudine to die; and continued toward Interstate 35. Halfway there, he spotted another police vehicle. Suddenly, they seemed to be everywhere. "A la madre," he muttered.

His heart galloped. The emergence of police cars was not something he had calculated into his plans. Suddenly, the thrill of execution was replaced by an awareness that the law was closing in on him. His hours seemed numbered. Whatever rage had bellowed in him earlier simmered to a simple, clear realization: it was time to end it all.

"How the fuck?" he said to Chelly. "I'm in the wrong exit. I don't know where the fuck I'm at."

He reached Interstate 35 and pulled in under the overpass, rolling the truck to a stop. Rain clouds blotted out the stars and moon, cloaking the night in inky darkness. Just beyond the overpass, rain fell in steady sheets through a thick, humid mid-70s night. Under the overpass, the night seemed even darker.

"Get out of my truck," Ortiz ordered. He and Chelly got out; his left hand gripped the .40-caliber H&K pistol.

Ortiz walked over to Chelly and waved the handgun toward one end of the underpass. "If you walk that way and make a left, you go to San Antonio." He waved the pistol in the other direction. "If you walk that way, the other way, you're going to go to Laredo."

The drive, the truck, the gun—all suddenly crystalized for Chelly. She was staring at the man who murdered her friends. But this ending seemed off script.

"Why are you letting me go?" she asked.

"I want you to relay a message," Ortiz told her. "You've heard about all of this shit that's been on the news de las dos viejas?"

"Sí."

"I'm the one that did that—but *ya*. That's it. I'm going to let you go and I'm going to take care of myself tonight."

"What do you mean?" Chelly asked.

"I'm going to take care of myself tonight," he repeated.

A plan had materialized in Ortiz's mind. He'd drive away, leaving Chelly behind on the highway, then take Interstate 35 south to the Walmart on San Bernardo Avenue, pull into a quiet spot in the parking lot, and put one of his .40-caliber jacketed hollow-point bullets through his brain. All the nightmares, all the pain, all the unholy impulses, would abruptly, sweetly cease.

"Why?" Chelly's voice brought Ortiz back to the darkened underpass.

The question confused him. "Walk away," he ordered.

"God loves you," she said. "God forgives you."

Anger and bewilderment rose in Ortiz.

"Chick, just go away, okay? Like, walk away. I'm telling you to walk away."

Chelly took a few slow steps away from Ortiz, then stopped, turned, and walked back toward him. Something inside of her didn't want to give up on him, gun or no gun.

Ortiz raised his handgun. "I'm telling you to walk away and you're not listening to me."

Boom. The sound of the gunshot echoed around the cement slopes of the overpass. The bullet barreled into the right side of Chelly's neck and exited the left. She collapsed to the pavement. Ortiz shot her again while she was on the ground. *Boom.* The second slug exploded into the left side of her neck. Later, a medical examiner would also report blunt force trauma to her head, including a 3.5-inch gash on the top of her scalp, a 4.5-inch gaping wound on the right side of her forehead, a bruised right eye, and a fracture in the midportion of the skull. The head injuries were so severe they led to bleeding in the brain, and they—not the gunshot wounds—were listed as the cause of Chelly's death.

Emotions and thoughts coursed through Ortiz as he climbed back into his truck and roared off. He ramped onto Interstate 35 and headed south, back toward the city. He was still gripped by an impulse to end his life, to blast a bullet in him and bring it all to an end. "It is all fucking over," he told himself. He also harbored an equally strong urge to continue erasing Laredo's illicit sex trade. Dawn was approaching, and someone would soon find the body under the overpass; his life would surely end, one way or another. Why not bring more undesirables with him? "Fuck it," he muttered. "Clean up the streets." As the lights of the city whizzed past, Ortiz coasted his truck off the interstate and headed back toward San Bernardo Avenue.

CHAPTER 16

Pat and Nora Roth were readying for a night out bowling when they heard tapping on the Relax Inn's bulletproof lobby window. *Knock, knock, knock.*

It was Janelle Ortiz, whom Pat teasingly called "Double-G," for the balled-up socks that passed for fake breasts under her sweater. She stood outside, gleaming with a confident smile.

It was just past 8:00 p.m. on Friday, September 14, and Janelle, who hadn't been able to afford a room on her own in weeks, had lined up a date who promised to pay her $300—the equivalent of several nights' earnings. As soon as she got the money, she told Pat, she would pay for a room and have enough left over for partying. But first, she needed to borrow some makeup from Nora, as well as a room in which to get ready. Pat unlocked the maintenance worker's room and let her in.

A sinewy five feet four inches, with wavy, shoulder-length black hair, cinnamon-hued skin, and small, cheery eyes, Janelle was one of a handful of transgender sex workers along San Bernardo. She was renowned for her smile, charisma, humor—and toughness. She had knocked out enemies and unscrupulous clients before with a signature move her father described as "la metralleta" (the submachine gun)—a series of quick, vicious jabs designed to inflict the most damage in the shortest span of time. She had an athletic build and a booming voice that could cower unexpecting johns or make friends laugh with loud, inappropriate jokes.

She also was one of the avenue's more spiritual workers, praying faithfully to Santa Muerte, a skeletal, grim reaper–like female deity with a passionate following across Latin America whom Janelle endearingly called "mi flaquita." Her bag clanged with votive candles emblazoned with the image of La Santísima, as the deity was known, and a tattoo of the spirit's skull covered her right shoulder. As Señora de la Noche, La Santísima is often invoked by those who dwell at night, such as taxi drivers, police officers, and prostitutes, and is believed to protect devotees from stabbings, gunshot wounds, beatings, and all forms of violent death.

That Friday night was ten days after Melissa's body had been found and the day after Claudine had been killed—both friends of Janelle's. San Bernardo was still mostly bereft of nightly activity, and the avenue's sex workers, shaken from the prospect of a serial killer on the loose and with rents and addictions looming, had little to feel good about. Janelle had lain low initially and warned her friends to be careful. But it was time to make money again, and she was in a buoyant mood at the thought of a new client.

Pat and Nora waited patiently as she showered, dressed in a black hoodie over a black T-shirt and tank top, black leather belt, and denim shorts, and meticulously applied makeup. When finished, she took a final approving glance at herself in the mirror and left the room.

"I'll bring you your money first thing in the morning," she told Pat. "I promise."

She strutted off into the night, giddy at the prospect of a big score.

———

JANELLE WAS BORN HUMBERTO GERMAN ORTIZ ON APRIL 25, 1990, in the Ladrillo section of Laredo, the second of five children to Armando Ortiz and Elva Enriquez Ortiz. Humberto was a happy, energetic kid and close to his mother, who called him "my little Humbo." His older brother, Armando, known as "Mandillo," tried to name him after his favorite animated character, Mickey Mouse, but flubbed the first name, instead calling him Ricky—a nickname that stuck for years.

From an early age, he showed a liking for dance and music and would imitate moves by Selena or Shakira. He loved reggaeton, that fusion of Latin hip-hop and Caribbean music. He would dress up his little sister, Rosenda, like reggaeton star Ivy Queen or Shakira and teach her to swing her hips like the pop stars.

As they got older, Humberto became very protective of Rosenda, who was nine years younger than him. He would walk her to elementary school or to the park. Along the way, he'd advise her, "Be a leader, not a follower," "Don't do drugs," and "Stay in school."

"Don't even go to summer school," he told her once. "Summer school is for flunkeros."

The advice would be easier to follow if the Ortiz home were stable. But home was a cauldron of chaos. The four brothers fought constantly. The twins, Ezekiel and Israel, would fight, and at times Humberto was pulled into the scrums. Mandillo fought with Israel, and Armando Sr. would pull them apart. Elva, meanwhile, worked as a biscuit maker and dishwasher at Red Lobster and ticket taker at the Laredo Entertainment Center, an eight-thousand-seat arena. She scraped enough together to pay bills and keep the family afloat, while Armando Sr. battled a drinking problem and struggled to hold down a job. Marital stress erupted into screaming matches. If Armando Sr. became too aggressive toward Elva, the brothers would jump him, too. Mandillo, Israel, and Ezekiel got in trouble at school and were in and out of juvenile facilities. Humberto and Rosenda steered clear of trouble and actually enjoyed school.

When he was eleven years old, his father taught Humberto "la metralleta" technique, a burst of quick, powerful punches designed to surprise and subdue an opponent.

As he entered Dr. Joaquin G. Cigarroa Middle School, Humberto was a bright, albeit unambitious, student who was teased by bullies for his effeminate mannerisms or because they suspected he was gay. Other boys called him "joto" and "verga." Fellow student Andy Garcia met Humberto at the start of sixth grade. Like Humberto, Andy harbored homosexual impulses but wasn't open with his sexuality— and was still teased unmercifully for it. Andy and Humberto bonded over their mutual love of early 2000s horror flicks, such as *Ghost Ship, House of 1000 Corpses,* and *Final Destination 2.* Andy admired how outgoing Humberto was, able to make an entire class laugh with a joke. Humberto was also starting to stand up to the bullying, whereas Andy shriveled under it.

One day in the courtyard during lunch, a classmate named Edgar, who had pestered both Humberto and Andy relentlessly throughout the sixth grade, repeatedly called Humberto a joto. Finally, Humberto turned and faced his tormentor.

"You need to stop messing with me, because I don't want to do this," he told him.

"¿Qué es lo que no quieres hacer, a ver?" Edgar answered.

"Dime 'joto' una vez más."

"Pinche joto."

As Edgar turned to leave, Humberto unleashed la metralleta, pelting him with a series of punches to his back and neck. Edgar turned around, and the two engaged in a brief, vicious fistfight, each landing sharp blows to the other's face and neck. When they were separated, both were bruised and bloodied about the face. Large red welts covered Edgar's face, and his lip was split. It was the last time he mentioned that word to Humberto.

From that day on, Andy and Humberto's friendship deepened. Another classmate, Augustine "Auggie" Contreras, also joined their circle, and the three became inseparable. After school, they'd walk to the nearby Freddie Benavides Sports Complex and splash down the waterslides or take the bus to the Best Buy off Interstate 35 to buy CDs. Humberto loved Destiny's Child and the Spanish girl group Las Ketchup. He would lend Andy or Auggie the handful of quarters left in his pocket so they could buy a Ring Pop or bag of Flamin' Hot Cheetos from the school's snack stand. "Humberto would always want to get you something," Andy remembered later. "No era codo."

Andy admired Humberto for his outgoing personality, his humor, and his toughness. But there was a sensitivity and emotional pain in his friend that few others saw. Midway through sixth grade, their class at Cigarroa Middle School prepared to take a field trip to the movies to see *School of Rock,* and students were asked to pool their money together and put it in an envelope. When the envelope went missing, someone accused Humberto of stealing it. He was made to stay in school while his classmates boarded buses and went to the movies.

Later, he approached Andy. "It wasn't me," Humberto told Andy, his eyes brimming with tears. Andy believed him.

===

DESPITE HIS CONFIDENT DEMEANOR, INNER CONFLICTS OVER his sexuality gnawed at Humberto. He and Andy both knew the other was gay and hinted at such, but neither outwardly said anything. In Humberto's corner of Laredo, it paid to keep such secrets sealed. As he entered high school, though, Humberto's persona darkened. He dressed in all black—black hoodie, black jeans, black Converse sneakers—and spent hours alone locked in his room. His musical taste shifted from the poppy Shakira to the angst rock of Evanescence, and he made friends with other students who dressed similarly and dabbled in drugs. During seventh grade, his mom noticed thin scars zigzagging across both his forearms and realized Humberto had been cutting himself. Alarmed, she took him to Border Region Behavioral Medical Center, Laredo's main mental health facility, where he was diagnosed with bipolar disorder and prescribed Prozac. The pills worked initially, and Humberto's demeanor brightened. He also enjoyed meeting with the social worker who visited him at home periodically. His grades improved. But the depression persisted.

One summer evening, when he was fifteen years old, Humberto walked in the kitchen as his mom and dad ate dinner. He slammed the door and turned to them.

"Soy gay," he told them in Spanish. "Haz lo que quieras hacer. No importa lo que digas. Yo soy lo que soy."

Elva looked at her son. He was voicing what she had suspected, and she accepted him.

"¡¿Qué?!" thundered Armando Sr., rising from the table. "¿Te gustan los hombres?"

An argument broke out between father and son, as Armando Sr. tried to reconcile the male toughness he thought he had instilled in his boys with the revelation that his second-oldest son was gay. Years later, Armando Sr. would confess that he was scared for his son—scared that he would be relentlessly teased, ostracized, and even harmed over his sexuality. He loved Humberto, but his actions that evening in the kitchen drove an immovable fissure between father and son. Humberto Sr. masked his inner turmoil by drinking more and deriding his son's effeminate appearance and mannerisms.

==

HOPING A CHANGE IN SCENERY WOULD IMPROVE THINGS AT home, the family used Section 8 housing vouchers to move into a beige two-story home in the chillingly named Ghost Town neighborhood of central Laredo. The house had a large, fenced-in yard of burnt grass and dirt, a small cement front porch, and a spray of bougainvillea next to a potted barrel cactus on the front lawn.

It also was, by some accounts, haunted. Family members reported unexplained movements in the home. Ezekiel felt a presence moving across his bedsheets at night and heard phantom steps trudging up and down the staircase. Doors would open and slam shut on their own. Elva felt rooms turn suddenly cold in the middle of summer.

Whether influenced by the supernatural, the Ortiz family's fate worsened at the Ghost Town home. Humberto's depression worsened and his anxiety ramped up. He abandoned Prozac and turned his attention to street drugs, such as Rohypnol, the powerful sedative better known as the date-rape drug "roofies" or, in border communities, "roches." He liked how the small white pills erased his pain and how he could self-medicate his anxiety away better than any doctor could. Roches escalated into cocaine and, later, heroin, which he began by snorting but was soon injecting for the more explosive high. His grades suffered as he missed classes and stayed out late partying with new, wilder friends. Close friends, such as Andy and Auggie, barely saw him in school anymore.

One day during their freshman year in high school, when Humberto was fourteen, Andy and another friend, Jorge, met Humberto at a friend's house in Laredo. "Stay right there!" Humberto said excitedly, a grin lighting up his face. "I'll be right back!" He disappeared inside, and when he returned thirty minutes later he was dressed in tight jeans, a dark woman's blouse, hoop earrings, and pumps. Mascara darkened his eyes, fire-engine-red lipstick shone on his lips, and blush streaked across his cheekbones. Humberto giggled uncontrollably. Andy and Jorge stared at their transformed friend, mouths agape.

"I'm Larissa," she purred.

———

Larissa later morphed to Janelle. Though she continued dressing as a boy for school, her dress and persona were predominantly female off campus. Janelle favored short denim shorts or miniskirts, and she went by Janelle Ortiz, although on Facebook she went by the stage name of Nikki Enriquez, a play on her childhood nickname and her mother's maiden name. Her Facebook profile picture showed her with jet-black hair cut short in a bob, dark gray eyes rimmed with dark eyeliner, rouge on high cheekbones, and full pink lips, while wearing a bright red tube top. She was now unabashedly Janelle.

Her focus shifted from school to exploring the nightlife of transgender women. She hung out with other trans women, including some known to prostitute themselves and sell and use drugs, and increasingly spent time on San Bernardo Avenue. One night two older men approached Janelle and a friend on the street and offered them cocaine if they would have sex with them. They agreed—introducing Janelle to a new, easy income stream.

Barely attending school anymore, Janelle was held back her freshman year. Then again the following year and again the next. Finally, as a seventeen-year-old incoming sophomore, she dropped school altogether. Fully immersed in the San Bernardo life, she began hustling for money and carved out a reputation as one of the tougher women on the strip. She didn't hesitate unleashing la metralleta on unsuspecting clients or roughnecks. From 2009 to 2018, she was arrested at least ten times, including five assault charges and twice for prostitution.

Meanwhile, her brothers, now nearly grown men, were also taking illicit drugs, including heroin, and staying out late, along with continuing their fistfights. On more than one occasion, the fights became so violent that neighbors called the cops. Janelle still lived at home but spent most of her time on San Bernardo. She would be gone for days at a time, then return for a hot meal or a decent night's sleep. At home, the brotherly brawls, drug use, marital stress, and financial instability all pressed heavily against Elva's fragile psyche. As her family spiraled out of control, anxiety and suicidal thoughts mauled at her nervous system. She felt constantly on the edge of a nervous breakdown.

One morning in September 2012, Elva got up early, packed her suitcase, and rustled Ezekiel awake. The stress of the house had become too much, she told him. She was leaving to visit family in northwest Indiana, and she wasn't sure when she'd be back. In the predawn darkness, Ezekiel walked her to a nearby Greyhound bus stop. He told her he understood she had to fix her mental health and that he loved her and wished her well. Ezekiel watched as the bus arrived and ferried his mother away, the last remnant of the family's stability vanishing into the twilight.

When she heard of her mother's abrupt exit, Rosenda, then thirteen, thought it'd be temporary. She'd come back, she thought; her mom wouldn't just abandon her at the start of her teens, left to decipher womanhood alone in a house full of men. She would visit her soon in Indiana, then mother and daughter could return to Laredo together. A few days after their mother left, Janelle came into Rosenda's room and shut the door behind her.

Out of all her siblings and close relatives, Rosenda was the one who had most accepted Janelle's transition and she loved her little sister for that. She knew their mom's departure would devastate her. She wanted to be the one to tell her.

"Mami's not coming back," Janelle told her sister.

Rosenda sat on her bed. "What do you mean she's not coming back?"

"I mean, she's not coming back," she said. "She has her life over there now. I'm going to be your second mother, okay?"

Janelle reached over to a small radio Rosenda kept on a shelf and played Michael Jackson's "You Are Not Alone." Rosenda started to cry, too.

"You can't see me as your brother anymore," Janelle told her. "But I'll be your sister—and mother."

The two sisters sat and hugged and cried as the song played out.

=====

FOR THE NEXT FEW YEARS, THE ORTIZ FAMILY LIVED IN TENUOUS circumstances. Rosenda went to school and got passing grades, despite the drugs and violence orbiting around her. Janelle, fully transitioned to womanhood, spent most of her waking hours on San Bernardo, returning each night to the house in Ghost Town to steal a few hours' sleep and check on Rosenda.

Armando Sr. struggled with the bills. His income slowed to a trickle, then stopped altogether. He fell behind on rent, and the landlord threatened to break the lease. The family split up: Rosenda went to live with an aunt; Mandillo and Israel moved in with cousins; Armando Sr. moved in with his girlfriend. Ezekiel joined Janelle on San Bernardo Avenue. The two siblings, each battling growing heroin habits, were officially homeless. They gravitated to the Relax Inn, where Janelle introduced her younger brother to Melissa, Chelly, and Claudine, as well as Pat and Nora. The two would hustle during the day, strolling through Walmart or Burlington Coat Factory on San Bernardo and shoplifting men's jackets, jeans, makeup kits, jumper cables—anything they could later sell on the street. Janelle started earning money as a sex worker. She had an array of designer dresses, pumps, top-shelf makeup, and the charm and sass to induce curious customers. Though there were male clients eager to pay for the services of a female sex worker with male genitalia, jobs didn't materialize as frequently or easily as with the other women. Janelle needed to constantly hustle to survive.

Left by her mother and shunned by her dad, Janelle turned to the inhabitants of San Bernardo Avenue as her new family. Able to fully be herself, she strutted proudly as a woman, favoring short denim shorts and gaining a rep as a loud, hilarious trans woman. The avenue not only accepted but encouraged the behavior. If she needed to bathe, she would swing by her friend Vanessa's home and ask to use the shower or borrow some makeup.

Early one morning, as he made his rounds at the Relax Inn, Pat found Janelle and Ezekiel dozing on the motel's pool furniture. Homeless and exhausted, the two had jumped a locked gate to steal a few hours' sleep on the lounge cushions. Instead of running them off the property, he made them a deal: help clean up around the motel and they could stay for free in one of the rooms. They grabbed brooms and went to work. Soon, they were fixtures at the Relax Inn, sweeping and cleaning up the property during the day, partying in the rooms at night. Pat gave them nicknames: Ezekiel became "EZ"; Janelle was "Double-G."

Janelle still tried to keep tabs on Rosenda, making sure she stuck it out in school. She also worried about how her brothers, mom, and dad were doing. Sharing beers one day with Big Mary, she told the fellow sex worker that she was motivated to work to help her family. "It's so hard. I'm struggling," she told Big Mary. "I'm trying to help my family. They're barely making it." So was she. Client money wasn't steady, and Janelle found herself in a daily struggle to survive. Increasingly, she turned to La Santísima for help.

Herbario La Luz was a small storefront botanica on San Bernardo Avenue, sandwiched between Lydia's Salon and Lily's Joyeria de Plata y Accesorios in the shopping strip anchored by Taco Mais, the popular taco stand frequented by many on the avenue. Inside La Luz, rows of votive candles dedicated to San Lazaro, San Benito, Nuestra Señora de Guadalupe, and a bevy of other saints and deities lined the shelves. Tinctures, shell bracelets, garlic oil, and rosaries used in Santeria and other religious ceremonies crowded a glass case. On the back wall, an entire shelf held an array of votive candles and wax figurines of the scythe-wielding La Santísima. Customers were encouraged to browse, buy, or, if so inclined, leave a small offering to La Santísima.

Janelle became a frequent visitor. She would stop in nearly every afternoon, her night shift still a few hours away, and drop a few coins in the small plate by the La Santísima figurine. She would murmur a few words, cross herself, thank the store owner, and walk out.

======

ANDY NEVER STOPPED THINKING ABOUT THE PLUCKY BOY HE met in sixth grade, now a woman, and with whom he had so many adventures. He had met some of his closest friends through Janelle in middle school. He owed most of his social circle to her. Andy still saw her occasionally around town. A few times, she wandered into the Popeyes where he worked while in high school, asking for a few bucks. If he had it, he would give her a ten- or five-dollar bill. When Andy got his first car, a 1992 Ford Escort, his junior year in high school, the first drive he took was to Janelle's house to pick her up. They drove to a nearby Whataburger and dined on burgers and shakes and chatted in Spanglish about their lives. It was a rare moment where Andy was able to meet and talk with Janelle without one of her new friends hanging nearby, and he cherished every moment. Janelle opened up to Andy, talking candidly about her drug use and sex work. She said she mostly did cocaine. "Le hago un poquito al pase."

Andy was careful not to preach to his friend but urged Janelle to be careful, to please use protection while having sex with strangers, and to not overdo the drugs. It was the best he could do.

"Don't worry," Janelle told him, "I know who I get into it with."

After high school, Janelle sightings became rarer. Andy got a job as a front desk clerk at a Holiday Inn Express, and his friend Jorge landed a similar position at the nearby Homewood Suites by Hilton. The two would carpool together to and from work. One night on their way home after a shift, they decided to drive down San Bernardo Avenue, just to see if they could spot their old friend.

As they drove south on San Bernardo, past the Walmart and Palenque Grill, they spied Janelle sitting on a bus bench with two other women.

Andy slowed the car to pull over, but Jorge recognized the other women. They were bad news, he said, notorious scam artists.

They decided to keep driving.

Still, Andy was determined to see his friend again. One night in June 2018, he thought he'd try his luck and video call Janelle via Facebook Messenger. To his surprise, she answered. Janelle was lying on her stomach on a bed in a darkened bedroom. She spoke about drifting from place to place and how she was currently staying with a relative. Andy, now openly gay, talked about trying to make his latest relationship work with his boyfriend. As they often did, they reminisced about the old days at Cigarroa Middle School.

Buoyed by the impromptu connection, Andy suggested they meet in person soon.

"Even if it's just you, me, and Auggie, we should get together," he said. "We were the original clique."

Janelle smiled in agreement. She'd like that, she said.

CHAPTER 17

September 2018 was not kind to Janelle Ortiz.

She was stunned and saddened by news that first Melissa, then Claudine, both close friends, were killed in remote parts of Webb County. She warned friends to be careful, carry a weapon, check out whom you're getting into a vehicle with.

The deaths of the two women, followed by an influx of police investigators prowling around San Bernardo and asking questions, also dried up much of the avenue's action. Clients were hard to come by. Janelle's life, already teetering on a razor's edge, became unhinged. She could no longer pay for motel rooms, and the little money she scraped together went to crack rocks or tiny foils of chiva. Unable to pay rent and no longer allowed to work for rooms at the Relax Inn, Janelle and Ezekiel were again homeless. For a while, they shared a soiled mattress under the concrete span over Zacate Creek, a spot popular with Laredo's homeless. When they could, they would shower at a relative's house or panhandle for a few bucks. Heroin had gripped them both hard by then, and they hustled constantly to stave off withdrawal sickness. When Ezekiel would head to the Walmart or Burlington Coat Factory to try to pilfer a few items to sell on the streets, Janelle urged La Santísima to look over him. "I'm worried," she told her little brother. "I'm praying for you."

Through the darkest hours, though, Janelle kept her mood high, assuring Ezekiel it would all work out, that better times were on the way. To Janelle, sleeping under a bridge or not eating for two days was just another life escapade. She made it feel "like it wasn't a struggle," Ezekiel remembered later. "It was just an adventure."

OF ALL THE PEOPLE JANELLE WOULD VISIT PERIODICALLY TO steal a shower or a meal from, Rosa Madrigal was near the top of her list. A longtime family friend who had seen Janelle and her brothers and sister grow from infants to rowdy teens to troubled adults, Rosa always invited Janelle in and cooked her favorite dish—nopalitos con huevos y chiles colorados—with no judgment or lectures.

On August 28, 2018, Janelle appeared on Rosa's doorstep, and the two sat and watched the funeral of Aretha Franklin on TV. Janelle swooned over the tea-length ruby-red dress with matching red pumps Franklin wore during her first day of viewing at Detroit's Charles H. Wright Museum of African American History.

"I want a dress like that when I die," she told Rosa.

"Be quiet," Rosa told her.

"I'm serious. I want that one."

Rosa agreed.

When Janelle asked about Rosa's sister's recent burial, she told her that her sister had asked to be cremated.

"Ooh, please don't do that to me," Janelle said.

A few weeks later, on the afternoon of Wednesday, September 12, Janelle reappeared at Rosa's house. She was hungry, and Rosa cooked up the usual plate of nopalitos con huevos and served it with a glass of orange juice. Janelle wolfed it down ravenously.

"I'll come back tomorrow to style and color your hair," Janelle told Rosa between bites.

After dinner, the two climbed into Rosa's truck, and she drove Janelle back to San Bernardo. On the ride over, Janelle appeared solemn. She mentioned she was thinking of leaving Laredo. She thought of moving to Corpus Christi, checking into rehab, and cleaning up.

"I'm not happy here," she said. "I want to rehabilitate myself and be able to live with people."

"Really?" Rosa said.

"Yes," Janelle said. "I want to do something good with my life."

Rosa told her that was the best news she'd heard in a while. "We'll talk about it tomorrow," she said. "Come to my house."

As Rosa pulled into a Conoco gas station on San Dario Avenue where Janelle asked to be dropped off, Janelle asked her friend to bless her. "Echa me la bendición."

"En el nombre del Padre, el Hijo, y el Espíritu Santo," Rosa said, crossing the air in front of Janelle with two fingers. "Ándale."

Janelle thanked her, got out of the truck, and headed under the overpass toward San Bernardo.

The next day, September 13, Janelle's aunt Patricia Ortiz scored a few hundred bucks on one of the myriad slot machines found in Laredo's gas stations and truck stops. Giddy, she set out to find Janelle and share some of her winnings with her. Like other Ortiz relatives, she got occasional visits from Janelle and knew her niece was going through a tough stretch. She looked forward to giving her a few bucks, maybe buying her lunch and brightening her day.

Patricia drove around the usual locales frequented by Janelle: the nearby park, motel parking lots, San Bernardo bus benches. She cruised and cruised. But no sign of Janelle.

At around the same time, Armando Sr. also tried locating Janelle. He had seen her a few days before, when his daughter appeared at a friend's house he was at. The two had dinner and watched a bigfoot documentary on the Travel Channel before Janelle vanished again. Janelle had seemed uncomfortable, and Armando Sr. sensed something was wrong. He set out to find her. He wandered through some of the same places Patricia had looked but, like his sister, couldn't locate Janelle. He gave up the search and headed home.

═══

ON FRIDAY, SEPTEMBER 14, JANELLE WAS EXCITED. HER LUCK— *finally*—seemed to be improving. She had met a client who had promised her $300 for a rendezvous at a motel. The payout would be a windfall compared with the crumpled tens and twenties she earned on a routine night. It would go a long way to easing her most pressing issues— including the gnawing pain of the onset of heroin withdrawal—and she could finally rent a hotel room, where she could bathe and get a decent night's sleep.

She showered and dressed at the Relax Inn, thanks to Pat and Nora's generosity, and bounded off to score her bounty. But a few hours later, at around 10:00 p.m., she returned, crestfallen, to the motel. The client called that he was running late, she told Pat. He could be blowing her off (jittery clients and last-minute cancellations were routine in her profession), but she was willing to give him some more time. After relaxing in the motel's air-conditioned lobby for a few hours, she took off once more down San Bernardo Avenue.

———

SOMETIME PAST MIDNIGHT, CHRISTOPHER CANALES WAS STROLL-ing down San Bernardo when he came upon Janelle sitting on the bus bench near Ugarte Street.

"Hey, give me a cigarette," she called out.

Christopher knew many of the women along San Bernardo and had known Janelle possibly the longest. The two had met a decade earlier in Webb County Jail, when Janelle was just eighteen and beginning to explore Laredo's dark crevices. She was one of the first transgender women he had ever met, and he respected how she hustled and stood her ground against the biases and meanness of others. Over the years, they had forged a friendship.

Christopher dug into his pocket and pulled out a single cigarette.

"Last one," he said. He sat next to Janelle and lit his final cigarette of the night.

As they passed the cigarette between them, she voiced a sense of dread that had been gnawing at her.

"I feel her calling me," Janelle said, blowing out a plume of silver smoke. "I feel my flaquita."

Christopher knew she was referring to La Santísima, knew that Janelle was a devoted follower of the deity.

"I feel her calling me," she continued. "I feel like I'm next."

Women on the avenue talked about death all the time: how to avoid it, how to deal with it when it came for friends. But Janelle's comments seemed too matter-of-fact, like she had some insight into her own impending demise. Christopher struggled with how to answer his friend when his girlfriend, Eva, emerged from around the corner. The two had been arguing most of the night, and Eva, stoned and still upset, again began yelling at Christopher. As the pair argued, Janelle stood and drifted away.

=====

IN THE EARLY-MORNING HOURS OF SEPTEMBER 15, STEPHANY Gonzalez, twenty-five, strolled along San Bernardo. A sex worker on the strip for years, she was keenly aware of what had happened to Melissa and Claudine and had talked it through with some of the other women on the avenue. For protection, she started carrying a pocketknife under her shirt. She needed the money, but she wasn't going to let some creep pull a gun on her without a fight. It had been a slow night, and Stephany was anxious for some action.

As she walked along San Bernardo, Stephany bumped into Janelle. The two walked together. The conversation inevitably turned to the killer targeting women on San Bernardo. Janelle joked that the murderer probably carried a list of his victims, and wondered aloud who was on it.

"Not funny," Gonzalez told her.

The two women parted ways.

=====

A LITTLE WHILE LATER, JUAN DAVID ORTIZ TURNED HIS WHITE Dodge truck down San Bernardo Avenue and headed south. It had been less than an hour since he had shot his last victim, Chelly, and left her to die under an overpass twenty miles away. Reason and guilt had fled his system; he was now gripped by a singular impulse: kill more sex workers.

The avenue was dark and generally bereft of activity. But as he drove past the Walmart and Palenque Grill, past Tacos Kissi and the Siesta Motel, he noticed a few people out and about. He drove past Ugarte Street, circled back, and pulled up next to Stephany. He rolled down his window.

"How much?" he asked her.

Stephany didn't know Ortiz. Something about him immediately seemed off to her. It was routine for clients to appear nervous during those early moments at the start of a transaction, but this one seemed extra jittery. He kept glancing around, as if ready to roar off in the truck at any moment. Her hand gripped her pocketknife. She needed the cash but had also come to trust her instincts, and her instincts were screaming at her not to get into that truck.

"I'm not working," she lied.

Ortiz sped off.

He drove a half block and turned down Ugarte to San Agustin Avenue. From where she stood on San Bernardo, Stephany could see the white truck stop along San Agustin and Janelle approach its passenger-side window.

====

ORTIZ HAD SEEN JANELLE BEFORE ALONG THE AVENUE AND THE two knew each other. In past days, he would buy her lunch at Taco Palenque or gift her one of the Bud Light tallies he had in his truck.

When he stopped on San Agustin at around 2:00 a.m. on September 15, Janelle walked right up to his window. She was hungry.

"¿Que honda?" she said. "Olle, pa', ¿me compras algo de comer como la última vez?"

Ortiz agreed to buy her something to eat. They could swing by a drive-through, he told her. Janelle climbed into the truck, and it rolled away down Ugarte.

As Ortiz steered the truck past San Bernardo and through several intersections toward Interstate 35, going by various fast-food restaurants,

Janelle grew suspicious. She looked around at the passing lights and shops around her.

"¿Pa' donde vamos?" she asked.

"Down this road," he said. "I'm just driving."

Suddenly, Janelle dropped her head into her hands as realization shivered through her. What heroin withdrawal, poverty, and hunger clouded just moments before became crystalline clear. She knew where they were headed.

"Aaaah," she said through her hands. "It's you, isn't it?"

"What?" Ortiz said.

"It's you. You're the one."

"No, dude," he answered. "What are you talking about?"

Ortiz had interacted with Janelle enough times in the past to know she still had the anatomy, and possibly strength, of a man. Though drugs and poor nutrition had whittled her body weight down to a waiflike 136 pounds, Ortiz worried that Janelle, unlike the others, might put up a fight.

Instead of driving the usual route to Exit 18 and onto Highway 83, a distance of seventeen miles from San Bernardo, Ortiz exited at Mile Marker 15, cutting the trip by four miles. Ortiz knew the area as where the CBP checkpoint used to be, before moving fifteen miles up the interstate. As he pulled off the highway, he drove into a desolate, widened expanse of the service road and weaved around barricades. Mounds of gravel were piled next to the roadway, where construction crews scooped and dumped as they expanded nearby roadways.

Ortiz brought the Dodge truck to a stop, gripped his .40-caliber pistol, and ordered Janelle out of the vehicle. She turned to face her killer.

"Okay," she told Ortiz. "Do what you've got to do."

"Hazte pa'ya," he told her, waving his gun away from his truck.

Janelle took a few short steps away from him, and Ortiz came up behind her and shot her once in the back of the head. *Boom.*

The bullet tore into the lower right side of the skull, opening as it went and mauling through skin, tissue, muscle, bone, and, finally, brain. It barreled through the left petrous bone at the base of the skull and came to rest just behind the nose. Death, more likely than not, arrived instantly.

===

ORTIZ KNEW LAW ENFORCEMENT OFFICERS WERE NOW ON HIS tail across Webb County. His entire life—everything he had built and coveted—was crashing down around him. Thoughts of suicide still clawed at him. But even stronger was a darker instinct to continue ridding the world of streetwalkers. With his wife two hours north in San Antonio, Ortiz headed back to San Bernardo. "Fuck it," he told himself. "Let's go do it again."

Ortiz gunned the truck and headed back into the city. He drove off Interstate 35 and down Santa Ursula Avenue. He made a right on Jefferson Street, then turned north onto San Bernardo Avenue, cruising the avenue near its end, then swinging a U-turn and driving back down. Suddenly, he passed a DPS state trooper SUV parked in the avenue's median. He looked in his rearview mirror and noticed two more troopers driving behind him some distance back.

"Chingamadre," he muttered to himself. "Ya se acabó todo el pedo. My God, this is where I check out. That's it. I'm out."

But when he glanced back at his mirror, the troopers were gone. Ortiz turned left into the Stripes convenience store at Jefferson and San Bernardo and pulled into the far left parking spot in front of the store. He exited his truck and went inside to use the bathroom, leaving his .40-caliber H&K pistol in its holster by the truck's driver's-side door.

===

EARLIER THAT NIGHT, DPS TROOPER JOHNHENRY BRADSHAW had pulled over a semitruck just north of Laredo on Highway 83, near Interstate 35, that had been weaving suspiciously. He let the driver off with a warning, and when he returned to his black DPS-issued 2017 Ford Expedition SUV, a string of text messages from a supervisor had piled up in his personal cell phone. They included the make and model of a white Dodge truck, its license plate number, and a driver's license photo of an intense-looking Hispanic male, along with a name: Juan David Ortiz. The messages warned that Ortiz was a suspect in the recent Laredo murders and was believed to be "armed and dangerous." "No one's going home until we find this guy," one message read. Bradshaw knew precisely what he meant.

At twenty-nine, Bradshaw was one of the younger and less experienced troopers on the force. Originally from nearby Harlingen, Texas, he had grown up visiting family in Laredo and other border communities. When he graduated from the academy in 2017, he was excited to be assigned to Laredo, which he knew well.

Shortly after joining DPS, Bradshaw was recruited to assist in Operation Secure Texas, a predecessor to Operation Lone Star, Governor Greg Abbott's multibillion-dollar attempt to use state resources to stem the flow of undocumented crossings. He was given the graveyard shift, working from 7:00 p.m. to 7:00 a.m. or 5:00 p.m. to 5:00 a.m. He spent the overnight hours patrolling the I-35 corridor and looking for vehicles suspected of smuggling people or drugs or both. He had heard about the murders from colleagues but didn't take part in the investigation.

However, shortly after Claudine Luera's murder, Bradshaw and another trooper were called into a supervisor's office at the DPS's Laredo headquarters and questioned. Had they seen any suspicious vehicles or activity? The gunman, whose identity was as yet unknown, had apparently traveled up Interstate 35—Bradshaw's area of coverage—on his way to the murder scene. Was there anything they remembered about that night that could help the investigation? The questioning had the unmistakable tinge of browbeating: the troopers, it was strongly implied, had let a serial murderer slip through their fingers. Bradshaw wasn't going to let that happen again.

After reading his supervisor's texts in his SUV, he pulled on a ballistic vest and grabbed his agency-issued DPMS AR-15 rifle out of the back of the vehicle. He returned to the driver's seat and cradled the assault weapon on his lap. He then gunned the SUV south on Interstate

35 toward Laredo. On the way, Bradshaw called his girlfriend's brother, a person he knew to be struggling with heroin and meth addiction and who was well acquainted with Laredo's criminal underbelly.

"Where would you go in Laredo if you were looking for prostitutes?" Bradshaw asked him.

The brother didn't hesitate: "San Bernardo."

=====

BRADSHAW COASTED OFF THE HIGHWAY AND HEADED SOUTH ON San Bernardo Avenue. He drove all the way down until the avenue ended at San Agustín Plaza, slowly lapped around the darkened plaza, looking for signs of a white truck, then headed north again on San Bernardo. He drove until the avenue's northbound lanes ended near Calton Road, then U-turned and headed back south.

Bradshaw peered into motel parking lots, convenience stores, and fast-food drive-throughs as he drove his SUV down San Bernardo. As he approached Jefferson Street, he looked to his left and caught a glimpse of what appeared to be a white truck in the far left parking spot of a Stripes convenience store and gas station. Probably nothing, Bradshaw thought, but worth a look. He turned left on Jefferson, then pulled into the gas station, parking diagonally behind the truck. The white truck's brake lights were still on, the driver still inside. As Bradshaw tried to make out the license plate, a stocky, dark-haired man exited the vehicle and walked casually toward the convenience store. As he went, he glanced up at Bradshaw and the two men's eyes caught for a moment. Then the driver looked down and continued walking into the store.

The trooper pulled up the text message with the photo. Was that him? He couldn't be sure. He entered the truck's license plate—324885DV— into the MobileCAD computer perched on his dashboard and, a few seconds later, the vehicle information scrolled up on the screen, including the name of the owner: Juan David Ortiz. This was him.

Bradshaw's heart galloped. He glanced at another screen on his dash showing the GPS locations of other troopers. All the dots on the screen seemed several miles away.

Oh shit, he thought.

He was about to confront a wanted murderer who was likely armed. By himself. He pulled his SUV around one of the pumps, as if he were just filling his tank, and called it in. "I have the suspect here at the Stripes," he said into his SUV's radio. In his nervousness, he forgot to say which one.

Bradshaw gripped the AR-15 on his lap and exited his vehicle. He walked behind the SUV, perched the weapon on the hood, and aimed it at the store. Peering through the rifle's EOTECH scope, he could place a small red dot—visible only to him—on Ortiz inside the store and watched as he walked to the back, then returned to the front of the store. No customers, only Ortiz and the worker at the counter. That was good, he thought. Fewer potential hostages to worry about.

Scenarios raced through Bradshaw's mind. What if Ortiz barricaded himself inside the store and took the employee hostage? What if he ran to his truck? Or came out shooting? His thoughts reached back to his training, especially the Lies, Threats, and Engagement Training he'd received just a few months earlier, which went over some of these very scenarios. He knew Ortiz needed to display a "clear threat" before Bradshaw could fire his weapon. A BOLO wasn't a strong enough threat.

=====

A FEW MINUTES EARLIER, DPS TROOPER ABIEL OBREGON HAD been driving along San Bernardo Avenue, also looking for Ortiz's white truck, when he noticed the taillights to a fellow DPS SUV pulling into the Stripes on Jefferson Street. On a hunch, he followed the taillights and pulled into the gas station moments after Bradshaw had positioned himself behind his vehicle. Obregon parked his DPS SUV directly behind Ortiz's truck, shining his headlights on the wanted truck.

Relief washed over Bradshaw. He knew Obregon. The previous week, Bradshaw's SUV had to go to the shop for maintenance, and he and Obregon had patrolled the graveyard shift together in Obregon's vehicle. Obregon had been with the agency longer and had military experience. He was glad to have him there; he walked over to his colleague.

"There's his truck right there," Bradshaw told Obregon, pointing at the Dodge truck. "He walked inside."

Obregon called in his position. "I'm with Bradshaw," he barked into the radio. "Making contact." Then he walked behind his SUV to pull his own agency-issued AR-15 rifle from the back. Just then, he heard Bradshaw's voice bellow nearby.

"Put your hands up!"

Obregon stepped toward the pumps and saw Juan David Ortiz standing just outside the store's front entrance, his hands slightly raised and a pained, puzzled look on his face.

Bradshaw repositioned behind his SUV and barked another order. "Turn around!" Again, louder: "Turn around!"

Ortiz slid two steps to his left. Obregon yelled, "Stop right there! Stop! Stop!"

The two troopers then began yelling competing orders at Ortiz, their words colliding with one another.

Bradshaw: "Stop walking away!"

Obregon: "Is this your truck?"

Ortiz, feigning bewilderment, asked, "What's going on?"

Obregon, again: "Is this your truck?"

Bradshaw: "Turn around!"

Obregon: "Turn around!"

Bradshaw: "Get on your knees!"

"You're freaking me out right now," Ortiz said.

This was it, Ortiz thought. This was the moment the night had been barreling toward. He looked at the two troopers, standing just twenty feet away, and calculated how fast he could pull out his pistol and shoot them before they shot him, maiming and possibly killing him. He might go down, but not without a fight.

Fuckers, he thought. I just want to shoot them.

It was time to check out.

He reached for his .40-caliber H&K pistol, then realized he had left it in the truck.

=====

Troopers Bradshaw and Obregon, believing the suspect was armed and dangerous, were trying to conduct what's known in law enforcement as a "felony stop." Typically in a felony stop, police order a suspect to put their hands on their head, turn around so that they're facing away from the agents, walk backward toward the police, then drop to their knees or lie facedown on the ground. The officers are trained to keep their distance during this phase and to stay highly vigilant of any weapon the suspect may have on them. Clear, concise commands are key components of a felony stop.

But the troopers' commands were so confluent that Obregon told his partner to let him take over. "Bradshaw, I'm going to do the talking."

Bradshaw gladly obliged. He knew Obregon had more experience and had interviewed suspects during his time in the military. Bradshaw, his AR-15 trained on Ortiz's torso, puzzled through different scenarios and came to some conclusions: if Ortiz reached his truck, he could pull out a weapon or jump in and possibly drive off, sparking a high-speed chase that could endanger others. He wouldn't allow Ortiz to reach his truck; he would either shoot out his tires or shoot at Ortiz or both. If he ran the other way, he wasn't posing an immediate threat, so he wouldn't shoot. The thoughts spun through his head in a matter of seconds.

Obregon turned back to Ortiz. "Sir, we have a positive ID . . . This truck right here is matching with the potential of . . . with the murders that had been happening within the past two weeks."

Ortiz, his hands up but palms skyward—more inquisitive than submissive—fidgeted and glanced around. He slid another step to his left.

Obregon continued: "We want to do an interview with you, we want to do some questioning. We just need you to cooperate with us, okay?"

"Okay," Ortiz said.

"All right, fine. Turn around and make [your] way this way."

Ortiz stared blankly at the officers. His final shootout with the police had been foiled by not bringing his weapon with him to the bathroom. Now he faced two troopers armed with high-caliber rifles. He considered his options. He could do as commanded—turn around, hands on head, and surrender—or . . .

He stalled, telling the troopers they were making him nervous. "Guys, you are really scaring the shit out of me," he said.

"Turn around," Obregon ordered again. "Just turn around. Turn around. Please."

Ortiz mumbled something else, turned his head slightly—then ran. He darted off to his left, toward Jefferson Street, away from the troopers and down the darkened streets beyond.

"Hey!" Obregon screamed. "*Hey!*"

Both troopers ran after him.

═══

ADRENALINE COURSING THROUGH HIM, ORTIZ SPRINTED ACROSS Jefferson Street, through the empty parking lot of the Sky-Palace Inn and Suites, and onto the I-35 service road.

Bradshaw ran close behind. The AR-15 was slung across his chest, and his belt clanged with his SIG Sauer 9mm service pistol, a Taser gun, an ASP expandable baton, handcuffs, a flashlight, and a tourniquet. Despite the added weight of his equipment, he closed in on the suspect. Ortiz had sprinted off with a forty-foot lead, but Bradshaw had narrowed that to thirty feet, then twenty-five, then twenty.

Ortiz made a right onto Constantinople Street toward San Bernardo Avenue. Bradshaw followed close behind, the sound of his hard-soled shoes on the pavement echoing down the quiet street. He knew he couldn't fire his rifle at a fleeing suspect. So, he slung the AR-15 behind him and, still running at full speed, pulled out his Taser. Bradshaw knew from experience that Tasers were effective if the suspect was standing still but notoriously hard to connect if the target was running or had on loose clothing. Bradshaw had discharged his Taser only once before, while chasing suspected smugglers who had ditched a car and run into thick brush. The prongs never caught, and the smugglers got away. Still, it was his best option.

As he aimed his Taser at a sprinting Ortiz, he lined up the red dot of the gun's sight on Ortiz's back and pulled the trigger. The prongs ejected and clacked to life but fell harmlessly to the ground. He lined up the dot again and pulled the trigger, discharging the gun's second cartridge. Again, the prongs shot forward; again, they clacked to life, then fell to the ground. Ortiz kept running.

He turned left onto San Bernardo, then, a half block south, made another quick left and sprinted up the ramp entrance to the parking garage of the Hotel Ava. The nine-story beige-colored hotel in the heart of San Bernardo had been known, until recently, as the Ramada Plaza hotel and had a four-story concrete parking garage adjoining it. Ortiz ran to the elevator and, his heart hammering in his chest, took it to the top floor. He got out, ran to the far end of the lot, and threw himself into the bed of a black GMC Sierra pickup truck parked there.

Still angry at himself for not having his weapon, Ortiz lay flat in the bed of the truck and waited.

———

BRADSHAW FOLLOWED THE SUSPECT ONTO SAN BERNARDO AND watched as he made a sharp left turn. Training had taught him never to follow an armed suspect blindly around sharp turns. It was the easiest way to get ambushed. He waited for a few moments until Obregon showed up. The two troopers then engaged in "pie-ing," a law enforcement technique for slowly looking around corners for hostile suspects, while presenting the smallest possible target, as if slicing up a pie into smaller pieces. They carefully peered around the corner to the ramp leading to the parking garage. But no one was there.

Ortiz had vanished.

Immediately north of the ramp was a cluster of low-slung concrete commercial buildings surrounded by a six-foot-tall chain-link fence. It was dotted with open patios and shrouded by trees and overgrown bushes. Inside the buildings, which appeared mostly abandoned, were stacks of yellowed boxes, ladders, dusty filing cabinets, upturned chairs, and various other junk piled high to the ceiling. On one of the buildings' west wall, a previous owner had scrawled "PACKS, BOXES, SUPPLIES" in hand-painted letters. Bradshaw pointed his flashlight beam into the darkened property. A few chairs were strewn on a small, cluttered patio at the San Bernardo entrance. The gate to the property was secured with a locked padlock. A few feet farther south on San Bernardo, a sign and arrow pointed toward the ramp and the Hotel Ava's parking garage.

Bradshaw calculated the speed at which Ortiz was running, his proximity to the suspect, and the few seconds it took for Obregon to show up, clear the corner together, and view the ramp. No way he had time to run all the way up the ramp and turn right into the garage, Bradshaw thought. He must've jumped left into the darkened property. Bradshaw jogged halfway up the ramp and raked his flashlight beam across the property, his back to the hotel.

Obregon agreed with Bradshaw's assessment. The troopers now believed they faced one of the most dangerous scenarios known to law enforcement: a desperate fugitive, wanted in a double murder and suspected of being armed, barricaded in a locked property.

Bradshaw trotted down the ramp and suggested they circle back around the block.

"No, bro," Obregon said, still struggling to catch his breath. "He's here." He pointed his flashlight beam at the darkened property behind the chain-link fence.

The two went to call in their position, then realized they had left their radios in their vehicles back at Stripes. Unwilling to stray from the site, Bradshaw waved down a passing car and ordered the startled couple inside to call 911. "Tell Laredo PD that Texas DPS is chasing a possible murder suspect and we're at this location," he said between ragged breaths. "We need backup." The couple agreed and sped off.

===

NEWS OF BRADSHAW AND OBREGON'S CONFRONTATION WITH Ortiz—and the suspect's dramatic flight on foot—spread quickly across the patrol radios of law enforcement agents throughout Webb County. Deputies and troopers rushed to the scene. As DPS SUVs and Webb County sheriff's trucks arrived at the scene, lights flashing, Obregon pointed the lawmen to the fenced property.

"He's in here, bro," he told one law enforcement agent after another as they arrived, pointing his handgun and flashlight at the property.

More DPS agents arrived and cased around the property, guns drawn and pointed at the ground. "David Ortiz—come out!" one bellowed as he walked up the entrance ramp. "State police!"

Sheriff's officials ordered a perimeter set up for two blocks in every direction. San Bernardo shut down in that vicinity, as did Constantinople and Santa Ursula. Bradshaw went into the Hotel Ava's lobby and asked the night clerk to see the property's security cameras, but the worker didn't know how to operate them. He told the clerk they were looking for a possible murder suspect and he should "lock the hotel down." The worker said he couldn't do that without his manager's consent. "Okay," Bradshaw warned, "but you might have a murderer sneaking into your hotel."

A block away, Obregon and a few other agents circled the darkened property a few times, peeking through the chain-link fence and shining their flashlights into its outer edges. Their beams shone on parked cars, shrubs, a dumpster. There was no sign of Ortiz.

"*Fuck!*" Obregon muttered under his breath. "Motherfucker."

CHAPTER 18

Rain drizzled steadily as Salinas and Calderon neared the sheriff's substation on Highway 59 at around 1:30 a.m.

It had been a long night, but they had received the best lead so far
on the identity of the San Bernardo killer. They were disappointed Juan
David Ortiz hadn't shown up at his house while they staked it out; that
could have ended the entire ordeal right then and there. But the lead was
solid and they felt they were close.

Most puzzling so far was Ortiz's occupation. Erika had repeatedly said her "David" was an oil field worker. Calderon had punched
in Ortiz's name and date of birth in the Texas Workforce Commission
website, which would normally give a person's employer and dates of
employment, but nothing had come up.*

As they pulled into the substation, Salinas received a call on his
cell phone from a DPS official. Two troopers had confronted Ortiz at a
Stripes convenience store on San Bernardo Avenue and Jefferson Street,
and the wanted suspect had fled on foot. They had made a positive ID
of the suspect and the truck. The killer was at large. Salinas threw his
vehicle's gears into reverse, pulled back out of the driveway, and gunned
his truck down Highway 59 toward the city.

They arrived at the Stripes along with swarms of other agents.
Members of DPS, Laredo Police Department SWAT and K-9 units,
Webb County sheriff's SWAT, and Border Patrol had flooded the streets
around the Stripes, around thirty law enforcement agents in all. Red
and blue lights from their assorted vehicles pulsed through the darkened shops and restaurants of San Bernardo Avenue. Calderon slung a

---

* Federal employees are not registered through the TWC portal.

ballistic chest plate over his shoulder and pulled out his 5.56mm AR-15 rifle. A sheriff's official debriefed him on the events: how the troopers confronted Ortiz, how he ran off, and how he had vanished as they chased him onto San Bernardo and Constantinople.

"What do you think? We might have our guy?" Calderon asked Salinas.

"Hopefully," he said, adding: "Hopefully, everything goes right." There had been enough bloodshed in Laredo without a shootout with a desperate military veteran.

=====

BRADSHAW STARED AT THE DARKENED PROPERTY NEXT TO THE ramp, and cold fear clawed at his heart.

Somewhere in there could be an armed suspect wanted for double murder. He could be behind any dark corner and could open fire at them as soon as they approached. He would have the advantage of position and surprise, and his eyes would be far more adjusted to the cramped, darkened space. It seemed almost suicidal to tromp through there looking for a gunman. Still, Bradshaw knew he needed to go in. His mind raced back to how Ortiz had likely driven past him when he drove Claudine to her murder site and the unhappy tone his supervisor used when he asked him about it. And how he had Ortiz in his sights, his AR-15 pointed squarely at his chest, and had let him run away; how he had seemed so close in the foot chase he thought he could tase him. But he had gotten away. This is my traffic stop, Bradshaw thought to himself. *This guy ran away from me.* He was going in.

He asked a few other agents there on San Bernardo—from DPS, Laredo PD, and other agencies—but all said they were unwilling or unauthorized to go into the property. Only Obregon agreed to go in with Bradshaw. The troopers approached Salinas and told him they wanted to go inside looking for Ortiz. Salinas told them they could join a Webb County SWAT team that was readying to go inside. On the way to meet up with the SWAT group, Bradshaw and Obregon ran into

Trooper Hernandez, who, after delivering Erika Peña to the substation, had joined the manhunt on San Bernardo. Hernandez said he wanted to go in, too. The three troopers pulled on heavier, level III bulletproof vests and Kevlar helmets and linked up with the SWAT commander.

Two teams of law enforcement agents—a mix of sheriff's SWAT, Laredo PD SWAT and K-9, and DPS troopers, eight agents total—entered the property just north of the Hotel Ava to search for Ortiz. The teams were ordered to "stack up," forming a single file of four agents, one behind the other, so as to offer the narrowest body mass to a hostile shooter. The agents hung a hand on each person's shoulder as they went. An agent with a ballistic shield led the way. They weren't quiet. The four-person teams tromped through the abandoned buildings, snapping loose boards, pushing aside piles of junk, and pointing flashlight beams and assault rifles around dark corners and at shadowy crevices, room by room. For around twenty minutes, they poked through piles of boxes and behind abandoned filing cabinets until the property was cleared.

Ortiz was nowhere to be found.

═══

Twenty miles north on Interstate 35, Sheriff's Deputy Robert Elisondo arrived at the Webb County interchange overpass near Mile Marker 20 to the scene of what was called in by a passerby as a possible auto-ped. He surveyed Chelly's crumpled body on the pavement, the blood pooling near her head, and caught a twinkle of brass on the pavement near the body. He pulled out his cell phone and called Calderon.

"It's not an accident," he told Calderon. "I think you have another crime scene out here."

"Why do you think that?"

Elisondo described the victim, her wounds, and the shell casings near her body.

"Are they .40 caliber?" Calderon asked.

Elisondo squatted for a closer look, careful not to get too close and disrupt evidence. Yes, he said, he thought they were.

Calderon thanked him and hung up the phone. He turned to Salinas and filled him in on their third victim. They agreed that they both needed to stay at the San Bernardo scene and the hunt for Ortiz. Salinas said he would send another Texas Ranger from Bexar County, which includes San Antonio, to process the third murder scene. They turned their focus back to finding Ortiz.

Calderon left the corner of Jefferson and Santa Ursula to help coordinate the manhunt, while Salinas stayed behind to inspect Ortiz's truck, still sitting in the far corner of the convenience store's parking lot. Pointing his flashlight beam into the vehicle, Salinas spotted several women's purses on the back floorboard, along with three tallboy cans of Bud Light. He looked in the front seat: there, by the center console, was an empty gun holster. He called Calderon with a warning: Ortiz may be armed.

He wasn't—Ortiz's .40-caliber H&K pistol was still tucked in the driver's door pocket, as yet undetected by investigators—but the revelation put the search teams on higher alert. A shootout with the suspect now seemed likely. For more than an hour, they combed through the property behind the chain-link fence, going through every darkened room of the abandoned buildings, rechecking the outdoor area and patio. Calderon walked to the top of the parking garage's ramp, where he could peer into the property and provide cover for the SWAT team below.

The teams returned from searching the property, secure in the knowledge that Ortiz was not hiding in there. They began packing up their equipment and prepared to relocate somewhere else.

"Hey, we're not done," Calderon called out to them. "Let's search the parking lot."

He motioned to the split-level covered garage on the other side of the ramp. The teams unpacked their gear and prepared to go into the garage.

———

POLICE UNITS WEREN'T THE ONLY ONES DRAWN TO THE SCENE.
As Calderon readied the SWAT teams to enter the garage, La Gordi-

loca pulled her truck into a lot on the west side of San Bernardo Avenue, just outside the perimeter, about a block down from the Hotel Ava. The number of police units with flashing lights and armed agents with assault rifles jogging about or squatting behind their vehicles for cover was rare and disconcerting, even by Laredo standards.

She parked, exited her truck, and stood behind it for protection. Then she pulled up her Facebook page on her smartphone, pointed its camera at the flashing lights and activity down the road, and started her broadcast. As usual, she was the only media present.

"Buenas noches," she began, greeting her viewers and telling them in Spanish where she was and the unusual number of armed lawmen around, before switching to English. "I don't know what's going on. All I know is that Texas Rangers, DPS, Laredo Police Department, Sheriff's Department are here at this time. Everybody has their firearms at hand. I honestly don't know what's going on. All I know is that everything is closed off. Everybody has their guns in their hands. Everybody's hiding behind their fucking truck. I don't know why I should be hiding behind my truck. I really don't know what the fuck is going on, but sounds serious to me."

She went on to speculate that it may have something to do with the "women who were killed in the ranches" outside Laredo. "I don't know what the fuck is going on—but this shit right here is serious."

The broadcast would go on for twenty-two minutes and draw more than thirty-six thousand viewers, including some of the victims' families, who, unable to sleep for days, had tuned in to La Gordiloca for the latest developments in the case.

From his perch at the top of the parking ramp, Calderon spotted La Gordiloca filming. A small crowd of followers was starting to form next to where she was broadcasting. He waved a deputy over and signaled to where La Gordiloca was. "Keep her back," he ordered.

═══

At around 2:14 a.m., Salinas walked over to the Hotel Ava and trudged up its parking ramp to join Calderon. He, too, had a ballistic chest plate and an AR-15 rifle slung across his chest. As he reached the top of the ramp, his phone rang. It was a DPS colleague from the BIC. After the BOLO was sent out, Ortiz's name had circulated through the intel center, and numerous people had recognized it.

"Are you sure?" Salinas barked into his phone. "Are you a hundred percent?"

He hung up and stared at Calderon.

"What?" Calderon asked. "What's going on?"

"The guy we're looking for—he's a BP agent."

Calderon's mind wobbled with the complexities and risks this latest detail uncorked. A federal agent and military veteran with weapons training. Wanted for murder. Likely armed. Barricaded somewhere nearby. And his men were moving in on him. This made the current scene explosively more dangerous. Calderon knew Border Patrol agents had to recertify their weapons proficiency at least once a year and visited the agency firing range four times a year. Their suspect was now an armed sharpshooter and military vet wanted for murder. Moreover, Ortiz likely was well versed in law enforcement tactics, so he probably knew every search and capture strategy the SWAT team would deploy against him and could possibly counter it.

Calderon was dumbstruck. He could hardly believe the serious sharp turn his case had just taken.

"You have to be shitting me," he said. "Are you serious?"

"One hundred percent," Salinas said.

=====

LYING IN THE BACK OF THE GMC SIERRA ON THE FOURTH FLOOR of the Hotel Ava's parking garage, Ortiz could hear the police manhunt for him mounting. He heard the sirens and squeals of tires as patrol units arrived and sped away. He heard lawmen shouting his name. He could hear them searching the adjoining property and padding up and down the entrance ramp.

He calculated it would be a matter of minutes before they entered the garage, made it up to the fourth floor, and found him in the bed of the truck. He pulled his iPhone from his jeans pocket and gripped it in his hand. When they showed up, he would pop out of the truck's bed and point the smartphone at them, holding it just as he was trained to do on the firing range: left hand cupping the right, arms taut and extended—mimicking the expert hold of a .40-caliber H&K pistol. The deputies, primed with adrenaline and squinting in the dim light of the parking lot, would surely answer with a fusillade of screams and high-velocity rounds that would tear through his body and end his life, hopefully instantly.

Lying faceup in the truck bed, he tapped the Facebook app on his phone and pulled up his profile. He typed a new post: "Doc Ortiz checks out. Farewell." Then, another: "To my wife and kids, I love u."

He lay back and waited for the storm of officers. Minutes stretched into excruciating minutes, which stretched into more than an hour. Text messages piled into Ortiz's iPhone from concerned Border Patrol and military buddies reacting to the Facebook posts.

"You okay brother?"

"Hey bro, what are you up to?"

"JD you okay?"

"Everything ok?"

Aizar Rodolfo Medina, an eleven-year veteran of Border Patrol who knew Ortiz from their time together in Cotulla, read Ortiz's Facebook posts and instantly thought his former colleague was considering suicide. After texting Ortiz and receiving no answer, Medina called another agent, Gabriel Macias, who had gone through the Border Patrol academy with Ortiz, and explained the situation. Macias immediately called Ortiz. "It's over," Ortiz told Macias, before hanging up.

Medina told Macias to contact Border Patrol's Laredo Sector headquarters, then tried calling Ortiz himself. He answered.

"Ortiz, is this you?" Medina said.

"Hey, bro, ya se acabó," Ortiz said.

"No se acabó nada," Medina told him.

Medina kept talking to him, trying to get Ortiz to tell him where he was, thinking of anything to keep his friend from dying by suicide. Ortiz wouldn't answer; the line went quiet.

Medina hung up and called his supervisor in Cotulla to report the phone call.

===

NEXT, ORTIZ CONTACTED HIS WIFE, DANIELLA, WHO WAS STILL waiting for him to join her and their children in San Antonio, wholly unaware of the night's events in Laredo involving her husband.

At 2:10 a.m., he texted her: "Don't come back to Laredo. . . . I love u and my babies . . . I'm sorry. U r the biggest blessing God could have given me."

Two minutes later, Daniella replied: "I love u . . . r u home?"

No reply. She followed up three minutes later with two more texts: "Please answer me" and "Don't do anything stupid. . . . Think of ur kids."

Still, Ortiz wouldn't reply.

Finally, he called her. He whispered into his iPhone, his voice straining with stress and adrenaline. "You and me were perfect in San Antonio," he told her. "Coming to Laredo was a big mistake."

Daniella tried to make sense of her husband's ramblings. He continued: "I should have never come here. We were a great family. Take care of my babies. Don't ever come back to Laredo."

Daniella was nearing hysterics, asking Ortiz what he meant by all this.

"Please don't come back to Laredo," he said. "They're going to the house."

He hung up.

===

AT THE BIC FOUR MILES AWAY, NEWS THAT A LAREDO-BASED Border Patrol supervisory agent was the lead suspect in the recent murders and a target of a multiagency manhunt swirled from one agent to the next. Agents were looking at Ortiz's ominous Facebook posts while hearing of the BOLO out for his arrest.

Gabriela Nuñez, a Border Patrol agent stationed in Laredo, knew Ortiz from working at the BIC. As a peer support specialist with the agency, she had worked with other agents in mental or physical distress, providing psychological support or stress management tips. She knew the signs of suicidal ideation and was instantly alarmed when she stumbled onto Ortiz's early-morning Facebook posts. She tried reaching Ortiz via phone call, text message, and Facebook Messenger. No answer. She called her station and told the supervisory agent on duty what was unfolding and that Ortiz may be on the verge of hurting himself. The agent told her there was a BOLO out on Ortiz and that he was the prime suspect in the recent murders.

Soon after hanging up, her cell phone rang. It was Ortiz. He was crying. Calling her from the bed of the pickup, with sheriff's SWAT teams closing in on him, Ortiz told her how his life had unraveled since moving to Laredo, how he should have stayed in Cotulla, how Laredo made him a "bad person." Ortiz told her how he was an Iraq War veteran and that he had killed people. Nuñez listened. He asked her for a favor: please call his wife and tell her not to come to Laredo. She jotted down her name and number as he relayed the details. Then they hung up.

Nuñez called Daniella, relayed the message, and asked her if she knew where her husband may be hiding in Laredo. Daniella said she did not. They hung up as well.

———

AS ORTIZ ANSWERED TEXTS AND MADE CALLS FROM THE BACK OF the Sierra, Calderon went over last-minute strategies with the search teams. After learning of his suspect's employment, Calderon had called his supervisors, including Sheriff Martin Cuellar, to alert them that they were now hunting a Border Patrol agent. By protocol, Cuellar would have to contact Homeland Security and other agencies to let them know what was happening. Calderon also told the sheriff's SWAT team what they were up against, bringing a higher level of alert and caution to the process. "You go from hypervigilant to hyper-hypervigilant," Calderon said later. "You're a little more on edge."

The agents, now led by the Webb County sheriff's SWAT unit, were ordered to stack up again in single-line formation, one behind the other. One group entered from the entrance ramp; another went in on the other side of the garage, mostly providing background to the main stack. Some wore Kevlar helmets; others had on baseball caps or no headgear at all. All wore some protection on the body. Stacked close together, they meticulously walked through the garage, using flashlights mounted on their assault rifles to peer around each concrete pillar, look between and under each car, and scour every corner as they slowly followed the ramp up from one floor to the next.

The SWAT team was in a vulnerable situation. Agents were out in the open plan of the parking garage, without much cover. A skilled gunman could shoot and wound and potentially kill several of them before they even knew where the gunfire was coming from. Agents made sure they were constantly looking in all directions as they went, guns ready, safeties off.

Obregon and Bradshaw were among them. If Bradshaw was unnerved by the prospect of heading into a dark, cramped, abandoned building looking for Ortiz, the openness and lighting of the parking garage posed their own threatening vibe. The suspect could be squatting behind any of the numerous cars parked there, waiting to spring out and open fire. He could be hiding behind a pillar or a wall. His heart racing, Bradshaw stuck close to his team, clearing one floor after another, meticulously peering behind cars and pillars.

On the third floor, they stopped and regrouped behind a concrete pillar. They radioed the second stack to learn where it was in its search. Sweat dripped from their hairlines and soaked T-shirts. They realigned in their stack and marched up the ramp. One floor to go.

As the ramp took them past the north side of the garage's fourth floor, they passed a black Sierra truck to their left. One of the SWAT team members shone a flashlight in the bed of the truck—and saw Juan David Ortiz lying there.

"Get down!" shouted Noe Gonzalez, head of the SWAT team.

The agents swarmed around the truck. One of the agents slammed open the tailgate as Gonzalez grabbed Ortiz by an arm and yanked him out of the truck. Ortiz landed on the concrete floor with a thud. As Gonzalez held on to his right hand, another SWAT team member twisted up Ortiz's left hand and placed a knee in the center of his back to immobilize him. Agents patted his waistline and pockets, looking for a weapon. They took off his boots.

"Where's the weapon at?" Gonzalez barked.

"In the truck," Ortiz said.

Agents looked in the black Sierra truck where Ortiz had been hiding but didn't see a gun.

"No, *my* truck," Ortiz said, meaning the Dodge Ram he had left at the Stripes.

"What's your name?" someone asked Ortiz.

"You already know," he said, breathing heavily.

His hands were placed behind his back and handcuffed. They pulled Ortiz to his feet and sat him on the Sierra's open tailgate. Someone in the group identified him with the photo in the BOLO. Laredo's serial killer was in custody.

———

MOMENTS AFTER THEY HAD HIM IN HANDCUFFS, CALDERON AND Salinas trotted up the ramp. Calderon looked at the agents, then at Ortiz, hands behind his back, sitting on the edge of the truck.

Someone started to read Ortiz his Miranda rights, but Calderon stopped him. No one was questioning Ortiz, so there was no need to read him his rights yet. From their combined three decades of experience chasing criminals and building legal cases, Calderon and Salinas knew the next few hours were crucial in making sure an indictment was approved and a suspect received justice for his actions. The slightest mis-step could derail the most airtight case.

"You already got him," Calderon told all the agents gathered. "Now, no one talks to him."

═══

AFTER GETTING THE KEYS FROM ORTIZ'S POCKET, DETECTIVES walked one block north to the Stripes and unlocked his Dodge Ram truck. Inside, they found a .40-caliber H&K handgun with nine live rounds in the clip, two loaded .40-caliber twelve-round magazine clips, an envelope with $200 in it, and a Coach handbag on the front passenger seat containing makeup, a pipe, and syringes. In the back seat, there was a makeup bag, a pair of Prada women's sunglasses, and three Bud Light tal-lies. A Tejano Mart store receipt for a Bud Light tally, Powerade, and pack of Marlboros was also crumpled in the back seat. The items were logged, bagged, and ferried to an evidence closet.

═══

ORTIZ WAS FAMILIAR WITH "TROPHY SHOTS"—THE IMPROMPTU, often unauthorized photos taken by law enforcement agents and mili-tary personnel of their captured enemy or suspect. Military buddies had taken their share of trophy shots of captured Iraqis during the Iraq War when Ortiz was there. And he had seen and taken a few himself during his time with the Border Patrol's Targeted Enforcement Unit.

As they wound down the parking garage ramp, Ortiz, hands still cuffed behind his back, turned to his captors.

"Take your trophy shot," he told them.

The agents refused to take the bait.

"We're not about that, bro," Gonzalez, the SWAT team leader, an-swered.

On the ground floor, he was placed into a waiting Webb County sheriff's truck and sped to the Highway 59 substation for questioning.

PART 4

CHAPTER 19

Before Saturday, September 15, 2018, Captain Federico Calderon had conducted more than one hundred interviews with suspects detained during his criminal investigations—and had extracted videotaped confessions from nearly all of them. Child molesters, domestic violence assaulters, embezzlers, and petty thieves had all met him in the interview room and left after volunteering a confession, which later helped in their conviction. Calderon never once pounded his fist on the table in front of a suspect, employed the good cop, bad cop strategy, or used any of the other tactics popular with scriptwriters of TV crime shows. His philosophy was simple: be as respectful and friendly and direct as possible to get the suspect talking—then keep him talking. About anything: his job, his marriage, the weather. That conversation, Calderon learned, inevitably veered to the alleged crimes and, more often than not, concluded with detailed confessions.

Calderon had read books on the interview process and attended seminars. He was intrigued by what made some suspects talk and others clam up. In his experience, hardened criminals—those with long records and repeated trips to the interview room—knew the process and often refused to utter a word without an attorney present. First-timers with less experience behind bars were often happy to talk. Men tended to talk more than women, and law enforcement agents thought they could talk their way out of anything. Eye contact was important; it put the suspect in a slight discomfort zone and made him vulnerable enough to talk.

As Calderon arrived at the sheriff's substation, he realized he faced the most important and daunting interview of his career. His suspect was a federal law enforcement agent and military veteran who knew the inner workings of criminal interviews and had likely conducted a few himself. Calderon already had amassed a decent amount of evidence against Ortiz, including shell casings at the crime scenes with the same caliber as his weapon, matching tire tracks at each scene, and the testimony of an escaped would-be victim. But a videotaped confession would firmly put this case to bed. The stakes couldn't be any higher.

Calderon felt he had a few things on his side: As far as he knew, this was Ortiz's first arrest. He was a law enforcement agent, which had its downsides but may line up with Calderon's theory of him thinking he could talk his way out of anything. And he was male. As he prepped for the interview, Calderon reminded himself of two key tactics to use with Ortiz: (1) Make eye contact. (2) Keep him talking.

He also made the crucial decision to leave his agency-issued SIG Sauer P226 .357 pistol in a drawer in his office instead of bringing it into the interview room. It put him in a vulnerable position inside the room next to a murder suspect. But he didn't want the possibility, albeit remote, of Ortiz somehow wresting the weapon away from him and causing more death or damage. He would conduct the interview unarmed.

=====

THE SUBSTATION, TYPICALLY QUIET AT THAT EARLY SATURDAY morning hour, hummed with activity. DPS troopers, including Obregon and Bradshaw, sheriff's deputies, and Border Patrol agents milled about in the parking lot, cased the hallways, or crowded into the room with the "Operation Stonegarden and Asset Room" sign on the door. Some of the agents still buzzed with the adrenaline rush of hunting and capturing Ortiz. Others were just curious; word that a Border Patrol agent had been arrested in connection with the murders had by then pinged through nearly every law enforcement radio and cell phone in the county. Webb County sheriff Martin Cuellar arrived and went straight for the asset room. Inside, six cushioned swivel chairs surrounded a large oval conference table, and a flat-screen TV mounted to the wall flickered with a closed-circuit live feed from inside the interview room, around the corner and down the hall. Agents streamed in and settled into the chairs or stood by the wall, all eyes glued to the screen.

In a neighboring room, Erika Peña wrapped herself in a blanket and stretched out on a cot. Oblivious to the commotion in the substation, made primarily by her doing, she dozed in and out of sleep.

====

ORTIZ WAS LED INSIDE THE INTERVIEW ROOM AT 2:51 A.M., HIS hands cuffed behind his back and his feet shackled, and was sat in one of the chairs. He faced a hidden camera on the wall directly in front of him. A microphone hidden in the ceiling above him picked up all sound. After a few minutes by himself, he asked to use the bathroom and was escorted out of the room, returning a short while later, this time with his hands handcuffed in front of his body. He sat again in one of the chairs. Thirty minutes later, Salinas and Calderon walked into the room and closed the door behind them. Salinas introduced himself, shook Ortiz's hand, and sat in a chair to Ortiz's right. Calderon introduced himself, then undid Ortiz's left handcuff and cuffed it to the arm of his chair, freeing his left hand. He sat in a chair directly across the table from the suspect, his back to the camera. Ortiz leaned over the table and rested his face on his left fist as Salinas started the questioning.

"What's your name?" he asked.

"You guys already know," Ortiz answered.

"Well, can you tell us?"

"You guys already know."

Ortiz looked bored as Salinas read him his Miranda rights. "Do you understand your rights?" he asked. Ortiz nodded yes.

"Okay," Salinas said, spreading out a document. "I just need your initials right here that you've understood your rights."

"No, I'm good."

"You don't want to sign that?"

"No."

Ortiz's general uncooperativeness continued. But when Salinas told him they planned to get a search warrant and go to his house, his demeanor shifted. Ortiz told them his wife was driving back from San Antonio, how she had gone there with their kids and he was supposed to meet them. He asked if someone could stop her before she reached Laredo. He gave her name and described the black Chevy Tahoe she was driving. He told them all the weapons he had at the house—the loaded Bushmaster AR-15 sitting on the kitchen island, the two shotguns in the garage, the .45-caliber Kimber pistol under his bed in the master bedroom—and asked they use the keys to enter instead of kicking in the door.

Ortiz asked them again to stop Daniella from coming to Laredo. He told them about his conversation with her earlier that night as he hid from the police in the garage, urging her not to come to Laredo.

"I was a squared-away motherfucker in San Antonio," he told the detectives.

They were less than twenty minutes into the interview, and one of the keys to Calderon's strategy was working. Ortiz was talking. And kept talking. He told them about being in the Border Patrol's Targeted Enforcement Unit and how he was promoted to the BIC. He talked about his eight years of active duty in the military and his time in Iraq. He told them about visiting the VA clinic in Laredo and the mix of eight medications he was prescribed. He talked about struggling with PTSD and having suicidal thoughts. He talked about the Canelo fight and planning to meet his wife and children in San Antonio. As he spoke, Ortiz leaned his left elbow on the table and looked down, as if speaking to the floor, the fingers of his left hand dancing nervously on the table with each word.

As the investigators tried to get him to go over the details of the previous night, Ortiz said he didn't remember.

"I'd like to know if you know why you are here?" Calderon asked.

"I have no idea," he said.

Ortiz denied recalling being at the Circle K earlier that night. He denied knowing Erika Peña, saying the only person he knew with that name was a girl from high school. He said he knew nothing about the deaths of Melissa and Claudine outside what he had seen on the news. He said he hadn't fired his service weapon in months.

The interview wasn't going exactly as Calderon envisioned, but he kept Ortiz talking. He talked some more about his days in the Targeted Enforcement Unit and about his time in Cotulla. He still didn't remember any involvement with Erika or other women, but he did recall working the Labor Day before Melissa's body was found and had worked a few days before his arrest.

A few minutes past 5:00 a.m., Ortiz was given a bathroom break, a bottled water, and a bag of Cool Ranch Doritos. Alone in the interview room, he bounced his leg in his seat, laid his head down on the table for a few minutes, tapped the table with his fingers, or covered his head with his free arm, rocking his body and moaning. A deputy was constantly standing just outside the door. Minute after minute went by, Ortiz alone with his thoughts.

When Calderon and Salinas returned nearly an hour later, they asked him about the Facebook posts he had made earlier that night. Ortiz said he was ready to end his life then. "If I would have had my firearm, I would have literally shot you guys," he told them. "I was ready to shoot myself back then. I've been wanting to do that a long time."

They had been speaking to Ortiz for over two hours, and though Ortiz had volunteered details of his life and seemed to remember a lot of specifics about his job, they were still no closer to having him confess to the murders.

Salinas pulled out eight-by-ten color head shots of each of the victims and spread them on the table before Ortiz. The victims were blood-splattered, recently killed. "Look at this one, please," Calderon said. Ortiz glanced down. "That's Melissa," Calderon said. ".40-caliber Smith & Wesson to the back of the head. More than once."

Salinas pulled out another photo.

"That's the same girl?" Ortiz asked.

"No, that's Claudine. .40-caliber Smith & Wesson, a big shot."

Calderon showed him pictures of Erika and Erika's floral purse left in the back of his truck. "That's not your wife's, right?" Salinas said.

"No," Ortiz said.

Still, Ortiz denied knowing Erika.

"I don't know who this person is."

"Then why is her stuff in your car?" Calderon said.

"I have no idea."

Ortiz kept looking at the floor, his head bobbing slightly up and down, up and down.

"Ortiz, look at me," Calderon said.

Ortiz looked up.

"Look at her, that's Melissa."

Ortiz's head bobbed up and down, his stare blank.

"You did this." Calderon pointed to Claudine's crime scene photo. "You did that."

Ortiz let out a low, barely audible whistle through his teeth.

"You did all of this," Calderon continued. Then, pointing to Erika's photo: "And you almost did it to her."

"If these allegations are true, then I'm fucked," Ortiz said, his voice barely above a whisper. "That's all there is to it."

Ortiz's story had suddenly veered from flat denial of any involvement to, if the allegations were true, no recollection of them. It was a slight but significant shift in his story.

Calderon put jailhouse mug shots of Melissa and Claudine next to their bloodied crime scene photos. "This is what Claudine looked like before," he said, pointing at the mug shot, "and this is what she looked like after she had an encounter with you."

Ortiz shrugged and bobbed his head. He kept looking down, pausing to take a sip of water. When he spoke, his voice quavered. "I have no recollection of what you say," he said. "That's all there is to it."

Through Ortiz's denials, his memory lapses, his shifts in story, Calderon's voice remained calm, low, and steady, almost warm. It was just past 6:00 a.m. The interview had been going on for over three hours. To Calderon, it was just getting started.

Isidro "Chilo" Alaniz was up early on Saturday, September 15, and readying for a weekend retreat on his ranch in eastern Webb County. As the elected district attorney, Alaniz had been busy the previous few weeks overseeing the prosecutions of child molesters, drug runners, and various other indicted criminals. He also, of course, was keeping tabs on the case of the serial killer of Laredo. Webb County sheriff's assistant chief Wayo Ruiz had called him twice in the past twelve days to alert him of the murders of first Melissa and then Claudine. It was an unnerving trend, and Alaniz hoped detectives would catch up with the killer. That Saturday morning, the plan was to head to the ranch early and clear some overgrown shrubs on the property. It was the best way for him to unwind.

Just before 6:00 a.m., his phone rang. It was Wayo again. He answered, expecting more bad news. Instead, Wayo told him deputies had arrested a suspect in the case and were questioning him at the substation on Highway 59. Also: the suspect was a Border Patrol agent.

Alaniz's heart took a mini flip. Of all the theories and possible suspects that had swirled in his head since the murders began, a Border Patrol agent as the gunman wasn't one of them. He scratched his plans for the ranch and drove to the substation. On the way, he called his deputy, Joaquin Rodriguez, who agreed to meet him there.

=====

A Laredo native, Alaniz was a popular figure in Webb County. Tall, clean-shaven, and charming, able to give speeches fluently in English and Spanish, he had easily won both his elections. Billboards around town with his likeness were constant reminders of his omnipresence: one showed him holding a football and urging residents to "Make the Right Call" and not drink and drive; another solicited their vote in his upcoming reelection.

The son of a federal probation officer, Alaniz spent summer afternoons as a boy in the federal courthouse with his dad, admiring how the attorneys ran the show, defending clients or sending criminals to prison.

After graduating law school, he got a job as an assistant district attorney in Laredo, then later worked at the Federal Public Defender's Office. He opened a private practice and ran it for a few years, representing defendants in federal court. But his heart was always in prosecuting. When the Webb County district attorney announced he was retiring in 2008, Alaniz jumped at the chance, running as a Democrat. The election went to a runoff—and Alaniz won handily. By 2018, he had been reelected three times.

As the lead prosecutor for two counties stretching 150 miles across the U.S.-Mexico border,* Alaniz oversaw cases ranging from the mundane to the tragic. He secured four life sentences for the killer of two-year-old Katherine Cardenas, who, in 2009, was raped, beaten, strangled, and left to die in an abandoned dresser in Laredo. He also got a ninety-nine-year prison sentence for a convicted murderer and fugitive who evaded capture for seven years in Mexico before being arrested and extradited to Laredo in 2018.

═══

As HE DROVE TO THE SUBSTATION SATURDAY MORNING, ALANIZ wrestled with the contours of his latest serial killer case. As a Border Patrol agent, the suspect was probably familiar with the inner workings of investigations. Alaniz had prosecuted first responders before, mainly firefighters and police officers, but on relatively minor charges of driving while intoxicated or domestic violence. Never a federal law enforcement agent facing capital murder charges. Alaniz knew the odds were slim of the suspect at the substation readily admitting to any role in the murders.

He knew a lot hinged on Ortiz's interview with investigators. Alaniz thought back to how, eighteen years earlier, he had traveled to Wyoming

* The district attorney for the Forty-Ninth Judicial District of Texas represents both Webb and Zapata Counties.

as a young lawyer to take a law course with celebrated trial attorney Gerry Spence and how the veteran lawyer stressed that in every person you should try to find "that thread of good." He tucked the concept away in his mind.

Alaniz arrived at the substation at the same time as Rodriguez, and they entered the building together. In a hallway inside, they ran into Salinas, who had already been interviewing Ortiz for several hours. Alaniz and Salinas had collaborated on cases before and knew each other well. Despite Ortiz's denials and shrugs, Salinas felt confident they were headed in the right direction.

"He's almost there," he told the prosecutors.

Alaniz and Rodriguez slipped into the asset room and watched the feed from the interview room on the flat-screen TV alongside DPS troopers and other agents. As the interview unfolded, Alaniz grabbed a legal pad and pen and began scribbling.

———

IN THE INTERVIEW ROOM, ORTIZ DETAILED HOW THE PILLS from the VA clinic made him feel detached from reality, how his time with the Targeted Enforcement Unit introduced him to the drug dens and prostitutes of San Bernardo Avenue, as well as more details about being a navy corpsman during his tour in Iraq.

Salinas and Calderon listened intently, encouraged by how much he was talking.

Down the hall in the asset room, Alaniz smoothed out a blank paper and wrote in clear, all-caps lettering: "HELP US UNDERSTAND. THERE HAS TO BE AN EXPLANATION. -THESE GIRLS, WERE THEY THREATENING YOU? -YOUR JOB? -YOUR WIFE? -YOUR REPUTATION?" He slid the sheet in a manila folder and gave it to a deputy to shuttle to Calderon.

Intermittently, Calderon and Salinas would exit the room and leave Ortiz alone for extended periods of time. Ortiz would fidget, stretch, stand up, hum, whistle bird noises, or mumble to himself. At one point, he stood up and leaned over his chair, to which he was still handcuffed, and muttered, "Ya se acabó el pedo."

Then, a minute later: "Chingadamadre . . . Ya se acabó el pedo."

Still, when Salinas and Calderon returned to the room and sat at the table, Ortiz wouldn't admit to any crimes or even knowing any of the women. "I didn't do any of this shit," he told them. They were approaching the five-hour mark of the interview and still had no confession.

Frustration and desperation were mounting in Ortiz. Even as he denied everything, he asked that, when he went to jail, he be placed in an isolated cell block, away from the general inmate population. Salinas pulled out the photo of Claudine.

"How many more of these pictures do you have?" Ortiz asked, picking up the picture and looking at the bloodied face.

"You tell us . . . you're the one who did it," Calderon said.

With his left hand, Ortiz crumpled up the photo and tossed it aside on the table.

Calderon and Salinas stood up to leave.

"You're the only one who can help yourself," Salinas told him. "No one else. We can't force you to help yourself."

Ortiz nodded, and the detectives left the room.

===

AFTER ORTIZ HAD BEEN ALONE ABOUT AN HOUR, A TEAM OF deputies entered the interview room. One deputy swabbed the inside of Ortiz's mouth for a DNA sample. Then they made him undress, took photos of the tattoos on his chest and arms, and ordered him to put on an orange short-sleeved prison shirt and pants. Then they recuffed both his hands.

Salinas and Calderon reentered the room, and Salinas told him the district attorney was in the building. Salinas took his same chair to the right of Ortiz. This time, however, Calderon pulled over a high-backed swivel chair that was sitting in the corner and rolled it over directly next to Ortiz. Calderon said they had called Ortiz's wife and asked her to return to San Antonio, as he'd requested, and were working on retrieving a picture of him and his children, taken last Father's Day, that he had asked for. Though they couldn't promise anything, they told Ortiz they were also asking for permission to place him in an isolated wing of the county jail, as requested.

Now, the detectives wanted some cooperation in return.

"Help us out," Calderon said.

"I didn't do anything, man," said Ortiz, staring at the floor, his right leg bouncing silently.

"Help yourself. Help us out with what happened."

"It's that I didn't do anything. That's it."

"Do the right thing, Ortiz."

"I've done nothing, okay?"

Ortiz dropped his face into his handcuffed hands, sniffling quietly, then wiped tears from his eyes.

Calderon inched closer to him. "J. D., look at me please . . . Let's start over."

"My mom is having a heart attack. She really is . . ."

"J. D., you've served your country."

"My mom is really, really going to have a heart attack . . ."

"You've served your country. You've continued serving your country through the U.S. Border Patrol. You're doing the right thing. Help us right now. Help us do the right thing."

═══

ALANIZ, WATCHING FROM THE ASSET ROOM, WROTE OUT ON A blank piece of paper, in all caps: "WE HAVE SHELL CASINGS FROM EACH CRIME SCENE." He tore it out, again slipped it into the manila folder, and again handed it to a deputy to take to Calderon. It was a bluff, of course. It would be weeks before a forensic lab would positively match the shell casings found at the crime scenes to Ortiz's handgun. But it seemed like a good card to play.

The door of the interview room was pried open, and the deputy handed Calderon the folder with the note from Alaniz. He looked it over, then inched closer to Ortiz.

"We're having information," Calderon said. "We're going to get there. Help your family."

Ortiz stared at the floor, his right leg bouncing, bouncing.

"J. D."

Ortiz kept staring at the floor.

"J. D."

He looked up.

"No te quedes como estamos. Help your wife. Help us so that we can get past this."

Ortiz gazed down at the floor. His shoulders sagged slightly, and, still looking down, he said, "Erika was in my house." Barely a whisper.

"Erika was in your house today?"

"Yes."

"Okay, what happened?"

Ortiz began unspooling the events of the past twenty-four hours: picking up Erika; her bringing up Melissa's death, then talking about Claudine; taking her to score drugs; driving her back to his house; Erika feeling nauseated and throwing up in his driveway; driving her to the Valero gas station on Bob Bullock Loop.

He told the detectives that he was just moving his gun and Erika freaked out. He tried grabbing her to calm her, but she yanked herself out of the truck and ran off topless.

For twenty minutes, Ortiz recounted his time with Erika, hedging the story in parts so it appeared more impulsive, less sinister. He admitted to knowing Melissa but didn't mention anything about her death or Claudine's.

Calderon told Ortiz they had recovered the casings from each scene, along with the bullets and casings from his gun.

"We got them," Calderon said, his gaze fixed on Ortiz, his voice low and steady. "What are you going to tell us on some of these slug shots?"

Ortiz looked down at the floor.

"Well?" Calderon said. "J. D., look at me."

Ortiz let out a shuddering sigh.

"It all started . . ." He paused and held up his handcuffed hands. "Can you please take these off? I'm not going to attack you."

A moment of tension swelled in the room. Calderon was unarmed and being asked to uncuff his murder suspect. Ortiz could attack him. But he knew Salinas had his weapon on him. Besides, there were more than a dozen armed agents just outside the door. He would play the odds. Calderon stole a quick glance at Salinas, then stood up, fished out a key from his jeans pocket, and removed Ortiz's handcuffs. Ortiz propped an elbow on the table and leaned his head on his left hand.

"Melissa was a friend of mine . . ."

CHAPTER 20

For the next thirty-seven minutes, Ortiz recounted, in vibrant and graphic detail, how he picked up, killed, and discarded the women of San Bernardo Avenue, starting with Melissa, then Claudine, then Chelly. He described what they were wearing, where he drove them, how many times and where he shot them, and what they said in their final moments. He told the detectives how Melissa fell asleep in his truck, how he drove home and went to bed with his wife after killing Claudine, how Chelly's legs smelled so bad he was forced to crack a window. He recounted how Melissa insulted him moments before he shot her, and the cold realization that swept over Claudine—how she repeated, "You were probably the killer!" over and over—seconds before shooting her, too.

He described each scene with a flurry of hand gestures and animated Spanglish flourishes ("Con esta no había nada de que I feel bad . . . No había nada de nada") and simulated how he lifted his gun and shot them, one after another, the way he might retell it to friends on a hunting trip.

Ortiz told them how, as he cruised down San Bernardo after Melissa's death, he was filled with an undeniable urge to rid the avenue of its sex workers. "This is where the monster came out," he told them. He remembered seeing some of them in La Gordiloca's videos, unbathed and jobless save for their solicitations with strangers, and how they filled him with inexplicable rage.

"They are all fucking mierdas," Ortiz said, adding: "This is going to sound stupid, but, like, I wanted to clean up the streets."

Ortiz sat with his legs uncrossed at the table, feet on the floor. His hands rested on his knees, both bobbing up and down in a nervous rhythm. His head slanted slightly down as he spoke.

Suddenly, he lifted his gaze to look at Salinas and Calderon.

"You guys haven't found this one," he said, his voice just above a murmur. "You literally need to send someone out."

He told them about Janelle: how he picked up someone whom he described as a "tranny" on San Bernardo, drove her to the exit off Mile Marker 15, marched her behind the gravel mounds, and shot her once behind the head.

═══

IN THE ASSET ROOM, JOAQUIN RODRIGUEZ'S MOUTH GAPED OPEN and his eyes widened as he turned to Alaniz. The room erupted with activity. Deputies and troopers sprang out of chairs, grabbed weapons and belts, and headed for their patrol units to jump on Interstate 35 and search for Janelle's body.

Alaniz and Rodriguez looked at each other. They had heard Ortiz's words but couldn't entirely believe what he was saying. He had admitted to committing the murders of three victims known to investigators in Webb County—then offered the location of a fourth. All captured on video. To prosecutors, it was an extraordinary, unexpected piece of self-incrimination.

Alaniz and Rodriguez stood and followed the deputies out the door. Before leaving, Alaniz checked in on Erika in the room next to theirs. He knocked, let himself in, and introduced himself.

"Thank you for what you did," he told her. "You were very brave." He added: "It's going to be okay."

"Thank you," Erika said.

═══

CALDERON AND SALINAS CONCLUDED THEIR QUESTIONING AT around noon. It had been nine long hours of mental gymnastics, but Ortiz had offered more than most law enforcement officials and prosecutors expected.

As they wrapped up, Calderon asked Ortiz if he was hungry and offered to bring him lunch. Sure, Ortiz said.

Calderon stuck out his hand. "Thank you."

Ortiz shook it. "I'm sorry," he said.

Salinas shook his hand next.

"I'm sorry," Ortiz said again.

Calderon left and asked a deputy to stand guard by the open door, leaving Ortiz alone and uncuffed. Thirty minutes later, he returned with a large Whataburger bag and set it on the table in front of him. Ortiz asked again for the picture of his kids and wife. Calderon said he would try to get it.

Ortiz pulled out a burger from inside the bag and hungrily tore into it.

===

MELISSA'S MOM, CRISTINA BENAVIDES, STRUGGLED WITH SLEEP. Since Melissa's death, she was haunted nightly with images of her daughter—her mischievous smile when she teased her mom about her outdated smartphone, her pained face when she came home bruised and bloodied—and her mind spun restlessly with unanswered questions about her murder. Could she have done more to find her, get her off the streets? Was her announcement a few days before her death that someone would shoot her just another vision? Or was someone actually after her? Were detectives any closer to catching her assailant?

In the predawn hours of Saturday morning, unable to sleep, she sat up in bed, flicked on her smartphone, and tapped the Facebook app. She still enjoyed looking at Melissa's profile, her smiling face gazing back at her. Sometimes it helped; other times it just deepened the pain. As she opened the app, she noticed La Gordiloca was broadcasting and tapped on her feed. Cristina sat up in bed, her eyes sharpening their focus on the small screen. She followed La Gordiloca's every word and image intently. She couldn't believe what she was seeing, as red and blue lights flickered on the tiny screen. Police were closing in on her daughter's killer.

=====

ON FRIDAY, SEPTEMBER 14, ARMANDO ORTIZ FELT THE FAMIL-iar pang of missing his daughter Janelle. Things had turned thorny be-tween them since she had transitioned to a woman in her late teens. But his heart still swelled with love and worry for her. He still called her "my puppy," a pet name he derived for her when she was just a toddler. He knew she needed help—getting off drugs, getting enough to eat and a place to sleep—and that primordial protective pull a parent never loses for a child drew him out of the house and into his car. He had tried to find her the previous day with no luck. He wanted to try again.

Armando cruised up and down San Bernardo, driving through some of the motel parking lots, side streets, and taco stands he knew Janelle frequented, but he couldn't find her. He asked a few other sex workers loitering on the avenue, but no one had seen or heard from Janelle. The following day, Saturday, as detectives questioned Juan David Ortiz at the substation, he tried again, taking a few laps around San Bernardo. Again, no sign of Janelle.

By Saturday evening, worry had morphed to mild panic. Word of La Gordiloca's early-morning broadcast from near the Hotel Ava was circulating around Laredo, and members of the Ortiz family were fear-ing the worst. Local media reports of a third and fourth victim, includ-ing a "male victim" next to the gravel mounds off Interstate 35 and Mile Marker 15, deepened their concern. Armando was at his home on San Francisco Avenue, strumming on his guitar to steer his mind away from his daughter's absence, when he received a panicked call from his sister, Patricia. "Mando, Mando!" she gasped, calling him by his nickname. "One of them is a guy!" She had called the police, but no one knew anything.

Armando tried next, calling the emergency number for the Webb

County Sheriff's Office and asking the operator if the body found on Interstate 35 was his son's.* The operator couldn't say but took down his phone number and said someone would call him back. No one did. For the next forty-eight hours, detectives would refer to the body discovered by the gravel mounds as "John Doe." From her home in Indiana, Janelle's mom, Elva Ortiz, had been following the Laredo murders closely and became distraught at the news of two more victims, paired with reports from the family that Janelle was missing. Unable to contribute much from northern Indiana, she turned to Facebook. "If you see my Janelle his [sic] been missing no one knows where she is plz call me I message me," she posted on her page, above a picture of a smiling Rosenda next to Janelle, the latter's hair flowing over her shoulders, her pink-colored lips in a slight smile.

The following day, Sunday, as the family gathered at Patricia's house, she received a call from the medical examiner's office. She handed the phone to Armando. An official there was returning their call to the sheriff's office and wanted to know if they could name any tattoos or other identifying marks on one of the bodies they had recovered from Interstate 35. It dawned on Armando that he didn't know any tattoos his daughter might have. Ezekiel, who was in the house, took the phone and described the La Santísima skull tattoo on Janelle's right shoulder. The official confirmed that she was the fourth victim and asked the family to come to the medical examiner's office on Highway 59 for an official ID.

When they arrived, only Armando was allowed to enter and see the body. He was escorted to the back receiving room, where, stretched out on an examination table, lay his daughter. She was faceup, with a sheet pulled up to her neck. Any blood and gore had been wiped away. Her eyes were closed and face serene, as if sleeping. It reminded Armando of how she looked when she napped as a child.

He dropped his face into his hands and wept.

---

* Armando still often slipped and called Janelle his "son."

=====

Joey Cantu was working at his job installing air-conditioning systems early Sunday morning when Sara, Chelly's daughter, reached him on his cell phone.

"Did you hear about Chelly?"

Joey had been so focused on his new job and staying in good standing with his parole officer that he hadn't heard of the murders plaguing Laredo, much less about his sister's involvement. The last time the two had spoken was several weeks earlier, when they had had a brief Face-Time chat.

"No, what about her?" he said.

"She's dead."

The medical examiner's office was able to identify Chelly through fingerprints that matched Webb County Jail records, but police were still more than forty-eight hours away from naming her publicly. Still, word had leaked down through those unofficial channels in Laredo and seeped into the motel rooms of San Bernardo, where Sara picked up on it. She knew her mom was the third victim before most of Laredo and the world did.

"Man, shut the fuck up," Joey told her, the facts not fitting into his reality. "Stop playing with me."

"I'm for real," she said. "They just found her."

Joey hung up and called his aunt Anna. She was hearing similar rumblings and feared it might be true. She told him about police arresting a Border Patrol agent who they thought committed the murders. Joey battled feelings that flowed between disbelief and crippling grief. He and his sister had been so close to reconnecting; he had been so close to getting his ankle monitor removed and finding her and pulling her off the streets. How had all those plans so quickly vaporized? He felt that familiar red rage, dormant for so long, rising in him.

Joey walked off his job site and stormed down the street. He was possessed by a single thought: to get arrested so he could confront that

Border Patrol agent in jail, then teach him what happens when someone hurts his sister.

=====

THE PRESS CONFERENCE ON MONDAY DREW MORE THAN A DOZEN journalists, including some from national outlets such as CNN, the *New York Times,* the Associated Press, and *USA Today,* everyone cramming into the second-floor reception area at the sheriff's Victoria Street head-quarters. Alaniz, increasingly the public face of the case as it shifted to the courts, stood next to Sheriff's Deputy Chief Federico Garza and described the broad outlines of the case: the victims, the chase, the man-hunt, the capture. A flat-screen TV flashed images of the victims, along with their names and ages, including Melissa Ramirez and Claudine Anne Luera. Chelly and Janelle were listed as "Jane Doe" and "John Doe," respectively. Standing next to Alaniz and Garza were members of the FBI and Carla Provost, the chief of Border Patrol, who called Ortiz a "rogue individual" and not representative of the thousands of agents who work in the region. She said Ortiz had one minor blemish on his record—the cigarette-snatching allegation from Cotulla—but noth-ing else pointing to worrisome behavior. "We do extensive background checks," she told reporters.

Behind the scenes, Salinas and investigators from the district at-torney's office were busy interviewing Ortiz's coworkers and poring through his personnel record, looking for any clues as to how and why a decorated war veteran and Border Patrol rising star would launch a kill-ing spree in Laredo. They interviewed Callahan, the woman who alleged a one-night stand with Ortiz a decade earlier. A detective from Corpus Christi reached out, wondering if Ortiz was involved in the unsolved murder of a transgender woman there, but nothing came of it.

The CBP's Office of Professional Responsibility, which investigates allegations of wrongdoing by Border Patrol agents, opened its own in-quiry into Ortiz, delving into his past at the agency and sharing records with Salinas and other investigators. Meanwhile, Ortiz was transferred to Webb County Jail and placed in an isolated wing. He was held there on $2.5 million bond.

═══

FUNERALS FOLLOWED.

Janelle's took place at the Aguero Funeral Home & Crematorium. Friends from school, relatives, and fellow sex workers streamed into the funeral home and walked past her open casket. Her mom, Elva, who took the thirty-hour Greyhound bus trip from Gary, Indiana, to Laredo to attend, marveled at the number of people who knew and cared for her daughter. The family dressed her in a red sequin dress, matching pumps, and red lipstick, emulating Aretha Franklin's final outfit as Janelle had requested days earlier. A flat-screen television flashed baby photos of Janelle. Her schoolmate Andy Garcia showed up, spent a long minute looking down at his old middle school friend, then walked over to Elva and cried.

Less than a mile away, family members, friends, acquaintances, and old boyfriends filled the Nieto Funeral Home and Crematory to pay respects to Claudine. Her face was so badly disfigured by the gunshots that the funeral home suggested a closed casket. The family agreed. The funeral home overflowed with more than three hundred people; some waited in line outside to get in. Luera relatives drove in from Hearne and Bryan, Texas. One former boyfriend drove in from Oklahoma to drop a rose on her casket. Relatives from Scotland, unable to make the journey, sent sprays of flowers. A Mass followed at Our Lady of Guadalupe Catholic Church. Claudine's youngest daughter, Malena Benitez, sixteen, gave the eulogy and sang songs by the Christian rock band Hillsong United, including "Oceans":

> You call me out upon the waters
> The great unknown where feet may fail
> And there I find You in the mystery
> In oceans deep my faith will stand.

The day after Janelle's and Claudine's services, the Aguero Funeral Home hosted Chelly's viewing. About 150 people showed up for a muted affair that drew mostly family members.

Cristina Benavides had held Melissa's funeral and Mass a few days after her body was discovered on September 3. Friends and family filled the Joe Jackson Funeral Chapel. One man, whom Cristina didn't know, cried over her casket, then bellowed, "I'm going to find out who did this to you!" Unable to afford the cost of burial, Cristina had her daughter's body cremated and her remains placed in a small wooden urn. Cristina placed the urn on a small wooden table in the kitchen of her mobile home in Rio Bravo, along with a framed photo of a smiling Melissa, draped with a wooden rosary, and a Bible opened to Psalm 91: "Whoever dwells in the shelter of the Most High will rest in the shadow of the Almighty." Melissa's final resting place was her mom's kitchen.

On Tuesday, September 18, friends and family members of Janelle, Melissa, and Claudine gathered at San Agustín Plaza downtown for a candlelight and prayer vigil. Some relatives wore pink T-shirts emblazoned with Melissa's photo or carried poster boards with a handwritten scrawl: "Justice for Melissa Ramirez." Malena, Claudine's daughter, wore a handmade sign around her neck with a picture of her mother. In the photo, Claudine is freshly made up, her hair is combed straight down, and she smiles for the camera. Around the photo, a handwritten message: "She is my mother." A local pastor prayed for the women in Spanish and said God was now looking over them. It was the first time some of the various victims' families met.

"I'm numb right now," Claudine's sister Colette said at the event. "It's just overwhelming to see that she's gone."

CHAPTER 21

As families mourned, District Attorney Alaniz prepared for what would be the biggest case of his career.

Four murders and an aggravated assault, with a federal law enforcement agent as the main suspect. The case transcended multiple jurisdictions and across local, state, and federal governments, with potential repercussions stretching from Laredo to Austin to Washington, D.C.

His investigators fanned out across Webb County, gathering evidence and interviewing Ortiz's former colleagues, looking for anything Calderon and Salinas may have missed or any new nuggets that could help the case. The evidence was already formidable: shell casings, matching tire tracks at each scene, an eyewitness, and, at its center, the nine-hour videotaped interview and confession. Another adage by Gerry Spence, Alaniz's trial lawyer mentor, sprang to mind: "The most effective structure for any argument will always be story." How would he be able to wrangle all the different sides of this story into a digestible narrative for jurors? He began mentally assembling the plot points of this drama.

The star of the story, of course, would be Erika Peña, the sole eyewitness who not only could describe Ortiz pulling a gun on her but could also offer details of his indulgence in the San Bernardo sex trade. Alaniz realized, however, that keeping tabs on her would be the case's biggest challenge. Her life already unstable, Erika spiraled in the weeks following her escape. Scared that Ortiz might still find her—or send someone to permanently quiet her—she jumped from friend's couch to friend's couch, scared to come home, since Ortiz knew where she lived. She confided to friends and family that she was still terrified, her nervous system unable to accept the fact that Ortiz was safely locked up in an isolated wing at the Webb County Jail. Her mother, Adriana Rodriguez, took her to a therapist, who diagnosed her with post-traumatic stress disorder. Erika found solace in the best place she knew: heroin-filled syringes and crack pipes. Old habits drew her back into dark corners of San Bernardo and trouble with the law. In May 2019, just as Alaniz was readying her for a pretrial hearing, she was arrested for criminal trespassing, then again two months later for resisting arrest.

Communicating mostly through her mom, a victim coordinator in Alaniz's office helped connect Erika with rehab services, affordable housing, and other support services. After her July arrest, as a condition of her release, Erika stayed at a halfway house, away from the seductions of San Bernardo. Alaniz needed her sober and focused. The defense lawyers had requested Ortiz's $2.5 million bond be lowered, and one of the most significant pretrial hearings was fast approaching. To counter the defense's motion, Alaniz requested an evidentiary hearing, essentially staging a "mini-trial" where witnesses would take the stand and evidence would be introduced. The tactic had two objectives: (1) to combat the motion for any bond reduction with some of the evidence against Ortiz; and (2) to get Erika's testimony on the record so that, if she vanished before the actual trial, it could be introduced as evidence and the jurors could read it. Alaniz prayed she would stick around—and steer clear of opioids—until at least the pretrial hearing.

━━

ON OCTOBER 13, 2019, ALANIZ AND HIS TEAM FILED INTO THE fourth-floor courtroom at the Webb County Justice Center in Laredo, followed by Ortiz's new court-appointed lawyer, Joel Perez, for the bond reduction hearing. Minutes later, Ortiz, dressed in a short-sleeved orange prison suit, hands and feet shackled, was led in and took a seat next to Perez. Colette, Cristina, Rosenda, and other victims' relatives watched from the gallery. A bailiff ordered everyone to rise, and 406th Judicial District Court judge Oscar Hale, black robe flowing, walked in and took his perch overlooking the courtroom. Mostly bald with tufts of jet-black hair running along the sides of his head, clean-shaven with wire-rimmed glasses, Hale was a veteran arbitrator of Webb County's drug courts and had seen some of the murder victims previously in his court as defendants. He had a reputation for being firm but fair, with a knack for problem-solving and transparency. He was the first judge in Webb County to allow cameras inside the courtroom and launched a Drug Court program aimed at getting drug offenders treatment and lowering their recidivism rate. He had smallish eyes set close together that always appeared to be smiling even when he was reprimanding an attorney or defendant. He spoke clearly and quickly, with a trace of a Spanish accent. After a few formalities, he asked Alaniz to proceed.

"The state calls Erika Peña," the prosecutor said.

The courtroom tensed. It was the first time in more than a year that the escapee would be in the same room as her assailant and face the person who had killed her friends—and nearly her.

Erika glided into the courtroom, her hair pulled up in a tight bun, wearing a black sweater and black-and-white-striped skirt. As she passed the defendant's table, she glared at Ortiz, held her stare for a few strides, then continued to the witness stand. She settled into her seat, smoothed out her skirt, and looked out around the courtroom, settling her gaze on Alaniz.

The district attorney asked her to introduce herself and went over some personal details, including her addiction to heroin, Xanax, and crack cocaine. Her voice was steady, clear, convincing. She said she had known Ortiz for about five months before the night he picked her up on September 14, 2018. Alaniz asked Erika whether she remembered if he had any tattoos.

"Yes, some flowers on his arm, some birds on his chest," Erika said, a smile creeping into her lips as she looked at Ortiz, who smiled slyly back.

Erika described how he had picked her up for the first time on San Bernardo, how she made money from him to support a drug habit. Alaniz asked if she ever had sex with Ortiz. "Yes," she said, again smiling. "A lot of kissing, sex. Mostly blow jobs."

"Did your relationship with him grow into something else?"

"Yes," Erika said, looking at Ortiz.

"Into what?"

"Into friendship," she said, her eyes welling with tears.

Led by Alaniz, Erika described the details of that night: how Ortiz picked her up on San Bernardo and drove her to his house, the sense of dread she felt when she realized he had murdered Melissa and Claudine and how she vomited in his driveway, the gun pointed at her chest behind the Circle K and how she escaped and alerted the state trooper. As she spoke, she kept her gaze steadily on Ortiz. The tears were gone, replaced with a dispassionate glare.

"I thought I was going to die," she told the court. "He pointed the gun right to my chest."

She described the murder weapon as a black pistol and told of how she spiraled into a cloud of fear and anxiety after the incident. Judge Hale listened intently until Alaniz finished with the witness.

During cross-examination, Joel Perez got Erika to concede she was harboring a $300-a-day drug habit and had been addicted for nine years. She described being arrested multiple times since she was eighteen and recounted how she had done heroin the day Ortiz picked her up. Erika was then dismissed.

Alaniz also called Captain Calderon, who went over some of the evidence against Ortiz, and Joel Perez called Ortiz's mom, Lupita Rocha; his good friend Jerry Solis; and an uncle of Ortiz's, all of whom recalled positive qualities of the defendant, including his devotion to his family and zest to join the military. Solis told the court how he noticed Ortiz's mood spiral when he began taking prescription pills.

It wasn't enough. After a brief recess, Hale denied the bond reduction.

Ortiz, for now, would stay in jail.

=====

MORE PRETRIAL HEARINGS FOLLOWED. THE HEARINGS, THOUGH emotionally draining, became a meeting point for the victims' families. Colette, Rosenda, Cristina, and Gracie Perez, Melissa's sister-in-law, attended nearly every hearing and grew to know one another. Women who would ordinarily not have much reason to interact were thrust together into a close-knit family. They began carpooling to hearings or meeting for coffee or lunch afterward, sharing the good memories of the women or the lingering pain their abrupt loss had brought them.

The case lumbered through 2019. Though united by their grief, the families were split over whether Ortiz should get the death penalty. In 2018, Texas easily led the nation in putting convicted criminals to death with 511. (Virginia was a distant second with 113, followed by Oklahoma with 112.) Some of the families wanted to see Ortiz die by lethal injection for killing his victims; others were more hesitant. Cristina Benavides seethed with anger over the loss of Melissa—at one pretrial hearing she stood and yelled, "¡Asesino maldito!" at Ortiz as bailiffs led him out of the courtroom. She wanted Ortiz to suffer for what he did but, devoutly Catholic, didn't believe in the death penalty. "Let God apply justice," she said at the time. "He's watching him." Kristian Montemayor, Claudine's niece who attended some of the hearings, would rather have seen him die for his actions. "He'll be in jail, comfortable, eating three times a day," she said. "He doesn't deserve to be alive."

═══

WHETHER PRO–DEATH PENALTY OR NOT, THE FAMILIES ALL agreed they wanted justice served swiftly. But they wouldn't get it. The case slogged from one pretrial hearing to the next. Motions were filed, heard, ruled upon. Then, just as trial dates were beginning to be discussed in early 2020, the coronavirus pandemic broke out, hitting Texas border communities particularly hard. In the pandemic's first year, more than 7,700 people died of COVID-19 in Texas border counties, making it one of the virus's deadliest regions in the United States. Texas border counties tallied 282 deaths per 100,000 people, compared with 166 deaths per 100,000 people in border counties in New Mexico. El Paso hospitals became so overwhelmed with the sick and dying that health officials set up ten mobile morgues to accommodate the dead. In Laredo, more than 600 people had died of the virus by February 2021, including 126 in January alone. By May 2021, three of the top six places in the United States with the highest rate of infection were Texas border communities. Laredo ranked sixth.

Courts, including the Webb County Courthouse, shut down, delaying hearings and trials. Dockets ground to a halt. Judge Hale engineered YouTube-based Zoom hearings between Ortiz and attorneys. But seating a twelve-person jury remained an ominous challenge, with no clear solution in sight. Court officials considered seating masked juries in spaced-out settings, such as the Fine and Performing Arts Center at nearby Texas A&M International University, and conducting trials there. But that idea fizzled.

Meanwhile, Joel Perez, Ortiz's attorney, filed a motion to suppress the nine-hour interview his defendant gave to Calderon and Salinas. It was denied. He also filed a motion to change venue, arguing that the case had become too publicized in Laredo and an impartial jury would be impossible to sit. In July 2022, under a sealed order, Hale agreed with the defense and ordered the trial be moved to a Bexar County courtroom in San Antonio. It was a stunning blow to the state's case. Besides having to haul their substantial cache of evidence, which by then included thousands of documents, shell casings, weapons, and a truck tire, two hours up Interstate 35 to another courthouse, it also shifted the trial to a city that was home to 250,000 military veterans and 80,000 active-duty military service members, many of whom worked at Joint Base San Antonio, the sprawling military complex that included Fort Sam Houston and Randolph and Lackland Air Force Bases. Finding a juror who wouldn't sympathize with a former navy corpsman, decorated Iraq War veteran, and U.S. Border Patrol agent became exponentially more challenging.

Shortly after Hale ruled on the change of venue, Alaniz gathered the victims' families into the fourth-floor jury room just outside Hale's courtroom. Those in attendance included Janelle's sister, Rosenda; Claudine's sister Colette; Claudine's daughter Ciara; Cristina Benavides and

Gracie Perez; Chelly's aunt Anna Sotelo; and Chelly's brother, Joey Cantu, three years removed from house arrest and free of any tracking devices.

Anger over his sister's murder seethed in Joey for weeks but slowly ebbed. Hate and anger had occupied his heart for so long that he no longer wanted them there. He thought back to 2018, just before he was released on parole. He had received a letter from the sister of the thirty-eight-year-old man he had murdered. She wrote that she heard he was being released on parole. The probation board had asked for her opinion, and she had supported his release, telling them he was just a kid when it happened and deserved a second chance. "You need to know that I forgive you for what you did and you need to forgive yourself," she wrote. As he read the letter, Joey felt an immense weight lifted from his chest. He realized the hate you carry serves no other purpose than to weigh you down.

Joey still wished to see Ortiz punished. But he had let the hate go.

In the jury room, everyone settled into seats around the conference room table, and Alaniz shut the door. He filled them in on the change of trial venue, assuring them it wouldn't affect how he attacked the case or the evidence he planned to present. He told them the district attorney's office would pay for their hotel rooms in San Antonio and help with their transport there, for those who wished to attend. Alaniz then turned the conversation to the death penalty. He stressed that, if he was going to pursue it, they needed to have a united front. It wouldn't work if he pushed the death penalty in court and then victims' family members gave TV interviews denouncing capital punishment. It needed to be all or nothing. He opened it up for discussion. Some family members voiced that they would still like to see Ortiz die for what he did; others said it was in God's hands. Colette recollected good memories about Claudine and said she would support what the district attorney decided. Family members wiped away tears as they went around the room, voicing thoughts.

Then Joey stood up. He had only recently started attending hearings, ever since his parole and terms of release loosened, and didn't know many of those gathered. He introduced himself as Chelly's big brother and recounted how he himself had gone to prison for murder as a teenager, spending two decades at the McConnell Unit and being released just a few months before his sister's murder. He told them how hard it is in prison.

"You hear grown men cry. You have grown men going crazy. Strong dudes, you see them going crazy. You wake up one morning and see them covered in their own shit, and you're like, 'What happened?'" Joey told the group. The room fell quiet, all eyes fixed on his hulking figure. "It's torture in there. Every day of your life, it's torture."

Joey told them he had made peace with Ortiz's horrific acts and had even forgiven him. If he dies, he wins, Joey told the other families. He'd rather have him live out his life in prison.

"I want to wake up and go to sleep every day and die knowing that that's what he's going through," Joey said. "The death sentence is a cop-out."

By the time he finished, all family members were in tears. Alaniz polled them, and every single one of them was behind Joey. They no longer wanted Alaniz to ask for the death penalty; they wanted Ortiz to spend the rest of his life in prison. Alaniz thanked them, and everyone shuffled out of the room. A few days later, he alerted the court of his intention to pursue the case as a "capital (non-death)" case. He also offered a plea deal to Ortiz through his lawyer: life without parole. No death penalty and no trial.

The response was prompt and unequivocal: Ortiz preferred to go to trial.

———

AT AROUND THE SAME TIME, ALANIZ GATHERED HIS TEAM OF deputies and investigators in the conference room of his fourth-floor offices at the Webb County Justice Center. For weeks, they had been packing up and filing all the evidence in the case. Now, they faced potentially the single most challenging task of pretrial prep: finding Erika Peña.

They hadn't heard from her at all since before the pandemic, as the coronavirus took its lethal sweep across South Texas. They had no idea whether Erika had vanished again, was homeless, had been arrested, or was even alive. Alaniz thought he had enough evidence without her to win the case. But nothing would give the case more gravitas and narrative depth than Erika on the stand, pointing to Ortiz and describing for jurors her brief armed abduction.

DA investigators again fanned out across the county, reaching out to sources they had contacted after Ortiz's capture, and the victim coordinator reached out to Erika's mom. After a few phone calls, they located her. She had been staying with her mom and was still struggling to stay off heroin. She had started taking methadone earlier in the year. She had even worked for a while cleaning rooms at the Residence Inn by Marriott in Laredo but later quit. Alaniz ordered his victim coordinator to keep close tabs on her. "If she needs assistance, if she needs treatment, let's get that for her," he told his staffer.

Alaniz faced a prosecutor's worst enemy: time. It had been four long years since the murders. In that stretch, victims easily vanish or die, memories fade, evidence gets lost. He was happy to locate Erika but knew that every minute counted. A few weeks before trial, officials brought her into his offices at the Webb County Justice Center to go over testimony, including questions he would ask, how Perez would likely cross-examine her, even the layout of the courtroom.

After he spoke, Erika asked Alaniz if he remembered when he checked in on her at the sheriff's substation the night of Ortiz's questioning. Alaniz had been so busy with trial prep he had forgotten that initial interaction. She told him she had really appreciated it.

Later, as he wrote up his opening remarks, Alaniz realized Erika was more than just a key witness. She was a key part of the *story*. His story would start with her.

Evidence crated up, hotel rooms booked, and strategy prepared, the prosecution team and victims' families readied to travel north to San Antonio. It was time to face Ortiz, and his defense team, in court.

CHAPTER 22

The Paul Elizondo Tower in downtown San Antonio stood eleven stories tall, a stout, modern, boxy building with pink granite panels and an ornate red sandstone veneer designed to complement the elegant nineteenth-century red sandstone of the Bexar County Courthouse next door. The building, also known as the Bexar County Justice Center, housed many of the county's courtrooms.

On the morning of Monday, November 28, 2022—four years and two months since Juan David Ortiz's arrest on murder and assault charges—family members of the victims and Ortiz, along with prosecutors and defense attorneys, milled outside courtroom 5 on the tower's fourth floor, waiting for the doors to open. Inside, the courtroom had wooden paneling, beige walls, high ceilings, and nine long wooden benches in the visitors' gallery, not much bigger in overall size than Hale's courtroom in Laredo. The judge's bench was to the right and back of the courtroom, and to the far left was a long, rectangular jury box with fourteen chairs. When the doors opened, the victims' families entered. Joey was there, as were Anna Sotelo, Cristina, Gracie, Colette, Ciara, and some of Claudine's sisters from Killeen and other Texas towns. Elva had taken an overnight Greyhound bus from Indiana to San Antonio to attend. Fourteen family members in total, or more than three times the number that attended pretrial hearings. Many wore matching white T-shirts emblazoned with pictures of all four victims on the front. On the back, in pink cursive lettering, was written: "They are Loved." Rosenda, Janelle's sister, was the sole exception. She wore a black hoodie with a picture of Janelle on the back and white cursive lettering underneath: "Justice for Janelle." They slid into the benches on the side of the gallery.

Ortiz's mom, Lupita Rocha, also walked in with Ortiz's uncle,

Pedro Gonzalez. They took the front-row bench on the right side of the gallery. Lupita settled into her seat, pulled a leather-bound Bible from her purse, and began to read. The media occupied all remaining spaces in the gallery and included journalists from the *San Antonio Express-News, Laredo Morning Times,* the *New York Times, USA Today,* and KSAT 12 in Laredo and a producer from *Dateline,* the popular NBC documentary show. Court TV, the cable network, was also broadcasting the trial, gavel to gavel, to hundreds of thousands of TV and online viewers across the country. Nestled among the media and onlookers was Liza Peña, a Laredo resident and self-published memoirist and poet (*Getting Up Even Stronger* and *The Girl Inside, the Woman Inside Me: Revelations of a Laredo Girl, Border Dreamer*), who harbored a professed fascination with serial killers and boasted of having access to Ortiz and his family that she planned to later parlay into a tell-all book.[*]

District Attorney Isidro Alaniz walked in wearing a dark suit and maroon tie, trailed by Chief Assistant District Attorney Joshua Davila and Assistant District Attorney Marisela Jacaman. District staffers rolled in six bankers boxes filled with documents and evidence. Joel Perez and his assistant, Raymond Fuchs, arrived next, and minutes later, two uniformed bailiffs escorted Ortiz into the courtroom from a side door. He was dressed in a black suit that hung loosely on his bony frame, a white shirt, and a dark tie, and his hair was closely shaven to his hairline. He was noticeably thinner than he was at pretrial hearings. The bulky figure who'd spent hours at Gold's Gym was replaced by a bookish, older-looking man wearing black wire-rimmed glasses framing a round, acne-scarred face.

Everyone stood as Judge Hale entered and sat in his seat, surveying the room and scanning a stack of papers in front of him. He called the

---

[*] At a pretrial hearing in 2019, bailiffs removed Peña from Hale's courtroom after she repeatedly used hand gestures in an effort to get Ortiz's attention.

case to order. The jury—ten women and five men*were brought in and took their seats in the jury box.

Alaniz began his opening arguments. He strode confidently in front of the jury, touching all ten tips of his fingers together. Speaking loudly and clearly, he recounted the events as if narrating a Hulu docuseries, promising jurors they'd soon be transported to the streets of Laredo as Ortiz picked up one victim after another, shooting them and leaving them for dead, all the way to Erika's escape from his truck in the Valero gas station. "Yes, we are in Bexar County," he said, jurors transfixed by his presentation, "but through pictures, through the evidence, we will take you to those dark and horrible places where this happened."

He held up poster-sized mug shots of each of the victims, starting with Melissa Ramirez. As he did, Cristina Benavides bowed her head and sobbed from the gallery. "This case, the evidence will show, is about a man who betrayed his badge, he betrayed his country, he betrayed his family, he betrayed his community, for his own selfish needs."

After speaking for about forty minutes, Alaniz sat down. Joel Perez took the floor.

"I won't be as long or as dramatic as Mr. Alaniz," the defense attorney said, his voice gravelly and several decibels lower than the prosecutor's. Several jurors leaned forward in their seats to better hear. Perez took a more legalese, less narrative approach to his arguments, questioning whether Ortiz understood his rights before giving the videotaped interview where he confessed and casting doubt on whether his truck—where the murder weapon was found—was legally searched. Perez talked about Ortiz being suicidal and suffering blackouts, taking psychoactive pills and drinking heavily. "This was a defeated man," he told jurors. He reminded them that Ortiz was a war veteran with a clean record, a "good husband who has children," prompting several audible

---

* Including three alternates, though the alternate jurors didn't know who they were.

sarcastic chuckles from the visitors' gallery. He pointed out how promises were made to Ortiz during his "coerced confession" with Calderon and Salinas, including telling him that Alaniz was in the building and a deal could be cut.

"I want you to listen to the evidence," Perez urged jurors. "Listen to the cross-examination. Listen to the investigation these police officers made. I believe you will find Mr. Ortiz not guilty." After just eighteen minutes, Perez sat down.

Alaniz called his first witness. "The state calls Erika Peña."

=====

IN THE WEEKS LEADING UP TO THE TRIAL, ALANIZ HAD QUES-tioned whether his star witness would actually show. Calls to her mother sometimes got his office in touch with Erika; other times she wasn't around. The Thursday before the start of the trial, Alaniz asked to meet with Erika to fine-tune a few final details on her testimony. His staff reached out to her mom. No, Erika replied, she didn't want to talk to Alaniz.

Somehow, they had made it to San Antonio, and Erika, her mom, and the other victims' families arrived on Saturday and checked into a block of rooms Alaniz's office had booked for them at the La Quinta Inn & Suites, just two blocks from the courthouse. Alaniz and his team checked into a string of rooms at the nearby Embassy Suites by Hilton on San Antonio's River Walk. On Sunday evening, the day before she was expected on the stand, Erika called Alaniz's victim coordinator. She wanted the district attorney to pay for dinner for her and her mom on the River Walk. Staffers initially denied the request, but Alaniz overruled them, ordering them to go ahead and do it. They escorted Erika and her mom to dinner among the throngs of tourists on the River Walk. The next day, staffers made sure Erika made the two-block walk to the courthouse.

=====

AFTER BEING CALLED, ERIKA WALKED SLOWLY INTO THE COURT-room. She wore a long-sleeved black-and-white patterned blouse that flowed down past her waist and white jeans. Her hair had been colored platinum blond, and she wore it straight down. She moved cautiously through the courtroom, flicked her hair off her neck, and stepped into the witness stand.

"You're under the same oath you were given earlier," Hale reminded her.

"Huh?" Erika said.

"You're under the same oath."

Erika stared at him for several moments, not moving or answering.

Hale repeated: "You took an oath today."

"A what?"

"An oath."

"Yes," said Erika, finally understanding. She sank slowly into her seat on the witness stand and pushed her hair away again. She surveyed the room, shooting a quick side glance toward Ortiz's table.

"Good morning," Alaniz said.

"Good morning," she answered. Her response was slow, her voice loud but syrupy. She looked around as if deciphering a dream. As Alaniz asked her questions, Erika inched closer to the microphone, periodically stealing a peek at Ortiz. Far from the clear, assertive witness who had strode into the Laredo courtroom in 2019, the Erika who showed up in San Antonio was slower to comprehend questions and muddled in her answers, her speech slurry, the effects of habitual methadone use clouding her responses.

Alaniz asked if she knew why she was there. Yes, said Erika.

"Do you know a person by the name of Juan David Ortiz?"

"Yes."

"Could you identify him here in the courtroom?"

Erika took a shuddering breath, turned slightly to her left, and lifted her left index finger slightly toward Ortiz.

"Do you see him?" Alaniz said.

"Yes. In black."

"Where is he seated?"

Her voice small, as if far away: "In the corner."

Alaniz led Erika through the events of September 14, 2018, ending with her fleeing Ortiz's truck and alerting Trooper Hernandez. She also talked about her murdered friends. She knew Melissa for four years. Claudine she knew for a year or two. She knew Chelly probably the longest, since starting in the escort business a decade earlier, but was closest to Janelle.

"Janelle was my best friend," Erika said, crossing her arms in front of her chest and rubbing her biceps. "Janelle was funny, very caring, had a lot of friends."

"Her personality?"

"Outstanding."

In the visitors' gallery, Rosenda sunk her face in her hands, crying. After a few minutes, she rose from her seat and walked out of the courtroom.

Erika went on to say that she and Ortiz indulged in sex, mostly of the oral variety, multiple times and in a variety of places: in his truck, behind motels, in the Walmart parking lot, in public parks at night. He would often pay for her drugs.

Alaniz passed the witness.

After a lunch break, it was Perez's turn to cross-examine. He went over Erika's drug habits at the time of the murders, including her $300-a-day black tar heroin habit, and how she shot up in Ortiz's home.

"Are you high right now?" Perez asked her.

"No."

"You're not here totally clear of head, are you?"

"Yes, I am."

"Are you under the effects of methadone?"

"Yes, I take methadone."

Erika said the methadone blocked her "triggers," but Perez retorted that methadone was in fact a synthetic heroin, to which Alaniz objected. Badgering the witness, he complained to the judge. Hale instructed

Perez to ask a question. Perez asked her about the night she was at Ortiz's house, when she heard a voice urging her to flee from the home. As he spoke, Erika rested her face on her right fist.

"You testified that you heard a voice?" Perez said.

"What I meant by that was my inner voice, my intuition."

"You testified, 'I heard a voice.' And I asked you, 'That said what?' 'For me to get out fast.'" Perez repeated the testimony from the pretrial hearing, asking Erika if she remembered how she had said the voice was of an ex-boyfriend who had died years earlier, who had told her, in Spanish, to leave. Alaniz objected, claiming the defense was fishing for a preferred response. "You're making it sound like if I'm crazy," Erika said, unprompted.

Under redirect examination from Alaniz, Erika told jurors how she was diagnosed with PTSD, depression, and severe anxiety after the incident with Ortiz. Alaniz wrapped up his questions, and Perez offered no further cross-examination. Erika, excused by Hale, made her way off the witness stand, strolled slowly across the courtroom, and sat down in the visitors' gallery between Rosenda and Brianna, Chelly's daughter. Ortiz, who had been staring straight ahead for most of the day, casually craned his head around and took a quick glance at his former lover.

=====

FRANCISCO HERNANDEZ, THE TEXAS STATE TROOPER WHO ENcountered Erika at the Valero station, took the stand next. After answering a few questions, Alaniz played the video footage from his bodycam showing a shirtless Erika running toward him, then her nervously recounting her story, then him calling Ranger Salinas to alert him of her. Erika and Hernandez flow constantly between English and Spanish, often mingling the two, with Erika saying, "Él me dijo si quisiera cigarros . . . I started getting very sick," and Hernandez telling her, "This is what's going to happen, uno de los officials de nostros will get you a shirt."

He ended by urging her to help Salinas in his murder investigation. "Cooperate with them like you're cooperating with me," he tells her in the video. "Maybe you could break a case of lo que está pasando ahorita." He added: "You never know."

══

THE NEXT FEW DAYS SAW MORE BODYCAM FOOTAGE, INCLUDING that of the two troopers—Bradshaw and Obregon—who confronted Ortiz at the Stripes on Jefferson Street and showed Ortiz fleeing from the scene, as well as that of SWAT team members as they searched for Ortiz, then found him hiding in the bed of a pickup truck.

Calderon was called to the stand and described the crime scenes, as Alaniz flashed crime scene photos on the large flat-screen TV behind the witness stand. As photos from Melissa's crime scene appeared, Gracie sobbed and shuddered uncontrollably in the visitors' gallery. When Claudine's pictures came up, Colette cried quietly and was comforted by a relative. A staffer from the district attorney's office shuttled from one grieving family member to the next, offering a Kleenex or soft word.

Ortiz kept his gaze down at a yellow notepad in front of him. Occasionally he would scribble notes on the pad; other times he would turn and swing a quick glance into the gallery, careful to avoid making eye contact with his mother and relatives sitting directly behind him.

══

NO MATTER HOW DRAMATIC OR SALACIOUS THE DETAILS OF A case may be, jury trials are inherently long, lumbering, tedious events, conducted in a legalese so opaque few average observers understand what precisely is going on. The Ortiz trial was punctured constantly with objections from both attorneys and requests to approach the bench. On one day, attorneys asked to approach Hale's bench more than a dozen times in an hour, slowing the proceedings to a crawl and leading to audible groans from the audience. Attorneys, bailiffs, court reporters, judge, jurors, and media all performed their tasks like muscle memory.

Families of the victims sat dutifully in the gallery, retraumatized each time a crime scene photo of their loved one flashed on the courtroom monitors.

On day four, Alaniz unveiled the crowning piece of his evidence cache: the nine-hour videotaped interview of Ortiz. Alaniz and Perez had agreed that, if they were to show jurors the videotape, they would play it in its entirety—all nine hours, not just the parts the state deemed most pertinent. Over the course of the next three days, the interview played nonstop on the courtroom's large flat-screen TV, including long stretches—forty-five minutes or more at times—where Ortiz sat alone in the interview room, strumming the table or bobbing his foot. Jurors sat and struggled to stay awake watching video of Ortiz sitting and struggling to stay awake.

Early in the video, Ortiz appeared cocky, joking with sheriff's deputies that he had outrun two troopers when he fled the Stripes gas station. "Hey, who's the trooper that smokes, man, the trooper that couldn't keep up with me, dude?" he asked a deputy just outside the interview room. "Tell him he needs to work out some more, man. Ha—two of them!"

But as the hours passed, Ortiz's mood shifted. Jurors could see him straining, stretching, standing up and sitting back down, mumbling to himself. At one point, he buried his head in the crook of his arm while sitting alone at the table. When he lifted his head, he wiped tears from his eyes. Then, slowly, he became more morose, more jittery, and asked to have his handcuffs removed—and began recounting how he orchestrated the murders. The jurors looked on with fresh focus.

Midway through that day's video, Perez approached Alaniz. They had evidence, he told him, that Ortiz had asked for an attorney during his interview but never got one. If true, that would derail the legality of the videotaped interview and strike it from the trial, removing the most significant piece of evidence in the prosecution's arsenal. Alaniz's heart jumped into his throat.

"What evidence?" he asked Perez.

In the confines of the empty jury room, the two legal teams huddled with Judge Hale. Perez explained that one of his investigators had heard on the videotape, during Ortiz's interview, the defendant mutter that he wanted an attorney, a request that was ignored by the detectives. Perez thought he had heard it, too. Hale slipped on a pair of earphones and listened to the section of the tape the defense team pointed to, but he couldn't make out any words from Ortiz. He called in one of his staffers from the courtroom. Without offering any explanation or context, he told the staffer to listen to the specific part of the interview and tell them if he could hear Ortiz say anything. The staffer listened. He also couldn't hear Ortiz mutter anything.

The judge overruled the defense's motion; the videotape was allowed to continue.

=====

DURING THE LUNCH BREAK ON THE TRIAL'S FOURTH DAY, MEDIA members received a stunning piece of breaking news: Joshua Davila, Alaniz's number two prosecutor who had questioned witnesses in the trial, had abruptly quit. He and Alaniz had disagreed on several tactical questions, and Davila had resigned. Outside the courtroom, Lupita, Ortiz's mom, gladly helped spread the news, hoping this latest development would somehow benefit her son's case. As the trial reconvened, questions swirled as to what impact Davila's departure would have on the case. Could this be grounds for a mistrial? Whatever feelings Alaniz harbored over the incident, his expression didn't betray them. His face was stern, focused, resolute. He paced around his team's table, making sure the video was cued up correctly, checking his notes. An old legal adage bubbled in his head: "Never let the jury see you panic." His mind became singularly focused on reaching a crucial moment in the videotaped interview.

Hale had advised the attorneys that they would break for the day sharply at 6:00 p.m. Alaniz needed to get to that scene before then. He checked his watch as Ortiz, in the video, told investigators how his mom would "have a heart attack" when she found out. In the gallery, Lupita shivered and cried, hugged by family members. A bailiff brought over a box of Kleenex. As Ortiz recounted how Chelly urged him not to kill himself, telling him under the overpass that God would forgive him, Joey sat and stared from the gallery, tears streaming down both cheeks.

The clock inched toward 6:00 p.m. At 5:55 p.m., Ortiz in the video described driving again down San Bernardo after killing Chelly. Jurors looked on attentively; some leaned forward in their seats.

"This is where the monster came out," he said.

Alaniz paused the video, and Hale adjourned for the day.

The next morning, the jurors, aptly enticed by the previous night's cliff-hanger, watched the court's monitor with renewed focus. In the video, Ortiz described the urge to assassinate more sex workers, his encounter with the troopers, and his escape. Then he revealed the existence of the fourth victim.

As the most damning piece of evidence against him played on the large flat-screen TV in front of the jurors, Ortiz sat at the defense table, at times blinking around the room as if confused by his surroundings. A few times, he whispered something to Fuchs or Perez in animated terms. Other times, he looked down and scribbled on his pad.

After the videotape concluded with Ortiz being led from the sub-station's interview room in shackles, Alaniz released Calderon, who had been translating the video's Spanish bits for jurors. During cross-examination, Perez went over the legal minutiae of the interview, asking Calderon what training he had had with interrogations, whether Ortiz understood his rights, whether the defendant may have been sleep deprived during the prolonged interview. Calderon answered each question steadily, his voice never rising above an utterance, as if he and Perez were chatting in a living room somewhere.

———

AFTER CALDERON WAS DISMISSED, ALANIZ SIFTED THROUGH various pieces of physical evidence, including the tire tread marks left behind by Ortiz's truck, the shell casings at the scene, and the full magazine clips found in his truck. Then he called up Dr. Corinne Stern, Webb County's chief medical examiner, a veteran coroner who had performed more than seven thousand autopsies in her two decades as a forensic pathologist. Dressed in a black-and-white-checkered dress suit and chartreuse cat-eye reading glasses, with curly henna hair flowing over her shoulders, Stern spoke in a loud, clear, professional tone as she described how bullets tore through bone and brain, killing their targets. As autopsy photos flashed on the screen, some showing the moist pinkish sheen of brain tissue, Stern described projectiles recovered from the "left sphenoid sinus" of one victim or the "cranial vault" of another.

As she described the color photo of a bullet wound that left a hole in Melissa's neck, one of the male jurors stiffened in his seat, leaned toward a neighboring juror, and passed out. Bailiffs and attorneys looked around, unsure what to do as the juror slumped to the floor. Stern, a licensed medical doctor, asked Hale if she could be excused from the witness stand. He allowed it, and she jumped from the stand and went over to the passed-out juror, crouching next to him and offering medical assistance.

After the juror was removed from the courtroom—and ultimately dismissed from duty—the trial continued.

Salinas's testimony came next, as he described the BIC and how Border Patrol agents, Texas Rangers, and other investigators worked in close proximity, often sharing tips and leads on investigations, raising the specter of Ortiz staying atop his own murder investigation. He testified that he found out that Claudine Luera was a friend of Melissa's on September 12, 2018, and placed a call into the BIC later that day to get information on her, including a possible address. The next day, Claudine was dead.

═══

ON DAY SEVEN OF THE TRIAL, PROSECUTORS PLAYED A JAILHOUSE phone call Ortiz placed to his wife, Daniella, on November 6, 2018, less than two months after his arrest. Perez objected to playing it, and Hale excused the jury as the two legal teams debated the issue near his bench. Finally, they played the call in the courtroom.

In it, Ortiz could be heard punching in Daniella's phone number and his PIN from inside the Webb County Jail, where he was awaiting trial. Daniella answered.

"Hi," she said. She was giddy, giggling. Kids could be heard playing in the background. As the two spoke, Daniella called him "mi amor" and "baby," urging him to keep faith and make the best of their "horrible" situation. She put two of their children on the phone to say hi to their dad. "I love you!" he told them. "See you soon!" one of his children replied.

Ortiz and his wife discussed Bible passages and using their faith to see them through his incarceration. He also stressed his growing concern that the videotaped interview he gave to Calderon and Salinas would be used against him in court someday.

"I want to make sure we're all on the same page, though," Ortiz told his wife. "If we're not, then I don't see the point of going through the whole [legal] process . . . I'm very concerned about the statement that was made . . . the confession."

In the courtroom, Ortiz blinked down at his desk, listening to the muffled sounds of his voice on the recording. About midway through the thirty-minute call, he removed his glasses, dropped his head on the table, and clasped his hands behind his neck, rocking slowly in his seat. When he lifted his head again, he wiped away tears. A bailiff handed him a box of tissues. It was the most emotion Ortiz had publicly shown in the four years since his arrest.

"God's timing is perfect," Daniella said on the call. Her voice was soft, cooing. "When we see a miracle, it may not be right after the trial. It may be years from now. I want you to have an open mind."

She continued: "More and more the whole situation is horrible, there's no other way to say it. It's horrible, but we know who you are. We know who you serve, our creator. Y ya . . . that's all we can do is hope."

"I love you," Daniella said as Ortiz's allotted thirty minutes ended and the call abruptly disconnected.

=====

SHORTLY AFTER THE JAILHOUSE CALL, AT 4:45 P.M. ON THE TRI-al's seventh day, having called twelve witnesses and submitted more than two hundred items of evidence, the state rested its case.

Then the defense team pulled one of the most surprising moves of the trial: it rested its case, too, without calling a single witness, paving the path to closing arguments.

=====

THE FOLLOWING MORNING, DECEMBER 7, 2022, THE COURT-room hummed with renewed activity. Sheriff Cuellar appeared. Lupita, Ortiz's mom, showed up with her grown twin daughters and another male relative. The number of media members swelled to more than twenty, and the number of victims' family members also multiplied, occupying over four rows of the left-hand side of the gallery.

Hale called the court to order, and the jury, now down to ten women and four men, filed in. Marisela Jacaman, now Alaniz's second-in-command, began closing arguments for the state, followed by Raymond Fuchs for the defense, before handing off to Joel Perez.

"We are a nation of laws," Perez began in his closing remarks. "The law matters."

He reminded jurors of the length of the interview Ortiz did with Calderon and Salinas and of some of the inducements promised to the defendant. He talked about Ortiz's struggles with mental health and other ailments. "He was broken: PTSD, migraines, headaches, insomnia, nightmares," he said, strolling in front of the jury box. "They induced him, they confronted him, they promised him all these things. It was improper inducement."

Because it was improperly obtained, the jurors should disregard the entire nine-hour interview with the police, Perez said. He recounted how Ortiz had an impeccable record until February 2018, when he began taking pills prescribed by the VA.

Looking directly at the jurors, Perez asked them to consider whether the state sufficiently eliminated all reasonable doubt to find Ortiz guilty of capital murder, or whether his circumstances and state of mind made him murder on impulse, which would make him guilty of the lesser crime of "ordinary murder."

It was a subtle but significant shift in Perez's strategy. He was no longer questioning whether Ortiz committed the murders but urging jurors to, if they found him guilty, consider checking the box on their verdict sheet for individual murders, which carries a lesser punishment.

"You really have to ask yourself: Is this guy really a serial killer?" he asked the jurors.

Finished, Perez walked back to his table, ending the defense's closing arguments.

===

ALANIZ STOOD UP AND STALKED TO THE FRONT OF THE JURY BOX.

"Mr. Perez stands up here and asks if Mr. Ortiz was a serial killer," he said. He removed his glasses and placed them on a table. "I'll answer that question."

He turned, took a few steps toward where Ortiz sat at the defense table, and pointed at the defendant. "Mr. Ortiz was a serial killer then," he bellowed, his voice booming through the courtroom, "and he's a serial killer *now*! This is what the evidence has shown."

Alaniz walked the jurors through the evidence brought before them the past seven days, how police officers preserved Ortiz's rights through his arrest and interview, how he described in front of a camera how he shot and left to die each of the women—and revealed a fourth victim detectives didn't even know about. He reminded them of how Ortiz returned to his wife's bed after one of the slayings.

"He played judge, jury, and executioner," Alaniz said.

Jurors looked on, locked in the presentation. One juror slowly nodded her head as Alaniz spoke. He reminded them how Ortiz had sworn to protect citizens as a U.S. Border Patrol agent and how he had busted that trust.

"It is terrifying to have the enemy within the ranks of law enforcement," Alaniz said.

He concluded his closing arguments.

======

AT 2:36 P.M., THE JURORS BEGAN THEIR DELIBERATIONS.

Perez had managed to get on the jury instructions extra boxes where jurors could check "murder felony 1" for each of the four slain victims. If those were unanimously selected, Ortiz would face a punishment of five to ninety-nine years in prison for each felony, rather than an automatic life in prison without parole that a capital murder conviction brings in the state of Texas. In theory, if the jury brought back the individual murder charge for each victim, Ortiz could be looking at a twenty-five- to thirty-year total prison sentence and could be eligible for parole in fifteen years—far less punitive than a capital murder conviction.

One hour bled into the next, as victims' families, lawyers, and journalists mingled outside in the hallway. Nervous small talk filled the space.

At 6:00 p.m., Hale received a note from the jury. Word of the note leaked into the hall. What did it mean? Was it a sign that the jurors were nearing their verdict? Or wedging further apart?

Actually, the jury had requested to see the transcript of Ortiz's interview with Calderon and Salinas. Perez had previously objected to allowing the jury a copy, arguing that some of the Spanish translations weren't accurate, and Hale had agreed. But now that the jury was specifically requesting it, he changed his order and sent a copy into the jury room. They continued deliberating.

At 7:34 p.m., just as families and attorneys wondered if deliberations would stretch through the night, jurors sent the judge another note: they had a verdict.

Everyone scrambled back into the courtroom. Judge Hale came in and sat in his perch. The jury was led back in, and a bailiff handed Hale a sheet with the verdict. Hale glanced at the paper, then ordered the defendant to stand in front of him. Ortiz walked over and stood directly in front of Hale, facing him; his attorney, Joel Perez, stood to his left. Extra bailiffs and court police officers filed into the courtroom and stood between the visitors' gallery and the defendant, their backs to the judge, ready to defuse any reaction the verdict may evoke.

Family members stiffened with tension. Four years of waiting, crying, shuffling from one pretrial hearing to the next, more waiting, endless legal wrangling, wondering which way justice would turn and for whom, then suffering the pain and agony of the COVID years—all of it reduced to the rustling of a single sheet of paper in the hands of the judge before them.

Hale read off the sheet: "We, the jury, find the defendant, Juan David Ortiz, guilty of the offense of capital murder as charged in the indictment."

Muffled cries erupted from both sides of the gallery. Ortiz stood and stared, head tilted slightly to the left, as his verdict was read. The jury was dismissed.

Hale asked Ortiz if he had heard the verdict. Yes, he said. Hale then asked if he wanted to make any final statements. He shook his head no. The judge informed him that the verdict carried an automatic sentence of life in prison with no possibility for parole. Hale also advised Ortiz that he could appeal the decision.

Then the judge opened the court for any statements from the victims' families. Ortiz stood to the right of the courtroom, in front of the desk where he witnessed his trial unfurl, facing the jury box. Convicted murderer and families of his victims would now face each other less than twenty feet apart. A stocky bailiff stood on either side of Ortiz, and two more flanked the family members. Hale would allow verbal statements, but he wouldn't stand for any physical outbursts in the courtroom.

Cristina Benavides and Gracie Perez went first. Reading from notes, Gracie said how her sister-in-law was funny, a loving mom, and a good friend and told Ortiz how much pain he had caused with his actions. "I hate you for what you did and I could never forgive you, nor do I think God will," she said, her voice rising in anger. "You deserve to die in prison and go to hell." She added: "Monsters like you don't even deserve to breathe." Cristina, reading in Spanish from handwritten notes, voiced questions many family members, attorneys, and detectives had wrestled with since the start of the killings—and remained mostly unanswered. "¿Por qué la mataste? ¿Por qué mataste a mi hija?" she said. "¿Por qué le quitaste la vida?"

As they left the area and walked back to the gallery, Gracie turned to Ortiz as she passed him and spat, "Fuck you, fucking coward!"

Colette and the rest of Claudine's family members went next, standing in front of Ortiz and expressing the pain and suffering the murders had inflicted on their family. Malena, Claudine's daughter, stood next to Ciara and spoke of how she was a seventeen-year-old junior in high school when she found out her mother had been killed. It plunged her and her brothers into a deep depression. "You didn't just kill women," she said. "You killed women who were loved by so many people."

As they cleared the area, Alaniz next called up the family of Guiselda "Chelly" Cantu. Joey Cantu stood up. The bailiffs tensed. Joey's head was clean-shaven, and he had a large, scruffy black beard. He wore a tight black short-sleeved button-down shirt that hugged a wide, muscular chest and bulging biceps decorated with tattoos. He ambled into the court area with a handful of other family members, glancing briefly at Ortiz as he passed him. The lead bailiff ordered an extra court officer to stand next to the defendant.

Joey read from his prepared notes: "My name's Joey Cantu, and Chelly Cantu was many things." His voice cracked with tears. "Yes, she was a drug addict, yes, she was a prostitute, and she was a felon. Maybe one day she may have ceased being these things, as her family always hoped, but you have forever robbed us of that hope that she would come back to us. You'll hear no clichés from me. My sister was a good person, yes, but she did bad things . . . She was sick, as were the rest of these girls."

He continued: "My sister was and always will be the six-year-old girl . . ." Joey stopped, trying to compose himself. He took a shaky breath, then lowered the paper he was reading. Tears welled in his eyes and his hands trembled. He looked up at Ortiz.

"She was all I had, bro," he said, his voice cracking. "She was all I had. You took the last living member of my family . . ." He glanced back at his sheet. "You know, she would always be the six-year-old girl who would walk her eight-year-old brother to the restroom because I was scared of the dark. She would always be the little sister who defended me from bullies, and she'll always be the little sister who cried because she saw me crying." He wiped away tears with the back of his hand.

"She was compassionate, as evident in what she told you before you killed her. She was trying to talk you out of suicide. She did not beg for her life, she begged for *your* life . . . That was my sister in a nutshell." He took a deep breath and continued, telling Ortiz about how his mother and father, and now his sister, had all been murdered. He talked about how he had spent twenty-two years in a Texas prison for murder and how the sister of his victim wrote him a letter, forgiving him.

"Now I stand in front of the man who killed my little sister, and I want you to know that I forgive you," he said, his voice small, "and I hold no ill will toward you, man. I pray one day you find the peace that you have ripped away from all of us."

Sobs and sniffs filled the courtroom. Family members dabbed their eyes or hugged one another. Brianna, Chelly's daughter, went next, the pages with her notes shaking in her hands as she read, followed later by Rosenda, Janelle's sister. Ortiz stood there, expressionless, occasionally glancing toward the sobs arising from his mother in the gallery.

"You had everything in life as a Border Patrol agent. How could you?" Rosenda said, her voice cracking with emotion. "You gave your word to protect the border, yet you failed. You betrayed your badge." She added: "I pray your family doesn't go through what we went through."

After Rosenda walked off, the judge asked if there was anything else from the defense.

"Nothing more," Perez said.

Hale adjourned court. Bailiffs handcuffed Ortiz and led him toward a side entrance. He nodded twice to his mother as he went and disappeared behind the door. Everyone stood as Hale left the courtroom. Then the victims' families slowly filed out, some arm in arm or wiping away tears, but buoyed by the verdict. They were followed by the prosecution and defense teams, then the media, then the bailiffs.

Only Lupita Rocha and her family remained in the gallery. She leaned over and cried, a daughter on either side of her, her sobs echoing through the empty courtroom.

A lot can happen in four years.

In the 1,544 days from when Juan David Ortiz was arrested on September 15, 2018, to his conviction of capital murder in a San Antonio courtroom on December 7, 2022, family and friends of the victims have grieved, moved, gotten jobs, grown families.

While waiting for her sister's killer's trial, Rosenda Ortiz, Janelle's sister, gave birth to two boys, Raul and Roel. Six months after the verdict, she gave them a baby sister, Roseline.

After landing in and out of jail in the wake of the murders, Erika Peña moved in with a new boyfriend, gifting her much-needed emotional and financial stability. In July 2023, seven months after testifying against her would-be murderer, she gave birth to a boy, Andrew. Her Facebook page is peppered with photos of her doting over her son and husband.

Ciara, Claudine's daughter, had a daughter of her own, Londyn—a stylized take on the English city where her grandparents met. In one of the more ironic twists of the saga, Ciara landed a job with the Webb County Sheriff's Office, the agency that pursued and caught her mother's murderer. She was recently promoted to intel analyst, where she monitors jailhouse phone calls for incriminating information and readies evidence for court.

Family members of the victims—thrust together into the darkest days of their lives—have shared Thanksgiving dinners and attended birthday parties for one another's kids. "It's kind of ugly and horrific the stuff we've bonded over, but we find joy in each other; we're not alone," Ciara told me outside the San Antonio courthouse hours before Ortiz's conviction. "That's a big thing: just knowing we're not alone."

For years after the murders, Ciara seethed with hate and rage.

Toward Ortiz. Toward his family. Toward everything that ripped her mom away from her, just as they had hoped to reconnect. Then she had Londyn in January 2022, and that anger simmered, replaced by an even stronger instinct to heal.

During a break in the trial, she approached Lupita, Ortiz's mom, in the hallway outside the courtroom—and apologized. She applauded her for showing up to the trial and commiserated with her predicament as a fellow mom. Lupita told her she prays every day, not just for her son but for Ciara and the other victims' families. Ciara cried. The two hugged. "I needed that," Ciara said later. "Everybody told me not to do it. But I needed it . . . I need to forgive. I need to be happy. I need to move on."

═══

EVEN AS CIARA AND OTHERS CONTINUE TO TRY TO UNPACK THE pain caused by the murders, a lingering question stands in the way of full recovery.

Why?

Why did Ortiz do it? And why did he target these four women specifically?

During five years of reporting for this book, I tried to find answers to those questions by unearthing every conceivable fact surrounding the murders, to discover as much as possible about the victims and about Ortiz's background. Still, a motive remained stubbornly elusive.

District Attorney Isidro Alaniz, who is intimately familiar with every nugget of evidence in this case, theorized to me that one of the women, possibly Melissa, may have known or done something that threatened to expose Ortiz's secret life on San Bernardo Avenue. His theory wasn't based on any evidence, Alaniz said, just informed hunches. But that wouldn't explain Claudine's murder or the spasm of violence in the early-morning hours of September 15, 2018, when Ortiz executed first Chelly, then Janelle, and planned to murder again.

Did his military service and deployment to Iraq play a role? Military veterans who turn to spree killing are uncommon but not unheard-of.

In his 2022 book, *Killer Data: Modern Perspectives on Serial Murder,* researcher Enzo Yaksic reports that, since 2011, eight serial murderers in the United States also served in the military (including Ortiz). Though some studies have found a possible link between military service and serial murder, that connection has been "long debated," Yaksic writes.

PTSD and polypharmacy no doubt revolved in Ortiz's orbit. But those don't, in and of themselves, generally motivate people to murder, let alone commit serial killings. If PTSD was truly prevalent, Ortiz's work would have also spiraled, said Robert Schug, a forensic psychologist at California State University, Long Beach, who teaches a class on serial killers and has studied the criminal mind for decades. Though Border Patrol colleagues reported increasingly bizarre behavior from Ortiz, nothing in his file suggested his work suffered. Schug said Ortiz's modus operandi reminded him of one of the most famous serial killers of all time, Ted Bundy, who continued killing even while knowing police were closing in on him. That type of murder suggests compulsive behavior, not entrenched mental instability, Schug said. One commonality the Ortiz case has with other serial killers: vulnerability of victims. "Given the facts of the case," he told me, "what [Ortiz] actually did doesn't suggest to me it was motivated directly and significantly by mental health."

WHERE ORTIZ'S ACTIONS LINE UP FIRMLY WITH PAST SERIAL killer patterns is his choice of victims. The FBI's ever-growing data on serial killers, which the agency describes as the murder of two or more people with a "cooling-off" period between kills, shows women account for three-fourths of the 1,398 known serial homicide victims in the United States since 1985, according to a 2018 report by sociologists Jooyoung Lee and Sasha Reid. The FBI data also shows that female sex workers are *eighteen times* more likely to be killed by a serial killer than someone who does not participate in sex work, according to the study.

As an underserved, vulnerable population—further shadowed by all-consuming substance abuse disorders and extensive rap sheets—the women of San Bernardo Avenue presented a statistically luring target for a lurking serial killer, said Schug. "The victimology lines up with many serial killers," he said.

=====

CAPTAIN FEDERICO CALDERON, CO–LEAD INVESTIGATOR ON the case who spent twelve days hunting Ortiz and nine hours in a room talking to him about the crimes, was equally stymied by motive. He could point only to moments in the interview where Ortiz mentioned "cleaning up the streets" as the vague contours of a motive. Beyond that, he was stumped. "The only person who really knows is Juan David Ortiz," he told me.

If Ortiz knows why, he's not saying. At least not yet.

From the first days I began looking into this case, I started sending letters to Ortiz as he awaited his trial in an isolated wing of the Webb County Jail and, through his lawyers and family members, requesting an interview. Even if he had agreed and we had met for an interview, I realized the odds of gleaning honest, factual information from him were nil to none. At that point, he'd be focused on his upcoming trial and opt to offer me versions that could help his case. Still, it was worth a shot. I sent five letters to him and family members, including his wife, and repeated emails to his lawyer, Joel Perez. None were answered.

After his conviction, when he was transferred to the Ramsey Unit, a Texas prison located in Rosharon, Texas, I used an inmate communication network to send Ortiz an email on May 2, 2023, again requesting an interview. I included a few extra virtual "stamps" so he could reply at no cost. The next day, I was surprised to see that he had. It was a one-line response.

"Mr. Jervis," Ortiz wrote, "Are you still employed by *USA Today*?" He signed off "J.D. Ortiz."

I replied, explaining that I still worked at *USA Today* but that this book was wholly independent from my job at that media outlet. Again, I included a few virtual stamps.

He replied on May 20. Starting again with "Mr. Jervis," Ortiz unleashed a litany of alleged wrongdoing by the Webb County Sheriff's Office, including a $1 million settlement for a wrongful death of an inmate—"Jailors denied medical care, destroyed evidence and falsified government records"—stating such activity was "common" in Webb County.

"Come on Mr. Jervis . . . look into the Webb County Sheriffs [sic] Office . . ."

He signed off "Respectfully, J.D. Ortiz."

In my reply, I told him I'd be happy to listen to any allegations he had against the Webb County Sheriff's Office if he'd agree to a sit-down interview.

That's the last I heard from him.

Lawyers for Ortiz appealed his case to the Eighth Court of Appeals in El Paso, and as of yet, he hasn't spoken publicly about the case. For now, any clues to motive are locked away with him in his cell at the Ramsey Unit in southeast Texas.

===

WHY ORTIZ DID WHAT HE DID IS AN IMPORTANT QUESTION AND left, perhaps, to the discretion of future interviewers. *How* he managed to do it while employed as a supervisory agent at the country's largest federal law enforcement agency poses an equally important conundrum.

While the actions of one agent obviously don't represent the more than twenty thousand agents employed at Border Patrol, as agency officials are apt to point out, there is little doubt that the agency tolerated an environment of misogyny and impunity within its ranks during Ortiz's tenure there. As part of his duties under Operation Secure Texas, Johnhenry Bradshaw, the DPS trooper who confronted Ortiz at the Stripes gas station, leading to his eventual arrest, had frequent interactions with Border Patrol agents. He would spend one week a month at the BIC, where Ortiz worked, mingling with Border Patrol agents and swapping tips and info on crimes, though he doesn't remember ever seeing Ortiz. He found many at the federal agency professional and easy to work with. Still, Border Patrol as a whole had the most questionable reputation of all law enforcement agencies operating in Laredo, he said. "We have a very complicated relationship with them," Bradshaw told me.

When DPS and local law enforcement agents began using body cameras around early 2018, Border Patrol agents, who still didn't have them, mocked the troopers, Bradshaw said, bragging that their union leaders would never allow that to happen to them.* In the field, Bradshaw assisted at a number of vehicle crash sites involving Border Patrol agents, who often refused to give a statement until they'd spoken to their union rep, or offered explanations that didn't always line up with the facts at the scene.

Ortiz's actions only heightened Bradshaw's suspicions of Border Patrol, he said. Ever since the murders, Bradshaw, who was later promoted to the Criminal Investigation Division in Beeville, Texas, has refused to return to the Laredo intel center.

=====

ONE OF THE MORE CONTROVERSIAL INCIDENTS INVOLVING BORDER Patrol occurred in the Laredo Sector just four months before the women of San Bernardo Avenue were discovered dead. On May 23, 2018, Claudia Patricia Gómez González, a twenty-year-old Guatemalan asylum seeker, crossed into Rio Bravo, the Laredo suburb where Melissa Ramirez grew up, with other migrants, when they were confronted by a U.S. Border Patrol agent. As some of the people in her group fled, the agent drew his handgun and opened fire, hitting Gómez in the

---

* The Biden administration began deploying bodycams to Border Patrol in 2021.

head and killing her. She was unarmed. U.S. Customs and Border Protection, which oversees Border Patrol, at first put out a statement saying migrants armed with "blunt objects" had attacked the agent. The agency later retracted that statement, saying only that the group had "rushed" the officer. The American Civil Liberties Union filed a civil lawsuit against CBP on behalf of Gómez's family; the group later settled with the federal government for an undisclosed amount. The FBI San Antonio Office and Texas Rangers opened their own investigations into the incident, as did CBP's Office of Professional Responsibility. As of December 2023, a CBP spokesperson said the incident was still under investigation. But the rangers' report, which concluded in 2022, describes how several Border Patrol officials, including a union representative, descended on the scene minutes after the shooting, shuttled the agent in question away, and moved the weapon from one location to another before it was finally recovered by rangers. The report reveals the FBI "concluded their investigation and determined the facts did not merit any civil rights violations," but says federal investigators had "discovered several inconsistencies" in the Border Patrol agent's story. Five days after the shooting, the agent was back at work.

Bradshaw said Gómez's shooting—followed by the gruesome serial killings four months later—corroded Border Patrol's image, at least in Laredo. "So much bad stuff happened in such a short amount of time, I don't know if they can recover," he said.

The tragic tales of Gómez and the four slain women are unconnected save for one fact: they all died at the hands of Border Patrol agents—one while on the job, the other while off duty. Motivations for each are undoubtedly vastly different. But did the culture at Border Patrol contribute in some way to the agents viewing these women similarly, as somehow subhuman or expendable? Did it nurture a false sense of impunity, even for the vilest deeds? These questions remain unanswered—and potentially unanswerable.

RON VITIELLO, A FORMER BORDER PATROL CHIEF WHO WAS ACTing director of Immigration and Customs Enforcement at the time of the Ortiz murders, was stunned to learn that someone in Border Patrol had been collared for the crimes. Shortly after Ortiz's arrest, he called several retired border officials and ruminated with them about how something like that could happen. Vitiello, who worked in the Laredo Sector earlier in his career, realized it was a blow to the agency's reputation. "It's disbelief first," he told me. "Then it's anger and frustration. How can someone on our team do something like that?"

Vitiello said he didn't think anything Ortiz did in the days and weeks leading to the murders—bragging to colleagues about picking up women, pointing out where prostitutes worked, complaining of overdrinking—likely warranted filing a formal complaint against the supervisory agent. And nothing in his work history pointed to any red flags. Still, Vitiello recognized the damage the event, however isolated, did to the agency. "We work hard to hold ourselves to account and make sure the public trusts us," he said. "It sets you back. The disbelief is overcome by frustration." He added: "No one knew. It's just a tragedy."

=====

UNFORTUNATELY NOT AN ISOLATED ONE AT THE BORDER PATROL's Laredo Sector.

As Judge Oscar Hale read the verdict in a San Antonio courtroom in December 2022, condemning Ortiz to life in prison, Alaniz, seated at the prosecutor's table, gave a quick fist pump. It was a brief, nearly indiscernible gesture but was the punctuation on four years of long work hours, countless interviews, struggles with witnesses, and promises made to victims' families. After the verdict, he met with them in a large fourth-floor conference room inside the Paul Elizondo Tower, where they hugged, addressed the media, and snapped selfies with one another. There were some tears, but mostly the room had the heady, elated feel of a Super Bowl victory party.

Afterward, Alaniz treated his legal team to dinner at the Double Standard restaurant on San Antonio's River Walk. They celebrated with beer and steaks and rounds of top-shelf tequila, everyone toasting to a job well done.

But there was scant time to revel in victory. Alaniz was already thinking of his next capital murder case—involving yet another Border Patrol agent. Ronald Anthony Burgos-Aviles, a supervisory agent with the Border Patrol's Laredo Sector, was accused of stabbing to death his lover, Grizelda Hernandez, twenty-seven, and their one-year-old son, Dominic, at a Laredo park in April 2018, five months before Ortiz embarked on his killing spree. Like Ortiz, there was nothing in Burgos-Aviles's official file to forecast the crime. Unlike Ortiz, the murder weapon was never found. Alaniz sensed this one would be a challenge.

The morning after the Ortiz verdict and River Walk celebration, Alaniz and his staff packed up their considerable files, got in their cars, and drove the two hours back to Laredo.

They had more work to do.

ACKNOWLEDGMENTS

On a Saturday afternoon, September 15, 2018, I received a call at home from an editor at *USA Today* alerting me to news emerging from Laredo, Texas: a U.S. Border Patrol agent had been arrested and charged with the murder of four women, all of them sex workers. A press conference was scheduled for that Monday morning.

I was less than thrilled with the idea of leaving my family on a weekend for work, but I also recognized the explosiveness and import of the story. The next day, I made the four-hour drive from Austin to Laredo to be able to attend the Monday morning presser. That was the start of the five-year odyssey that culminated with this book.

Along the way, many, many people lent a hand, showed support, dug up a document, shared their insight, and opened their homes and hearts in ways I'm still marveling over. This book couldn't have been done without their collective goodness.

This story is anchored in the honest, often painful retelling of some of life's darkest moments by the victims' friends and family. Cristina Benavides, Cesar and Gracie Ramirez, and Emily Varela all shared their most intimate memories of Melissa Ramirez. Colette Mireles, Angie Perez, and Ciara Munguia were admirably honest in their retelling of the life of Claudine Luera. Rosenda Ortiz, Ezekiel Ortiz, Elva Enriquez Ortiz, Armando Ortiz, and Patricia Ortiz all opened up about Janelle Ortiz. And Joey Cantu, Anna Sotelo, and Javi and Gustavo Montemayor weaved a powerful story about Chelly Cantu. I'm in awed appreciation for how they opened their lives to me.

Staffers at the Webb/Zapata County District Attorney's Office were incredibly helpful—and patient—with my requests, as I pestered them week after week, year after year, for more details and documents in the case. District Attorney Isidro Alaniz was immensely helpful and led a team of professionals, including Marisela Jacaman and Joaquin Rodriguez. Brigette Garay was particularly valuable.

The Webb County Sheriff's Office was also seminal in telling this story. Sheriff Martin Cuellar's cooperation was essential in helping me secure key interviews and documents. Captain Federico Calderon was gracious in his time and knowledge and pivotal to understanding the inner gears of the investigation that led to Juan David Ortiz's arrest. Victoria Luna was professional and helped organize many of the interviews. Kimberly Moreno at the Webb County Clerk's Office was always cheery and professional as she helped me secure public documents and replied to an endless stream of emails from me. Ranger E. J. Salinas and DPS spokesmen Travis Considine and Sgt. Erick Estrada helped bring the DPS angle to light.

The residents of Laredo—especially those around the San Bernardo Avenue corridor—were also remarkably helpful and welcoming. Pat and Nora Roth were invaluable in introducing me to the San Bernardo scene. Many of the sex workers, pushers, and hustlers along Sanber overcame their suspicions of a stranger asking questions and shared their remarkable stories. Some—like Cassy and Big Mary—bravely did it on the record; others did it more anonymously. All shared the horror and pain of having four close friends violently ripped away from them.

Jerry Thompson, Laredo's vaunted historian, helped me forge and ensure the accuracy of all the intriguing historical details of that city. From the minute I broached the idea with them, my editors at *USA Today* have also been endlessly supportive and nurturing: Cristina Silva, Kristen Go, Nicole Carroll—all rock stars. Josh Susong, editor extraordinaire, gave my manuscript a deep read and offered key suggestions and edits, as did Cristina. Rafael Carranza, resident border expert at the *Arizona Republic*, also helped review chapters.

Kelley and Tom French at Indiana University gave the manuscript an early read and made some key suggestions. Amma Szal was a huge help with Spanish edits and general grammar corrections; Nancy Tan also gave it a masterful copyediting sweep.

My literary agent, Matt Carlini of Javelin, was the first to recognize the potential this story had for deeper digging and a longer tell (he was on to something . . .) and offered limitless guidance and encouragement. Matthew Daddona brought the project home to Dey Street/HarperCollins. There, I was blessed with the talents and vision of Stuart Roberts, Dey Street's executive editor, who polished, sculpted, and willed my manuscript into its final form. Forever indebted.

The Jones/Cottrell family, particularly Phoebe and Frances, graciously opened their soul-soothing home to me, allowing me to drag the manuscript across the finish line.

Lastly, three souls in particular deserve my deepest gratitude:

Elle and Isla filled my heart with joy and inspiration each day, even as I mined the darker chambers of humanity. And Elena was—and will always be—my rock, an immovable force as I bobbed through the turbulent currents of this project. Love you all endlessly.

SPANISH-ENGLISH GLOSSARY

PROLOGUE

Tengo una girl: "I have a girl."

barbacoa: barbecued meat

seguros de auto: car insurance

tía: aunt

primo: cousin

cacahuates: peanuts

conchas: shell-shaped pastries

pan dulce: sweet bread

colonia: housing development, often with subpar services, found along the Texas-Mexico border

En el nombre del Padre y del Hijo y del Espíritu Santo: In the name of the Father and of the Son and of the Holy Spirit

Me van a matar: "They're going to kill me."

Así es como me matarán: "This is how they'll kill me."

el mundo espiritual: the spirit world

chancletas: flip-flop sandals

picadillo: seasoned ground meat

Cállate: "Be quiet."

Vamos a porriar: "Let's party."

CHAPTER 1

Ventas Especiales: "Special Sales"

Almuerzo Caliente: "Hot Lunch"

Oye, guey, do you have a white troca que tenga un radio that works well?: "Hey, man, do you have a white truck with a radio that works well?"

Si, patrón, we have a nice troca para que veas in the back lot: "Yes, boss, we have a nice truck for you to see in the back lot."

¿Quieres probar el especial de hoy?: "Would you like to try today's special?"

rancheros: ranchers

bandidos: bandits

parrilladas: grilled meat

tequileros: tequila smugglers

CHAPTER 2

el heladero: the ice cream truck

Gordo: fat person (term of endearment)

abuela: grandmother

lesbiana: lesbian

sancha: other woman

Gracias, mi'ja: "Thank you, daughter."

¿Cómo se llama usted?: "What is your name?"

¿Y cuántos años tiene usted?: "And how old are you?"

Cincuenticuatro: "Fifty-four."

Usted es muy mayor para ella: "You're too old for her."

Meli, llámame: "Meli, call me."

¡Órale!: "Okay!"

¿Has visto a Melissa?: "Have you seen Melissa?"

Lo siento: "I'm sorry."

CHAPTER 3

¿Qué rollo?: "What's up?"

CHAPTER 4

¿Cómo?: "What?"

Mataron a mi hija: "They killed my daughter."

Mi Meli: "My Meli."

CHAPTER 5

Ministerio Restauración y Poder: Ministry of Restoration and Power

Estudiantina Juventud: Musical Youth Group

CHAPTER 7

coyotes: human smugglers

CHAPTER 9

Ay pa', dame dinero para ir agarrar algo: "Hey dude, give me money to get something [drugs]."

Hey, ¿andas bien o todavía andas junto con la Erika?: "Are you cool or still with Erika?"

No'mbre, buey: "No, dude."

¿Dónde chingao ando?: "Where the fuck am I?"

¡Párate a la verga!: "Fucking stop!"

No'mbre, ¿pa' qué, bro?: "Nah, for what, bro?"

¿Pero pa' qué, buey?: "But for what, dude?"

CHAPTER 11

carne guisada: beef stew

CHAPTER 12

Sal de la casa . . . ¡Vete ya!: "Get out of the house . . . Leave now!"

la muerte anda cerca: death is near

¿Qué chingao traes?: "What the fuck is with you?"

Tranquila: "Relax."

Tengo miedo, sir: "I'm scared, sir."

We started talking about the muchachas que acaban de fallecer: "We started talking about the girls who were recently killed."

¿Las que dumpiaron allá?: "The ones that they dumped over there?"

CHAPTER 13

She knows who they are, esas muchachas: "She knows who they are, those young women."

¡Ahí está!: "There it is!"

Sí, esa casa: "Yes, that house."

CHAPTER 15

Me dió un chingazo . . . Mira: "He hit me . . . Look."

A la madre: "Crap!"

de las dos viejas: of the two women

CHAPTER 16

la metralleta: the submachine gun

mi flaquita: my skinny one

flunkeros: students who flunk out of school

joto: derogatory slang for "homosexual"

verga: derogatory slang for "penis"

¿Qué es lo que no quieres hacer, a ver?: "What is it that you don't want to do? Let's see."

Dime joto una vez más: "Call me 'joto' one more time."

Pinche joto: "Fucking joto."

No era codo: "He wasn't a cheapskate."

Soy gay . . . Haz lo que quieras hacer. No importa lo que digas. Yo soy lo que soy: "I'm gay . . . Do what you want. It doesn't matter what you say. I am what I am."

¡¿Qué?! . . . ¿Te gustan los hombres?: "What?! . . . You like men?"

Le hago un poquito al pase: "I use a little cocaine."

CHAPTER 17

nopalitos con huevos y chiles colorados: prickly pear with scrambled eggs and red chili peppers

Echa me la bendición: "Bless me."

Ándale: "Go."

¿Qué honda? . . . Olle, pa', ¿me compras algo de comer como la última vez?: "What's up? . . . Hey, dude, can you buy me something to eat like last time?"

¿Pa' dónde vamos?: "Where are we going?"

Hazte pa'ya: "Go over there."

Chingamadre . . . Ya se acabó todo el pedo: "Motherfucker . . . This is all fucking over."

CHAPTER 18

Buenas noches: "Good evening."

Hey, bro, ya se acabó: "Hey, bro, it's over."

No se acabó nada: "Nothing's over."

CHAPTER 19

No te quedes como estamos: "Don't leave this like this."

CHAPTER 20

Con esta no había nada de que I feel bad . . . No había nada de nada: "With this one, there was none of that, 'I feel bad' . . . There was nothing about nothing."

mierdas: pieces of shit

CHAPTER 21

¡Asesino maldito!: "Damn murderer!"

CHAPTER 22

Él me dijo si quisiera cigarros: "He asked if I wanted cigarettes."
uno de los officials de nostros will get you a shirt: one of our officials will
   get you a shirt
Maybe you could break a case of lo que está pasando ahorita: "Maybe you
   could break a case of what's been happening."

CHAPTER 23

mi amor: "my love"
Y ya: "And that's it."
¿Por qué la mataste? ¿Por qué mataste a mi hija? . . . ¿Por qué le quitaste la
   vida?: "Why did you kill her? Why did you kill my daughter? . . . Why
   did you take her life?"

A NOTE ON SOURCING

This narrative is based on extensive interviews with family members of the victims, law enforcement officials, and residents of Laredo who live and work around San Bernardo Avenue, as well as more than one thousand pages of documents gleaned from the Webb/Zapata County District Attorney's Office, the Webb County Sheriff's Office, the Webb County Medical Examiner's Office, the Texas Center for Border Economic and Enterprise Development, the United Independent School District Records Management Office, and the Texas Department of Public Safety. I also conducted a jailhouse interview from the John B. Connally Unit state prison in South Texas with an inmate who knew one of the victims and was with her in her final hours. All unattributed passages and dialogue come from those interviews and documents. One interview source was identified with a pseudonym.

Some of the narrative and dialogue, especially of the victims' final moments, also arise from the nine-hour videotaped interview Juan David Ortiz gave to investigators following his arrest, where he recounted, in surprisingly vivid detail, how he orchestrated each of the murders. I also drew from witness testimonies and exhibits from Ortiz's trial. Any other source material that contributed to the body of this narrative has been duly cataloged in endnotes.

No current officials of U.S. Customs and Border Protection agreed to be interviewed for this book.

NOTES

CHAPTER 1

15 **In April 1790, a band of Lipan Apaches:** John A. Adams Jr., *Conflict and Commerce on the Rio Grande: Laredo, 1755–1955* (College Station: Texas A&M University Press, 2008), pp. 23–25.

15 **In the winter of 1836:** Ibid., p. 55.

16 **Native Americans routinely attacked:** Kathleen da Camara, *Laredo on the Rio Grande* (San Antonio, TX: Naylor, 1949).

16 **"Everything is in a state of siege":** Adams, *Conflict and Commerce on the Rio Grande,* p. 85.

20 **"Protests from residents":** "Oust Prostitutes Off San Bernardo Is City Order," *Laredo Times,* July 7, 1937.

20 **"Your attack on the San Bernardo Ave.":** *Laredo Times,* letter to the editor, July 27, 1937.

21 **heroin seizures in its area soar:** Houston division of U.S. Drug Enforcement Administration.

21 **Overdose deaths in Laredo:** City of Laredo Health Department.

CHAPTER 2

33 **In a blurry cell phone video:** Video footage from Cristina Benavides's smartphone.

CHAPTER 3

41 **Just then, Rene Arce:** Maria Eugenia Guerra, "Serial Killer's Bloody Trail Went Cold While Webb Deputies, Rangers Raid North Laredo Home & Interrogate LPD Officer for 6 Hours," *LareDOS,* September 18, 2018, https://laredosnews.com /2018/09/18/serial-killers-bloody-trail-went-cold-while-webb-deputies-rangers -raid-north-laredo-home-interrogate-lpd-officer-for-6-hours/.

46 **Arce had returned home:** Guerra, "Serial Killer."

46 **Outside, Webb County sheriff's deputies:** Ibid.

47 **In 2017, she posted allegations:** Molly Hennessy-Fiske, "The 'Crazy Fat Lady' Reports on Crime from the Texas Border. Cops Say She's Gone Too Far, and Now She's Facing Charges," *Los Angeles Times,* January 24, 2018, https://www.latimes.com /nation/la-na-lagordiloca-laredo-20180124-story.html.

48 **Villarreal went live:** Guerra, "Serial Killer."

CHAPTER 4

55 **He told them he was:** Ibid.

CHAPTER 5

65 **The group met each Thursday:** Author interviews with members of Youth Alive Bible Study.

65 **One passage Ortiz often repeated:** Ibid.

66 **The Porter High School yearbooks:** Gladys Porter Early College High School yearbooks, 1998–2001.

67 **he enlisted in the U.S. Navy:** Juan David Ortiz U.S. Navy records.

69 **Ortiz would treat the marines:** Author interviews with marines at Twentynine Palms.

70 **In October 2001:** "The U.S. War in Afghanistan, 1999–2021," Council on Foreign Relations, https://www.cfr.org/timeline/us-war-afghanistan.

71 **Intel officers estimated U.S. casualties:** Michael S. Groen et al., *With the 1st Marine Division in Iraq, 2003: No Greater Friend, No Worse Enemy* (Quantico, VA: Marine Corps University, 2006), pp. 27–29, https://www.usmcu.edu/Portals/218/With%20the%201stMarDiv%20in%20Iraq%2C%202003.pdf.

CHAPTER 6

72 **In all, 138 U.S. troops:** Michael E. O'Hanlon and Adriana Lins de Albuquerque, "Iraq Index: Tracking Variables of Reconstruction & Security in Post-Saddam Iraq," Brookings Institution, January 19, 2005, https://www.brookings.edu/wp-content/uploads/2017/11/index20050119.pdf.

72 **Corpsmen had legs blown off:** Ibid.

72 **Then he ran over to where:** Transcript of Juan David Ortiz interview with Federico Calderon and Ernesto Salinas, Webb County Sheriff's Office, Laredo, TX, September 15, 2018.

73 **civil-military operations center:** Groen et al., *With the 1st Marine Division*.

76 **By 2009, about 12 percent:** Institute of Medicine Committee on the Initial Assessment of Readjustment Needs of Military Personnel, Veterans, and Their Families, *Returning Home from Iraq and Afghanistan: Preliminary Assessment of Readjustment Needs of Veterans, Service Members, and Their Families* (Washington, D.C.: National Academies Press, 2010), https://pubmed.ncbi.nlm.nih.gov/25032369/.

77 **Of the 1,200 marines who deployed:** Dave Philipps, "In Unit Stalked by Suicide, Veterans Try to Save One Another," *New York Times*, September 19, 2015, https://tinyurl.com/4tkpmd5e.

78 **The next day, a story appeared:** Criselda Valdez, "U.S. Soldier Returns Home to Brownsville," *Brownsville Herald*, August 2, 2003.

78 **They were married:** Marriage record, County Clerk Office, Cameron County, TX.

79 **One day in the summer of 2008:** Summary of transcript of Amanda Callahan interview with DPS investigators on January 7, 2019.

79 **In eight years of military service:** Ortiz U.S. Navy records.

CHAPTER 7

81 **At the Border Patrol's academy:** Skip Hollandsworth, "The Hunt for the Serial Killer of Laredo," *Texas Monthly*, October 2019, https://www.texasmonthly.com/true-crime/serial-killer-border-patrol/.

81 **To coworkers, Ortiz seemed smart:** Transcripts of U.S. Border Patrol agents interviews with DPS and Webb County District Attorney investigators.

82 **The Laredo Sector's 1,800 employees:** "Southwest Land Border Encounters (By Component)," U.S. Customs and Border Protection, last updated December 22, 2023, https://www.cbp.gov/newsroom/stats/southwest-land-border-encounters-by-component.

83 **The year Ortiz arrived:** "U.S. Border Patrol Monthly Apprehensions (FY 2000–FY 2019)," U.S. Customs and Border Protection, https://tinyurl.com/54v4uza5.

84 **Backed by local and state law enforcement:** Transcript of Ortiz interview with Calderon and Salinas.

84 **With the freedom afforded to a supervisor:** Transcripts of Border Patrol agents interviews with DPS and Webb County District Attorney investigators.

86 **He woke up four, sometimes five:** Transcript of Ortiz interview with Calderon and Salinas.

87 **Spurred by his friend, Ortiz tried:** Ibid.

87 **"Veteran describes childhood":** Veterans Affairs clinical assessment, February 12, 2018.

88 **In the office, Ortiz whistled:** Transcript of Juan Flores interview with DPS and Webb County District Attorney investigators, January 17, 2019.

88 **Pedro "Pete" Gutierrez:** Transcript of Pedro Gutierrez interview with DPS and Webb County District Attorney investigators, January 17, 2019.

89 **Another Border Patrol colleague, Joseph Peralta:** Transcript of Joseph Peralta interview with DPS and Webb County District Attorney investigators, January 23, 2019.

90 **"Veteran describes self":** Veterans Affairs clinical assessment, February 26, 2018.

90 **Between February and September 2018:** Juan David Ortiz medical records, U.S. Customs and Border Protection.

90 **Psychopharmacology first emerged:** S. Nassir Ghaemi, ed., *Polypharmacy in Psychiatry* (New York: Marcel Dekker, 2002), pp. 7–8.

91 **The percentage of patients:** Sheldon H. Preskorn and David Flockhart, "2006 Guide to Psychiatric Drug Interactions," *Primary Psychiatry* 13, no. 4 (2006): 35–64.

91 **"we know an awful lot":** Author interview with Sheldon Preskorn, May 19, 2023.

91 **Attorneys for Lindsay Clancy:** Kay Lazar, John R. Ellement, and Laura Crimaldi, "Lindsay Clancy's Lawyer Said She Was on 13 Different Drugs for Mood Disorders, Anxiety, and Psychosis. Was She Over Medicated?," *Boston Globe,* February 3, 2023.

92 **Whatever the reasoning:** Sanjay Kukreja, Gurvinder Kalra, Nilesh Shah, and Amresh Shrivastava, "Polypharmacy in Psychiatry: A Review," *Mens Sana Monograph* 11, no. 1 (Jan.–Dec. 2013): 82–99.

94 **Instead, on August 27, 2018:** Juan David Ortiz personnel record, U.S. Border Patrol, U.S. Customs and Border Protection.

CHAPTER 8

95 **The agreement shrank Mexico's border:** Greg Grandin, *The End of the Myth: From the Frontier to the Border Wall in the Mind of America* (New York: Metropolitan Books, 2019).

95 **when Congress created the Border Patrol:** Kelly Lytle Hernández, *Migra! A History of the U.S. Border Patrol* (Berkeley: University of California Press, 2010).

96 **In his 1983 book:** John Crewdson, *The Tarnished Door: The New Immigrants and the Transformation of America* (New York: Times Books, 1983), p. 166.

96 **Beginning in 1971, investigators:** Ibid.

97 **Border Patrol agents apprehended:** "U.S. Border Patrol Total Apprehensions (FY 1925–FY 2020)," U.S. Customs and Border Protection, https://tinyurl.com/52 jdk9b2.

97 **New recruits flooded Border Patrol stations:** Garrett M. Graff, "The Green Monster: How the Border Patrol Became America's Most Out-of-Control Law Enforcement Agency," *Politico,* November/December 2014, https://tinyurl.com/y9nnodxr.

97 **All told, the United States government:** "The Cost of Immigration Enforcement and Border Security," American Immigration Council, January 20, 2021, https://www.americanimmigrationcouncil.org/research/the-cost-of-immigration -enforcement-and-border-security.

98 **Unlike the FBI, which requires all applicants:** James F. Tomsheck and James Wong, brief of *amici curiae, Jesus C. Hernandez, et al. v. Jesus Mesa, Jr.,* August 9, 2019, p. 13.

98 **Between 2004 and 2014:** Andrew Becker, "Border Agency's Former Watchdog Says Officials Impeded His Efforts," *Washington Post,* August 16, 2014, https://tinyurl.com /579nvh3a.

98 **Arrests for general misconduct:** Graff, "The Green Monster."

98 **An audit report:** *DHS Needs to Improve Its Oversight of Misconduct and Discipline,* Office of Inspector General, U.S. Department of Homeland Security, June 17, 2019, p. 2.

98 **Out of 809 complaints:** Daniel E. Martínez, Guillermo Cantor, and Walter A. Ewing, "No Action Taken: Lack of CBP Accountability in Responding to Complaints of Abuse," American Immigration Council, May 2014, https://tinyurl.com /5a38be9r.

98 **From 2006 to 2014:** Graff, "The Green Monster."

99 **Kerlikowske learned firsthand:** Author interview with Gil Kerlikowske, August 22, 2022.

101 **From 2003 to 2017:** Alex Nowrasteh, "Border Patrol Agent Deaths in the Line of Duty," Cato Institute, November 27, 2017, https://www.cato.org/blog/border -patrol-agent-deaths-line-duty.

102 **"There is a certain way":** Author interview with Vicki Gaubeca, August 9, 2022.

102 **After graduating with honors:** Author interview with Jenn Budd, August 7, 2020.

103 **Agents posted jokes and memes:** A. C. Thompson, "Inside the Secret Border Patrol Facebook Group Where Agents Joke About Migrant Deaths and Post Sexist Memes," ProPublica, July 1, 2019, https://www.propublica.org/article/secret-border-patrol -facebook-group-agents-joke-about-migrant-deaths-post-sexist-memes.

104 **CBP officials denounced:** Ted Hesson and Cristiano Lima, "Border Agency Knew About Secret Facebook Group for Years," *Politico,* July 3, 2019, https://tinyurl.com /yc2u92ta.

104 **In October 2021, the U.S. House Committee:** *Border Patrol Agents in Secret Facebook Group Faced Few Consequences for Misconduct,* staff report, Committee on Oversight and Reform, U.S. House of Representatives, October 2021, https://ti nyurl.com/38vnmu48.

CHAPTER 9

110 **Ortiz was also a repeat customer:** Transcript of Anna Karen Herrera interview with Texas Ranger, January 15, 2019.

110   **His questioning often turned:** Richard Cooke, "A Serial Killer at the Border—and the Women Who Stood Up to Him," *Guardian,* May 9, 2019, https://tinyurl.com/23kpvkzu.

111   **From his house on the corner:** Author interview with Robert DeLeon, July 23, 2019.

118   **Juan Flores, another Ortiz colleague:** Transcript of Juan Flores interview with DPS and Webb County District Attorney investigators, January 17, 2019.

CHAPTER 10

127   **Between 2011 and 2018:** Claudine Luera records, Webb County Criminal Records.

132   **"Hey mamas, what you up 2?":** Text messages from Ciara Munguia's smartphone.

CHAPTER 11

136   **he aspired to rid Laredo:** Transcript of Ortiz interview with Calderon and Salinas.

137   **Unlike past drives:** Ibid.

137   **"Yeah, I heard about that shit":** Ibid.

138   **She gathered her things:** Ibid.

138   **the jacketed hollow-point bullet mushroomed:** Report, Webb County Medical Examiner.

138   **At daybreak on September 13:** Investigation notes of interview, Webb County Sheriff's Office CID.

139   **"Just calm down":** Author interview with Rey Veliz, July 24, 2019.

141   **The tall grass was littered:** Crime scene photos, Webb County Sheriff's Office.

CHAPTER 12

145   **The next morning, at 8:21 a.m.:** César Rodriguez, "DPS: Woman Found Critically Wounded off Roadway in Webb County Dies," *Laredo Morning Times,* September 14, 2018, https://www.lmtonline.com/local/crime/article/DPS-Woman-found-critically-wounded-off-roadway-13229325.php.

149   **At 5:50 p.m. that day:** Interview notes, Webb County Sheriff's Office Criminal Investigation Division.

152   **They drove first to a drug house:** Transcript of Ortiz interview with Calderon and Salinas.

154   **"I feel strange":** Ibid.

154   **As they settled into the patio chairs:** Erika Peña testimony at pretrial hearing, Webb County District Court, Laredo, TX, October 3, 2019.

CHAPTER 13

159   **"Fuck this shit":** Transcript of Ortiz interview with Calderon and Salinas.

160   **Ortiz surveyed the weaponry:** Ibid.

CHAPTER 14

169   **Early on the morning of September 7:** "Woman Murdered; Cops Arrest Suspect," *Laredo Morning Times,* September 8, 1985; "Cantu Services Set for Tuesday," *Laredo Morning Times,* September 9, 1985.

170 **At fifteen, he was tried as an adult:** José "Joey" Cantu records, Texas Department of Criminal Justice.

172 **In February 2013, Chelly was picked up:** Guiselda Alicia "Chelly" Cantu records, Texas Department of Criminal Justice.

CHAPTER 15

177 **On June 18, 2018, Joey walked out:** Joey Cantu records, Texas Department of Criminal Justice.

180 **Blood trickled from a corner:** Transcript of Ortiz interview with Calderon and Salinas.

182 **"Why are you letting me go?":** Ibid.

182 **The bullet barreled:** Report, Webb County Medical Examiner.

183 **"It is all fucking over":** Transcript of Ortiz interview with Calderon and Salinas.

CHAPTER 16

190 **From 2009 to 2018, she was arrested:** Janelle Ortiz records, Webb County Criminal Court.

CHAPTER 17

202 **"Aaaah," she said through her hands:** Transcript of Ortiz interview with Calderon and Salinas.

202 **"Okay," she told Ortiz:** Ibid.

203 **"Chingamadre," he muttered to himself:** Ibid.

207 **"Put your hands up!":** DPS trooper Abiel Obregon bodycam footage.

207 **Fuckers, he thought:** Transcript of Ortiz interview with Calderon and Salinas.

211 **Bradshaw trotted down the ramp:** Trooper Obregon bodycam footage.

212 **A block away, Obregon:** Ibid.

CHAPTER 18

219 **Text messages piled into Ortiz's iPhone:** Investigation notes, Webb County Sheriff's Office CID.

219 **Aizar Rodolfo Medina, an eleven-year veteran:** Transcript of Aizar Rodolfo Medina interview with DPS and Webb County District Attorney investigators, January 17, 2019.

220 **Finally, he called her:** Transcript of Ortiz interview with Calderon and Salinas.

221 **Gabriela Nuñez, a Border Patrol agent:** Transcript of Gabriela Nuñez interview with DPS and Webb County District Attorney investigators, January 28, 2019.

223 **"Where's the weapon at?":** Webb County Sheriff's Office SWAT team bodycam footage.

224 **Inside, they found a .40-caliber H&K:** Investigation notes, Webb County Sheriff's Office CID.

CHAPTER 19

234 **He secured four life sentences:** Jason Buch, "Killer of 2-Year-Old Gets Four Life Sentences," *San Antonio Express-News,* April 4, 2012, https://www.kgns.tv/content /news/Man-on-the-run-for-seven-years-is-now-behind-bars-497117651.html.

234 **He also got a ninety-nine-year prison sentence:** Rudy Maya, "Victim's Family Speaks Out on Victor Palomo's Arrest," KGNS, October 11, 2018, https://tinyurl .com/3a94emyp.

CHAPTER 21

250 **In May 2019, just as Alaniz:** Erika Peña records, Webb County Criminal Court.

253 **In 2018, Texas easily led:** "Facts About the Death Penalty," Death Penalty Information Center, last updated November 30, 2023, https://dpic-cdn.org/production /documents/pdf/FactSheet.pdf.

253 **Texas border counties tallied 282 deaths:** René Kladzyk, Phil Galewitz, and Elizabeth Lucas, "Why COVID-19 Killed Texas Border Residents in Shocking Numbers," *El Paso Matters,* June 22, 2021, https://elpasomatters.org/2021/06/22/why-covid -19-killed-texas-border-residents-in-shocking-numbers.

254 **In Laredo, more than 600 people:** Simon Romero, "The 'Dr. Fauci' of the Texas Border Is Counting the Dead," *New York Times,* February 1, 2021, https://tinyurl.com /4wbe96wh.

254 **By May 2021, three of the top six places:** "Monitoring the Coronavirus Outbreak in Metro Areas Across the U.S.," *New York Times,* May 24, 2021, https://tinyurl.com /bdv8m6bu.

254 **Besides having to haul their substantial cache:** Megan Rodriguez, "With 80,000 Active-Duty Personnel, Bexar County Ranks Highest in Number of Military Deaths," *San Antonio Current,* June 7, 2018, https://tinyurl.com/ms3akauw.

EPILOGUE

281 **In his 2022 book:** Enzo Yaksic, *Killer Data: Modern Perspectives on Serial Murder* (Abingdon, UK: Routledge, 2022), p. 118.

281 **according to a 2018 report by sociologists:** Jooyoung Lee and Sasha Reid, "Serial Killers and Their Easy Prey," *Contexts* 17, no. 2 (Spring 2018): 46–51.

285 **But the rangers' report:** Texas Department of Public Safety, Texas Rangers: Report of Investigation: Officer-involved shooting/Webb County/Claudia Patricia Gómez González/May 23, 2018, p. 106.

ABOUT THE AUTHOR

Rick Jervis is a Pulitzer Prize–winning journalist with more than two decades of experience working at the *Miami Herald*, the *Wall Street Journal Europe*, the *Chicago Tribune*, and *USA Today*, where he has worked since 2005. He lives in Austin, Texas. *The Devil Behind the Badge* is his first book.